The Archaeology of Ca
Contexts

CONTRIBUTIONS TO GLOBAL HISTORICAL ARCHAEOLOGY

Series Editor:
Charles E. Orser, Jr., New York State Museum, Albany, New York, USA

A Continuation Order Plan is available for this series. A continuation order will bring delivery of each new volume immediately upon publication. Volumes are billed only upon actual shipment. For further information please contact the publisher. For more information about this series, please visit: www.Springer.com/Series/5734.

Sarah K. Croucher · Lindsay Weiss
Editors

The Archaeology
of Capitalism in Colonial
Contexts

Postcolonial Historical Archaeologies

 Springer

Editors
Sarah K. Croucher
Assistant Professor of Anthropology,
Archaeology, and Feminist
Gender & Sexuality Studies
Wesleyan University
06459 Middletown, CT, USA
scroucher@wesleyan.edu

Lindsay Weiss
Archaeology Center and Department
of Anthropology
Stanford University
94305 Palo Alto, CA, USA
lw2004@caa.columbia.edu

ISSN 1574-0439
ISBN 978-1-4614-3004-9   ISBN 978-1-4614-0192-6 (eBook)
DOI 10.1007/978-1-4614-0192-6
Springer New York Dordrecht Heidelberg London

Springer is part of Springer Science+Business Media (www.springer.com)

This book is dedicated to our advisors, especially:

Eleanor Casella
Tim Insoll
&
Lynn Meskell

Preface

This volume results from a session at the 2008 *Society for Historical Archaeology* meeting in Albuquerque, New Mexico. Our motivation was feeling that at the time that there was little discussion in postcolonial directions in histories of capitalism occurring within historical archaeology. Yet, we were both inspired to analyze our archaeological materials by these same postcolonial histories, and were animated by the direction they offered in fracturing the often teleological discussions of the development of capitalism offered by historical archaeologists. As a result of these conversations, we organized a session which produced an exciting grouping of papers and conversations on the topic. We seem to have been timely in our desire to integrate insights from postcolonial theory more thoroughly into the discipline, since this has occurred more frequently since our original session. Notably Liebmann and Rizvi's *Archaeology and the Postcolonial Critique* (2008) and Lydon and Rizvi's *Handbook of Postcolonial Archaeology* (2010) have been directed at more forcefully integrating postcolonial theory within archaeology, albeit into the field more generally and not simply within historical archaeology which is the target of the papers included in this volume. The plenary session at the American Theoretical Archaeology Group conference in 2010 was also notable for bringing the noted theorist Homi Bhabha into a conversation with archaeologists (http://www.proteus.brown.edu/tag2010/7261). Discussions within historical archaeology itself, particularly in the nontraditional areas of the field, are also pushing forward explicit discussions as to the problems of applying the usual discussions of the progression of capitalism into new contexts, as we discuss in our introduction.

Nevertheless, the grouping of these papers at the time of the 2008 meeting seemed a novel one, and we felt that a volume resulting from this session would produce a timely contribution to the field, and it is with this premise we pursued the publication of the papers within the session. Since then, the chapters have been swollen with the introduction of Alistair Paterson's work adding a segment of the discussion from an Australasian perspective. Several of the original participants who were vital to the original discussions are also not included in this volume, and we would like to acknowledge their input (Heather Atherton, Jenna Coplin, Chris Matthews, and Kathryn Sikes).

Several people have been particularly instrumental in bringing this volume to actuality. We are indebted to the support of Martin Hall, who provided insightful commentary to our original session (Hall 2008) which he has updated to the commentary chapter included in this volume. Nan Rothschild also kindly read the original commentary at the SHA session. Charles Orser has also been a continual supporter of the project, particularly in shepherding us through inclusion in the *Global Directions in Historical Archaeology* series. Teresa Krauss at Springer has also been generous in her support of our volume, and she has been instrumental in bringing this project to fruition. We would also like to thank the two anonymous reviewers of our book proposal, whose comments ensured a tightening of the direction of the volume, our arguments in the introduction, and ensured that we had as great a global spread as has been possible. Many others have also inspired us with ideas and comments for our chapters, and are acknowledged in individual chapters. All errors and admissions are, of course, our own.

This book is also the product of the early years of our career, spanning the first years of the tenure track for Sarah Croucher, and the completion of the dissertation and a move to a postdoctoral position for Lindsay Weiss. Many of our ideas have been provoked by our advisors, and it is to them we would like to dedicate this volume, for their continual mentoring and support.

Middletown, CT   Sarah K. Croucher
Palo Alto, CA   Lindsay Weiss

Contents

About the Contributors

Matthew A. Russell has been an Archeologist with the US National Park Service's Submerged Resources Center (SRC) since 1993. His education includes an MA in Maritime History and Nautical Archaeology from East Carolina University and a BA in Cultural Anthropology from University of California, Santa Barbara. Since 1993, he has participated in or directed numerous projects in national park areas, and for state, federal, and international agencies. He was Deputy Field Director for the *H. L. Hunley* Recovery Project in 2000 and is Project Director for the USS *Arizona* Preservation Project. He has been a member of Society for Historical Archaeology since 1992, is past-Chair of SHA's UNESCO Committee, and is currently Chair of the Advisory Council on Underwater Archaeology (ACUA). In addition to a variety of monographs on SRC's work in national parks, he has published in *Historical Archaeology*, *Journal of Field Archaeology*, and *International Journal of Nautical Archaeology*. He is currently a PhD candidate at the University of California, Berkeley where he is integrating maritime and terrestrial archaeology into a synthetic collaboration to examine culture contact between the shipwrecked crew of a Spanish Manila Galleon and indigenous Coast Miwok in Point Reyes, California in 1595.

Audrey Horning is Professor of Archaeology in the School of Geography, Archaeology and Palaeoecology at Queen's University Belfast. Her research addresses the comparative archaeology of British expansion, with particular attention to Ireland and the Chesapeake in the sixteenth and seventeenth centuries. She is also interested in historical memories of colonialism as they impact upon contemporary perceptions and divergent presentations of the archaeologies of the last 500 years in Ireland (north and south), the USA, and the United Kingdom. She is a founding member and Newsletter Editor for the Irish Post-Medieval Archaeology Group; Secretary for the Society for Post-Medieval Archaeology; and is an Associate Editor for the journal *Historical Archaeology*. In 2001, she received the John Cotter Award of the Society for Historical Archaeology in recognition of her research contributions. Books include *Ireland and Britain in the Atlantic World* Wordwell, Dublin (co-edited with Nick Brannon 2009); *Crossing Tracks or Sharing Paths?*

Future Directions in the Archaeological Study of Post-1550 Britain and Ireland (co-edited with Marilyn Palmer, Boydell and Brewer 2009); *The Archaeology of Post-Medieval Ireland, 1550–1850* (co-edited with Ruairi Ó Baoill, C.J. Donnelly, and Paul Logue; Wordwell, Dublin, 2007) *In the Shadow of Ragged Mountain: Historical Archaeology of Nicholson, Corbin and Weakley Hollows* Shenandoah Natural History Association (2004).

Aron L. Crowell, Anthropologist and Director of Alaska programs for the Smithsonian Institution's Arctic Studies Center, has focused his work on archaeological, traditional, and contemporary cultures of Alaska and Siberia. His diverse projects – ranging from historical archaeology to prehistoric maritime adaptations to museum-based ethnography and material culture studies – have produced numerous publications and exhibitions. His books include *Crossroads of Continents: Cultures of Siberia and Alaska, Looking Both Ways: Heritage and Identity of the Alutiiq People, Archaeology and the Capitalist World System: A Study from Russian America*, and *Archaeology and Coastal Dynamics of Kenai Fjords National Park*. Crowell's current archaeological research and recent publications focus on the Alutiiq and Tlingit regions of southern coastal Alaska. Crowell's PhD in Anthropology is from the University of California, Berkeley.

Lynda Carroll is currently a doctoral candidate at Binghamton University in the Department of Anthropology. She is also a Project Director and Coordinator of the Community Archaeology Project at the Public Archaeology Facility, Binghamton University. She is also one of the Co-Directors of "Engaging Diverse Communities Through Visual Representation and Heritage Preservation," which is being developed by the Public Archaeology Facility and Department of Anthropology at Binghamton University. Carroll received her MA in Anthropology from Binghamton University in 1997, and her BA in Anthropology from Queens College, CUNY in 1992. Her research interests include postmedieval archaeology (Turkey and Jordan), historical archaeology (US), consumption studies, ceramic, landscape studies, and the archaeology of nomadic populations. Publications include "Commodities in Global Perspective" (1999, Guest Editor, International Journal of Historical Archaeology), "An Historical Archaeology of the Ottoman Empire" (2000, Co-Editor with Uzi Baram), and "Sowing the Seeds of Modernity on the Ottoman Frontier: Agricultural Investment and the Formation of Large Farms in Nineteenth-Century Transjordan" (2008, Archaeologies). She has received research grants from the Social Science Research Council, the American Research Institute in Turkey and the Institute for Turkish Studies.

Mark W. Hauser is an Anthropological Archaeologist who specializes in the material culture of the African Diaspora and social inequality and identity in the Caribbean. His work pays special attention to understanding the everyday life and material world of enslaved laborers. His first book entitled *An Archaeology of Black Markets: Local Ceramics and Economies in Eighteenth-Century Jamaica* explores these issues by focusing on Yabbas, a kind of pottery made by people of African descent in Jamaica, to draw out how solidarities were built and maintained in the everyday by enslaved Jamaicans in the eighteenth century. *An Archaeology of Black Markets* demonstrates that by lending rigorous attention to the intensity of social relations and the densities of material connections, we can construct an analysis of political control that is not only sensitive to issues of sovereignty, but also to the ways in which individuals mediated colonial regimes, including slavery. Hauser has published numerous scholarly articles and chapters on the archaeology of informal and unexpected economies; methodological considerations for understanding colonial landscapes and identity formation; and the centering of craft industries in Caribbean political economy. He co-edited a special issue of the *International Journal of Historical Archaeology* on issues of scale in Caribbean archaeology. He is an Assistant Professor in Anthropology and an affiliated faculty of African American Studies at Northwestern University.

Felipe Gaitán-Ammann is currently a PhD candidate in the Department of Anthropology, Columbia University. For the last 10 years, he has been conducting archaeological research in the central highlands and the Caribbean coast of Colombia. His current work focuses into the material life of slavers and slaves in late seventeenth-century Panama, for which he has carried out extensive archaeological research in the UNESCO World Heritage site of Old Panama. His research interests include the historical archaeology of the Spanish colonies in the Americas, material culture theory, museum anthropology, and the politics of archaeological heritage in Latin America.

Sarah K. Croucher is an Assistant Professor of Anthropology, Archaeology, and Feminist, Gender & Sexuality Studies at Wesleyan University, Connecticut, and a 2010–2011 Weatherhead Fellow at the School for Advanced Research, Santa Fe. Her research centers on nineteenth-century East Africa, exploring themes of Omani colonialism which was embedded in new forms of capitalist trade. She has conducted survey and excavation work on Zanzibar and in mainland Tanzania, examining archaeological contexts of the nineteenth-century caravan trade and of clove plantations. Her PhD (University of Manchester) won the Society for Historical Archaeology 2008 dissertation prize and is currently being revised for publication. She has published articles in the *Journal of Social Archaeology* and *The International Journal of African History*, and chapters in several edited volumes. She is also the Co-Author (with E. Casella) of *The Alderley Sandhills Project: An Archaeology of Community Life in (Post)Industrial England* (2010, Manchester University Press).

François G. Richard (PhD, Syracuse University 2007) is a Historical Archaeologist and Historical Anthropologist studying the intersection of materiality, cultural practices, and power in West Africa over the past 1500 years. His current work examines the political changes that have taken place in coastal Senegal during the Atlantic era, how those were manifested in social landscapes, and how they shaped the historical experiences of rural societies into the postcolonial era. Another ongoing project examines the history of Catholic missionaries in the small province of Siin (Senegal), especially the nature of their relationship with the French Colonial State and African communities they sought to convert.

Lindsay Weiss is a Postdoctoral Scholar in the Archaeology Center and the Department of Anthropology at Stanford University. Her research specializes in the politics of postcolonial heritage, and the nineteenth-century diamond rush in South Africa. Lindsay earned her doctorate at Columbia University in 2009. Her doctoral research explores the history of the late nineteenth-century South African diamond rush and the role that speculative culture played in establishing apartheid conditions on the Diamond Fields. Her archaeological research examines the social and political significance of changes in material culture before and after segregation.

Professor Alistair G. Paterson is an Archaeologist at the University of Western Australia. His research and teaching covers culture contact, historical archaeology in maritime and terrestrial settings, European colonization, historical rock art, and archaeological and historical methodology. Much of his work is located in northern Western Australia, including regional studies of Australia's Northwest, the uses of coast and offshore islands in colonial and precolonial settings (in collaboration with the Western Australian Museum), and early colonial settlements across the state. He is the Author of *A Millennium of Cultural Contact* (Left Coast, 2011), *The Lost Legions: Culture Contact in Colonial Australia* (Alta Mira, 2008) and Editor with Jane Balme of *Archaeology in Practice: A Student Guide to Archaeological Analyses* (Blackwell Publishing, 2006). He is past-President of the Australian Archaeological Association (2005–2007), and has been involved with editing for, and publishing in, key archaeology journals, including *Archaeology in Oceania*, *Australasian Historical Archaeology*, and *Australian Archaeology*.

Matthew Palus completed a doctoral degree in Anthropology at Columbia University in 2010. He holds a Master's degree in Applied Anthropology from the University of Maryland College Park, and has worked with Archaeology in Annapolis and the University of Maryland's Archaeology Field School since 1999. He is Co-Author, with Paul Shackel, of *They Worked Regular: Craft, Labor, and Family in the Industrial Community of Virginius Island* (University of Tennessee Press, 2006).

Martin Hall is Vice-Chancellor of the University of Salford. He is also Professor Emeritus, University of Cape Town, where he is affiliated with the Graduate School of Business. Previously, Professor of Historical Archaeology, he was inaugural Dean of Higher Education Development and then Deputy Vice-Chancellor at UCT (from 1999 to 2008). He is a past-President of the World Archaeological Congress and is a Fellow of the Royal Society of South Africa and of the University of Cape Town. He is an accredited mediator with the Africa Centre for Dispute Settlement.

He has written extensively on precolonial history in Southern Africa, on the historical archaeology of colonialism and on contemporary public culture. He currently carries out research on the intersection of the public and private sectors, entrepreneurship, and the role of "knowledge organizations" in advancing development in highly unequal societies.

Recent publications include "Identity, memory and countermemory: the archaeology of an urban landscape" (*Journal of Material Culture* 11(1–2): 189–209, 2006),

Historical Archaeology (edited with Stephen Silliman; Oxford, Blackwell, 2006), *Desire Lines: Space, Memory and Identity in the Post-Apartheid City* (edited with Noeleen Murray and Nick Shepherd; London, Routledge, 2007), "Transformation and continuity in the university in Africa" (*Social Dynamics* 33 (1):181–198, 2007), "Stitch Wise: Strategic Knowledge Management for Pro-Poor Enterprise on South Africa's Goldfields" (in *The Business of Sustainable Development in Africa: Human Rights, Partnerships, and Alternative Business Models*, 2008), and *The Next 25 Years? Affirmative Action and Higher Education in the United States and South Africa,* edited with Marvin Krislov and David L. Featherman, University of Michigan Press, 2009. A full list of publications, as well as current work, is available at http://www.salford.ac.uk/vc.

Contributors

Lynda Carroll Public Archaeology Facility, Binghamton University, Binghamton, NY, USA

Sarah K. Croucher Assistant Professor of Anthropology, Archaeology, and Feminist, Gender & Sexuality Studies, Wesleyan University, Middletown, CT, USA

Aron L. Crowell Arctic Studies Center, National Museum of Natural History, Smithsonian Institution, Washington, DC, USA

Felipe Gaitán-Ammann Department of Anthropology, Columbia University, New York, NY, USA

Martin Hall University of Salford, Salford, Greater Manchester, UK

Mark W. Hauser Department of Anthropology, Northwestern University, Chicago, IL, USA

Audrey Horning Queens University Belfast, Belfast, UK

Matthew Palus Department of Anthropology, University of Maryland, College Park, MD, USA

Alistair G. Paterson School of Social and Cultural Studies, The University of Western Australia, Perth, WA, Australia

François G. Richard Department of Anthropology, University of Chicago, Chicago, IL, USA

Matthew A. Russell Department of Anthropology, University of California, Berkeley, CA, USA

Lindsay Weiss Archaeology Center and Department of Anthropology, Stanford University, Palo Alto, CA, USA

Chapter 1
The Archaeology of Capitalism in Colonial Contexts, an Introduction: Provincializing Historical Archaeology

Sarah K. Croucher and Lindsay Weiss

> *A key question in the world of postcolonial scholarship will be the following. The problem of capitalist modernity cannot any longer be seen simply as a sociological problem of historical transition (as in the famous "transition debates" in European history) but as a problem of translation, as well.*
>
> (Chakrabarty 2008 [2000]: 17)

> *Colonialism is* the *major cultural and historical fact of the last 500 years and to some extent the last 5000 years, although it is said that we now live in a post-colonial world. . . When colonialism is viewed comparatively it is disruptive of our views of people, power and objects. By looking at the varying forms power can take we learn much about the past and unlearn much about the present.*
>
> (Gosden 2004: 6)

Introduction

Historical archaeology, if we were to choose to use such dramatic language, could be said to be facing something of a crisis. This seems to come as something of a shock to a discipline which, despite debates about method and links to historical and archaeological theory (e.g., Beaudry 1988; Beaudry et al. 1991; Little 1994; South 1978; Schmidt 1990, 2006), has remained relatively constant in terms of the idea of historical archaeology as a field (cf. Dawdy 2010), particularly when compared to the almost ongoing nature of epistemic crises in other areas of anthropology (Behar 1995: 3;

S.K. Croucher (✉)
Assistant Professor of Anthropology, Archaeology, and Feminist, Gender & Sexuality Studies, Wesleyan University, Middletown, CT, USA
e-mail: scroucher@wesleyan.edu

S.K. Croucher and L. Weiss (eds.), *The Archaeology of Capitalism in Colonial Contexts*, Contributions To Global Historical Archaeology, DOI 10.1007/978-1-4614-0192-6_1, © Springer Science+Business Media, LLC 2011

Comaroff 2010; Comaroff and Kohl 2010; Ortner 1984; Trouillot 1991: 17). As the discipline globalizes, those working in the margins throw forward critique as to the flattening effects of the use of mainstream definitions and theoretical concepts (Funari et al. 1999; Reid and Lane 2004; Stahl 2007). This being the case, a volume that draws together diverse perspectives on two of the key themes of historical archaeology, debating their relevance and resisting their potentially muting discourses, seems a timely contribution to emerging debates.

The opening quotation from Chakrabarty frames perfectly the debates of this volume. We take as our central tenets two of the "universals" of historical archaeology: capitalism and colonialism. But we question what it means to discuss these formations in a variety of contexts, and in so doing show the problems inherent in taking these historical categories as always-already everywhere the same. Beyond archaeology, as we discuss below, postcolonial theory has provided scholarship on the issues of engaging with capitalism while simultaneously grappling what it means to examine this without the usual developmentalist historicity of Western scholarship.

By placing the two quotations together, each proclaiming the primacy of different universals (capitalist modernity, colonialism) as vital for analyzing the past, we highlight the continued importance of engaging with both, particularly when these are placed in historical contexts where global connections are impossible to ignore. They each also illustrate the place of the present in analyzing the past; postcolonial scholarship, through contemporary critique, has enabled a turn to history as a source of social justice and alternative possibilities in the present (Bissell 2011; Kearns 1998; Prakash 2000: 221), and historical archaeology has often been motivated by comparable aims (McDavid 2002; Wood 2002). While all are rooted in the past, every chapter in this volume is also in dialogue with the present, often through the persistent voice of local communities whose positions demand inclusion, along with more generalized aims to utilize archaeology for the purpose of social justice through examining historical roots of inequalities. Opening dialogue around the past in this way enables a certain emancipatory potential for the future (Weiss 2007).

In this introduction, we sketch out the contours of why a specifically postcolonial project is required in historical archaeology at the present time. This includes a genealogy of the analysis (or lack thereof) of capitalism and colonialism in the field. Drawing out specific lines of postcolonial theory, we suggest new directions for scholarship in these areas. Moving scholarship forward also presents some methodological implications for historical archaeology as a field that provides a specifically material dimension to the study of social aspects of political and economic formations of the last few hundred years. After introducing the content of each chapter, we provide some thoughts on future directions for postcolonial historical archaeologies (see also Hall, this volume). In the writing of this chapter and assembling this volume, we are not simply attempting to set out a new theoretical paradigm into which archaeologists can step, possibly adding "postcolonial" as an extra "haunt" of historical archaeology (*sensu* Orser 1996). Instead, we hope readers will take away a renewed sense of difference within the scope of historical archaeology. It is through embracing the varied subjects, power relations, and materialities of the recent past that historical archaeologists may engage in comparative discussions where different contexts may be written about as coeval and in which the "modern world" is not reducible to the confines of the Atlantic World.

Historical Archaeology's Haunts: Capitalism and Colonialism

To discuss the importance of capitalism and colonialism within historical archaeology is effectively to reiterate some of the broader points in the foundational definitions of our discipline. We are not interested in trying to create a new definition here to replace these,[1] and it suffices for us to say that the contributors to this volume all address contexts dating to the last several hundred years for which there is some form of historical evidence. Definitions are, however, instructive in following the genealogy of capitalism and colonialism as areas for analysis within historical archaeology. Beginning where most do, with Deetz (1996: 5), we could recall the usual "spread of European cultures definition." The words of the oft-cited phrase of defining the field are not so important; far more instructive is the expansion that Deetz provides beyond definition alone. He views colonialism as a process occurring directly between the Old and New worlds, as "Two worlds that had been separate from each other for millennia suddenly were brought into close contact." In these words, colonialism is confined within the panorama of the Atlantic Ocean. Absent from Deetz's definition is any specific mention of capitalism. Although he goes on to sketch out a narrative of modernity, this is one which happens largely in America, despite British cultural roots, and is not framed in any kind of Marxist terminology or with any particular reference to capitalism (Johnson 1996: 206).

This definition was originally sketched out in 1977, and was little revised for the update of *In Small Things Forgotten* produced in the mid 1990s. At the same time this updated version of a popular text was being printed, another archaeologist was attempting to redefine the field, based on the observation of changes in the scope and theoretical interests of historical archaeologists. Charles Orser's four "haunts" of historical archaeology have come to stand in as the most recent pop-definition of the field. *A Historical Archaeology of the Modern World* was written at a time when historical archaeology as so constituted here, was being practiced in more widely geographically spaced locales than ever before. As this was the case, Orser (1996: 27)

---

[1] We recognize the contentions over the scope and use of this term (see particularly Moreland 2001; Reid and Lane 2004; Schmidt and Walz 2007), however we apply it in the general sense meant by those who are members of the Society for Historical Archaeology, the annual meeting of which the papers in this volume were first aired. The concise definition on their website states: "Historical archaeology is the study of the material remains of past societies that also left behind some other form of historical evidence. … These sites [in the New World] document early European settlement and its effects on Native American peoples, as well as the subsequent spread of the frontier and later urbanization and industrialization. By examining the physical and documentary record of these sites, historical archaeologists attempt to discover the fabric of common everyday life in the past and seek to understand the broader historical development of their own and other societies." (Society for Historical Archaeology 2007) This definition is problematic in terms of a global discourse within the discipline, but we shall leave it to other authors to contribute new defining terms.

was attempting to find a way to tie together the field in a meaningful definition and dialogue that did not purely rest upon the history of North America. In choosing the themes of capitalism, colonialism, modernity, and Eurocentrism, Orser highlighted the epochal change he saw between the "modern world" of historical archaeology and the eras of earlier archaeology. He was wary of "unrestricted" definitions of the field based merely upon the presence of oral or documentary histories precisely because of the temporal split that he viewed as all important to the bounded nature modernity, highlighting that the world of prehistory was a "vastly different place" which was "inherently different" from earlier periods, and that the "things" of historical archaeology are those which seem "to be easily and readily understandable today" (ibid: 15, 16, 25). Such a rendering of historical archaeology, now widely accepted (and thus also critiqued) as the benchmark definition of the field, calls our attention to the fact that its boundaries are those of time, a decisive split between the Us of modernity and the Them of all earlier epochs, particularly prehistory (Dawdy 2010; Thomas 2004).

Colonialism in historical archaeology. At a general level, capitalism and colonialism are thus embedded as broad themes that help to mark off the epoch of "historical archaeologies of the modern world." But when we delve a little more deeply into each element, the boundaries are not so clear, showing perhaps that an epochal moment within historical archaeology is perhaps not so easy to delineate. Beginning with colonialism, we see immediately that this has a much larger timeframe than that of historical archaeology, and that even within historical archaeology, the precise edges of where colonialism begins and ends – the pre- and post-colonial periods – are really not so clear (Burbank and Cooper 2010; Horning, this volume; Palus, this volume; Russell, this volume; Silliman 2005; Stein 2005a). Stretching back in time for at least two millennia, colonial formations and encounters can be characterized as "a widespread, cross-cultural process" (Stein 2005b: 5). Despite this general point of agreement, comparative work across different time frames has been relatively rare, although seems to be increasing in frequency within the fields of archaeology and history, possibly motivated by a growing interest in the analytic of capitalism driven by postcolonial theory (Cooper 2005).[2] Within this general field as scholars look to examine the differences in colonialism over time, they struggle to see clear chronological epochs in colonialism.[3] Although historical archaeologists have participated in these debates a little, they tend to be written by scholars whose work focuses on periods of colonialism prior to the second half of the second

---

[2] In these comparisons, archaeologists are, in fact, trying to mark off their territory as the only discipline in which truly long-term comparison can take place, since archaeology "is the only discipline that can cover the full temporal range of colonial forms over the millennia." (Gosden 2004: 6)

[3] Stein (2005b: 4) notes, drawing on a seminar and edited volume of work by archaeologists attempting cross-cultural comparisons in the archaeology of colonialism that there is a lack of consensus by anthropologists as to: "(1) what colonies are, (2) how and why colonies vary from one another, (3) how colonies function as social, economic, and political entities, (4) what colonial relations are like with indigenous host communities, and (5) how ethnic identities are transformed in colonial situations." Within this discourse, even the terminology of colonies, colonization,

millennium AD – that is, prior to "modern" colonialism – as they figure in how their work might fit within broader discourse of colonial scholarship based upon postcolonial theory.

Definitions of colonialism in historical archaeology are hard to come by, and this in itself is telling.[4] Colonialism is at once everywhere, but it is also tightly delineated. Almost always when colonialism is referred to in historical archaeology it marks out Spanish or British colonialism, with rare forays into French colonialism (Richard, this volume). No scholar denies that colonialism existed before the "modern world," but the specificity of European colonialism (as marked by Deetz and Orser, among others) seems to mark the epoch of that particular colonialism of modernity, ushering in a particular set of relations between the West and the Rest tied in to such apparatus as the founding of anthropology as a discipline solidifying the very identity of the West (Trouillot 1991).[5]

Since colonialism is such a given, it is perhaps no surprise that the main attempt to segment off colonialism in a framework combining chronology and cultural relations is that of Gosden (2004). This work is not only aimed at the period of historical archaeology discussed here, but his work has been rapidly cited within historical archaeology as a key definition. Prior to splitting colonialism into a typological system, Gosden first claims a definition of it on archaeological grounds:

> Colonialism is a particular grip that material culture gets on the bodies and minds of people, moving them across space and attaching them to new values. These values often have a centre . . . but this is a symbolic centre, as much as a geographical one. Power emanates from artefacts and practices connected to that centre, rather than from the metropolis and its economic or military superiority. The new symbolic centre has power by virtue of the fact that it is associated with novel, but compelling, sets of materials and practices (Gosden 2004: 3).

---

and colonialism are contested ground. Within history, there has been a challenge for rigor in the use of the term colonial as a phenomenon outside of what might more narrowly be termed empires or true imperial formations, the use of which may result in "a diminished ability to make distinctions among the various forms of discrimination and exclusion [existing outside of colonialism] and a tendency to look away from the actual histories of colonization toward a homogenized coloniality." (Cooper 2005: 26; cf. Palus, this volume). Even within a more narrowly defined sense of colonialism, the changes and temporalities of colonialism can be hard to capture: "Although distinguishing empires with chronological labels – "modern," "premodern," or "ancient" – is tautological and unrevealing, empires did change over time and in space. Empires' capacities and strategies altered as competition drove innovations in ideas and technology and as conflicts challenged or enhanced imperial might." (Burbank and Cooper 2010: 17, cf. Gosden 2004 on the periodization of colonial formations)

[4]A lack of dialogue on the nature of colonialism within the field may also relate to postcolonial amnesia in some quarters (Gandhi 1998: 4) as well as the usual north-Atlantic-centric assumptions on the part of historical archaeology more generally.

[5]For a narrative of colonialism ordered chronologically which distinctly unseats this epoch of specifically Western and European colonialism as the only form of the last 500 years see Burbank and Cooper (2010: Chaps. 6–11).

Thus, colonialism is claimed as something that is comparable purely for the dispersed quality and power of its materiality; not simply because of the fact that European powers sailed over oceans and claimed new lands, or that classical civilizations expanded into new territories around Europe and the Mediterranean. Gosden's argument is provocative for archaeologists and those of other disciplines in calling for us to be attuned to the fact that colonialism should, according to this definition, always have a clear materiality to its expression of power.[6] He goes on to split off epochs of colonialism dependent upon social relations to "simplify a large and confusing reality" (Gosden 2004: 25). The period which seems to exist only in premodern periods is colonialism "within a shared cultural milieu," with a second category of colonialism in the "middle ground" spanning precapitalist and capitalist periods (Gosden 2004: 31–32). The latest epoch of colonialism is that of *Terra nullius*, where land could be taken, racial categories hardened, local power systems ignored, and with the exploitative requirements of capitalism at its base (ibid: 27). Of interest here is the fact that Gosden's epoch of modernity, as defined only within a chronology of colonialism, falls later than that which is usually defined as historical archaeology, instead, he sees a split when capitalism becomes a dominant economic formation, calling forth new colonial forms in order that plantations, mines, and colonies could be utilized to procure the raw materials for industry. Thus, we can read into Gosden's work the fact that he does see a modern world epoch, albeit one which is defined through capitalism, as brought into being by the possibilities of colonialism. In viewing colonialism of the past 500 years in a longer comparative framework, which focuses on cultural practices and politics of colonialism, and not on the economics of capitalism, Gosden (2004: 4) argues that within this historical archaeological time zone, "chaotic early contacts [of European colonialism] gave way to a new system of global culture set up after 1750, which really did span the whole world."

In broad archaeological discourse about colonialism we can see the embedded definitions of an epoch of European colonialism in the modern world, which seem to assume some form of break in the colonial patterns of the last 500 years (see for example also Hall 2000). Within historical archaeological definitions the very lack of discourse about the nature of colonialism seems to implicitly convey that there is some singular form of colonialism marked by modernity. Yet this is set against broader dialogues of colonialism about the *longue durée* of colonialism that see

---

[6]This definition can be compared to that of a recent comparative volume written by historians: "Empires are large political units, expansionist or with a memory of power extended over space, polities that maintain distinction and hierarchy as they incorporate new people . . . empire reaches outward and draws, usually coercively, peoples whose difference is made explicit under its rule. The concept of empires presumes that different peoples within the polity will be governed differently." (Burbank and Cooper 2010: 8) This definition shares with Gosden attention to the power of the colonial or imperial formation. But Gosden is not concerned, in his general definition, to pay attention to differences between empire and state power; he is concerned only with the operation of power within expansive political formations. Burbank and Cooper, by contrast, are writing from the perspective of modern historians, where a distinction between nation-states (which may also be expansive) and empires is required; in this they find that the marking of difference in colonial subjects (whether or not this has material registers, for this is not their concern) rather than the shared citizenship of nation-states, is the fundamental premise of colonial power.

connections in political forms of rule and the deployment of power between different contexts (Burbank and Cooper 2010; Stein 2005a). In these larger comparative frameworks, and in the suggestion that colonialism may change when in relation to capitalist economic relations, we see that perhaps the boundaries of colonialism within our field and that of other periods are murky, and this seems to call for attention to consider what it might mean to place colonialism into a larger discursive framework.

The epoch of capital. Capitalism, on the contrary, seems as though it should be far more straightforward to define. And yet, this is not so; historical archaeology struggles with its relationship to capitalism. Historical archaeology could be said to be a discipline founded on plantation studies, with canonical sites of the mid twentieth-century emergence of the discipline as such often plantations or closely connected with these institutions, such as Flowerdew Hundred (Deetz 1993) and Monticello (Kelso 1997). Sites such as these could be expected to be vital in forming a contribution toward understandings of the materialities of early capitalist formations. For outside of archaeology, scholars have discussed that experiments and developments in commodity production are perhaps exemplified most perfectly in the history of plantations, particularly as leading to the British plantations of the mid seventeenth century (Mintz 1985: 44). Drawing on a legacy of Marx, debates have turned over the issue of what it might mean to *be* capitalist, taking this as emanating from productive relations with social effects. As boundary drawing is attempted around what capitalism *is*, plantations occupy the borderlands. They are acknowledged to be embedded in relations of production that are capitalist (Mintz 1985: 50; Wallerstein 2000; Williams 1994 [1944]) and yet due to the fact that they are not based upon industrial production in the manner of that which emerged in eighteenth-century Europe and that they use enslaved labor, historical interpretation that centers on capitalism as presented by Marx relegates plantations to the introduction to the history of capitalism rather than as central to the narration of its form (Harvey 2010: 298, 305; Wolf 1997 [1982]: 87).

As plantations of early European colonialism prior to the late eighteenth century are such a contested point in the broader dialogue on the nature of capitalism, we might expect that historical archaeologists would be at the center of this conversation. Yet in much of the literature on plantations in archaeology leaves capitalism as a strangely absent force, particularly when the focus is on enslaved communities (Deetz 1993; Wilkie and Farnsworth 2005; cf. Croucher, this volume; Hauser, this volume), with the exception of work on Jamaica, influenced by the scholarship of B.W. Higman (1987, 2000) which focuses on the landscapes of plantations as capitalist forms (Delle 1998; see also Hauser, this volume, 2008). Agrarian forms, as part of the historical archaeology of capitalism, tend to focus more on Euro-American forms of tenant farming (Purser 1999; Wurst 1999) or the transformation of plantations in postbellum America (Orser 1991, 1999), or in the enclosure of landscapes in England (Johnson 1996). Instead, much of the focus of historical archaeology has been on "cultural issues pertaining to the growth of Anglo-American society," meaning that "Even now, historical archaeology has contributed little to the debate concerning the emergence of capitalism in the New World" (Mrozowski et al. 2000: xvi).

By far the clearest debates in historical archaeologies of capitalism have been directed at periods of industrial capitalism in USA. These engage with the development of class relations within new industrial settlements (Mrozowski 2006) and the changes in settlements as capitalist relations of the nineteenth century became sedimented (Leone 1999b; Leone et al. 2000 [1987]; McGuire 2008; Wurst 1999). Within this discourse, capitalism is defined quite clearly a "a social system in which the people who won and control the fields, factories, machines, tools and money do not assume the brunt of the work. Other men and women, who must sell their labor as if it were a commodity, perform the work." (Leone 1999a: 13) Wage labor here is the defining feature of a capitalism that stays faithful to the definitions set forth by Marx. Once this boundary of capitalism is passed, archaeologies defining themselves as being about capitalism become more numerous, showing the potential of our focus on materiality to engage with, for example, early consumer culture and its racialized aspects (Mullins 1999a, b). In their relationship to wider North American history, these archaeologists are attuned to the intersections of capitalist relations, particularly as they intersect with race and gender (Delle et al. 2000; Wall 1999). Despite this intersectionality, narratives of capitalism in historical archaeology have a tendency to be tautological, asking only why *the* industrial or *the* consumer revolution happened only in England, Europe, or America, and therefore effectively asking only why the history of the West happened in the West (Appadurai 1996: 72).[7]

The lack of attention to broader questions of capitalism in debates occurring outside of historical archaeology is a crucial epistemological issue of historical archaeology. Alison Wylie (1999: 26) has noted the danger in this:

> [T]his prescient commitment to humanistic and critical initiatives encourages a return to particularism, fostering a historical archaeology of capitalism that is about capitalism only in the narrow sense that many of the periods and subjects of interest to historical archaeologists are, by default, components of a capitalist world system. If the archaeological study of capitalism is framed as a series of narrow case studies with no movement beyond concrete particularities, and no analysis of the encompassing processes and structural conditions that give rise to these particularities, it cannot be expected to provide an understanding of these subjects as capitalist.

Outside of US scholarship, the situation is a little better. In examining early histories of capitalism, the work of the British historical archaeologist Matthew Johnson (1996) has been exemplary in demonstrating the complexities of the *longue durée* of those aspects we think of as the package of capitalism. His work has been accompanied by a number of other British historical archaeologists who have engaged with historical debates in offsetting the epochal moment of the industrial revolution, and producing a complex narration of British archaeology of the last 500 years in which industrialization was a drawn out process, involving rural populations and varying dialogues other than that of the totalizing ideas of capitalism alone (Belford and Ross 2004; Casella and Croucher 2010; Casella and Symonds 2005; Palmer and

---

[7] A flip side to this is the assumption of the place of the West as viewed from the side of the Rest, often allowing for discourses about the place of the Occident to go unchallenged (Carrier 1992).

Neaverson 2005; Tarlow 2007). Work in Britain has begun to engage with the diversity of narratives, but has yet to provincialize itself; capitalism and industrialization have become more complex in the West, but they remain resolutely Western.

In those few pockets of historical archaeology engaging with capitalism as occurring outside of the North Atlantic, scholars have begun to increasingly seek links to social scientific theory that seems to offer a framework of capitalism that can encompass the global relations we see, and yet leave enough space for the particularisms of the local. In this, the influence of Wallerstein's world-systems theory must be acknowledged. The discourse of this is complex, and was worked out over many years. Crucially however, it was a social scientific framing of a singular system of nomothetic principles. He viewed human history as progressive. But he did not see this progression as a trajectory but instead as an analytical variable where trends are "uneven or possibly indeterminate" and do not necessarily result in the "transformation toward some inevitable end-point" (Wallerstein 2000 [1987]: 146). Despite the fact that Wallerstein's work attempted to move away from a teleological analysis of capitalism – indeed he was indebted to the work of Fanon and influenced by incipient ideas in postcolonial scholarship – in seeing capitalism as a clear epoch (Wallerstein 2000 [1974]: 75) and in his insistence in the law-like properties of the relations between core, semi-periphery, and periphery (ibid: 86) capitalism becomes a *thing*, an analytical solidity which has come into being in a historically specific time.

In contrast to this point of view, we argue that there is no definition of capitalism in the singular. To engage with capitalism is to attempt to interpret the logics of its formations, the resistance to these, and the multiple elements of social action through which it is enacted at any one time. No single discipline has the "answer" to the question what, epistemologically or practically, delimits or defines the enactment of capitalism, since no set of evidentiary constraints that any discipline applies to itself – ethnographic, documentary, oral historical or archaeological – can be treated as only secondary and dispensable to any other (Wylie 1999: 28). It is easy to succumb to the idea of the "capitalist monolith," which seems all eclipsing – as we might note in those studies of capitalism in nineteenth- and twentieth-century North America – but capitalism is something which is continually emerging (Tsing 2005: 77). This move of seeing capitalism only as a formation, always shifting and never complete, is drawn out further by our use of Chakrabarty discussed below. It is an important one in a altering our ideas of the history of capitalism as a "flattening narrative" (Horning, this volume) in which we rely on such an analytic frame only to provide a thread of interpretation for which the answers are already known.

Postcolonial Theory and Its Implications

Postcolonial theory is a diverse body of work, and it would be impossible to cover it completely here. Directed by the literature of authors such as Fanon, Césaire, and Memmi, the scholarship of postcolonial critique is recognized to as emerging with the publication of Edward Said's *Orientalism* (1995 [1978]). This text drew on poststructuralist theory, particularly a critical treatment of Foucault's idea of discourse, to demonstrate the role of the Orient as a consistent foil to the Occident. Scholarship in this realm is often seen to exist largely in the field of literary studies, or at least those of the humanities, focusing mostly on the deconstruction of texts in terms of representations of coloniality and colonial thought (e.g., Bhabha 1994; Spivak 2000; Young 1995). However, at around the same time as this scholarship on the place of colonialism in literary representation, other disciplines were also grappling with the legacies of colonialism within their own fields, drawing forth the continued presence of colonial modes of thought and representation, and inter-rogating the colonial past from new critical directions. We discuss the place of history in this below, but cultural anthropology has, of course, had a broad ranging dialogue on its role in colonialism (e.g., Asad 1973), the continuation of colonial thought within anthropology (e.g., Fabian 2002 [1983]; Trouillot 1991), and the role of anthropological perspectives in understanding the colonial past (e.g., Comaroff and Comaroff 1991).

Archaeologists' engagement with postcolonial studies has been more recent. But postcolonial theory has a growing role in the theoretical framework as a discipline, particularly through work engaged with the World Archaeological Congress (e.g., Lydon and Rizvi 2010; Meskell 2009; Shepherd 2008). There are several strands to the role of postcolonial theory in archaeology, and these relate to the diversity of the theoretical work upon which this archaeological scholarship draws. All are refer-enced within this volume. They can be summarized into three distinct areas (Liebmann 2008: 4); of interpreting colonialism in the past (which all of the chap-ters in this volume do to a greater or lesser extent), in studying archaeology's role in the construction of colonial discourses (Horning, this volume; Russell, this vol-ume), and in the role of the theory in helping to methodologically decolonize the discipline in an attempt to move away from the colonial discourse contained within archaeology itself (see below). All of these areas are gaining greater and greater traction, and all are discussed in different ways within this volume. Our primary interest, however, is the utilization of postcolonial theory as it pertains to helping to understand the complex and intertwined role of capitalist and colonial formations over the past several hundred years, and as can be argued to continue into the present.

Postcolonial theory has not been absent from historical archaeology. On the American continent several studies have shown the way in which indigenous com-munities and colonizers had deep and sustained relations with one another, resulting in changes in daily lifeways and identities for *all* involved (see for example Deagan 2001; Ferguson 1992; Hall 2000; Lightfoot et al. 1998; Loren 2005; Rubertone 2000). While the differential power relations of these colonial engagements cannot be understated and had deep constraints on the forms in which changed identities could take place (Silliman 2005), at the same time archaeologists are increasingly coming to realize the importance of investigating the multidirectional nature of colonialism (Lawrence 2003). Such scholarship is deeply embedded in approaches ushered in by a general move toward postcolonial scholarship, even if not directly referenced as such.

We have been deeply influenced by the historical writings of the Subaltern Studies collective, particularly in moves to write history as a political practice, where capitalism is seen to include the heterogeneity of the conflicts, contradictions, and ambivalence of colonial history (Prakash 2000: 236). The historians of this group can be seen as part of the wider framework of postcolonial theory, which has worked to examine the representations of coloniality, past and present, and to break down binaries between colonizer and colonized (e.g., Bhabha 1994; Spivak 2006 [1987]; Young 1995). Its use in archaeology is relatively young, with much of its application being directed to specifically colonial periods, the place of archaeology in helping to construct European colonial discourse, and to the decolonization of knowledge (Dietler 2005; Hall 2000; Liebmann 2008: 4; Liebmann and Rizvi 2008; Lydon and Rizvi 2010; Patterson 2008; Shepherd 2002; van Dommelen 2005). As a field deeply influenced by Foucault and the deconstruction of knowledge (Said 1995 [1978]), it is perhaps no surprise that later iterations of postcolonial history within the field of Subaltern Studies came to be framed by locating the inadequacies of Marxist historiography.[8] Through trying to use the idea of "history from below," subaltern studies historians came to find that Indian peasants were always cast in a developmentalist framework, where they were "prepolitical," never able to be the full subjects of capitalist history in the manner of, for example, the British working class (Pandey 2000, cf. Gaitán-Amman, this volume on the use of precapitalist). Such dialogue brought out a tension that Marxist historical theory could not adequately account for "the nature of power in non-Western colonial modernities" (Chakrabarty 2002: 14).

The move of this school of history in the late twentieth century was, therefore, not only deeply concerned with representations of history – via the resurrection of subalterns in historical narrative – but also became a project of decolonizing history itself; first in narratives of Indian history, but also in the project of Dipesh Chakrabarty (2008 [2000]) to "Provincialize Europe" through attacking the historicist roots of history to make a theoretical move whereby Indian history and that of Europe during capitalism became coeval through a process of recognizing the incompleteness of the universal history of capital within Europe itself. In order to do this, Chakrabarty distinguished two parts of history that are always present within any analysis. The first of these (which he terms History 1) is an analytical category – capital in this instance, but we could, with qualifications, expand this argument to many "universals". This category of history, through its nature abstracts tending eventually "to make all places exchangeable with one another" (Chakrabarty 2008 [2000]: 71). But a second kind of history, one formed out of the practices and experiences of life (termed History 2) is also *always* present, and "beckons us to more *affective* narratives

---

[8]It should be noted that postcolonial theory and Marxism have a complex relationship; postcolonial scholars are indebted to a theoretical genealogy of Marxist scholarship, particularly coming through Foucault to Said, but they simultaneously are able to take apart the Marxist historical framework of the idea of the West and its Others (Gandhi 1998: 25; Patterson 2008: 30).

of human belonging where life forms, although porous to one another, do not seem exchangeable" (ibid). In our recognition that it is not only the "peripheries" of capitalism that are the bearers of these second kind of histories, we see that the history of capitalism everywhere is a balance between these two acts. This is demonstrated through, for instance, the fact that cultural categories (an example is given of a pianist and tastes in music as being a vital precursor for the capitalist production of pianos) are always interacting with even the most abstract operations of capital, which we may be tempted to see as progressing outside of local realms of experience and practice (ibid: 66). Even in the heartland of historical archaeology, such as the city of Annapolis (Palus, this volume), we must, therefore, be aware that we are not looking at *the* history of capital, but rather *a* history of capital. Chakrabarty concludes, in a passage that is vital for us to think through what a provincialized historical archaeology might consist of:

> To provincialize Europe in historical thought is to struggle to hold in a state of permanent tension a dialogue between two contradictory points of view. On one side is the indispensable and universal narrative of capital . . . [providing us with] energizing glimpses of the Enlightenment promise of an abstract, universal but never-to-be-realized humanity. . . On the other side is thought about diverse ways of being human, the infinite incommensurabilities through which we struggle – perennially, precariously, but unavoidably – to "world the earth" in order to live within our different senses of ontic belonging. These are the struggles that become – when in contact with capital – the History 2s that in practice always modify and interrupt the totalizing thrusts of History 1 (Chakrabarty 2008 [2000]: 254).

Through taking on board this lesson, we can see a path toward a postcolonial historical archaeology, and this project will involve – through a process which is in effect decolonizing knowledge – "provincializing" the field through making us realize that the usual tautological narratives of capitalism where, for instance, modern American individuals come into being in modern America, is but one part of the complex history of capital. It allows us to bring into being globalized historical archaeologies which engage with the manner in which capitalism and colonialism were part of the lives of the subjects being examined, but without using these contexts to flatten out narratives of these periods, since we know that any experiences within the formations of capitalism are a complex relationship between a formation which is *never* complete (even in industrial England or America), and local, particular, scales of knowledge and practice. Thus this volume engages not only with globalizing historical archaeology (*sensu* Orser 1996), but also moves the center of the discipline away from its United States heartland and the Atlantic world. In decentering geographically, including so-called peripheral sites (those removed from traditionally held centers of industrialization and imperialism, and those of indigenous populations under colonialism), and in shifting our epistemological starting place for the very terms through which we think about capitalism, we make an vital generative move in terms of prompting critical discussion about how historical archaeological research may redress some of the limits of our Eurocentric theory and historical accounts. This is driven by postcolonial theory and feeds into the aims of postcolonial archaeological scholarship in terms of producing archaeological narratives which seek to redefine the often implicit colonial representations of a developmentalist history of capitalism within historical archaeology, particularly in the way that most non-Western contexts are always viewed through a prism of underdevelopment, and in an attempt to produce a decolonized narrative of historical archaeology which redefines the general discourse of our field through an appreciation of global relations based upon postcolonial scholarship.

The move to postcolonial theory as a frame for understanding archaeologies of capitalism in colonial contexts also provides a route out of the usual framings of relations of power. Historical archaeology has largely taken a top down approach to the exercise of power, examining the manner in which hegemonic power is exerted in material form, influenced by critical theory (Leone et al. 2000 [1987]). Within colonialism, the imperative has been to find the hybrid identities between colonizer and colonized, often locating resistance and agency of colonized subjects within this process (e.g., Fennell 2007; Silliman 2001; cf. Liebmann and Murphy 2011 on limiting the use of resistance). Drawing upon Chakrabarty's work in particular, and in taking a broader influence from the discussion of concepts of hegemonic power in anthropology and histories of colonialism (Sivaramakrishnan 2005), we show the instability of the operation of power. If we are to take the insistence of "History 2s" – those localized historical pathways to any moment – seriously, then the exercise of power by capital and colonialism can never be complete. This is not simply because of a spring back of resistance. Instead, it is through the impossibility of the full exercise of hegemonic power in any one context (e.g., Richard, this volume).

Theoretical Implications

Several implications arise from the theoretical directions that we take here. These range across the different areas of scholarship that postcolonial theory tends to invoke; examining the history of the field, representation within current discourse and attempts to decolonize theory and practice. Issues of delving into the history of historical archaeology to find the roots of colonialist thought have begun to be sketched out above. In drawing out the genealogy of scholarship on capitalism and colonialism within this realm, we have begun to show how this is couched only in a sense of historical archaeology based on the Atlantic World, with particular bias toward the Americas. If archaeologists assume, based on geographical privilege, that they are in a context where they see the *complete* iteration of any universal, then they risk flattening out the particularities of the dialectic between universal and singular that always exist. History 1 – our universals and metanarratives – may be easy to find. But we must never accept that these are fully formed, or that they unfold in the absence of History 2s.

We suggest that historical archaeology has fallen prey to the seductive explanatory promise of grand narrative, seeing capitalism and colonialism as isolable forces that can be examined in every context on the same terms. As Hauser (this volume) points out, grand narratives of capitalism, modernity and race can produce singular interpretations of the archaeology of slavery in the Caribbean. We would extend this to say that singular interpretations of (usually Spanish or Anglo) colonialism and capitalism are widely (re)produced across the discipline (see Horning, this volume for further critique). By shifting the geography of historical archaeology into a wider range of contexts, we are able to demonstrate that an overarching narrative of either of these terms is impossible. An attempt to solve this diversity by grouping together regions does not work either; taking a single continent of case studies in this volume, that of Africa (Croucher; Richard; Weiss, this volume) we see the variance of both capitalism *and* colonialism.

Colonial rule is not that which we are used to invoking in historical archaeology; Crowell shows us an "off-center" study of Russian colonialism in Alaska, Carroll that of the Ottoman Empire (and here colonial rule is still drawing on Enlightenment thought), and Croucher of the Omani Sultanate in Zanzibar. This list is but the beginning of the manner in which these chapters pick apart the usual binary of European colonizer/indigenous colonized in historical archaeology. The history of capitalism as a singular thing is similarly problematized by taking a diverse perspective via our case studies. We discussed earlier the attempts to bound off capitalism at particular epochs within Marxist thought. But capitalist relations defy any easy periodicity within this set of chapters. Hauser (this volume) for instance shows us an almost nested capitalist economy on Jamaica; that of African-Jamaicans, unfree and free, engaging in commodity exchange of locally produced ceramics. This economy is closely related to that of colonial Jamaica through the limits on enslaved participation in the wider economic life of the island and the requirements of daily life of this population. Yet it is also not defined by it; the economy of higglers seems to defy the hegemonic economic control of the island by British rulers. Similarly, Richard (this volume) shows how the Serer in Senegal practiced a complex, even hybrid, economy whereby precolonial production and that promoted by French colonial rule were able to come together in a solution which worked to the Serer's advantage. Capitalist production does not thrive merely by its own logic in colonial situations, where the holding of industrial technology and large landholdings is destined for success. Paterson (this volume) demonstrates the interrelationship between Anglo-settlers and local Aboriginal populations in Australia for the large scale pastoralist farming.

Making a move into global dialogue also produces new issues in terms of the translation of regional traditions of scholarship into the larger frame. We have argued that it is imperative for non-Anglo-European contexts to have voice within the wider narrative of historical archaeology. But these all come with diverse histories of scholarship that we have to engage with, being aware of terminology that might seem problematic when it becomes placed into a global dialogue of scholarship. Ignoring such difference could risk that postcolonial theory itself simply becomes the new grand narrative, ignoring the particularisms that are in fact so crucial to recognizing difference. Writing from one regional tradition, Gaitán-Ammann, for instance, characterizes the New Granada economy as in some ways still "premodern" in the late nineteenth century, owing to the cultural resistance of postcolonial nationalism to some capitalist economic structures. This kind of developmentalist segmenting off of aspects of capitalism would be antithetical to the work of current trends in the postcolonial historical scholarship discussed above, but draws upon a history of postcolonial scholarship on the nature of economic and cultural history in Latin America. Such instances demonstrate the potential problems in writing across disciplinary and area-studies, but in these moments of theoretical incompatibilities, our attention is drawn toward ideas that we might take for granted, forcing us to question these and to sustain our arguments. These disparities may arise from important aspects of historical trajectories in these different regions, and may have import that exists in this area but does not translate well into the wider field, providing us with limits to being able to simply take theory and place it into any context. Moving into this wider discourse and attempting not to gloss over difference but to engage with it offers further possibilities for recognizing colonial trajectories of scholarship. To conclude our introduction we offer up some future directions for postcolonial historical archaeologies, but we are first going to introduce the scope of the volume, in order that those reading these suggestions may understand a little more of the content of the case studies upon which our arguments are informed.

Volume Overview

The chapters that follow have been structured into a roughly chronological order. Much as with our provocation to problematizes any monolithic reading of either capitalism or colonialism, the purpose of this is not to suggest that there is some kind of history unfolding through time, but to demonstrate the continual ebb and flow within this apparent chronology of modernity. One immediate point that our readers may notice is that these chapters are scattered around much of the world, with very little from the "heartland" of historical archaeology. As discussed above, this is a key reason that we think that each author, and the volume as a whole, is able to challenge the general narrative structure of historical archaeology. Of eleven chapters in total, three are based on sub-Saharan African contexts, two are from North America, and then the following relate to the Middle East, Australia, the Caribbean, South America, and Europe. This continental diversity, along with that of the temporal dimension (contexts range from the sixteenth century through to the twentieth century in archaeological material, and include twenty-first century discourse around archaeology), means that a productive dialogue emerges around questions of how the two universals we are all engaging can be examined in each study. The chapters are, therefore, intended to be read together, to force our readers to confront the diversity constituting these very universals, and to consider that their analytical legitimacy may lie precisely within this multiplicity.

Chapter 2 is written by Matthew Russell, and presents an interesting mix of maritime and land-based archaeology in the study of culture contact in early Spanish colonialism at the (now Californian) site of *tamál-húye*. This is an "event oriented archaeology" in that it is focused on a sixteenth-century Spanish shipwreck, almost

200 years prior to European colonialism of the region. Russell's chapter presents several interesting ideas about the factoring in of such a short-term "event" to address the *longue durée* of indigenous-European relations and colonialism in California.[9] Russell's chapter is not about the simple question of what happened in the event of the Spanish shipwreck on a little-known coast. He utilizes this moment, and the potential of archaeological and historical traces of this, to explore whether this early culture-contact had any clear effect on the indigenous peoples who came into contact with the ship itself and its material remnants.

In addressing the themes of capitalism and colonialism, Russell explores the borderlands of each to trouble any clear epochal moment in which the Tamal (the indigenous peoples living around *tamál-húye*) were drawn into wider structures of capitalism and colonialism. Wolf (1997 [1982]) is used as a framework to place Tamal and European intercultural engagements as part of larger processes taking place on a global scale, since from this perspective the histories of Tamal and European peoples were interconnected from the point of encounter onward. Such encounter has potential to be viewed as part of the emergence of colonial rule in this area, but can also be taken within the frame of culture-contact rather than colonialism (Silliman 2005), allowing Russell to address whether the short-term shipwreck events he is addressing, thus introducing foreign material culture, "was a possible source of long-term cultural change, or whether extended entanglement from later, eighteenth- and nineteenth-century colonialism was necessary for significant social transformation to occur." (Russell, this volume: 42). World-systems theory is used as an heuristic aid in this analysis, since it emphasizes, for Russell, the fact that within the growth of capitalist worldwide economic relations, such as those driving European vessels to be sailing near the Californian coast, societies were increasingly interconnected through a particular economic imperative. However, Russell also cautions against the potential essentialization of "core" and "peripheral" groups in such a framework. By drawing together the ideas of microhistorical, event-oriented, perspectives to examine the long term, recognizing the interconnectedness of societies in the expansion of capitalism, along with the differences between culture-contact and colonialism, Russell produces a chapter which immediately challenges the epochal terrain of historical archaeology's break with prehistorical or precolonial pasts, forcing readers to immediately confront whether there is any clear rupture into periods of capitalist and colonial archaeologies. By refusing the prehistory/historical divide in archaeology, and demonstrating the need for contiguous analyses across these periods, Russell reminds us of the importance of a diachronic framework that recognizes the importance of the social continuum across so-called "breaks" in historical time; the events at *tamál-húye* were epochal for neither indigenous nor European peoples. The archaeological examination of cultural structure both before and after the events Russell examines demonstrate that the European

---

[9]This idea of taking short-term events as a perspective within archaeology to write longer-term histories (*sensu* Ginzburg 1990 [1982]) has also been explored from the perspective of microhistory, see Brooks et al. (Eds., 2008) for a range of studies on this approach.

shipwreck off the Californian coast was in no way culture changing for Tamal people, and that the use of shipwreck-derived material culture was determined on the terms of Indigenous peoples rather than on those of European traders. In this interpretation, strongly supported by archaeological evidence and oral histories, Russell also contributes to wide-ranging attempts to address Eurocentrism within historical archaeology (Orser 1996; Schmidt and Walz 2007), sympathetic with the postcolonial theoretical position of *Capitalism in Colonial Contexts*. By focusing his archaeological studies on indigenous society, and not *presuming* that European culture-contact would have an impact, Russell's (this volume: 40) chapter opens up a new arena of thinking of "postcontact, precolonial Indigenous society," and in so doing effectively engages in efforts to decolonize method and theoretical orientation within archaeology as a whole (Liebmann 2008).

Audrey Horning's contribution (Chap. 3) elaborates some of the themes from Russell's chapter, in that she addresses the problems of the baggage of theoretical assumptions that so often come along with the recognition of colonialism and capitalism in historical archaeology, leading all too-often to "totalizing narratives" on these topics. Time is of the essence in Horning's work, as she presents the crux of her critique through the contemporary political context of Northern Irish and Irish discourse about the colonial past, along with the situating of Ireland within wider current historical archaeological narrative. Late in her chapter, we are introduced to her role as an archaeologist on a panel organized by Belfast City council in 2009 to respond to the quadricentennial of Ulster Plantation histories. Archaeological evidence of these contexts has demonstrated for Horning the reality of a shared history of plantation between the Irish and colonial British settlers. For instance, "Irish-built cooking pot fragments, wheel-thrown, gravel tempered pottery from North Devon, and English and Dutch pipestem fragments" are the types of assemblages found that suggest "a significant degree of material exchange" between different residents of sixteenth-century Ireland (Horning, this volume: 79), as does evidence of alcohol consumption, which demonstrates "intimacy of relations between the London Company settlers and the Irish whom they were supposed to be supplanting" (ibid). The archaeological identification of shared practices, unsettling the often binary history between Irish and plantation villages shows the impossibility for Horning, as an archaeologist informed by evidence, to allow her work to prop up either unionist or nationalist versions of minority history in Northern Ireland. Here, Horning's authority as an archaeologist provides here with a potential responsibility to share "the convoluted history and ambiguous material evidence" from plantation sites in Northern Ireland, providing her audience with "a greater opportunity to decide for themselves what matters most about the events and human experience of Plantation" (Horning, this volume: 80). In this vein, Horning articulates the emancipatory potential for historical archaeology to contribute to a decisionist (*sensu* Chakrabarty) role. That is, the potential to use historical narrative to offer choices about the future; why should the future for Northern Ireland be divided when the past has not always been so. In this potential, however, she tempers her optimism with her reflexivity, worrying that she questions for whom she speaks, even as her statements are recognized as authoritative by public audiences.[10] Such reflexivity is vital within postcolonial archaeologies, as we attempt to decolonize the very voice of narrative within our discipline (Liebmann 2008).

The complexity of the Northern Irish plantation past is key to Horning's critique of the place of capitalism and colonialism as often thoughtless metanarrative within historical archaeology. She takes inspiration from postcolonial theory in her work, but worries that this still has the potential to emphasize binary oppositions between colonizer and colonized in the past, as exemplified by the recognition of historical similitude between Native Americans and the Irish demonstrated through discourse surrounding the repatriation of a canoe from a Galway museum. The colonial settlement of Irish plantations, and the capitalist relations of the sixteenth century are not a simple history of domination and resistance in Horning's reading of the past. Yet she finds as she reads the majority of archaeology which sets up global linkages in the discourse of the universals of capitalism and colonialism, that there are glib uses of these terms, eliding interpretive rigor, and (re)producing "totalizing narratives" about the sameness of colonized and working class oppression everywhere (Horning, this volume: 65). Readers will find it impossible to finish Horning's chapter with anything but a series of thoughts that push for critical rigor while we use those all-too-dangerous "universals" of capitalism and colonialism, risking erasing the qualities of each case study we examine by sloppy excesses of meta-level theory.

The first two interpretive chapters of the volume may be familiar territory for historical archaeologists, drawing us into the earliest prehistory of Spanish colonialism in California and the archaeology of plantations in Ireland. Chapter 4, by Aron Crowell, moves us into more unfamiliar territory, with an "off-center" view of colonialism in Russian Alaska from the mid-eighteenth century to the US purchase of Alaska in 1867. Crowell's chapter is fascinating in demonstrating the "not-quite" quality of capitalism in this region (*sensu* Chakrabarty) as he leads us through the contested relations of daily life and capitalist production and extraction on a remote frontier of the Russian Empire. He situates this within a world-systems framework of analysis, where this region might be seen as peripheral, yet still integral to the whole, of the world-system of capitalism. However peripheral, Russian Alaska was clearly deeply enmeshed in various productive relations that were, at least in part, structured by the imperatives of capitalism. These ranged through forced and (minimally) paid labor and trading relations with indigenous groups, and can be viewed in archaeological contexts such as the nineteenth-century Russian colonial capital of Novo-Arkhangel'sk, which was "a hub of colonial industry" with a "diversity and abundance of goods" (Crowell, this volume: 97). Such sites challenge the very terrain of what it might mean for archaeologists to write regions off as "peripheral," when life in Novo-Arkhangel'sk must surely have seemed anything but.

---

[10] The issue of scholarly positionality is a key one in postcolonial theory, as articulated in the seminal piece 'Can the Subaltern Speak?' (Spivak 1988). See also Fontein (2010: 315) and Battle-Baptiste (2010: 390) for specific discussion of the place of position (both emic and etic) and representation in postcolonial archaeological scholarship.

In addressing the two core themes of the volume, Crowell's work challenges readers to think about the diversity of capitalism and colonial relations. Our attention is drawn to the particularism of capitalism in this region, structured by the Russian-America Company and their corporate investment and risk, which resulted in a set of colonial power relations simultaneously singular and analogous to those of other regions and periods. Crowell's chapter is one of the most detailed of the volume in terms of the depth of archaeological evidence he presents, summarizing evidence from a range of sites, spanning the years of Russian colonial rule, to show the diversity of cultural practices under the single colonial-capitalist structure of the Russian-America Company. The result of his data analysis is to show the force of hybridity in the face of strict regulation as to how the relations of this structure should exist. As with many other colonial situations the power relations of colonialism were played out in the nervous terrain of the boundaries between ethnic and racial identities and sexual relations between colonizers and natives.[11] While supposedly clearly policed, sexual relations between Russian settlers resulted in a large Creole population within Russian-Alaska, and the everyday politics of new categories and boundaries of identities intersected along racialized/ethnic and class lines. Class segregation should have mirrored a clear division between upper- or middle-class/Russian, middling- or lower-class/Creole, and poor native populations. However, as Crowell shows from archaeological findings at a variety of sites, the economic striations and the cultural boundaries of capitalist and colonialist relations in Russian Alaska were far from clear. Crowell also presents his archaeological work as squarely in a contemporary frame, as the postcolonial politics of archaeological research in Alaska take place in a context where historical legacies of ethnic discourse continues today, such as the change in ethnonym for the peoples of Kodiak Island from the Russian-conferred "Aleuty" or "Alutiiq" to the current Sugpiaq, meaning "real people." The politics of historical archaeology in the wake of such complexities can never be easy, as Crowell (this volume: 86) reminds us of the context of his work beneath "blue Orthodox domes that float above scores of southern Alaskan villages from Kodiak to the Yukon River."

The following chapter spins the globe almost a half-turn, yet in what we might also think of as usually off-center-stage in terms of historical archaeology; the colonial and capitalist relations of the Transjordan under Ottoman colonial rule during the second half of the nineteenth century. While unfamiliar to many readers (although see contributions to Baram and Carroll 2000), Carroll (this volume: 105) reminds us that the Ottoman Empire was "one of the Great Powers of the early modern period," covering large swathes of the Middle East, North Africa, and the Balkans at its height during the sixteenth century. By the nineteenth century, the period of Carroll's

---

[11] One of the strongest analogies to the system in place in Russian Alaska may be found in Spanish colonialism in the Americas. See in particular Voss (2008) for a full length study of attempts to regulate ethnicity versus on-the-ground ethnogenesis. See also Deagan (1973, 1998) and Loren (2005) for further discussions of ethnicity and colonialism in Spanish America. For a more general discussion on issues of sexuality and identity within colonial relations, see McClintock (1995) and Cooper and Stoler (1997).

(this volume: 108) study, the Transjordan region she is examining was under the influence of *Tanzimat* reforms, which were "based on Enlightenment ideals . . . linked to discourses of progress and modernity." The nomadic Bedu who lived in the Transjordan were viewed as antithetical to these reforming moves of the Ottoman state, and were to be forced to adopt more settled modes of life along with the arrival of merchant settlers from Palestine.

Archaeological evidence from a single site, Qasr Hisban, in the Transjordan, is utilized by Carroll to explore the terrain of these new relations of self-consciously modernizing colonialism and the shift to more intensified crop production to export this in commodity form out of the region. On one level, the use of new architectural styles and the settled farm complex at Qasr Hisban seem to show a "top-down model of change" where the Bedu were passive recipients of the forced changes of *Tanzimat* reform. However, the archaeological evidence from caves near this settled farm-stead show active spaces of resistance within this period, as the Bedu utilized these spaces to hide goods from tax collectors, to deal directly with merchant settlers so as to link into newly expanding urban networks of trade, and to serve as a local political center.

Thus, Carroll's chapter seems to offer only an unfamiliar setting for familiar themes of the study of capitalism in colonial contexts; imposition of new power structures and local resistance to these – perhaps a risk of the "totalizing narratives" of which Horning warns. Carroll (this volume: 107) is, however, well aware of these issues; although she squarely situates herself within the framework of global histori-cal archaeology (*sensu* Orser 1996), she notes that "there is a danger that Ottoman archaeology could be constructed as just one more study of how the West material-ized itself in yet another non-Western setting, whether through so-called capitalist penetration, or through colonial encounters." Such concerns directly echo Horning's, recognition of the dangers in taking those ever-present universals of global histori-cal archaeology too far. To know capitalism and colonialism in one location is *not* to know the complex relations between Bedu, Palestinian settlers, and the Ottoman state in the nineteenth-century Transjordan. Carroll (this volume: 107) sees postco-lonial theory as a route through some of these issues, since it offers the ability "to provide alternative stories about the past," and has an "emphasis on particularisms in the face of the global structures of capitalism and colonialism." The site of Qasr Hisban itself presents these particularisms, while situating these in attempts to deploy capitalist economic and settler-colonial power structures. In taking the Transjordan as her context, Carroll performs important scholarship within postcolo-nial historical archaeology not only in revealing attempts of nineteenth-century Transjordan Bedu to form new alliances with settlers and to find ways to carve out their own paths through impositions of power, but also through the fact that she is concerned with carrying out historical archaeology of "the Ottoman state itself." For there is very little to be said of non-Western European colonialism within historical archaeologies, despite the fact that these were a fundamental part of the terrain of colonial rule in the last few hundred years. In taking such a stance, Carroll's chapter should be taken here with Crowell's and Croucher's in thinking through the diversity of these "other" colonialisms, and figuring them into a broadened discourse as to what colonialism was and is.

Mark Hauser's chapter explores the market contexts of colonial Jamaica, where his work focuses on European plantations of the eighteenth century, operating via the use of enslaved labor. He immediately notes, as with other authors, that there have been key metanarratives to frame historical and archaeological investigations of the period: capitalism, modernity, race. While recognizing the importance of these frames of investigation, Hauser (this volume: 121) also cautions that they may reduce life in the Caribbean at this time to "a by-product of rather monolithically conceived forces unleashed in the metropole." To try to recognize their importance, and yet to investigate an archaeology of eighteenth to nineteenth-century plantations on Jamaica that is not simply another iteration of the same metanarratives over and over, Hauser turns to question the lives of enslaved laborers as "subjects of capitalism" and "conscripts of modernity" within the broader themes of capitalism and colonialism. Colonial rule by Europeans is taken as a given here, since this was a key area in fashioning ideas of delineated and segmented state rule (Delle 1998; Higman 1987), and since European – specifically British – rule, was the generative legal power structure for the lives of enslaved laborers on Jamaica. However, enslaved persons on Jamaica were capable of autonomous lives, and so Hauser attempts to question whether these same persons followed the same "mercantile logics" of Europeans in their attempts to accumulate wealth and deploy labor. Questions on this front are examined through the linking of archaeological, textual and oral historical data which addresses the role of local ceramic (*yabbas*) production and consumption on Jamaica.

Through this complex web of evidence, Hauser (this volume: 124) shows that colonial law on the island circumscribed economic activity for the enslaved, and also set up an "opposition between formal and informal markets: those run by property-owning (renting) white merchants who must pay taxes, and those (implied as people of African extraction) who [were] not subjected to the same demands." Within this legal framework, Hauser moves on to explore the archaeology of *yabbas* ceramics to attempt to establish the economic participation of the majority enslaved population. Hauser's evidence shows that there was a limited number of centers of production for such wares (probably only three), but that these were a crucial part of the everyday lives for the enslaved of Jamaica. This concentration of production which was able to market out to a wide network demonstrates that an economic network was in place out of the control of the planter, and yet still conforming to the logic of commodity markets in that goods were not exchanged in a barter network. Instead, local traders who sold these wares were "higglers" (Hauser, this volume: 134), who were able to derive good profits from a limited and – literally – captive market. Hauser's analysis of capitalism in this colonial context provides some fascinating insights into the potential for networks of capital, showing that these can at once conform to the logic of capitalism, and yet be far removed from the type of metanarrative world-systems approach so often used to investigate such economic relations. Thus the final interpretation of eighteenth and nineteenth-century ceramic trading on Jamaica shows the potential for hidden-transcripts within capitalist historical archaeologies, which also highlight networks of social relations that would have gone on alongside trading itself. This is a vital factor in helping establish archaeological interpretations of the potential for social independence and interrelationships within the harsh conditions of enslavement. It also presents an expansion of the way in which we think of capitalism. Yet Hauser (this volume: 135) also cautions that we should not think of this as an "alternative economy," but instead as a "local manifestation of the kind of social relations which enabled capital accumulation and growth, and yet are hidden or ignored in the grand narratives on empire, capitalism, and modernity."

This theme of the complexities of capitalism and its local iterations continues in the next of our case-study chapters by Felipe Gaitán-Ammann, as he takes us to the postcolonial context of New Granada (present day Columbia). The archaeological narrative to the chapter is viewed through the finding of ceramic sherds from the home of one of the newly composed postcolonial national elites of a New Granada independent of Spain in the nineteenth century. Gaitán-Ammann utilizes consumption patterns of Uribe family to begin to take us on a narrative, via the trail of ceramic sherds and documentary history, into the contradictions and complexities of the economic life of independent citizens of Bogotá and their positioning as postcolonial subjects. Although locally made mass-produced refined industrial whitewares were available in Bogotá, and were printed with local designs which highlighted national pride, this local capitalist productive venture failed; both in continuation of production, and in the fact that the wares from this pottery were not found in the waste of the Uribe household. Instead, they chose plain whitewares which were manufactured in England, and yet were also stamped with the mark of the Bogotá ceramic importer, from whom they would have been procured. Gaitán-Ammann takes this consumption choice to show the fact that bourgeoisies in Bogotá were echoing consumption practices in metropoles of the nineteenth-century capitalist world, such as New York (Wall 1999), demonstrating their cosmopolitan tastes. Gaitán-Ammann takes us on another step in this historical archaeological narration by tracing the life of the ceramic merchant, Leonidas Posada Gaviria. Moving away from archaeological evidence to that of documentary history inspired by the ceramic finds, we learn of Posada Gaviria's thriving shop in late nineteenth-century Bogotá, perhaps prompting echoes also of the growth of consumer culture in Europe and North America. However, despite his flourishing mercantile business, Posada Gaviria did not reinvest his profits in expanding his business, but instead spent his money on becoming a landowner and philanthropist, a route which allowed him to ascend to become mayor of Bogotá.

Through this narration, Gaitán-Ammann shows us the contradictions of capitalism as the elites of New Granada struggled to define themselves within the nationalist context of their postcolonial state. On one side is the clear linkage with capitalist practices in terms of the ability to amass wealth through mercantile ventures and in the desires of consumers, which mirror those of elites in other nineteenth-century cities. Problematizing a reading of Bogotá as a straightforwardly capitalist city, we see the importance of alternative local structures of power, in which landholding and "precapitalist" "feudal" relations are the route to political rule rather than simply the generation of capital and ever increasing reinvested surplus as the pathway to authority. Although this is very much a microhistory account derived from an archaeological context (Brooks et al. 2008), Gaitán-Ammann is deeply attuned to the theoretical context particularly, as discussed above, the relationship between this case study and understandings of nineteenth and twentieth century Latin American economics derived from world-systems theory. From this chapter the theme of the continuity of the past in the present is felt through the ramifications of how understanding the sociocultural relations of capitalist economics in nineteenth-century New Granada society may also help to formulate deeper understandings of current global economic inequalities. The elites and merchants of Bogotá resist any easy temporal pigeon-holing in this narrative, since they are at once the contemporary of elites in any other metropolitan city of the nineteenth century, and simultaneously restricted in social and economic action through the postcolonial nationalist culture of New Granada.

Sarah Croucher's examination of capitalism within colonial Zanzibar (Chap. 8) has echoes with that of Mark Hauser's in that it also deals with the archaeology of plantation sites. Further linkages to other chapters are found, however, in the fact that this is not European capitalism, since nineteenth-century Zanzibar was under Omani colonial rule, thus echoing Carroll's examination of the Ottoman Empire. As with Gaitán-Amman, Croucher traces her archaeology through the path of mass-produced imported ceramics. Thus the richness and complexity of the diversity of the comparative chapters of the volume begins to take shape as we tie in economic forms (plantations), ties between religion and colonialism (Islam), ceramics, and – in historical archaeological terms – another out-of-the-way place. The Omani run plantations of Zanzibar have clear differences with those of Hauser's work in that they are run by an Islamic colonial elite, but beyond this the differences are perhaps not clear.[12] A key issue for Croucher becomes, therefore, to what extent nineteenth-century Zanzibari plantations can be seen as equally as capitalist as those of Jamaica, or as only peripheral to global capitalist systems of the nineteenth century.

In examining the brightly colored bowls found on all plantation contexts – including enslaved workers and plantation owners – Croucher utilizes a commodity chain analysis to show the diverse aspects of capitalism (as loosely tied via the plantation context and the tracing of mass-produced commodities) in operation within Zanzibar and through global networks. Upon the islands of Zanzibar themselves Croucher argues that mass-produced ceramics were utilized in reciprocal relations, usually in the form of loans at times of social necessity, between elites and the poor – including enslaved laborers. At a time when the relations of enslavement were being contested between the requirements of plantations for chattel slaves and prior social relations of client-patron relations between slaves and slave-owners, Croucher suggests that this reciprocity in imported goods may demonstrate that material realms were one

---

[12]The plantation landscape of Zanzibar was also very different to that of the spatially ordered modern landscapes of Jamaican plantations as discussed by Higman (1987) and Delle (1998), thus adding to the complexity of our understandings of what plantations are. See Croucher (2007, in prep) for detail on plantation landscapes and their relationship to capitalist production on Zanzibar.

level on which reciprocal relations were still recognized, even as the labor of enslaved persons was pressed into greater demand for the production of commodities on plantations. Contrasting with this, the multiethnic colonial society of Zanzibar was also, in part, understood as such through the monetary exchange of these goods, since Indian traders (living apart from plantations and viewed by various elements of plantation society as associated with monetary trade) were the merchants via which mass-produced ceramics were purchased. This singular mercantile role of Indian traders may have been a route through which the alienation of commodity exchanges with strangers became entangled with the homogenization of an "Indian trader" identity on Zanzibar.

The final part of Croucher's commodity chain analysis takes us off the islands of Zanzibar, linking us into wider global capitalist relations. She argues that the ceramics consumed on Zanzibar – large open bowls with bright floral and painted line decorations – were a product manufactured purposefully for the tastes of Indian Ocean consumers. For those alienated commodity producers in the factories of Europe (*sensu* Marx 1976 [1867]), Croucher suggests that manufacturing mass-produced goods was not only an act of blind labor. Instead of the interchangeability of labor in factories suggested by Marx, Croucher's arguments make the case that manufacturing goods specifically for colonial markets was one way in which factory workers came to understand difference with colonial Others, albeit on a vague level with no face-to-face interactions. In showing the contemporaneous nature of all of these dimensions that a single category of commodity, its production and exchange, Croucher (this volume: 186) makes an argument for the coeval nature of diverse capitalist relations that cannot be slotted into historicist narratives. Colonial Zanzibar shows us, via this archaeological analysis, that "it is impossible to adopt any simple evolutionary type approach to understanding the manner in which capitalist practices and meanings pass into colonized societies."

Staying in nineteenth-century Africa, but moving from east to west, François Richard's chapter brings us to Francophone colonialism in the Senegambia. In this move, Richard reminds us of the Anglo-centrism of historical archaeology (see also Dawdy 2008) as he points out the importance of the material past of colonial French West Africa for the discipline. By examining different regimes of colonial rule, Richard (this volume: 194) performs a "decentering gesture" forcing us to think about the metonymy of capitalism within the discipline, as it is so often invoked to reflect only British, or Anglo-American colonial in form. This call for decentering is important, particularly given the paucity of Francophone colonial archaeology. As discussed above, this point also resonates with the diversity of capitalisms and colonialisms in the plural presented in this volume, allowing Richard's decentering gesture to be amplified almost to a centrifugal power within the wider conversation.

Richard's blend of historical ethnography and material evidence is centered on the Siin region of Senegal. He focuses on the tensions between French attempts to draw the residents of the Siin region, the Serer, into a productive role within the colonial state. The Serer present an interesting case study in the selective use of capitalist production by indigenous Africans within a colonial regime, in that they were simultaneously successful at growing a new cash crop, peanuts, and yet also did this in a flexible manner, retaining traditional forms of production which ensured a flexible agropastoral economy. This flexibility allowed them to make use of some imported commodities, where it suited them, but also to remain outside of the "web of colonial dependence" (Richard, this volume: 208).

The result of this flexibility can be read on one level as almost a success for the Serer, since they were able "to maintain a delicate balance between growing food and peanuts, acquiring objects while honoring matrilineal obligations, paying taxes and the costs of social reproduction while avoiding debt or famine, working within the terms of freehold property without giving up their notions of inalienable land" (Richard, this volume: 212). In the contestations of colonialism, this seems, on the surface, to be a positive outcome: the Serer are able to maintain cultural continuity in the face of French colonialism, while also integrating new elements of a capitalist cash-crop economy through the partial introduction of peanut farming. However, this very selectivity has worked to the disadvantage of the Serer within the construction of the contemporary postcolonial nation state of Senegal. Richard argues that the French rulers' perception of the Serer as not fully integrated into the commerce of colonial Senegal, allowed them to be viewed as premodern, an image that has continued into the present day where the Serer now face a marginal position in the "modern" nation. Richard (this volume: 213), therefore, reminds us of the saliency of his work in the present for producing alternative histories that reflect positively on the Serer, thus enabling historical archaeologists/ethnographers to "illuminate current postcolonial predicaments without invoking essentializations of culture or history inherited from earlier periods." Multiple readings of the place of the Serer in colonial history are available, and Richard presents a decisionist (*sensu* Chakrabarty) possibility for the role of scholarship in this vein in replacing colonial pasts in contemporary imaginaries.

The third chapter in the volume which focuses on an African context is that of Lindsay Weiss, as she examines the social relations of diamond mining in South Africa. Under British colonial rule, Weiss suggests that these mining sites in the two decades after their discovery in the 1870s prior to the monopolization of mining may be read in terms of the genealogy of contemporary "casino capitalism." By framing the nineteenth-century South African diamond rush in this way, Weiss is able to reflect on the importance of recognizing colonial roots in contemporary practices of speculative economics.[13] A crucial component of this genealogy is the role of relationships between black and white speculators on the diamond fields, as colonial rulers became increasingly concerned with policing fears of illegal diamond selling by black laborers. In the "lawless" diamond fields, fantasies of wealth and potential respectability were also always present, structuring the social relations of social spaces in this context.

---

[13] The historical roots of speculative capitalism and their legacy of global inequalities while presenting the specter of possible riches are also addressed in Tsing (2005), *Friction*, through the Bre-X scandal in Indonesia.

Weiss' research is focused around public spaces, such as the Half-Way House Hotel, a road-side hotel and canteen near the diamond diggings, tracing changes in "canteen-culture" that reflected wider social issues. Early in the use of the Half-Way House, mismatched sets of dining ware were in use, suggesting to Weiss (this volume: 229) that no one single set of cultural practices were being enacted in the canteen, but rather the assemblage represents "the broader culture of a mobile and hybrid community." Respectability was inscrutable within this phase of the use of the canteen, since all those frequenting the space mixed across class and color lines. However, from the late 1880s, as large companies imposed racial segregation of miners and housed African laborers in compounds, the archaeological assemblage recovered from the Half-Way House also shifted, suggesting a change in canteen-culture in relation to the new spatial politics of mine labor. Plainer "hotel wares" and tureens were found in this phase of the site, and regular dining wares for individual servings increased in numbers. Weiss (this volume: 234) suggests that this shift in the habits of dining at the canteen "could be described as shifting from a domestic and informal atmosphere, to a more service-oriented and recognizably hotel-like assemblage, which more than likely coincided with a far less diverse clientele as a result of the segregation of the fields."

Weiss' chapter presents to us an important case study through which to consider contemporary capitalist relations and their colonial histories. The relationship between the inherently speculative space of colonial rush and modes of controlling labor (or controlling risk more generally), illustrates the importance of the colonial landscape in understanding contemporary divisions. The changing character of public life on the diamond fields helps us to understand the *longue durée* of contemporary capitalism, particularly showing the racialized roots of segregating cheap labor into corporate controlled spaces (cf. Mrozowski 2006).

In the penultimate case-study chapter in the volume Alistair Paterson stays within the temporal context of the nineteenth century, but we move this time to Australia. Paterson compares the archaeology of two pastoral sheep stations, one in Central Australia, and one located in the Pilbara region of Northwest Western Australia. In comparing these areas, Paterson is able to examine the complexities of the changing relations of pastoralism as a mode of expansion in search of capitalist profit of the Australian colonial state. In the initial stages of rural capitalism in Central Australia, archaeological studies show the reliance of European colonizers on indigenous knowledge of water, and on Aboriginal labor, as sheep farming remained a marginal activity. During this phase, little difference is found in the access to material goods for Aboriginals and Europeans working on the station. However, as industrial capitalism made its incursions into this region, in the form of railways bringing technological aids to problems of water resources, Paterson shows the shifts in archaeology that accompanied a shift to seasonal-only labor requirements on the pastoral station, and the differentiation in material culture between Aborigines and Europeans. Paterson also ties documentary history into the narration of the changing history of pastoralism in Central Australia, utilizing documents and photographs to relate European historical renderings of relationships to those shown in the landscape and artifactual record.

Contrasting to this is the archaeology in the Northwest of Australia, where colonization occurred later and was thus bolstered by colonial laws already in place to facilitate cheap labor from the indigenous population. Clear divisions appeared to exist here between the Aboriginal and European populations, but so too did they *within* the European population, with the manager of one pastoral station having greater access to luxury goods than other European workers on the station. These varied histories of the colonial relations of pastoral stations in nineteenth-century Australia are utilized by Paterson to argue that the myth of an egalitarian past in rural Australia must be contested. This was a world where Europeans often relied on Aboriginal populations and worked with them to achieve economic success, while simultaneously attempting to exploit them, and where class divisions also existed within the white population. Paterson highlights a difference to many other colonial situations, however, in the fact that despite close relations, little ethnic creolization between Europeans and Aborigines appears to have occurred, despite the – often forced – hybridity of lives through the labor of profitable pastoral farming. Such contrasts with other contexts of capitalist labor and colonial rule are crucial in enabling us to further map out terrains of difference across these two structural facets. These dimensions of shared and divided histories across multiple lines of ethnicity, race, and class continue to resonate in the politics of Australia today, thereby making the archaeological narratives that are drawn out from Paterson's study hold an important place in the negotiation of postcolonial life in Australia today.

The final chapter in our volume, by Matthew Palus, moves us into the twentieth-century and the USA. For historical archaeologists we are on familiar territory; the outskirts of the city of Annapolis (see Leone 2005 for summary of long-term archaeological projects in Annapolis). Less familiar is the argument that the east coast of USA may be read as a site of colonialism. Palus drawing upon the work of Foucault makes a convincing case for readers to attend to the links between structures of governance and colonial rule. He traces the multilayered government relating to twentieth-century Eastport, a predominantly African-American suburb of Annapolis. Here federal (nation-wide), state, and municipal (town-wide) governmental structures were all attempting to "colonize" the lives of the citizenry. Palus suggests that the late nineteenth and early twentieth century were key periods in shifts in this governmentality, as local structures of patronage increasingly gave way to liberal governance and the political-economic power structures of the contemporary USA. He highlights the importance of figuring Eastport into this frame, since it began as an area in which African-Americans, discriminated against through social and legal factors, were able to live in a largely African-American settlement which was independent of the white dominated Annapolis municipal government.

On an archaeological register, Palus suggests that this type of context – the extension of services from the nineteenth century through to the present day (with services in developing countries having particular contemporary relevance to this topic and transnational structures of neoliberal governance and capital) – is one in which we can trace the attempt by government to colonize the lives of citizens. As Palus (this volume: 271) argues:

> "Utilities traced out existing relationships between people and institutions, and just as importantly they fixed those relationships in new ways with material forms . . . [T]he infrastructural networks that penetrated homes and at some point inevitably articulated with

bodies also established an entirely new relationship between persons, things, and wider society. As material culture, the apparatuses for moving sewage and clean drinking water around the city performed in ways that material culture never had before."

If we are to accept the claim that governmentality be seen as an analogous practice to colonialism, and that the shape of this power can be traced through the materialization of infrastructure – and we feel that Palus makes a sound argument for this relationship – then we are left with the question of how these practices played out in Eastport. The archaeological and documentary evidence that Palus presents shows that Eastport was slow to be connected to municipal services from Annapolis. In discussing this finding, he argues that there is no easy answer as to precisely why this is so. On the one hand, it might show discrimination in provision on the part of the municipal government, but on the other it might show the Eastport residents resistance to the powers of surveillance and control afforded by this infrastructure, in a small area of USA in which they had carved out some degree of autonomy. Ultimately, Palus (this volume: 288) argues for this latter point, viewing the Eastport community as achieving "a measure of autonomy and self-determination" through their resistance to being connected to the wider grid of sewerage and service provision. Whichever argument we are to follow, Palus' chapter makes a sound conclusion to the grouping of chapters in terms of moving us forward to seeing a radically different field site – the networks of services that impinge on most of our lives – as a potential present iteration of colonialism extending into the present day.

Thoughts on the Future: Provincializing Historical Archaeology

It seems to me that it is the duty of the scholar to be subversive of received truths, and that this subversion can be socially useful only if it reflects a serious attempt to engage with and understand the real world as best we can (Wallerstein 2000: i).

Many directions could be taken in attempts to decolonize historical archaeology, not the least of which is to recognize the inherent coloniality of thought within much of the field. The debate about the use of the "history" in historical archaeology (Funari et al. 1999; Moreland 2001; Schmidt and Walz 2007) has initiated important discussions within the discipline, and yet these have perhaps obscured more important debates about the framing of temporality within historical archaeology, and the epochal way in which colonialism, capitalism, and other facets of a structure of modernity are viewed (*pace* Dawdy 2010; Silliman 2005). While many of the authors write here about the issues of universals, none reject wholly the idea of the productive nature of debate between those working in the same temporal framework, even if this works to demonstrate difference and divergences. As a postcolonial project, such dialogue has the potential of actually challenging the assumptions of the field in utilizing often implicit models of global universals of colonialism and capitalism which employ a historicist perspective.

A pressing critique which emerges from a reading of postcolonial scholarship within historical archaeology is the uneven temporality of different cultural groups (as called by archaeology) within the timeframe of modernity. Colonialist thought has a crucial role in the terms of this temporal delineation, as widely discussed in cultural anthropology (Fabian 2002 [1983]; Trouillot 1991; see also Cobb 2005; Cobb and Loren 2008 for a discussion of this within historical archaeology). The anthropological present of historical archaeology was a realm in which, in association with the voyages of merchant capitalists and early settler colonists, non-Western peoples increasingly "produced material analogies for those curiosities of the Old World such as thunderstones." (Lucas 2004: 112) While the Portuguese, Spanish, French, British, and Dutch were being the subjects of historical archaeology, therefore, a multitude of Others became temporally segregated into *pre*historical archaeology. This temporal disparity within single chronological frames is something that a postcolonial approach in historical archaeology calls us to address. Partly, this is through changing the interpretations of such contexts where Europeans seem to sweep in changes to indigenous populations, seeming to irrevocably bring cultural change and to draw indigenous peoples into modernity. Instead, such archaeologies can be reframed to try to produce narratives which examine these types of contexts through a more equal lens, whereby culture contact or colonialism (dependent upon situation) has effects for *both* parties, in ways which are not predetermined by the exigencies of European colonialism and capitalism (Paterson, this volume; Richard, this volume; Russell, this volume; Silliman 2009). Another direction that this can take is to recognize that Europeans were not the only power brokers of the last 500 years. Within the *same* global formations of capital, non-European powers also vied for their interests, sometimes in expansive relations of colonialism (Carroll, this volume; Croucher, this volume). Within colonial societies, economic relations were not always those imposed by hegemonic colonialism (Hauser, this volume; Richard, this volume). In postcolonial nations, capitalist relations were messily defined in terms of new discourses of nationality which attempted to erase the colonial past, and yet were simultaneously embedded in their then-current global relations (Gaitán-Ammann, this volume).

Temporality is also at issue within the stakes of postcolonial representation. Here we see that the past is increasingly powerful in terms of the maneuvers for placing pasts as good or bad in the terminology of the capitalist and postcolonial present. Our representations which seek to challenge the normative historical archaeological representations of capitalism and colonial power as being always within the realm of Western societies have a part to play in this. But the use of archaeology as a space of discourse about such pasts is also hugely important:

> As group pasts become increasingly parts of museums, exhibits, and collections, both in national and transnational spectacles, culture becomes less what Pierre Bourdieu would have called a habitus (a tacit realm of responsible practices and dispositions) and more an arena for conscious choice, justification, and representation, the latter often to multiple and spatially dislocated audiences (Appadurai 1996: 44).

For the authors of many of the chapters within this volume (see particularly Crowell; Horning; Paterson) the ongoing engagement between the work of archaeology and contemporary communities has a power in the present, in that it is able to redefine pasts in a postcolonial world.[14] The audiences for these pasts are, indeed, diverse, and may be engaged through a virtual realm (Hall 2000, Chap. 8; McDavid 2002). Materiality, in the fact that archaeology seems to offer pasts which are undoubtedly "real" through their physical presence, offers a potent arena for negotiations of what the past might mean in terms of contemporary stakes to descendent communities. Drawing out the issue of representation from postcolonial theory is of vital importance here, since these new discourses between archaeologists and communities are often about the renegotiation of received pasts in the present. Archaeology may be an arena in which varied scales and groups of individuals and communities are able to articulate new pasts through the findings of archaeology, and to use archaeological projects as a starting point for engaging in dialogue about how history has been represented via colonialist thought, and what this means for present day community relations, political power, and identity politics.

As we engage in these new directions of representation, we also have to be wary. The history of depictions of the past as mired in colonialist thought and the silences that this can produce (*sensu* Trouillot 1995) sounds a warning to rush forward into new representations that have the potential for eliding particular pasts in new ways. Reflexivity and critical reflection about this process becomes crucial here. In this volume, Horning warns us, in a reflexive discussion about her own work in Northern Ireland, to think carefully about the question of "for whom" we speak. New areas of historical archaeology give rise to new issues of balancing representation, as seen in Carroll's (this volume: 108) attempt to "provide voice" to the Ottoman state in her work, since this has been a "silence" of historical archaeology, and yet simultaneously to ensure that the Bedu, the colonized subject of Ottoman rule in the Transjordan, are also given voice through archaeological interpretation.

We offer this volume as a commitment to historical archaeologies of capitalism and colonialism, not to understand either conceptual category within universalist terms, but to see each as formations that had effects and affects for those subjects of our studies. The diversity of discourse in postcolonial scholarship and current anthropological scholarship examining the contours of globalization provides us with exciting jumping off points for taking historical archaeology to a level in which we make thoughtful contributions to wider scholarship. We are materially based, but this is our strength, for the discipline is not just about counting potsherds. Instead, we bring a material sensibility which is informed by anthropological theory to historical periods (Richard, this volume: 198). The archaeologies written within this vein will not necessarily conform to the directions of strict archaeological science that has been advocated by the field, although some may do so. Authors within this volume demonstrate some of the diverse ways of

---

[14]One thing that should also be noted is the potential for the renarration of heritage within the terms of neoliberal capitalism as heritage increasingly becomes a potential commodity (Hall and Bombardella 2005; Horning, this volume).

writing about archaeological pasts where material culture may form the basis of interpretation (e.g., Crowell, this volume), or may be more of a jumping off point for a wider narrative blending archaeological, ethnographic, and historical material (e.g., Gaitán-Ammann; Richard, this volume). Archaeologists examining the last several hundred years are also able to be engaged with those pasts which many living communities see as their own pasts, allowing the affective force of materiality and the presence of archaeology to enable us to dialogue about the past as it seems to rupture the present through the fact of being here with us (González-Ruibal 2008). The political stakes of the discipline of historical archaeology are high, since the nature of the periods we engage tend to make us see them as a close genealogy to contemporary social and political formations. Without historical perspectives, anthropology falls short of its full capability of engagement with social phenomena (Mintz 1985). Thus, as anthropology takes increasingly a material turn, those of us who deal with the materialities of these histories have a crucial role to play within broader disciplinary conversations outside of historical archaeology. As Hall (this volume) comments on the chapters as a whole, we have a potential to make greater contributions to understanding the past through our engagement with sensory modes of knowledge and representation. Perspectives from postcolonial theorists remind us of the dangers of temporal displacements within colonial regimes, and the continual refusal of admittance for non-Western subjects as fully participant in the formations of capitalism.

The varied papers within this volume throw up no simple epoch of historical archaeology, no bounded idea of where capitalism begins and who can be included within its web and no solution to the issues of the diversity of colonial forms even within the 500 years spanned by this small collection. No definitions can capture the diversity of the social formations we present, and yet there are factors connecting them; shadowy and often volatile configurations of power that are continually in motion. We chase these universals as horizons of possibility, understanding that they can never be quite fully formed, never static things, but ongoing relations as lived in materialities of past and present worlds. As Horning (this volume: 80) points out: "To know the archaeology of inequality and oppression in one part of the modern world is *not* to know it in another, except in the most superficial of fashions." This is, in part, the provincialization we call for in historical archaeology. All too often, North American frameworks are taken as "knowing" all other areas touched by capitalism and colonialism. To take this stance is to ignore the variability within coeval time periods of the last several hundred years. From the indistinct configurations that tie together varied contexts comes a historical archaeology that is not defined by simplistic definitions. Complex relationships weave through all of the chapters within this volume, and these are impossible to sum down to a few lines of characterizations of what historical archaeology is. In putting together this volume, we hope to contribute to a growing discourse of decentered diversity within the field, where no place – be it Annapolis, Bogotá, or Zanzibar – can stand in for all other contexts.

References

Appadurai, Arjun. 1996 *Modernity at Large: Cultural Dimensions of Globalization*. University of Minnesota Press, Minneapolis.

Asad, Talal (editor). 1973 *Anthropology and the Colonial Encounter*. Humanities Press, New York.

Baram, Uzi, and Lynda Carroll (editors). 2000 *A Historical Archaeology of the Ottoman Empire: Breaking New Ground*. Springer, New York.

Battle-Baptiste, Whitney. 2010 An Archaeologist Finds Her Voice: A Commentary on Colonial and Postcolonial Identities. In *Handbook of Postcolonial Archaeology*, edited by J. Lydon and U.Z. Rizvi, pp. 387–391. World Archaeological Congress Research Handbooks in Archaeology, Vol. 3. Left Coast Press, Walnut Creek, CA.

Beaudry, Mary C. (editor). 1988 *Documentary Archaeology in the New World*. Cambridge University Press, Cambridge.

Beaudry, Mary C., Lauren J. Cook, and Stephen A. Mrozowski. 1991 Artifacts and Active Voices: Material Culture as Social Discourse. In *The Archaeology of Inequality*, edited by R.H. McGuire and R. Paynter, pp. 150–191. Blackwell, Oxford.

Behar, Ruth 1995 Introduction: Out of Exile. In *Women Writing Culture*. R. Behar and D.A. Gordon, eds. pp. 1–29. Berkeley and Los Angeles: University of California Press.

Belford, Paul, and R.A. Ross. 2004 Industry and Domesticity: Exploring Historical Archaeology in Ironbridge Gorge. *Post-Medieval Archaeology* 38(2): 59–62.

Bhabha, Homi K. 1994 *The Location of Culture*. Routledge, London.

Bissell, William Cunningham. 2011 *Urban Design, Chaos, and Colonial Power in Zanzibar*. Indiana University Press, Bloomington and Indianapolis.

Brooks, James F., Christopher R. N. DeCorse, and John Walton (editors). 2008 *Small Worlds: Method, Meaning, and Narrative in Microhistory*. School for Advanced Research Press, Santa Fe, NM.

Burbank, Jane and Frederick Cooper. 2010 *Empires in World History: Power and the Politics of Difference*. Princeton University Press, Princeton, NJ.

Carrier, James G. 1992 Occidentalism: The world turned upside down. *American Ethnologist* 19(2): 195–212.

Casella, Eleanor Conlin, and Sarah K. Croucher. 2010 *The Alderley Sandhills Project: An Archaeology of Community Life in (Post)-Industrial England*. Manchester University Press, Manchester.

Casella, Eleanor Conlin, and James Symonds (editors). 2005 *Industrial Archaeology: Future Directions*. Springer, New York.

Chakrabarty, Dipesh. 2002 *Habitations of Modernity: Essays in the Wake of Subaltern Studies*. The University of Chicago Press, Chicago.

Chakrabarty, Dipesh. 2008 [2000] *Provincializing Europe: Postcolonial Thought and Historical Difference*. Princeton University Press, Princeton, NJ.

Cobb, Charles R. 2005 Archaeology and the "Savage Slot": Displacement and Emplacement in the Premodern World. *American Anthropologist* 107(4): 563–574.

Cobb, Charles R., and Diana DiPaolo Loren. 2008 The Earth of the Modern. *Archaeologies* 4(1): 11–23.

Comaroff, John. 2010 The End of Anthropology, Again: On the Future of an In/Discipline. *American Anthropologist* 112(4): 524–538.

Comaroff, Jean, and John L. Comaroff. 1991 *Of Revelation and Revolution, Volume One: Christianity, Colonialism and consciousness in South Africa*. The University of Chicago Press, Chicago.

Comaroff, John, and Karl-Heinz Kohl. 2010 Introduction to "In Focus: (Not) The End of Anthropology, Again? Some Thoughts on Disciplinary Futures". *American Anthropologist* 112(4): 522–523.

Cooper, Frederick. 2005 *Colonialism in Question: Theory, Knowledge, History*. University of California Press, Berkeley and Los Angeles.

Cooper, Frederick, and Ann Laura Stoler (editors). 1997 *Tensions of Empire: Colonial Cultures in a Bourgeois World*. University of California Press, Berkeley and Los Angeles.

Croucher, Sarah K. 2007 Facing Many Ways: Approaches to the Archaeological Landscapes of the East African Coast. In *Envisioning Landscape: Situations and Standpoints in Archaeology and Heritage*. edited by D. Hicks, L. McAtackney, and G. Fairclough, pp. 55–74. One World Archaeology Walnut Creek, CA: Left Coast Press.

Croucher, Sarah K. in prep Capitalism and Cloves: *A Critique of Historical Archaeology*. New York: Springer.

Dawdy, Shannon Lee. 2010 Clockpunk Anthropology and the Ruins of Modernity. *Current Anthropology* 51(6): 761–793.

Dawdy, Shannon Lee. 2008 *Building the Devil's Empire: French Colonial New Orleans*. The University of Chicago Press, Chicago.

Deagan, Kathleen. 1973 Mestizaje in Colonial St. Augustine. *Ethnohistory* 20(1):55–65.

Deagan, Kathleen. 1998 Transculturation and Spanish American Ethnogenesis: The Archaeological Legacy of the Quincentary. In *Studies in Culture Contact: Interaction, Culture Change and Archaeology*, edited by J.G. Cusick, pp. 23–43. Visiting Scholar Conference Volumes. Southern Illinois University, Center for Archaeological Investigations (Occasional Paper No. 25), Carbondale.

Deagan, Kathleen. 2001 Dynamics of imperial adjustment in Spanish America: ideology and social integration. In *Empires: Perspectives from Archaeology and History*, edited by S.E. Alcock, T.N. D'Altroy, K.D. Morrison, and C.M. Sinopoli, pp. 179–194. Cambridge University Press, Cambridge.

Deetz, James. 1993 *Flowerdew Hundred: The Archaeology of a Virginia Plantation*. University of Virginia Press, Charlottesville, VA.

Deetz, James. 1996 *In Small Things Forgotten: An Archaeology of Early American Life*. Anchor Books, New York.

Delle, James A. 1998 *An Archaeology of Social Space: Analyzing Coffee Plantations in Jamaica's Blue Mountains*. Pleunum Press, New York.

Delle, James A., Stephen A. Mrozowski, and Robert Paynter (editors). 2000 *Lines That Divide: Historical Archaeologies of Race, Class, and Gender*. The University of Tennessee Press, Knoxville, TN.

Dietler, Michael. 2005 The Archaeology of Colonization and the Colonization of Archaeology: Theoretical Challenges from an Ancient Mediterranean Colonial Encounter. In *The Archaeology of Colonial Encounters: Comparative Perspectives*, edited by G.J. Stein, pp. 33–68. School of American Research Press, Santa Fe, NM.

Fabian, Johannes. 2002 [1983] *Time and the Other: How Anthropology Makes its Object*. Columbia University Press, New York.

Fennell, Christopher C. 2007 *Crossroads and Cosmologies: Diasporas and Ethnogenesis in the New World*. University Press of Florida, Gainesville.

Ferguson, Leland. 1992 *Uncommon Ground: Archaeology and Early African America, 1650–1800*. Smithsonian Institution Press, Washington D.C.

Fontein, Joost. 2010 The Efficacy of "Emic" and "Etic" in Archaeology and Heritage. In *Handbook of Postcolonial Archaeology*, edited by J. Lydon and U.Z. Rizvi, pp. 311–322. World Archaeological Congress Research Handbooks in Archaeology, Vol. 3. Left Coast Press, Walnut Creek, CA.

Funari, Pedro Paolo, Martin Hall, and Siân Jones (editors). 1999 *Historical Archaeology: Back From the Edge*. Routledge, New York.

Gandhi, Leela. 1998 *Postcolonial Theory: A Critical Introduction*. Edinburgh University Press, Edinburgh.

Ginzburg, Carlo. 1990 [1980] *The Cheese and the Worms: Cosmos of a Sixteenth-Century Miller*. J. Tedeschi and A. Tedeschi, transl. The Johns Hopkins University Press, Baltimore.

González-Ruibal, Alfredo. 2008 Time to Destroy: An Archaeology of Supermodernity. *Current Anthropology* 49(2): 247–279.

Gosden, Chris. 2004 *Archaeology and Colonialism: Cultural Contact from 5000 BC to the Present*. Cambridge University Press, Cambridge.

Hall, Martin. 2000 *Archaeology and the Modern World: Colonial Transcripts in South Africa and the Chesapeake*. Routledge, New York.

Hall, Martin, and Pia Bombardella. 2005 Las Vegas in Africa. *Journal of Social Archaeology* 5(1): 5–24.

Harvey, David. 2010 *A Companion to Marx's Capital*. Verso, London.

Hauser, Mark W. 2008 *An Archaeology of Black Markets: Local Ceramics and Economies in Eighteenth-Century Jamaica*. University Press of Florida, Gainesville.

Higman, B.W. 1987 The Spatial Economy of Jamaican Sugar Plantations: Cartographic Evidence from the Eighteenth and Nineteenth Centuries. *Journal of Historical Geography* 13(1): 17–39.

Higman, B.W. 2000 The Sugar Revolution. *The Economic History Review* 53(2): 213–236.

Johnson, Matthew. 1996 *An Archaeology of Capitalism*. Blackwell, Cambridge, MA.

Kearns, Gary. 1998 The Virtuous Circle of Facts and Values in the New Western History. *Annals of the Association of American Geographers* 88(3): 377–409.

Kelso, William M. 1997 *Archaeology at Monticello: Artifacts of Everyday Life in the Plantation Community*. Thomas Jefferson Foundation, Charlottesville, VA.

Lawrence, Susan (editor). 2003 Archaeologies of the British: Explorations of Identity in Great Britain and its Colonies, 1600–1945. Routledge, London.

Leone, Mark. 2005 *The Archaeology of Liberty in an American Capital: Excavations in Annapolis*. University of California Press, Berkeley and Los Angeles.

Leone, Mark. 1999a Setting Some terms for Historical Archaeologies of Capitalism. In *Historical Archaeologies of Capitalism*, edited by M.P. Leone and P.B.J. Potter, pp. 3–20. Contributions to Global Historical Archaeology. New York: Kluwer Academic/Plenum Publishers.

Leone, Mark. 1999b Ceramics from Annapolis, Maryland: A Measure of Time Routines and Work Discipline. In *Historical Archaeologies of Capitalism*, edited by M.P. Leone and P.B.J. Potter, pp. 195–216. Kluwer Academic/Plenum, New York.

Leone, Mark, Parker B. Jr. Potter, and Paul A. Shackel. 2000 [1987] Toward a Critical Archaeology. In *Interpretive Archaeology: A Reader*, edited by J. Thomas, pp. 458–473. Leicester University Press, London.

Liebmann, Matthew. 2008 Introduction: The Intersections of Archaeology and Postcolonial Studies. In *Archaeology and the Postcolonial Critique*, edited by U.Z. Rizvi and M. Liebmann, pp. 1 – 20. AltaMira Press, Lanham, MD.

Liebmann, Matthew, and Melissa S. Murphy. 2011 Rethinking the Archaeology of "Rebels, Backsliders, and Idolaters. In *Enduring Conquests: Rethinking the Archaeology of Resistance to Spanish Colonialism in the Americas*, edited by M. Liebmann and M.S. Murphy, pp. 3–18. School for Advanced Research, Advanced Seminar Series. School for Advanced Research Press, Santa Fe, NM.

Liebmann, Matthew, and Uzma Z. Rizvi (editors). 2008 *Archaeology and the Postcolonial Critique*. AltaMira Press, Lanham, MD.

Lightfoot, Kent G., Antionette Martinez, and Ann M. Schiff. 1998 Daily Practice and Material Culture in Pluralistic Social Settings: An Archaeological Study of Culture Change and Persistence from Fort Ross, California. *American Antiquity* 63(2): 199–222.

Little, Barbara J. 1994. People with History: An Update on Historical Archaeology in the United States. *Journal of Archaeological Method and Theory* 1 (1): 5–40.

Loren, Diana DiPaolo. 2005 Creolization in the French and Spanish Colonies. In *North American Archaeology*, edited by T.R. Pauketat and D.D. Loren, pp. 297–318. Blackwell Studies in Global Archaeology. Blackwell, Malden, MA.

Lucas, Gavin. 2004 Modern Disturbances: On the Ambiguities of Archaeology. *Modernism/modernity* 11(1): 109–120.

Lydon, Jane, and Uzma Z. Rizvi (editors). 2010 *Handbook of Postcolonial Archaeology*. Left Coast Press, Walnut Creek, CA.

Marx, Karl. 1976 [1867] *Capital: A Critique of Political Economy, Volume One*. B. Fowkes, transl. Penguin Books, London and New York.

McClintock, Anne. 1995 *Imperial Leather: Race, Gender and Sexuality in Colonial Contest*. Routledge, New York.

McDavid, Carol. 2002 Archaeologies that Hurt; Descendants that Matter: A Pragmatic Approach to Collaboration in the Public Interpretation of African-American Archaeology. *World Archaeology* 34(2): 303–314.

McGuire, Randall H. 2008 *Archaeology of Political Action*. University of California Press, Berkeley and Los Angeles.

Meskell, Lynn. 2009 Introduction: Cosmopolitan Heritage Ethics. In *Cosmopolitan Archaeologies*, edited by L. Meskell, pp. 1–17. Duke University Press, Duke, NC.

Mintz, Sidney W. 1985 *Sweetness and Power: The Place of Sugar in Modern History*. Penguin Books, New York.

Moreland, John. 2001 *Archaeology and Text*. Duckworth, London.

Mrozowski, Stephen A. 2006 *The Archaeology of Class in Urban America*. Cambridge University Press, New York.

Mrozowski, Stephen A., James A. Delle, and Robert Paynter. 2000 Introduction. In *Lines That Divide: Historical Archaeologies of Race, Class, and Gender*, edited by J.A. Delle, S.A. Mrozowski, and R. Paynter, pp. xi-xxxi. The University of Tennessee Press, Knoxville, TN.

Mullins, Paul R. 1999a "A Bold and Gorgeous Front": The Contradictions of African America and Consumer Culture. In *Historical Archaeologies of Capitalism*, edited by M. Leone and P.B.J. Potter, pp. 169–195. Contributions to Global Historical Archaeology. Kluwer Academic/Plenum Publishers, New York.

Mullins, Paul R. 1999b *Race and Affluence: An Archaeology of African America and Consumer Culture*. Kluwer Academic/Plenum Publishers, New York.

Orser, Charles E. Jr. 1991 The Continued Pattern of Dominance: Landlord and Tenant on the postbellum Cotton Plantation. In *Archaeology of Inequality*, edited by R.H. McGuire and R. Paynter, pp. 40–54. Blackwell, Oxford.

Orser, Charles E. Jr. 1996 *A Historical Archaeology of the Modern World*. Plenum, New York.

Orser, Charles E. Jr. 1999 Archaeology and the Challenges of Capitalist Farm Tenancy in America. In *Historical Archaeologies of Capitalism*, edited by M. Leone and P.B.J. Potter, pp. 143–168. Contributions to Global Historical Archaeology. Kluwer Academic/Plenum Publishers, New York.

Ortner, Sherry B. 1984 Theory in Anthropology since the Sixties. *Comparative Studies in Society and History* 26(1): 126–166.

Palmer, Marilyn, and Peter Neaverson. 2005 *The Textile Industry of South West England: A Social Archaeology*. Tempus, Stroud, UK.

Pandey, Gyanendra. 2000 Voices from the Edge: The Struggle to Write Subaltern Histories. In *Mapping Subaltern Studies and the Postcolonial*, edited by V. Chaturvedi, Mapping, published in association with New Left Review. Verso, New York.

Patterson, Thomas C. 2008 A Brief History of Postcolonial Theory and Implications for Archaeology. In *Archaeology and the Postcolonial Critique*, edited by M. Liebmann and U.Z. Rizvi, pp. 21–34. Archaeology in Society Series. AltaMira Press, Lanham, MD.

Prakash, Gyan. 2000 Can the 'Subaltern' Ride? A Reply to O'Hanlon and Washbrook. In *Mapping Subaltern Studies and the Postcolonial*, edited by V. Chaturvedi, pp. 220–238. Mapping, published in association with New Left Review. Verso, New York.

Purser, Margaret. 1999 Ex Occidente Lux? An Archaeology of Later Capitalism in the Nineteenth-Century West. In *Historical Archaeologies of Capitalism*, edited by M. Leone and P.B.J. Potter, pp. 115–141. Contributions to Global Historical Archaeology. Kluwer Academic/Plenum Publishers, New York.

Reid, Andrew, and Paul J. Lane. 2004 African Historical Archaeologies: An Introductory Consideration of Scope and Potential. In *African Historical Archaeologies*, edited by. A.M. Reid and P.J. Lane, pp. 1–32. Contributions to Global Historical Archaeology. Kluwer Academic/Plenum Publishers, New York.

Rubertone, Patricia E. 2000 The Historical Archaeology of Native Americans. *Annual Review of Anthropology* 29: 425–446.

Said, Edward W. 1995 [1978] *Orientalism: Western Conceptions of the Orient*. Penguin Books, London.

Schmidt, Peter R. 1990 Oral Traditions, Archaeology and History: A Short Reflective History. In *A History of African Archaeology*, edited by P. Robertshaw, pp. 252–270. London/Portsmouth (N.H.): James Currey/Heinemann.

Schmidt, Peter R. 2006 *Historical Archaeology in Africa: Representation, Social Memory, and Oral Traditions*. AltaMira, Lanham and New York.

Schmidt, Peter R., and Jonathan R. Walz. 2007 Re-Representing African Pasts through Historical Archaeology. *American Antiquity* 72(1): 53–70.

Shepherd, Nick. 2008 WAC at a Crossroads. *Archaeologies* 4(1): 1–7.

Shepherd, Nick. 2002 The Politics of Archaeology in Africa. *Annual Review of Anthropology* 31:189–209.

Silliman, Stephen W. 2005 Culture Contact or Colonialism? Challenges in the Archaeology of Native North America. *American Antiquity* 70(1): 55–74.

Silliman, Stephen W. 2001 Agency, Practical Politics and the Archaeology of Culture Contact. *Journal of Social Archaeology* 1(2): 190–209.

Silliman, Stephen W. 2009 Change and Continuity, Practice and Memory: Native American Persistence in Colonial New England. *American Antiquity* 74(2): 211–230.

Sivaramakrishnan, K. 2005 Some Intellectual Genealogies for the Concept of Everyday Resistance. *American Anthropologist* 107(3): 346–355.

Society for Historical Archaeology. 2007. *What is Historical Archaeology?* Electronic document, http://www.sha.org/about/whatis.cfm, accessed October 18 2010.

South, Stanley. 1978 Pattern Recognition in Historical Archaeology. *American Antiquity* 43(2): 223–230.

Spivak, Gayatri Chakravorty. 1988 "Can the Subaltern Speak?" In *Marxism and the Interpretation of Culture*, edited by C. Nelson and L. Grossberg, pp. 271–313. University of Illinois Press, Urbana.

Spivak, Gayatri Chakravorty. 2000 Thinking Cultural Questions in 'Pure' Literary Terms. In *Without Guarantees: In Honour of Stuart Hall*, edited by P. Gilroy, L. Grossberg, and A. McRobbie, pp. 335–357. Verso, New York.

Spivak, Gayatri Chakravorty. 2006 [1987] *In Other Worlds: Essays in Cultural Politics*. Routledge, New York.

Stahl, Ann Brower. 2007 Entangled Lives: The Archaeology of Daily Life in the gold Coast Hinterlands, AD 1400–1900. In *Archaeology of Atlantic Africa and the African Diaspora*, edited by A. Ogundiran and T. Faloda, pp. 49–76. Indiana University Press, Bloomington and Indiana.

Stein, Gil J. (editor). 2005a *The Archaeology of Colonial Encounters: Comparative Perspectives*. Santa Fe: School of American Research Press, Santa Fe.

Stein, Gil J. 2005b Introduction: The Comparative Archaeology of Colonial Encounters. In *The Archaeology of Colonial Encounters: Comparative Perspectives*, edited by G.J. Stein, pp. 3–32. School of American Research press, Santa Fe.

Tarlow, Sarah 2007 *The Archaeology of Improvement in Britain, 1750–1850*. Cambridge University Press, New York.

Thomas, Julian. 2004 *Archaeology and Modernity*. Routledge, London & New York.

Trouillot, Michel-Rolph. 1991 Anthropology and the Savage Slot: The Poetics and Politcs of Otherness. In *Recapturing Anthropology: Working in the Present*, edited by R.G. Fox, pp. 16–44. School of American Research Advanced Seminar Series. School of American Research Press, Santa Fe, New Mexico.

Trouillot, Michel-Rolph. 1995 *Silencing the Past: Power and the Production of History*. Bacon Press, Boston.

Tsing, Anna Lownhaupt. 2005 *Friction: An Ethnography of Global Connection*. Princeton University Press, Princeton.

van Dommelen, Peter. 2005 Colonial Interactions and Hybrid Practices: Phoenician and Carthaginian Settlement in the Ancient Mediterranean. In *The Archaeology of Colonial Encounters: Comparative Perspectives*, edited by G.J. Stein, pp. 109–142. Santa Fe, NM: School of American Research Press.

Voss, Barbara L. 2008 *The Archaeology of Ethnogenesis: Race and Sexuality in Colonial San Francisco*. University of California Press, Berkeley and Los Angeles.

Wall, Diana di Zerega. 1999 Examining Gender, Class and Ethnicity in Nineteenth-Century New York. *Historical Archaeology* 33(1): 102–117.

Wallerstein, Immanuel. 2000 *The Essential Wallerstein*. The New Press, New York.

Weiss, Lindsay 2007 Heritage-Making and Political Identity. *Journal of Social Archaeology* 7(3): 413–431.

Wilkie, Laurie A., and Paul Farnsworth. 2005 *Sampling Many Pots: An Archaeology of Memory and Tradition at a Bahamian Plantation*. University Press of Florida, Gainesville.

Williams, Eric. 1994 [1944] *Capitalism and Slavery*. University of North Carolina Press, Chapel Hill.

Wolf, Eric R. 1997 [1982] *Europe and the People Without History*. Second Edition. University of California Press, Berkeley and Los Angeles.

Wood, Margaret C. 2002 Moving Towards Transformative Democratic Action through Archaeology. *Historical Archaeology* 6(3): 187–198.

Wurst, LouAnn. 1999 Internalizing Class in Historical Archaeology. *Historical Archaeology* 33(1): 7–21.

Wylie, Alison. 1999 Why Should Historical Archaeologists Study Capitalism? The Logic of Question and Answer and the Challenge of Systemic Analysis. In *Historical Archaeologies of Capitalism*, edited by M. Leone and P.B.J. Potter, pp. 23–50. Contributions to Global Historical Archaeology. Kluwer Academic/Plenum Publishers, New York.

Young, Robert C. 1995 *Colonial Desire: Hybridity in Theory, Culture and Race*. Routledge, New York.

Chapter 2
Precolonial Encounters at *Tamál-Húye*: An Event-Oriented Archaeology in Sixteenth-Century Northern California

Matthew A. Russell

Introduction

During a brief span in the late sixteenth century, Indigenous hunter-gatherers on the northern California coast met European voyagers, both Spanish and English, for the first time. The Coast Miwok-speaking Tamal people, inhabitants of what is now coastal Marin County, California, were not isolated before the meetings. They had long-standing interaction and exchange with nearby village communities who spoke their language, as well as neighboring California Indians from other language groups. They participated in a complex trade network that moved coastal goods, such as clam and abalone shell inland in exchange for raw materials not available on the coast, such as obsidian and steatite (soapstone). The Tamal's encounters with the sixteenth-century European visitors were unprecedented; however – not only were they very different than regular visits with neighboring California Indian groups but they also had potentially significant long-term implications, and they foreshadowed Spanish and Russian colonization of northern California more than 175 years later.

This essay highlights the brief intersection of European mercantile (precapitalist) expansion and northern California Indian culture in the late-sixteenth century, using short-term engagements between English and Spanish seafarers and Coast Miwok-speaking Tamal hunter-gatherers in 1579 and 1595 to explore how brief, precolonial encounters can contribute to broader anthropological inquiries of cultural change and persistence. The 1579 and 1595 encounters at *tamál-húye*, the Indigenous name for the area now encompassing Drakes Bay in Point Reyes National Seashore (Barrett 1908: 307; Collier and Thalman 1996: 14) (Figs. 2.1 and 2.2), represent two of the earliest intersections of Europeans and California Indians on the US Pacific coast. Research is examining the potential long-term implications of short-term events, in this case by focusing on a brief visitation by Sir Francis Drake and his crew to

M.A. Russell (✉)
Department of Anthropology, University of California, Berkeley, CA, USA
e-mail: matthew_russell@berkeley.edu

S.K. Croucher and L. Weiss (eds.), *The Archaeology of Capitalism in Colonial Contexts*, Contributions To Global Historical Archaeology, DOI 10.1007/978-1-4614-0192-6_2, © Springer Science+Business Media, LLC 2011

Fig. 2.1 Point Reyes Peninsula and *tamál-húye*, or Drakes Bay. Map by the author

tamál-húye in 1579, followed by the wreck of the Spanish Manila galleon *San Agustín*, under the command of Sebastián Rodríguez Cermeño, in the same area in 1595. These encounters represent the earliest cross-cultural encounters between Europeans and native peoples in northern California, and the last for more than 175 years until the Spanish colonized northern California beginning in 1769. I use these encounters to illustrate the analytical value of short-term events in archaeological research, and as a way to highlight the historical archaeology of postcontact, precolonial Indigenous societies, which have not received a great deal of attention from historical archaeologists studying processes of culture contact and colonialism (although see Lightfoot and Martinez 1995; Torrence and Clarke 2000a). This work contributes to ongoing efforts to reduce Eurocentric bias in historical archaeology

Fig. 2.2 Drakes Bay in Point Reyes National Seashore, an area called *tamál-húye* in the Coast Miwok language, and the location of sixteenth-century encounters between California Indians and European voyagers. Photo by author

(e.g., Harrison 2002; Harrison and Williamson 2004a; Jordan and Schrire 2002; Torrence and Clarke 2000a) by focusing inquiry on native sites and Indigenous cultural practices in the context of cross-cultural encounters (see also Lightfoot 1995).

Silliman (2005) recently highlighted the importance of making clear distinctions between archaeologies of culture contact (short-term events) and colonialism (long-term entanglements) (see also Hill 1998). Using Silliman's terminology, many archaeological studies have focused on investigating native responses to European capitalist and colonial enterprises and, therefore, emphasize the importance of long-term cross-cultural entanglements for culture change and continuity (e.g., Deagan 1983; 1995; Kirch and Sahlins 1992; Lightfoot 2005b; Lightfoot et al. 1991; 1997). Fewer archaeological inquiries have focused on the long-term implications of short-term events (e.g., Duke 1992; Gibbs 2002, 2003; Nutley 1995; Staniforth 1997, 2003a), especially in contact situations. An examination of the encounters at *tamál-húye* using an historical anthropological framework that rests on an archaeological foundation but that incorporates other types of evidence (historical, oral, ethnographic), therefore, presents an opportunity to approach issues of culture contact from a different perspective than previous studies. No material culture can be definitively attributed to the earlier Drake encounter, although the historical and ethnographic aspects of that encounter are a key component of the overall study. Archaeological research, however, focuses on artifacts from the 1595 *San Agustín* shipwreck. After the shipwreck, the Spaniards were only present in *tamál-húye* for a short time before they continued their voyage to New Spain (Mexico) in a small boat.

When the Spanish departed, they left behind the *San Agustín* and its cargo. Archaeological evidence from extensive excavations around *tamál-húye* during the 1940s–1970s indicates that Tamal villagers took advantage of the body of introduced material culture from *San Agustín* by salvaging objects from the shipwreck and incorporating them into their cultural practices. Salvage of the ship's cargo provides an exceptional opportunity to examine the choices made by the Tamal people in selecting specific objects for reuse in Indigenous contexts. In this case, the focus is how the Tamal actively selected European materials for salvage from a diverse range of goods, rather than selecting objects whose availability was mediated by early traders and colonists as is often the case in colonial contexts. Beyond the initial exchanges that took place with the Tamal, the Spanish were not present to structure use of European and Asian materials from the shipwreck.

Current research focused on the encounters at *tamál-húye* utilize the body of existing archaeological data from previous excavations, and a historical anthropological approach that incorporates multiple lines of evidence and a holistic framework (Lightfoot 2005b), to evaluate how the Tamal people incorporated material culture from the shipwreck into their cultural practices, as well as to assess whether this short-term, precolonial event, and the material culture introduced as a result, was a possible source of long-term Tamal cultural change, or whether extended entanglement from later, eighteenth- and nineteenth-century colonialism was necessary for significant social transformation to occur. I examine these questions by reconstructing previous archaeological excavations through analysis of museum collections, archival excavation records, original field notes, and published reports from the earlier investigations, and by incorporating additional data from ethnography, historical documents, and native oral traditions. Using the wreck of *San Agustín* as a unique case where contact was mediated almost entirely through introduced material culture, my research considers a variety of evidence to reflect on how the Tamal may have negotiated these sixteenth-century cross-cultural encounters, how they may have recontextualized introduced material culture from *San Agustín* and integrated it into their daily lives, and if there were long-term implications of events that took place nearly 200 years before Spanish colonialism reached the region.

In this essay, I first outline the historical background of the encounters between the English seafarers, and later the shipwrecked Spanish voyagers, with the native Tamal. I explore how the world-views of the English, the Spanish, and the Tamal may have structured the encounters at *tamál-húye*, as well as subsequent Tamal salvage and reuse of material from *San Agustín*, highlighting the role of Indigenous agency. Although the interaction I discuss here took place during the period of sixteenth-century mercantilism, a precursor to the industrial society of fully fledged capitalism (Johnson 1996: 8), and it preceded Spanish colonialism in California by almost two centuries, I next frame how the encounter at *tamál-húye* can be considered part of a larger body of work on archaeologies of capitalism in colonial contexts that examines how indigenous societies negotiated capitalist world system expansion across the globe. Following Wolf (1982), I underscore the fact that the intercultural engagement between the English, Spanish, and Tamal did not take place in a vacuum, but was an aspect of larger processes taking place on a global scale. European and

Tamal history intersected on the beaches of *tamál-húye* on two brief occasions in the late-sixteenth century, and the histories of each were interconnected from that point forward. Finally, by focusing on a short-term, precolonial encounter, I highlight the archaeology of the event, and I examine how an event-oriented archaeology can contribute to broader studies of cultural change and continuity.

The Encounters at *Tamál-Húye*

Beginning in 1565, regular trade between the Philippines and New Spain (Mexico) became an important aspect of the global Spanish mercantile system. Silver from Mexican and South American mines was shipped from Acapulco to Manila, exchanged for Chinese luxury goods highly sought after by European elites, and then shipped back to Acapulco via a return route that passed northern California after a north Pacific crossing (Schurz 1939). The English, with a limited presence in the Pacific in the sixteenth century, sought to make inroads against their Spanish rivals with incursions by privateers and fortune hunters like Sir Francis Drake. Both the English and Spanish had encountered Indigenous peoples on many occasions and in many settings for more than a century before the encounters at *tamál-húye*, so they had a well-developed cultural sense of the Indigenous "other," and how such meetings could unfold (see, for example, Schieffelin 1991). The voyages of Drake and Cermeño are the only two documented European voyages that made landfall in northern California before the eighteenth century. Sir Francis Drake was the first in the summer of 1579, during a global circumnavigation in which he spent 5 weeks on the California coast preparing his ship for a long Pacific crossing and eventual return to England (Drake 1854 [1628]; Hakluyt 1854 [1600]). Scholars debate the precise location of the landfall, but most agree it was within the territory of Coast Miwok-speaking inhabitants of the northern San Francisco Bay Area, encompassing Marin and southern Sonoma Counties today; it was most likely, it was in what was called *tamál-húye* in the Coast Miwok language, which Drake called Nova Albion (Heizer 1947, 1974; Heizer and Elmendorf 1942; Wagner 1926). Accounts of Drake's interactions with the Tamal (or another Coast Miwok group) are documented in several detailed accounts (Nuttall 1914; Vaux 1854), and the episode is compelling because the Drake texts record a series of unusual and highly ritualized scenes after the English arrived in California (see below). After these events, Drake departed California and sailed on to England, leaving little or no significant material component of his visit – no archaeological remains have been conclusively associated with events in 1579 – although the rich historical account detailing aspects of the interaction indicate he may have made a lasting impression in other ways.

From an archaeological perspective, another interaction that took place just 16 years after Drake's visit is more intriguing. The Spanish Manila galleon *San Agustín*, carrying a diverse cargo of Chinese trade goods including porcelain, silk, and other luxury items, wrecked in *tamál-húye* in November 1595 while sailing from Manila to Acapulco. Cermeño and an 80-member crew left the Philippines on July 5, 1595 aboard the *San Agustín*. After a 4-month Pacific crossing, they reached California in early November and anchored their vessel in a large, sheltered bay called the *La Bahia de San Francisco* (later renamed Drakes Bay) for reprovision and for assembling a small launch for coastal exploration. The *San Agustín* was driven ashore during a storm before they completed their tasks and became a total loss, forcing the Spaniards to modify the launch to accommodate the entire crew for their return to Acapulco. For more than a month, both before and after *San Agustín*'s wreck and while completing modifications to the launch, Cermeño's crew interacted with the Tamal population (Cermeño 1924 [1596], 2001 [1596]). The Spanish voyagers quickly departed *tamál-húye* for Acapulco after the shipwreck event, but they abandoned the galleon and its cargo, leaving a considerable body of material culture behind.

The Tamal, on the contrary, had no exposure to Europeans before Drake and Cermeño's visits. The Tamal and their ancestors had occupied and exploited the Drakes Bay area and its adjacent estuaries for at least 2,500 years, probably much longer. The Coast Miwok-speaking Tamal and their neighbors (whose descendents still reside in the area today as the federally recognized Federated Indians of Graton Rancheria) were hunter-gatherers who exploited a variety of terrestrial, estuarine, and marine resources. They occupied a series of permanent and seasonal habitation sites, hunted terrestrial game and sea mammals, foraged for wild plants, and collected shellfish and other coastal resources (Stewart 2003). California was inhabited by a dense population of complex hunter-gatherers organized as a series of small, independent polities, sometimes referred to as village communities (Kroeber 1925: 831), tribelets (Kroeber 1932: 258–259, 1962: 29–33), or tribes (Milliken 1995). Village communities in California, such as larger tribes in other regions of North America, were autonomous, self-governing polities that controlled a loosely defined territory for resource exploitation (Kroeber 1925: 831, 1962: 29, 49). Each community claimed the territory surrounding its settlements, often a portion of one or more watersheds, and maintained exclusive access to the available resources. Although surrounded by as many as a dozen village communities who shared the same language, the Tamal were an independent polity whose territory included the Point Reyes Peninsula (Emberson et al. 1999: 42).

The Tamal people shared a number of cultural characteristics with their fellow Coast Miwok-speaking neighbors, as well as neighboring ethnolinguistic inhabitants of surrounding areas, such as the Pomo (Kroeber 1925: 275). The Tamal also likely shared a common world view with surrounding village communities, and engaged in similar religious practices. California Indian cosmology was similar throughout the central part of the state, including the San Francisco Bay Area, although there are clear distinctions made by individual tribes. In general, central California Indians had an animistic world-view, believing that not only humans but also all of nature (animals, plants, rocks, celestial phenomena, features on the landscape, etc.) had spirits that formed the complex tapestry of life. Ghosts also played an important role in the spiritual beliefs of California Indians (Loeb 1926: 302–303). California Indian religious practices included a variety of community ceremonial observances meant to benefit the entire community (Kroeber 1907: 321). Ritual practice in Native California followed a rich and complex ceremonial calendar, and many rites were performed by "secret societies," whose members had access to spiritual knowledge not available to nonmembers. Each tribal group had a distinctive set of dances, ceremonies, and rituals that they performed throughout the year, but there was a common thread that ran throughout central California connecting the various tribes through a shared system of belief. Ceremonies likely practiced by the Tamal included secret society initiation ceremonies and specific tribal dances or ceremonies performed for a variety of purposes, but that generally ensured balance in the natural world. (Kroeber 1907: 335). The secret society initiation ceremonies included those that are part of the Kuksu cult system, north-central California Indian phenomena characterized by a series of ceremonies performed by society members who impersonated supernatural figures, including the mythological character Kuksu (Kroeber 1907: 336, 1932: 399–400, 423). The purpose and social function of the secret societies, as well as the specifics of the dances and enactments, varies between California Indian tribal groups (Kroeber 1932: 394), but seemed to center on the initiation and instruction of new members, and on the performance of healing rites (Kroeber 1932: 394, 396; Loeb 1926: 354). Numerous other dances and rituals were performed along with the Kuksu rites on a regular schedule throughout the year (Collier and Thalman 1996; Kelly 1978). The cultural context of the Tamal, especially their religious observances and world-view, likely influenced the way in which they perceived and interacted with the first European voyagers they encountered in the late-sixteenth century.

Although we can never know their true perceptions of these early encounters, there is at least one native oral tradition recorded about precolonial European encounters in northern California that offers some insight. It comes from the Kashaya Pomo, closely related neighbors of the Tamal to the north, as told by elder Essie Parrish to Berkeley linguist Robert L. Oswalt in 1958. As the story goes,

> In the old days, before the white people came up here, there was a boat sailing on the ocean from the south. Because before that they had never seen a boat, they said, 'Our world must be coming to an end. Couldn't we do something? This big bird floating on the ocean is from somewhere, probably from up high. Let us plan a feast. Let us have a dance.' They followed its course with their eyes to see what it would do. Having done so, they promised Our Father [a feast] saying that destruction was upon them…. When they had done so, they watched [the ship] sail way up north and disappear. They thought that [the ship] had not done anything but sail northwards because of the feast they had promised. They were saying that nothing had happened to them – the big bird person had sailed northward without doing anything – because of the promise of a feast; because of that they thought it had not done anything. Consequently they held a feast and a big dance…(Oswalt 1966: 245–247).

This tradition provides a glimpse into the California Indian perspective on early encounters, albeit filtered through many generations of oral tradition, and illuminates how at least one California Indian group made sense of their initial contact with European outsiders. Native perceptions of early encounters with European voyagers may be the product of an Indigenous cosmology or world-view that is very different than a European perspective. Interpreting archaeological remains that resulted from the encounters needs to consider that native populations may have thought about introduced material culture in very different ways than the Europeans who were the primary consumers of the objects.

Based on anthropological assessment of the historical accounts, the encounter with Drake and his crew in 1579 may have had important ritual connotations for the Tamal (Heizer 1947; Kroeber 1925: 276–278; Meighan 1981). After anchoring the *Golden Hind*, a lone individual in a canoe approached the ship and addressed Drake and his crew in an oratory greeting. After landing, the English crew observed that the assembled native inhabitants appeared to weep and scratch their faces in an elaborate display of anguish. Later, both sides participated in a ceremony in which the California Indians "crowned" Drake as their "king" (at least in the eyes of the English chronicler), followed by more ritualizing crying, shrieking, weeping, and face-scratching. While it is not known for certain, many scholars argue the native inhabitant's actions may represent a variation of the Kuksu ceremony, or the ghost ceremony, both of which took place during the summer months. In this context, the encounter has been interpreted as the Tamal perceiving the English as returned spirits or ghosts of dead ancestors (Heizer 1947; Kroeber 1925: 276–278; Meighan 1981), or in a more nuanced interpretation, as symbolic individuals who had arrived in *tamál-húye* to participate in the ceremonial context of the Kuksu performances (Lightfoot and Simmons 1998).

From the Tamal perspective, the Spanish departure was likely just the beginning of their interaction with the shipwreck itself, as small-scale collecting, opportunistic salvage, or possibly systematic exploitation likely continued for some time. The Tamal salvaged and incorporated many objects from *San Agustín* into their cultural practices, and many of these have been recovered archaeologically. Together, evidence for the encounters at *tamál-húye* gives us the raw material for a rich historical anthropology of the interactions and a starting point for assessing the long-term implications of short-term events.

The *San Agustín* shipwreck itself has not yet been located, so archaeological evidence for the encounters at *tamál-húye* consists of objects from the ship excavated from Tamal sites on land. Archaeologists from a variety of institutions excavated, tested, or surface collected a number of sites in *tamál-húye* between 1940 and 1973 that produced a significant quantity of blue and white underglaze Chinese export porcelain, iron ship's fasteners, and other objects of possible sixteenth-century origin found in wholly native contexts (Beardsley 1954a, b; Heizer 1941; King and Upson 1970; Meighan 1950, 2002; Meighan and Heizer 1952; Treganza 1959; Treganza and King 1968; Von der Porten 1968, 1972). The projects generated extensive museum collections and a vast archive of original field notes, artifact catalogs, and publications. Despite this rich record, however, there has been little published on the excavations that focuses on Tamal cultural practices or engages with the data from a contemporary, culture contact perspective.

Previous interpretations of Tamal interactions with Drake and his crew in 1579, in particular the possibility that the Europeans were perceived in supernatural or ceremonial terms, provide the cultural context for how the native peoples may have subsequently viewed the material remains from the *San Agustín* in 1595. Lightfoot and Simmons (1998: 160) suggest that after the shipwreck and the Spaniard's departure, Tamal individuals may have collected porcelain vessels, ceramic fragments, iron spikes, and other material because they were valued as symbols of the previous

Drake encounter, and as objects that signified unknown worlds. This interpretation is based on the Tamal world-view, and it relies on a culturally informed view of history that preserves Indigenous agency and culture (Sahlins 2000). In this interpretation, it is "more apt to speak of an incorporation of the world system into the local polity than the reverse" (Thomas 1990: 64). It was not the English or the Spanish who drew the California Indians into the nascent world capitalist system with the interactions at *tamál-húye*, rather it was the Tamal who drew the Europeans into their own world system through retention and reuse of introduced material culture from the shipwreck in their cultural practices. Examining how that process unfolded and in what ways the introduced material culture was incorporated into Tamal cultural practices offers a window into the ways the foreign goods can be recontextualized in local contexts, and if there are long-term consequences (Thomas 1991).

Culture Contact and Colonialism

While the encounters at *tamál-húye* represent a precolonial intersection of European capitalism and Indigenous northern California culture, my examination of the cross-cultural encounters is situated within the larger body of work on archaeologies of culture contact and colonialism, especially as related to the expansion of mercantilism and capitalism in the early modern period. For many decades, up until the 1980s, archaeologists interested in studying processes of culture change during cross-cultural encounters often used established anthropological frameworks of culture contact, such as acculturation theory (e.g., Broom et al. 1953; Foster 1960; Linton 1940; Redfield et al. 1936; Spicer 1961) and world systems theory (e.g., Chase-Dunn and Mann 1998; Hall and Chase-Dunn 1993; Kardulias 1999; Kohl 1987; Kristiansen 1987; McGuire 1989). Both have been severely critiqued and are rarely applied today, although there are aspects of these early approaches that are important to acknowledge in our study of intercultural interactions (Cusick 1998). Models based on Wallerstein's (1974) world system theory, in particular, have had a significant impact on the study of intercultural interactions. In addition to the overall historical perspective world systems approaches bring to the archaeology of cross-cultural encounters, part of their heuristic value is to reinforce the idea that societies are interconnected and cannot be evaluated in isolation (Rowlands 1987). This heuristic value is diminished, however, when its application inadvertently obscures past socio-economic relations by essentializing groups as either core or periphery (Dietler 1989: 127; see also Dietler 2005; Rice 1998; Schortman and Urban 1998) or assuming a priori relationships based on economic inequality. Given the numerous critiques of Wallerstein's model, appropriate archaeological application of world systems theory may be limited to research that examines relationships between European powers and their colonies in the sixteenth to nineteenth centuries (e.g., Williams 1992) – indeed, such approaches are still used today (e.g., Delgado 2009). In general, however, these examples fall outside the boundary of what are normally considered culture contact studies.

Despite widespread criticism of world systems theory in anthropology, most contemporary researchers acknowledge that local archaeological cases can only be understood fully when placed within a broader regional context. There is both theoretical and analytical value to the study of structural forces as long-term undercurrents that powerfully influence people's lives, and they do not need to be portrayed as deterministic – these structures are in turn shaped and transformed by historically situated events (Sahlins 1981b: 111). For my current purposes, we cannot simply assume that the Europeans dominated interaction and exchange with the Tamal people or directed subsequent outcomes. This may be particularly true in my study because of the unintentional nature of the encounter at *tamál-húye* – when shipwrecks are the reason cultures come into contact, structural dynamics of the engagements may shift significantly from what would be expected in a world systems framework (see, for example, Keate 2002 [1788]). This is one of the reasons maritime archaeology can make such important contributions to the archaeology of intercultural interaction (see below).

Moving beyond world system approaches, a more productive framework for assessing brief, precolonial encounters like that at *tamál-húye* is one that not only discards the assumption that Europeans always dominated relations with non-Europeans during early encounters but also acknowledges that contact situations are simultaneously part of a larger global process, as well as historically contingent and situated within specific contexts. Like Wallerstein, Wolf (1982) argues that world history is systemic, but he suggests that the system should not highlight European expansion at the expense of other cultures. Instead, all peoples and cultures are part of an interconnected system that developed as Europeans drew together numerous preexisting local exchange networks into a global complex. As this process unfolded, the histories of all peoples became inextricably linked into a shared, common history. Some societies prospered, others were decimated, but all were touched in some way. Thus, writes Wolf, "the history of these supposedly history-less peoples is in fact a part of the history of European expansion itself" (Wolf 1982: 194). In this sense, the Tamal were briefly touched by European contact in the sixteenth century, but we do not know if there were long-term implications of that contact. From the point of contact onward, however, as the Tamal salvaged and incorporated Chinese porcelain vessels and other objects into their cultural practices, their history became part of the history of global connections.

From an archaeological perspective, Stein (2002, 2005) has attempted to synthesize principles shared by contemporary archaeologists studying cross-cultural encounters and colonialism, and offers a way forward. He has suggested that recent scholarly attention to intercultural engagements and colonial encounters has seven interconnected elements that draw it together. These include a combination of processual and postprocessual approaches; a rejection of unilinear models, such as acculturation and core–periphery (world systems); a multiscalar approach; recognizing patterned variability in power relations; recognizing that individual societies are heterogeneous and cannot be essentialized; acknowledging internal dynamics as well as external forces for change; and consideration of human agency as well as larger structural constraints. These principles acknowledge that contact situations and colonial entanglements are historically contingent and situated within specific contexts, which makes an all-encompassing theory of culture contact unrealistic and inappropriate. Yet, there are enough similarities between cross-cultural encounters that a broadly comparative approach, which recognizes the distinctive nature of individual intercultural engagements, can be productive (Alexander 1998; Lightfoot 2005a; Stein 2005).

Stein's principles underlie my study of the encounters at *tamál-húye*. The unique circumstances of the Tamal people's encounter with Drake in 1579, which may have included a ritual or ceremonial element, and of their salvage of material from the *San Agustín* after a brief set of interactions with the Spanish and Filipino crew following the shipwreck in 1595, require a research approach that highlights an Indigenous understanding of the events to examine both the immediate effects and potential long-term implications on California Indian society. A more nuanced approach such as this can combine both macroscale and microscale perspectives, and may consider episodes of culture contact as dynamic zones of cross-cutting social interaction and active identity construction. Negotiating identities will be archaeologically visible in innovative transformations of material culture adoption and use on both sides of the encounter, and by interpretations that allow for the active use of material culture to create new social identities and foster cultural interactions (Lightfoot and Martinez 1995).

In addition, my research highlights an approach that explicitly acknowledges that processes of culture contact and colonialism, as well as the long-term implications of each, can span both prehistory and history – and oftentimes may reside in the liminal "protohistoric" zone. Understanding this calls into question the usefulness of the sharp disciplinary divide between "prehistoric" and "historical" archaeology that exists today (Lightfoot 1995; Rubertone 2000). This problematic dichotomy is especially evident in cases where Indigenous cultural practices continued virtually unchanged into the colonial period, even with incorporation of introduced material culture (e.g., Colley 2000; Duke 1992). Both prehistoric and historical archaeologists can work to dispel this separation by using a long-term perspective that highlights the dynamic nature of culture, continuous change over time, as well as cultural persistence and continuity, as part of a natural rhythm. This approach does not see the arrival of Europeans or other outsiders as a sharp break with the past, but rather contextualized within a diachronic framework, prehistory and postcontact are part of a single historical continuum (Lightfoot 1995; Torrence and Clarke 2000b; Williamson 2004). In addition, the artificial divide between prehistory and history can be obscured by focusing attention on a variety of "traditional" archaeological site-types, such as middens, rock shelters, lithic scatters and rock art, as I do in this project. As is the case at *tamál-húye*, these sites often persisted into the historical period, and although some may not contain obvious signatures of contact such as quantities of European-made artifacts, they can nonetheless contribute to an Indigenous perspective on cross-cultural encounter (Colley 2000; Torrence and Clarke 2000b).

Event-Oriented Archaeology

As I previously mentioned, what makes the project at *tamál-húye* unique, however, is that it is not focused on long-term colonial encounters, but instead focuses on two brief, maritime events. The first encounter with Drake may have had singular significance because of the cultural context in which it occurred, while the second, the *San Agustín* shipwreck, was also unprecedented because of the significant material element. Because of this, the project is an example of the unique contributions that event-based archaeologies, which can include shipwrecks but that can focus on a variety of historical site-types, can make to anthropological scholarship. Maritime archaeology in particular, however, is often uniquely positioned to address broad anthropological questions about large-scale social processes, such as the study of culture contact and colonialism (Dellino-Musgrave 2006). Shipwrecks can be indicative of larger patterns of trade and commerce, and may often give distinctive insight to the expansion and movement of people around the world. In addition, however, shipwrecks can be touchstones to specific moments of cross-cultural engagement and can help us understand how these interactions unfolded. Shipwrecks and their cargos, like other material remains from early cross-cultural encounters, can contribute a unique perspective to understanding these engagements (e.g., Campbell 1997; Campbell and Gesner 2000; Fallowfield 2001; Gesner 2000; Illidge 2002). While I interpret the particular historical contingencies of the encounter at *tamál-húye* as an early example of the intersection of native California with European mercantilism, one of the most distinctive aspects of shipwreck events, including that of the *San Agustín*, is that they were entirely unintentional. This makes shipwrecks unique archaeological sites, and it positions maritime archaeology to address the effects of interaction between Indigenous populations and Europeans and their material culture in specific locations *before* the advent of formal colonial enterprises (see Gibbs 2003, 2006). Shipwrecks also represent the kind of unintentional interaction that can significantly alter the power dynamics of cross-cultural encounters between native societies and Europeans. Due to the unintentional nature and historical contingencies of the encounter, the brief Tamal interaction with the English and Spanish at *tamál-húye*, and their later salvage of the *San Agustín*, provides an example of how shipwrecks can significantly alter the dynamics of cross-cultural encounters between native societies and representatives of the expanding world capitalist system.

Investigating a short-term, precolonial encounter between the sixteenth-century world capitalist system and Indigenous hunter-gatherers in northern California demonstrates how an event-based perspective can contribute to broader studies investigating issues of cultural change and continuity. An approach that considers the long-term implications of short-term encounters has a theoretical foundation based on Marshall Sahlins' "event-oriented anthropology" (Sahlins 1981a, 1985, 1991, 2004, 2005), a term used by Biersack (1991: 7) to describe Sahlins' standpoint. Along with the work of other practice-oriented scholars (e.g., Sewell 2005), Sahlins emphasizes the importance of the "event" in history. Similarly, an archaeologically based research perspective that focuses on brief, precolonial intercultural interactions can be termed an "event-oriented archaeology." Several previous archaeological studies have focused on the "archaeology of the event" (e.g., Duke 1992; Gibbs 2002, 2003; Nutley 1995), but Staniforth's *Annales*-based approach (Staniforth 1997, 2003a, b), which emphasizes shipwrecks as unique events representing cultural continuity, is the most explicit example.

Archaeologists began incorporating ideas from the French *Annales* school of historiography in the 1980s (Bintliff 1991a; Knapp 1992b). The *Annales* school has its foundation in the 1930s as an interdisciplinary approach merging history, sociology, anthropology, geography, psychology, and archaeology in a multifaceted methodology for studying premodern societies. Although *Annales* lacks a single, unifying framework, important themes include a focus on the daily lives of ordinary people, population demography, analysis of class structure, patterns of diet and health, and ideologies and world-view (Bintliff 1991b). Fernand Braudel, representing the second generation of *Annales* scholars, has been the most influential *Annaliste* for archaeologists. Braudel's most important contribution is his "wavelength" historical framework, characterized by a well-known tripartite scale of history, which includes the *longue durée*; a medium-term wavelength; and a short-term wavelength, highlighting the history of events (Braudel 1972: 20–21). While recognizing multiple levels of time, Braudel's attention is mostly focused on the long and medium terms, which act as structuring influences that both constrain and enable human action. Braudel equates the event, on the contrary, with traditional, narrative political history (Knapp 1992a: 6). A more serious attention to historical events is taken up in more detail by third generation *Annalistes*, including Jacques Le Goff and Emmanuel Le Roy Ladurie.

An archaeological approach that specifically draws on third-generation *Annales* emphasis on the event is Mark Staniforth's "archaeology of the event" (Staniforth 1997, 2003a, b). This is an innovative perspective with a foundation in maritime archaeology, highlighting shipwrecks as particular events. Staniforth suggests that while certain types of archaeological evidence may not be suited to investigation at the level of the individual event, shipwrecks, which result from a specific event, may be uniquely suited to just that role (Staniforth 1997: 18). Focusing on colonial-period shipwrecks in Australia, Staniforth demonstrates that wreck events are tied to larger structural processes, such capitalism, consumerism, and colonialism (Staniforth 1997: 20). Using a broadly comparative theoretical framework, Staniforth argues that successful British colonization of Australia required expanding trade networks to supply colonists with appropriate consumer goods that allowed them to maintain their familiar British social system and identity. Using individual shipwreck events and the material culture carried on board as representations of broader British attitudes and world-views, Staniforth demonstrates an effort by colonists to maintain cultural continuity. Staniforth (2003b: 2) notes that "[i]n the colonial context, cultural continuity was one of the critical ways in which people established order in their world." Recognizable architecture, alcohol, food and beverage helped maintain that order. Staniforth's "archaeology of the event," therefore, uses events to show how culture is reproduced and maintained. At heart, it demonstrates cultural continuity. Staniforth's *proximate* object of study is material culture from shipwreck events, but his *ultimate* object of study is the structure that produced them. In this way, by using events (shipwrecks) to reflect larger structures (British world-view), Staniforth's approach may actually have as much in common with a Braudelian perspective as it does the third generation *Annales* scholars.

An Event-Oriented Archaeology

Like Staniforth, my research focuses in part on a specific shipwreck event, although I approach an event-oriented archaeology from a different perspective. An alternative way to view the relationship between structure and events (rather than events reflecting larger structures) is to acknowledge that there is a dialectic between the two, in which structure both enables and constrains events, while events both reproduce and transform structure (Giddens 1979: 5). A view of events rooted in theories of practice in which they play an active role in cultural transformation is essential to what I term an "event-oriented archaeology," a perspective based on Sahlins' theoretical analysis of the event, which views short-term events – whether shipwrecks or cross-cultural encounters – as "turning points" that stimulate cultural change (e.g., Sahlins 1981a).

An event-based anthropology foregrounds the importance of short-term "events" and places them on equal theoretical footing with the broader concept of "structure." Like Giddens, Sahlins' work highlights the recursive relationship in which events produce and reproduce structure (Sahlins 1981a, 1985). Structure is shaped by history and events, and events are directly linked to cultural transformation (Sahlins 1985: vii). While cultural reproduction results in ongoing societal transformation, significant cultural transformation can occur in the interaction between structure and event, that is, when a group's underlying cultural logic (structure) is confronted by an entirely unique circumstance (event) that it must make sense of and incorporate into its realm of understanding (Sahlins 1981a: 8). This is especially true when cultural groups encounter one another for the first time – each approaches the other with its own cultural logic and through such encounters both are transformed in a "structure of the conjuncture" – a new structure that results from a revised cultural understanding (Sahlins 1981a: 68). An important question is what makes an event historically significant, and when and under what circumstances it fundamentally transforms cultural practice (Sahlins 1991, 2004, 2005). Sahlins suggests that "[a]n event becomes such as it is interpreted. Only as it is appropriated in and through the cultural scheme does it acquire an historical *significance*" (Sahlins 1985: xiv, emphasis original). An event's significance is entirely situated within particular cultural contexts; each situation is unique and must be evaluated with reference to its historically contingent condition (Sahlins 1991: 44–45). What constitutes a historically significant event can only be understood through a detailed analysis of cultural context. An event has the power to engender change because of how it is interpreted, and an interpretation of an event as significant enough to cause change depends on the cultural context in which the event occurs. In other words, the event is dependent on structure for significance, and when significant, can result in structural change.

Further, rather than social change solely occurring through gradual production and reproduction of cultural practices, specific events can redirect historical trajectories in ways not predictable from knowledge of what came before (Sewell 2005: 227). In practice, to argue that short-term events can initiate structural change, it is necessary to effectively demonstrate how structure has been altered. Demonstrating structural change requires a detailed grasp of structure both before and after the event under study to know how structure has been changed, which requires in-depth knowledge of the historical details surrounding the event in question (Sewell 2005: 219).

An analysis of significant events and their impact on culture change can, in certain circumstances, be investigated through a historical anthropology based on archaeology (Beck et al. 2007). The late-sixteenth century intercultural engagement between the Tamal people of northern California and European voyagers shipwrecked in the *San Agustín* may be one of these unique events that give us a window into processes of culture change and continuity. The key concern here is whether the short-term shipwreck event and resulting introduction of foreign material culture precipitated culture change, or if later, long-term colonial entanglement was necessary for such change to occur. For my purposes, an event-oriented archaeology is one that attempts to trace cultural change, whether internally or externally generated, to a specific or short-term event. Archaeologically, one effective way to do this is by a methodology similar to Le Roy Ladurie's (1979) structure–event–structure model. That is, to examine key variables that provide insight into structural conditions before an event, and look for fundamental change, steady continuity, or perhaps some combination, after the event. When events are given equal theoretical footing as structure, it restores people as the primary force in historical change, a view that links key theoretical concepts of agency and event. Combining historical and maritime archaeology may offer a unique opportunity to address such questions about culture change.

Archaeology of the Encounters at *Tamál-Húye*

Since the *San Agustín* shipwreck has not yet been located, current archaeological evidence for the encounters at *tamál-húye* consists of nearly 800 blue and white underglaze Chinese export porcelain sherds, earthenware and stoneware fragments, iron spikes, and a handful of other small objects from the shipwreck that were found among traditional California Indian artifacts in wholly native contexts in Tamal village and midden sites during excavations from the 1940s to 1970s (Fig. 2.3). At least 15 sites have been investigated in *tamál-húye* that may include material culture from the *San Agustín* shipwreck. Previous researchers either viewed Tamal reuse of the porcelain ceramics either in a strictly utilitarian way, assuming typical Western uses such as food preparation, serving, and storage, or that they were collected as simple curiosities, although they did note a few porcelain fragments that had been modified into bead blanks and pendants, or flaked as bifacial tools (Fig. 2.4) (Heizer 1941; Treganza 1959; Treganza and King 1968; Von der Porten

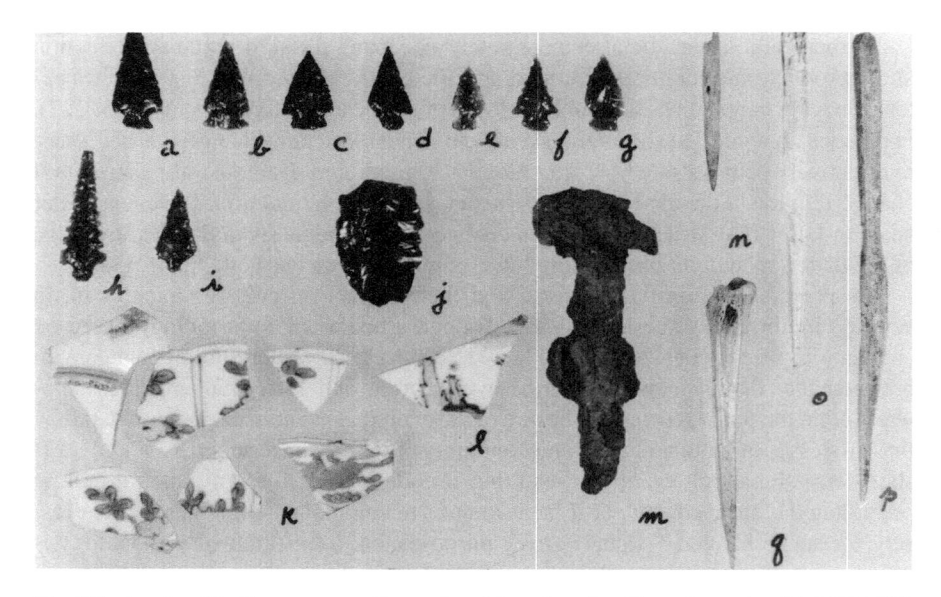

Fig. 2.3 A mix of indigenous-manufactured and introduced artifacts from site CA-MRN-308, now in Point Reyes National Seashore, excavated by Adan E. Treganza and San Francisco State College in 1959. Photo courtesy of the Phoebe Apperson Hearst Museum of Anthropology and the Regents of the University of California (Ms283)

1968). My current project uses multiple lines of evidence, built on an archaeological foundation, to evaluate competing hypotheses that view Tamal perception of introduced objects as either utilitarian vessels or "merely trifles," or alternatively as powerful objects imbued with symbolic meaning, as suggested by Lightfoot and Simmons (1998).

To evaluate Tamal recontextualization of introduced material culture from the *San Agustín* shipwreck, I utilize existing museum collections and archival field data from previous archaeological excavations, some nearly 70 years old, as my primary data source. I use these collections and the accompanying data to reconstruct the previous excavations and reanalyze the data to address my research questions. In this way, while the research can be broadly considered historical archaeology, at the same time it is archaeological history. My archaeological analysis follows two primary lines of inquiry. First, I reconstruct the excavation from six primary sites at *tamál-húye* within a Geographic Information System (GIS) framework, and I conduct exploratory spatial data analysis (ESDA) to look for intrasite patterning. In particular, I evaluate whether introduced objects are clustered in statistically significant ways with native artifact-types or features representing specific cultural practices. I also evaluate whether the layout and use of space within sites changed after introduction of the sixteenth-century material culture. Second, I conduct a detailed analysis of introduced objects from all 15 sites that have yielded material

Fig. 2.4 Some of the few porcelain fragments excavated at Point Reyes that were modified into Indigenous artifact-types, compared to native forms. At left, abalone (*Haliotis* sp.) pendants; at right, clamshell (*Saxidomus nuttalli*) disk bead blanks, with a whole *Saxidomus nuttalli* shell in the center. The large majority of porcelain fragments recovered archaeologically from Point Reyes sites were not modified. Photo by Carola DeRooy

from the *San Agustín* to look for clues as to how Tamal individuals incorporated them into their cultural practices.

At present, this research remains a work in progress. The GIS study is ongoing and results are not yet available. Preliminary evidence from examining the museum collections, however, may offer some insight into how the Tamal perceived the introduced objects from *San Agustín*, in particular the Chinese porcelain. As suggested by previous excavators, one way that Tamal individuals may have used introduced artifacts is for pragmatic or utilitarian purposes. New objects such as ceramic vessels may have been incorporated into existing cultural practices in ways that resulted in no significant change to their daily lives. For example, the Tamal may have used porcelain plates, bowls, and other ceramic vessels from the shipwreck as food preparation, serving, and storage containers, which they discarded as they broke (Heizer 1941). If this interpretation is correct, then Tamal people may have used ceramic vessels as an equivalent to baskets and food platters that were simply made from a new, previously unknown material. One archaeological finding that would support this premise is if particular vessel forms were selected more frequently than others. A preference for selecting hollowware versus flatware vessels, for example, may indicate utilitarian incorporation of porcelain ceramics into existing native foodways that favored stews, porridges, and gruels (Cabak and Loring 2000;

Table 2.1 Comparison of vessel forms from archaeologically excavated porcelain fragments and beach-collected porcelain fragments

Vessel form	Archaeological assemblage (MNV = 209)		Beach-collected assemblage (MNV = 102)	
	Number	Percentage	Number	Percentage
Flatware (plates and saucers)	65	31	28	27
Hollowware (bowls)	84	40	46	45
Unknown open vessels	51	24	27	26
Bottles and vases	5	2.5	0	0
Unknown closed vessels	5	2.5	1	1

Farnsworth 1996; Voss 2008). To test this, I compared percentages of Chinese porcelain vessel forms carried to Tamal village sites, and later recovered during archaeological excavations to the percentages of available vessel forms on the shipwreck. I reconstructed available ceramic vessel-types from a collection of more than 420 beach-collected porcelain sherds that have washed ashore seasonally from an offshore site, presumably from the shipwreck site itself. This beach-collected assemblage of porcelain represents a random sample of vessels available on the shipwreck, and may be used as a control to compare to culturally selected items. During my examination of the collections, I determined the archaeological assemblage of porcelain fragments includes a total of 692 sherds, representing a minimum number of vessels (MNV) of 209, while the beach-collected assemblage includes 420 individual porcelain fragments representing an MNV of 102. While examining the assemblages to determine MNV, I also recorded vessel type, distinguishing between open and closed vessels, and dividing open vessels into flatwares and hollowwares when possible. Results of the analysis (Table 2.1) indicate very similar percentages of vessel forms from both the excavated and beach-collected assemblages, which may indicate the Tamal had no preference for selecting specific vessel forms for salvage from the *San Agustín*. This may indicate that pragmatic or utilitarian concerns were not a top priority for Tamal villagers when they collected porcelain vessels and fragments.

Next, I addressed the question of Tamal reuse and recontextualization of the artifacts through detailed examination of each artifact. I carefully examined all objects for evidence of Californian Indian reuse, including modification into traditional artifact classes such as bifaces, beads, and pendants. Understanding the variability in artifact modification is a critical component of addressing my primary research questions pertaining to utilitarian versus nonutilitarian artifact use. I found that out of a total of 692 porcelain fragments from archaeological contexts on the Point Reyes Peninsula, just 46, or 6.6%, showed any indications of cultural modification. This included a number of sherds used as possible bead blanks, pendants, and medallions, although the majority are simple bifaces. Results of this analysis indicate that a large majority, almost 94% of the porcelain fragments, show no sign of modification. This could support the idea that the Tamal people collected the porcelain fragments because of symbolic meaning, although it does not rule out the hypothesis that they were collected as simple curiosities. Additional material research, as well as the intrasite spatial analysis, may offer additional lines of evidence for evaluating various ideas of Indigenous recontextualization of the introduced objects, as well as whether there were long-term implications.

Conclusions

An archaeological examination of the encounters at *tamál-húye* asks whether the wreck of the *San Agustín*, the intercultural interaction with European voyagers, and recontextualization of introduced goods into Indigenous cultural practice was a historical "event" for the Tamal people – if it resulted in measurable changes to their cultural practices. In this regard, the project may be considered an "event-oriented archaeology." This approach is rooted in the work of practice-based scholars whose analyses consider "events" to be as theoretically rich as the "structures" that shape them, suggesting in fact that events mold structure as much as structures transform events. According to this viewpoint, unique events, whether shipwrecks or short-term intercultural engagements, can represent "turning points" that precipitate cultural change.

Silliman (2009) offers a cautionary note regarding this line of inquiry. He suggests that researchers should not automatically assume that cross-cultural encounters resulted in either change *or* continuity as two mutually exclusive outcomes. Silliman writes,

> [F]or social agents, communities, or households to move forward, they must change *and* remain the same. But to have moved forward means to have carried on. Therefore, the incorporation of so-called 'European/Euro-American' objects into Indigenous cultural practices in ways that insure their survival as individuals, families, and communities should not lead us to interpret them in terms of loss or passive acquiescence (Silliman 2009: 226).

This is an important point for my study, which although examining the long-term implications of the intercultural interaction and recontextualization of introduced material culture by looking for change in cultural practices triggered by or associated with the introduced objects, is not asking these questions within a research framework that suggests that the Tamal population were passive recipients of new technologies and imposed cultural transformation (Harrison and Williamson 2004b). Rather, since the event under study is a short-term encounter rather than a long-term colonial entanglement, I would suggest that any change to Tamal cultural practices occurred within the structure and logic of their own cultural practices, world-view, and cosmology, and was due to active engagement by native populations, with the sixteenth-century cross-cultural encounters and the introduced material culture from the *San Agustín* simply an impetus that allowed them to "move forward" after the encounters in their own culturally informed way (see also Thomas 1997, 2002).

Sewell remarks that what makes events such as the encounters at *tamál-húye* unique is the particular cultural context in which they occur:

> The specific nature of the structure of the conjuncture will, of course, be different in every event. But if Sahlins's theory of the event is correct, it should always involve a novel conjuncture of structures. Hence, we cannot predict in advance what structure of the conjuncture will shape the novel acts of reference that constitute the core of a given event. But we do know what to look for: a conjunction of structures that sets off a synergetic inter-action between actors attempting to make structural sense of a highly volatile situation (Sewell 2005: 223).

Given this starting point outlined by Sewell, the sixteenth-century intercultural interactions on the Point Reyes Peninsula are an exceptional set of circumstances in which to look what types of cultural change may be precipitated by short-term events. In this case, this approach uses short-term engagements between English and Spanish seafarers and Coast Miwok-speaking Tamal hunter-gatherers in 1579 and 1595 to investigate how brief, precolonial encounters can contribute to broader anthropological inquiries of cultural change and continuity.

References

Alexander, R. T. 1998 Afterword: Toward an Archaeological Theory of Culture Contact. In *Studies in Culture Contact: Interaction, Culture Change, and Archaeology*, edited by J. G. Cusick, pp. 476-495. Occasional Paper No. 25. Center for Archaeological Investigations, Southern Illinois University at Carbondale, Carbondale, IL.

Barrett, S. A. 1908 The Ethno-Geography of the Pomo and Neighboring Indians. *University of California Publications in American Archaeology and Ethnology* 6(1):1–332.

Beardsley, R. K. 1954a *Temporal and Areal Relationships in Central California Archaeology, Part One*. University of California Archaeological Survey Report No. 24. Department of Anthropology, University of California, Berkeley.

Beardsley, R. K. 1954b *Temporal and Areal Relationships in Central California Archaeology, Part Two*. University of California Archaeological Survey Report No. 25. Department of Anthropology, University of California, Berkeley.

Beck, R. A. J., D. J. Bolender, J. A. Brown and T. K. Earle. 2007 Eventful Archaeology: The Place of Space in Structural Transformation. *Current Anthropology* 48(6):833–860.

Biersack, A. 1991 Introduction: History and Theory in Anthropology. In *Clio in Oceania: Toward a Historical Anthropology*, edited by A. Biersack, pp. 1-36. Smithsonian Institution Press, Washington D.C.

Bintliff, J. (editor). 1991a *The Annales School and Archaeology*. New York University Press, New York.

Bintliff, J. (editor). 1991b The Contribution of an *Annaliste*/Structural History Approach to Archaeology. In *The Annales School and Archaeology*, edited by J. Bintliff, pp. 1-33. New York University Press, New York.

Braudel, F. 1972 *The Mediterranean and the Mediterranean World in the Age of Philip II*. Translated by S. Reynolds. Volume 1. Harper & Row, New York.

Broom, L., B. J. Siegel, E. Z. Vogt and J. B. Watson. 1953 Acculturation: An Explanatory Formulation. *American Anthropologist* 56(6):973-1000.

Cabak, M. and S. Loring. 2000 "A Set of Very Fair Cups and Saucers": Stamped Ceramics as an Example of Inuit Incorporation. *International Journal of Historical Archaeology* 4(1):1-34.

Campbell, J. 1997 Eighteenth Century Wooden Clubs from HMS *Pandora*: A Preliminary Analysis. *Bulletin of the Australian Institute for Maritime Archaeology* 21(1 & 2):1-8.

Campbell, J. and P. Gesner. 2000 Illustrated Catalogue of Artifacts from the HMS Pandora Wrecksite Excavations 1977-1995. *Memoirs of the Queensland Museum Cultural Heritage Series* 2(1):53-159.

Cermeño, S. R. 1924 [1596] The Voyage to California of Sebastian Rodriguez Cermeño in 1595. Translated and edited by H. R. Wagner. *California Historical Society Quarterly* 3(1):3-24.

Cermeño, S. R. 2001 [1596] Log and Account of the discovery made by Sebastian Rodriguez Cermeño, by order of his majesty, from the Philippines to *Cedros Island*. Translated and edited by J. P. Sanchez. *Colonial Latin American Historical Review* 10(2):223-251.

Chase-Dunn, C. and K. M. Mann. 1998 *The Wintu and Their Neighbors: A Very Small World-System in Northern California*. University of Arizona Press, Tucson.

Colley, S. M. 2000 The Colonial Impact? Contact Archaeology and Indigenous Sites in Southern New South Wales. In *The Archaeology of Difference: Negotiating Cross-Cultural Engagements in Oceania*, edited by R. Torrence and A. Clarke, pp. 278-299. Routledge, London.

Collier, M. E. T. and S. B. Thalman (editors). 1996 *Interviews with Tom Smith and Maria Copa: Isabel Kelly's Ethnographic Notes on the Coast Miwok Indians of Marin and Southern Sonoma Counties, California*. Miwok Archaeological Preserve of Marin, Occasional Paper No. 6, San Rafael, CA.

Cusick, J. G. 1998 Historiography of Acculturation: An Evaluation of Concepts and Their Application in Archaeology. In *Studies in Culture Contact: Interaction, Culture Change, and Archaeology*, edited by J. G. Cusick, pp. 126-145. Occasional Paper No. 25. Center for Archaeological Investigations, Southern Illinois University at Carbondale, Carbondale, IL.

Deagan, K. (editor). 1983 *Spanish St. Augustine: The Archaeology of a Colonial Creole Community*. University Press of Florida, Gainesville.

Deagan, K. (editor). 1995 *Puerto Real: The Archaeology of a Sixteenth-Century Spanish Town in Hispaniola*. University Press of Florida, Gainesville.

Delgado, J. P. 2009 *Gold Rush Port: The Maritime Archaeology of San Francisco's Waterfront*. University of California Press, Berkeley, CA.

Dellino-Musgrave, V. E. 2006 *Maritime Archaeology and Social Relations: British Action in the Southern Hemisphere*. Springer, New York.

Dietler, M. 1989 Greeks, Etruscans, and Thirsty Barbarians: Early Iron Age Interaction in the Rhone Basin of France. In *Centre and Periphery: Comparative Studies in Archaeology*, edited by T. C. Champion, pp. 127-141. Unwin Hyman, London.

Dietler, M. 2005 The Archaeology of Colonization and the Colonization of Archaeology: Theoretical Challenges from an Ancient Mediterranean Colonial Frontier. In *The Archaeology of Colonial Encounters: Comparative Perspectives*, edited by G. J. Stein, pp. 33-68. School of American Research Press, Santa Fe.

Drake, S. F. 1854 [1628] The World Encompassed by Sir Francis Drake. In *The World Encompassed by Sir Francis Drake, Being his next Voyage to that to Nombre de Dios*, edited by W. S. W. Vaux, pp. 1-162. The Hakluyt Society, London.

Duke, P. 1992 Braudel and North American Archaeology: An Example from the Northern Plains. In *Archaeology, Annales, and Ethnohistory*, pp. 99-111. Cambridge University Press, Cambridge.

Emberson, G., S. Thalman and D. Theodoratus. 1999 Point Reyes National Seashore Cultural Affiliation Report, NPS Cooperative Agreement No. 1443-CA-8530-97-017. Federated Coast Miwok Cultural Preservation Association, Novato, CA.

Fallowfield, T. 2001 Polynesian Fishing Implements from the Wreck of HMS *Pandora*: A Technological and Contextual Study. *Bulletin of the Australian Institute for Maritime Archaeology* 25:5-28.

Farnsworth, P. 1996 The Influence of Trade on Bahamian Slave Culture. *Historical Archaeology* 30(4):1-23.

Foster, G. M. 1960 *Culture and Conquest: America's Spanish Heritage*. Viking Fund Publications in Anthropology No. 27. Wenner-Gren Foundation for Anthropological Research, New York.

Gesner, P. 2000 HMS *Pandora* Project - A Report on Stage 1: Five Seasons of Excavation. *Memoirs of the Queensland Museum Cultural Heritage Series* 2(2):1-52.

Gibbs, M. 2002 Maritime Archaeology and Behaviour During Crisis: The Wreck of the VOC Ship *Batavia* (1629). In *Natural Disasters and Cultural Change (One World Archaeology 45)*, edited by R. Torrence and J. Grattan. Routledge, London.

Gibbs, M. 2003 The Archaeology of Crisis: Shipwreck Survivor Camps in Australasia. *Historical Archaeology* 37(1):128-145.

Gibbs, M. 2006 Maritime Archaeology at the Land-Sea Interface. In *Maritime Archaeology: Australian Approaches*, edited by M. Staniforth and M. Nash, pp. 69-81. Springer, New York.

Giddens, A. 1979 *Central Problems in Social Theory: Action, Structure and Contradiction in Social Analysis*. University of California Press, Berkeley.

Hakluyt, R. 1854 [1600] Extracts from Hakluyt's Voyages. In *The World Encompassed by Sir Francis Drake, Being his next Voyage to that to Nombre de Dios*, edited by W. S. W. Vaux, pp. 219-226. The Hakluyt Society, London.

Hall, T. D. and C. Chase-Dunn. 1993 The World-Systems Perspective and Archaeology: Forward into the Past. *Journal of Archaeological Research* 1(2):121-143.

Harrison, R. 2002 Archaeology and the Colonial Encounter: Kimberley Spearpoints, Cultural Identity and Masculinity in the North of Australia. *Journal of Social Archaeology* 2(3):352-377.

Harrison, R. and C. Williamson (editors). 2004a *After Captain Cook : The Archaeology of the Recent Indigenous Past in Australia*. AltaMira Press, Walnut Creek, CA.

Harrison, R. and C. Williamson (editors). 2004b Introduction: 'Too many Captain Cooks'? An archaeology of Aboriginal Australia after 1788. In *After Captain Cook: The Archaeology of the Recent Indigenous Past in Australia*, edited by R. Harrison and C. Williamson, pp. 1-13. AltaMira Press, Walnut Creek.

Heizer, R. F. 1941 Archaeological Evidence of Sebastian Rodriquez Cermeno's California Visit in 1595. *California Historical Society Quarterly* 20(4):315-328.

Heizer, R. F. 1947 Francis Drake and the California Indians, 1579. *University of California Publications in American Archaeology and Ethnology* 42(3):251-302.

Heizer, R. F. 1974 *Elizabethan California*. Ballena Press, Ramona, CA.

Heizer, R. F. and W. W. Elmendorf. 1942 Francis Drake's California Anchorage in the Light of the Indian Language Spoken There. *Pacific Historical Review* 11:213-217.

Hill, J. D. 1998 Violent Encounters: Ethnogenesis and Ethnocide in Long-Term Contact Situations. In *Studies in Culture Contact: Interaction, Culture Change, and Archaeology*, edited by J. G. Cusick, pp. 146-171. Occasional Paper No. 25. Center for Archaeological Investigations, Southern Illinois University at Carbondale, Carbondale, IL.

Illidge, P. 2002 The Tahitian Mourner's Costume: A Description of Use, Composition and Relevant Artefacts from HMS *Pandora*. *Bulletin of the Australian Institute for Maritime Archaeology* 26:65-74.

Johnson, M. 1996 *An Archaeology of Capitalism*. Blackwell, London.

Jordan, S. and C. Schrire. 2002 Material Culture and the Roots of Colonial Society at the South African Cape of Good Hope. In *The Archaeology of Colonialism*, edited by C. L. Lyons and J. K. Papadopoulos, pp. 241-272. Getty Research Institute, Los Angeles.

Kardulias, P. N. (editor). 1999 *World-Systems Theory in Practice: Leadership, Production, and Exchange*. Rowman & Littlefield Publishers, Lanham, MD.

Keate, G. 2002 [1788] *An Account of the Pelew Islands*, edited by K. L. Nero and N. Thomas. Leicester University Press, London.

Kelly, I. 1978 Coast Miwok. In *Handbook of North American Indians*, edited by R. F. Heizer, pp. 414-425. vol. 8, California. Smithsonian Institution, Washington D.C.

King, T. F. and W. F. Upson. 1970 Protohistory on Limantour Sandspit: Archaeological Investigations at 4-Mrn-216 and 4-Mrn-298. In *Contributions to the Archaeology of Point Reyes National Seashore: A Compendium in Honor of Adan E. Treganza*, edited by R. E. Schenk, pp. 114-194. Treganza Museum Papers No. 6, San Francisco State College.

Kirch, P. V. and M. Sahlins. 1992 *Anahulu: The Anthropology of History in the Kingdom of Hawaii*. 2 Vols. University of Chicago Press, Chicago.

Knapp, A. B. 1992a Archaeology and *Annales*: Time, Space, and Change. In *Archaeology, Annales, and Ethnohistory*, edited by A. B. Knapp, pp. 1-21. Cambridge University Press, Cambridge.

Knapp, A. B. 1992b *Archaeology, Annales, and Ethnohistory*. Cambridge University Press, Cambridge.

Kohl, P. 1987 The Ancient Economy, Transferable Technologies and the Bronze Age World-System: A View from the Northeastern Frontier of the Ancient Near East. In *Centre and*

Periphery in the Ancient World, edited by M. Rowlands, M. Larsen and K. Kristiansen, pp. 13-24. Cambridge University Press, Cambridge.

Kristiansen, K. 1987 Center and Periphery in Bronze Age Scandinavia. In *Centre and Periphery in the Ancient World*, edited by M. Rowlands, M. Larsen and K. Kristiansen, pp. 74-85. Cambridge University Press, Cambridge.

Kroeber, A. L. 1907 The Religion of the Indians of California. *University of California Publications in American Archaeology and Ethnology* 4(6):319-356.

Kroeber, A. L. 1925 *Handbook of the Indians of California*. Bureau of American Ethnology, Bulletin 78. Smithsonian Institution, Washington D.C.

Kroeber, A. L. 1932 The Patwin and Their Neighbors. *University of California Publications in American Archaeology and Ethnology* 29(4):253-423.

Kroeber, A. L. 1962 The Nature of Land-Holding Groups in Aboriginal California. In *Two Papers on the Aboriginal Ethnography of California*, pp. 19-58. Reports of the University of California Archaeological Survey No.56. University of California Archaeological Survey, Department of Anthropology, University of California, Berkeley, CA.

Le Roy Ladurie, E. 1979 *The Territory of the Historian*. University of Chicago Press, Chicago.

Lightfoot, K. G. 1995 Culture Contact Studies: Redefining the Relationship Between Prehistoric and Historical Archaeology. *American Antiquity* 60(2):199-217.

Lightfoot, K. G. 2005a The Archaeology of Colonization: California in Cross-Cultural Perspective. In *The Archaeology of Colonial Encounters: Comparative Perspectives*, edited by G. J. Stein, pp. 207-236. School of American Research Press, Santa Fe.

Lightfoot, K. G. 2005b *Indians, Missionaries, and Merchants: The Legacy of Colonial Encounters on the California Frontiers*. University of California Press, Berkeley.

Lightfoot, K. G. and A. Martinez. 1995 Frontiers and Boundaries in Archaeological Perspective. *Annual Review of Anthropology* 24:417-492.

Lightfoot, K. G., A. M. Schiff and T. A. Wake (editors). 1997 *The Archaeology and Ethnohistory of Fort Ross, California, Vol. 2: The Native Alaskan Neighborhood A Multiethnic Community at Colony Ross*, Contributions of the University of California Archaeological Research Facility No. 55. University of California, Berkeley.

Lightfoot, K. G. and W. S. Simmons. 1998 Culture Contact in Protohistoric California: Social Contexts of Native and European Encounters. *Journal of California and Great Basin Anthropology* 20(2):138-170.

Lightfoot, K. G., T. A. Wake and A. M. Schiff. 1991 *The Archaeology and Ethnohistory of Fort Ross, California, Vol. 1*. Contributions of the University of California Archaeological Research Facility No. 49. University of California, Berkeley.

Linton, R. (editor). 1940 *Acculturation in Seven American Indian Tribes*. D. Appleton-Century, New York.

Loeb, E. M. 1926 Pomo Folkways. *University of California Publications in American Archaeology and Ethnology* 19(2):149-405.

McGuire, R. H. 1989 The Greater Southwest as a Periphery of Mesoamerica. In *Centre and Periphery: Comparative Studies in Archaeology*, edited by T. C. Champion, pp. 40-66. Unwin Hyman, London.

Meighan, C. W. 1950 *Excavations in Sixteenth Century Shellmounds at Drake's Bay, Marin County*. University of California Archaeological Survey Report No. 9, Papers on California Archaeology No. 9. Department of Anthropology, University of California, Berkeley, CA.

Meighan, C. W. 1981 "This is the Way the World Ends": Native Responses to the Age of Exploration in California. In *Early California: Perception and Reality*, pp. 45-74. William Andrews Clark Memorial Library, University of California, Los Angeles.

Meighan, C. W. 2002 The Stoneware Site, A 16th Century Site on Drakes Bay. In *Essays in California Archaeology: A Memorial to Franklin Fenenga*, edited by W. J. Wallace and F. A. Riddell, pp. 62-87. Contributions of the University of California Archaeological Research Facility No. 60. University of California, Berkeley.

Meighan, C. W. and R. F. Heizer. 1952 Archaeological Exploration of Sixteenth-Century Indian Mounds at Drake's Bay. *California Historical Society Quarterly* 31(2):99-108.

Milliken, R. 1995 *A Time of Little Choice: The Disintegration of Tribal Cultue in the San Francisco Bay Area 1769-1810*. Ballena Press, Menlo Park, CA.

Nutley, D. 1995 More Than a Shipwreck: The Convict Ship Hive - Aboriginal and European Contact Site. *Bulletin of the Australian Institute for Maritime Archaeology* 19(2):17-26.

Nuttall, Z. (editor). 1914 *New Light on Drake: A Collection of Documents Relating to his Voyage of Circumnavigation, 1577-1580*. The Hakluyt Society, London.

Oswalt, R. L. 1966 *Kashaya Texts*. University of California Publications in Linguistics No. 36. University of California Press, Berkeley.

Redfield, R., R. Linton and M. J. Herskovits. 1936 Memorandum for the Study of Acculturation. *American Anthropologist* 38(1):149-152.

Rice, P. M. 1998 Contexts of Contact and Change: Peripheries, Frontiers, and Boundaries. In *Studies in Culture Contact: Interaction, Culture Change, and Archaeology*, edited by J. G. Cusick, pp. 44-66. Occasional Paper No. 25. Center for Archaeological Investigations, Southern Illinois University at Carbondale, Carbondale, IL.

Rowlands, M. 1987 Centre and Periphery: A Review of the Concept. In *Centre and Periphery in the Ancient World*, edited by M. Rowlands, M. Larsen and K. Kristiansen, pp. 1-11. Cambridge University Press, Cambridge.

Rubertone, P. E. 2000 The Historical Archaeology of Native Americans. *Annual Review of Anthropology* 29:425-446.

Sahlins, M. 1981a *Historical Metaphors and Mythical Realities: Structure in the Early History of the Sandwich Islands Kingdom*. Association for the Study of Anthropology in Oceania, Special Publication No. 1. University of Michigan Press, Ann Arbor.

Sahlins, M. 1981b The Stranger King, or Dumezil among the Fijians. *Journal of Pacific History* 16(3):107-132.

Sahlins, M. 1985 *Islands of History*. University of Chicago Press, Chicago.

Sahlins, M. 1991 Return of the Event, Again; With Reflections on the Beginnings of the Great Fijian War of 1843 to 1855 Between the Kingdoms of Bau and Rewa. In *Clio in Oceania: Toward a Historical Anthropology*, edited by A. Biersack, pp. 37-99. Smithsonian Institution Press, Washington D.C.

Sahlins, M. 2000 Cosmologies of Capitalism: The Trans-Pacific Sector of "The World System". In *Culture in Practice: Selected Essays*, pp. 415-469. Zone Books, New York.

Sahlins, M. 2004 *Apologies to Thucydides: Understanding History as Culture and Vice Versa*. University of Chicago Press, Chicago.

Sahlins, M. 2005 Structural Work: How Microhistories Become Macrohistories and Vice Versa. *Anthropological Theory* 5(1):5-30.

Schieffelin, E. L. 1991 Introduction. In *Like People You See in a Dream: First Contact in Six Papuan Societies*, edited by E. L. Schieffelin and R. Crittenden, pp. 1-11. Stanford University Press, Stanford.

Schortman, E. M. and P. A. Urban. 1998 Culture Contact Structure and Process. In *Studies in Culture Contact: Interaction, Culture Change, and Archaeology*, edited by J. G. Cusick, pp. 102-125. Occasional Paper No. 25. Center for Archaeological Investigations, Southern Illinois University at Carbondale, Carbondale, IL.

Schurz, W. L. 1939 *The Manila Galleon*. E. P. Dutton & Co., Inc., New York.

Sewell, W. H. 2005 *Logics of History: Social Theory and Social Transformation*. University of Chicago Press, Chicago.

Silliman, S. W. 2005 Culture Contact or Colonialism? Challenges in the Archaeology of Native North America. *American Antiquity* 70(1):55-74.

Silliman, S. W. 2009 Change and Continuity, Practice and Memory: Native American Persistence in Colonial New England. *American Antiquity* 74(2):211-230.

Spicer, E. H. (editor). 1961 *Perspectives in American Indian Culture Change*. University of Chicago Press, Chicago.

Staniforth, M. 1997 The Archaeology of the Event - The Annales School and Maritime Archaeology. In *Underwater Archaeology*, edited by D. C. Lakey, pp. 17-21.

Staniforth, M. 2003a *Annales*-Informed Approaches to the Archaeology of Colonial Australia. *Historical Archaeology* 37(1):102-113.

Staniforth, M. 2003b *Material Culture and Consumer Society: Dependent Colonies in Colonial Australia*. Kluwer Academic/Plenum Publishers, New York.

Stein, G. J. 2002 From Passive Periphery to Active Agents: Emerging Perspectives in the Archaeology of Interregional Interaction. *American Anthropologist* 104(3):903-916.

Stein, G. J. 2005 Introduction: The Comparative Archaeology of Colonial Encounters. In *The Archaeology of Colonial Encounters: Comparative Perspectives*, edited by G. J. Stein, pp. 3-32. School of American Research Press, Santa Fe.

Stewart, S. 2003 An Overview of Research Issues for Indigenous Archaeology for the PRNS-GGNRA. In *Archaeological Research Issues for the Point Reyes National Seashore - Golden Gate National Recreation Area*, edited by S. Stewart and A. Praetzellis, pp. 49-246. Anthropolological Studies Center, Sonoma State University, Rohnert Park, CA.

Thomas, N. 1990 Taking People Seriously: Cultural Autonomy and the Global System. *Critique of Anthropology* 9(3):59-69.

Thomas, N. 1991 *Entangled Objects: Exchange, Material Culture, and Colonialism in the Pacific*. Harvard University Press, Cambridge.

Thomas, N. 1997 Partial Texts: Representation, Colonialism, and Agency in Pacific History. In *In Oceania: Visions, Artifacts, Histories*, pp. 23-49. Duke University Press, Durham.

Thomas, N. 2002 Colonizing Cloth: Interpreting the Material Culture of Nineteenth-Century Oceania. In *The Archaeology of Colonialism*, edited by C. L. Lyons and J. K. Papadopoulos, pp. 182-198. Getty Research Institute, Los Angeles.

Torrence, R. and A. Clarke (editors). 2000a *The Archaeology of Difference: Negotiating Cross-Cultural Engagements in Oceania*. Routledge, London.

Torrence, R. and A. Clarke (editors). 2000b Negotiating Difference: Practice Makes Theory for Contemporary Archaeology in Oceania. In *The Archaeology of Difference: Negotiating cross-cultural engagements in Oceania*, edited by R. Torrence and A. Clarke, pp. 1-31. Routledge, London.

Treganza, A. E. 1959 The Examination of Indian Shellmounds in the Tomales and Drake's Bay Areas With Reference to Sixteenth Century Historic Contacts (MS283). In *Collection of Manuscripts from the Archaeological Archives of the Phoebe Hearst Museum of Anthropology*. Phoebe Hearst Museum of Anthropology, University of California, Berkeley.

Treganza, A. E. and T. F. King (editors). 1968 *Archaeological Studies in Point Reyes National Seashore*. San Francisco State College Archaeological Survey and Santa Rosa Junior College.

Vaux, W. S. W. (editor). 1854 *The World Encompassed by Sir Francis Drake*. The Hakluyt Society, London.

Von der Porten, E. P. 1968 *The Porcelains and Terra Cottas of Drakes Bay*. Unpublished manuscript by Drake Navigators Guild, Point Reyes, CA.

Von der Porten, E. P. 1972 Drake and Cermeño in California: Sixteenth Century Chinese Ceramics. *Historical Archaeology* 6:1-22.

Voss, B. L. 2008 *The Archaeology of Ethnogenesis: Race and Sexuality in Colonial San Francisco*. University of California Press, Berkeley, CA.

Wagner, H. R. 1926 *Sir Francis Drake's Voyage Around the World: Its Aims and Achievments*. John Howell, San Francisco.

Wallerstein, I. 1974 *The Modern World-System I: Capitalist Agriculture and the Origins of the European World-Economy in the Sixteenth Century*. Academic Press, New York.

Williams, J. S. 1992 The Archaeology of Underdevelopment and the Military Frontier of Northern New Spain. *Historical Archaeology* 26(1):7-21.

Williamson, C. 2004 Contact Archaeology and the Writing of Aboriginal History. In *The Archaeology of Contact in Settler Societies*, edited by T. Murray, pp. 176-199. Cambridge University Press, Cambridge.

Wolf, E. R. 1982 *Europe and the People Without History*. University of California Press, Berkeley.

Chapter 3
Subduing Tendencies? Colonialism, Capitalism, and Comparative Atlantic Archaeologies

Audrey Horning

Introduction: Scales of Analysis

Historical archaeologists have long emphasized capitalism and colonial discourse in examining commonalties in the archaeologies of the "modern world," yet have struggled to avoid the muting effect of totalizing narratives. Is archaeology really necessary if all we have to say is that capitalism breeds poverty and wealth and that objects and landscapes encode dominance and resistance? At one level, our interpretive difficulty is clearly rooted in the ongoing struggle to reconcile our scales of analysis – "from the local to the global" – but at another level it betrays our own unresolved relationship with the political and ethical implications of globalization as well as the fact that our discipline is itself immersed in capitalism and embedded in the structures of colonialism. Critique is implicit in historical archaeologies of capitalism and colonialism, yet to what purpose?

The ways in which past individuals negotiated economic and political inequities in locally rooted ways provide a means to challenge the subduing tendencies of "archaeologies of capitalism" while also questioning dichotomies of structure and agency. Drawing from my work in Ireland, I explore the challenges of a multiscalar approach to the archaeology of colonial entanglements by focusing upon the relationship between the historical contexts of capitalism and colonialism and their palpable legacies. Here, a European context provides an opportunity to reevaluate the centrality of North American approaches to global historical archaeology, while also addressing the challenge of scales.

Ireland sits awkwardly in global histories of colonialism, given its integral role in the imperial projects of the nineteenth-century UK as well as its economic and political subordination within the UK, a position often understood through the lens of colonialism. As noted by the geographer David Harvey (2001: 326), the anomalous position of Ireland even posed a problem for Karl Marx: "The politics of the Irish question forced him to confront regional and cultural divergence as fundamental to

A. Horning (✉)
Queens University Belfast, Belfast, UK
e-mail: ajh64@leicester.ac.uk

S.K. Croucher and L. Weiss (eds.), *The Archaeology of Capitalism in Colonial Contexts*, 65
Contributions To Global Historical Archaeology, DOI 10.1007/978-1-4614-0192-6_3,
© Springer Science+Business Media, LLC 2011

class struggle." Yet Marx remained chiefly concerned about the role Ireland could play in the liberation of the English working class rather than exploring the ramifications of the particularities and peculiarities of history and identity in Ireland. In his estimation, the English working class "will never be able to do anything decisive here in England before they separate their attitude towards Ireland quite definitely from that of the ruling classes, and not only make a common cause with the Irish, but even take initiative in dissolving the Union... this must be done not out of sympathy for Ireland, but as a demand based on the interests of the English proletariat" (Marx to Ludwig Kugelmann, 29 November 1896, Marx and Engels Collected Works [MECW] 43, 1988: 390).

For Marx, an Irish worker in the British Empire facilitated his own oppression through being "a tool of his aristocrats and capitalists against Ireland" (Marx to Sigrid Meyer and August Vogt, 9 April 1870, MECW 43, 1988: 474–475). Such a formulation rests on several premises. Beyond categorizing the Irish working class as dupes crippled by false consciousness, it also presumes the existence of an "authentic" cultural Ireland that could be freed not only from capitalist oppression but from British colonial domination. Both perceptions are worth challenging in the interests of progressing a multiscalar understanding of past human experience, but also in aid of dismantling the problematic construction of Ireland as colony which underpinned the use of violence throughout the period of the Troubles and continues to influence unrest into the present.

In common with other authors in this volume, I take some inspiration from postcolonial theory in seeking to understand how individuals and groups interact with one another and engage with the broader structures of colonial and capitalist entanglements, but suggest that, when incautiously applied, postcolonial rhetoric runs the same risk of serving as a totalizing narrative as do interpretations which take capitalism as a central theme. In their simplest formulations, both rely upon binary oppositions: oppressor and oppressed; metropole and colony, even when the best of postcolonial thought endeavors to subvert such binaries by exploring the ambiguous spaces in between (e.g. Bhabha 1994), or in challenging the solidity of the center (e.g. Naipaul 1967). Nevertheless, to become "postcolonial" presumes having been "colonial," however that state of being may be defined. Here, the history and archaeology of the north of Ireland, a place where the label of "colonial" remains strongly contested, serves as a cautionary tale.

Finally, in considering the challenges of interpreting capitalism and colonialism and their contemporary relevance, I have also endeavored to be overt about my own positionality in acknowledgement of Martin Hall's (2009: 13) response to my original conference paper in which he queried my claim to address the problematic presence of the past without acknowledging "on whose behalf" did I speak and "behind whom" did I stand. The need for self-reflexivity and an explicit ethical position is a necessity for responsible archaeology in a postcolonial, postmodern age, yet I've always hoped that my own position was obvious in the questions I ask. I want to prioritize other people's stories over my own, but accept that as a kind of self-justifying subterfuge suggestive of a latent attachment to scientific objectivity exacerbated by an over-developed (Western?) sense of privacy. It is a question of balance – if we employ personal narrative we run the risk of further privileging the author's voice while exposing individual agendas. I hope to make my own approach explicit in the following discussion, albeit without dominating the conversation.

Uniform Interpretations and Subduing Tendencies

Before I further explore the convoluted legacies of capitalism and colonialism in Ireland, it is useful to revisit the ways in which historical archaeologists have traditionally endeavored to interpret these processes. Sarah Tarlow (2007: 10) has expressed concern that "archaeologies of capitalism always ask the same question: what does this or that aspect of the material past tell us about relationships of power between social groups?" I see nothing wrong with this particular question, insofar as it can be tackled at multiple scales of analysis and insofar as "power" can be interpreted in many different ways. My discomfort with foregrounding capitalism in our enquiries is less about the questions asked than about the sameness of the answers given, with the endless rehashing of material inequities too often producing worrying uniform interpretations of diverse assemblages: "We identify these activities, artifacts, and features of African American historical material culture as a critique of the dominant white cultural order" (Matthews et al. 2002: 122); "workers may have spoiled knives intentionally…as a way to regain some degree of autonomy on the shop floor, where hierarchy must have seemed immutable for many" (Nassaney and Abel 2000: 268); "by continuing to apportion upland grazing as they done in the past…small holders…were contesting the acquisitive agrarian capitalists' schemes" (Frazer 1999: 96). Everywhere in the world, historical actors can be found resisting capitalist-inspired inequality. The totalizing character of – for want of a better term – archaeologies of capitalist inequality is further underlined by this assertion by Charles Orser (1999: 274): "Much of what I knew about the archaeology of African-Americans could be almost directly transferred to the study of Irish peasants." If that were really true, why study Irish peasants?

An historical archaeology which persists in explicating the existence of capitalism through imprinting domination and resistance on every artifact; or through repetitious descriptions of institutional buildings adhering to Foucauldian surveillance principles; or through carefully selected case studies of known class violence comes very close to meeting Jim Deetz's (1991: 1) paraphrased definition of historical archaeology as "the most expensive way in the world of finding out what we already know." Few would deny that capitalism was inextricably linked with the processes of colonialism in the post-1550 world. Historical archaeology should not be about proving the obvious, but rather ought to be an exploration of past human experiences that acknowledge the constraints of structure without denying humanity. The intricacies of capitalism and colonialism in the early modern world, and their contemporary legacies, represent incalculably serious issues. Capitalism and colonialism demand attention, but also demand interpretive rigor.

My concern about the totalizing character of capitalist-based interpretations of human interrelationships in the modern world hardly represents a radical departure. Pedro Funari, Siân Jones, and Martin Hall (1999: 7) have expressed similar unease: "The prioritization of capitalism as a focus of study situates its emergence, spread, and domination as an inevitable process, lying beyond the consciousness or control of social actors, particularly subordinate groups." Funari (1999: 45) argued most articulately for shifting focus from capitalism: "the complexity of modern historical societies provides us challenging evidence of non-capitalist features."

In 2000, Laurie Wilkie and Kevin Bartoy published a spirited, if not fully thought out, critique of what they saw as the totalizing tendencies of critical archaeology by the "members" of the "Annapolis School." Their article occasioned fierce rejoinders including one accusing Wilkie and Bartoy, in their overemphasis on individual agency, of becoming dupes of the New Right political order soon to be personified by George W. Bush (Thomas 2000: 770). Debate was silenced. More recently, Gavin Lucas (2006: 39) risked a return to this acrimonious discussion: "For historical archaeology, the danger in producing 'totalising' histories lies not only in a privileging of European perspectives, but also in the attendant flattening out of local diversity and particularly histories. And yet an equal danger lies in shifting to another extreme – rejecting grand narratives, and conducting archaeologies that only produce highly specific, localized narratives whose broader relevance is missing."

This seemingly dichotomous debate also reared its head in the responses to a discussion article I wrote for *Archaeological Dialogues* in which I questioned the efficacy of interpreting modern Ireland through the lens of colonialism (Horning 2006). According to one discussant, "Neoliberal, centrist archaeologists have always sought to mischaracterize global historical archaeology. They have raised objections to the archaeological investigation of capitalism, claiming that it constitutes a metanarrative and thus is off-limits. The recognition of overarching schemes and designs is somehow anathema to serious archaeological research in the postprocessual era" (Orser 2006). So there I found myself cast out into that neoliberal centrist Giddens-inspired desert, wearing a scarlet "*NLC*", with only Laurie Wilkie and Kevin Bartoy to keep me company! Given my aversion to the policies of George W. Bush and the fact that elsewhere I have been (rather more flatteringly) described as a "post-Marxist" (Palus et al. 2006: 91) this characterization came as a bit of a shock.

From my perspective, I had not denied the structures of economic and social inequality that gave rise to today's divided Ireland. Where I had chosen to prioritize the discussion of structure, however, was not to explain every past action and artifact as part of an antagonistic discourse with capitalism, a relatively easy task, but to consider these structures through their impact upon archaeological practice. In terms of reading the past, I have come to prefer ambiguity to the certainty of narrowly interpreted Marxian rhetoric. In so doing, I align myself with many of the authors in this volume in finding inspiration in notions of hybridity, syncretism, and creolization to explore colonial entanglements in the early modern Atlantic "world", while at the same time eschewing understandings of the Irish past as a straightforward colonial narrative. The resultant "messy" past is one that I find holds great promise for reenvisioning the present. Similarly, I find Charles Orser's (2009) more recent call for a "dialectical multiscalar" approach to historical archaeology a productive avenue to resolve the tension between local and global approaches.

Despite my discomfort with "archaeologies of capitalist inequality", my focus upon the present-day implications of interpretations of colonialism and capitalism clearly owes a strong debt to critical archaeology. Reacting to archaeology's deep roots in capitalism and colonialism, critical archaeologists have explicitly cast their work as political activism, particularly in opposing capitalist inequalities. What remains unclear is how we are supposed to effect a radical reordering of capitalism and social hierarchies in the modern world while maintaining our own grasp on our privileged positions as archaeologists. I have not witnessed a mass Marxian exodus from the halls of academe nor do there seem to be any ivory towers sporting "to let" signs. I am uncomfortable with the "top-down" manner in which archaeology selects "audiences" for its critiques, yet as a university-based archaeologist who is occasionally allowed out "into the field," I am implicated in this practice.

For as much as I wholeheartedly agree with the need to communicate with (not just "to") communities outside what McGuire (2006: 137) rightly labels as the "the traditional middle-class community that the discipline [of archaeology] usually serves", I find the approach of the Colorado Coal Field project (McGuire and Reckner 2005), in targeting a monolithic "working class" as the recipients of their archaeological insights about the Ludlow massacre, problematic. In McGuire's words, "the project's message is simple. Labour's rights to a safe workplace, benefits, reasonable wages, a forty-hour week and dignity were won with blood. They were not freely given by capitalists but bought with the lives of working people like those who died at Ludlow" (McGuire 2006: 141). Fine, but I doubt that this message, as important as it is, requires archaeology with all its attendant expenses. And what about those people who died at Ludlow? I question whether being used for the purposes of the contemporary Union movement is necessarily how they would concoct their own epitaphs.

Any useable past constructed by archaeologists to serve particular constituencies today is by its very nature an exclusive past. I am wary of useable pasts, particularly in colonial/postcolonial contexts. I would find more interest in a consideration of the Coal Field project that tackled the ways in which the archaeologists are being used by labor organizers for the union movement's own self-aware purposes. I suspect a *quid pro quo*: academic archaeologists obtain the capital they require in the form of publications and publicity, and the union organizers gain another means of increasing their membership and public support. Perhaps that is an appropriate exchange. But where in all this are the people of the past and their experiences? Where should the balance between responsibilities to the past and to the present fall? Who has the right to place an exchange value on past human lives? As a union member (University and College Union), I do not denigrate the importance of the issues at stake, nor do I question the value of the Ludlow archaeology itself. My critique is not intended to suggest that somehow I have found a way to do things "better", whether operating from my exile in the "neoliberal desert" or from the more trendy environs of the post-Marxist café. Instead, the questions I am concerned with highlight the contradictions and uncertainties which to me are the logical outcome of critical considerations of colonialism, capitalism, and their contemporary legacies in the place where I pursue archaeology: Northern Ireland.

The archaeology I conduct in Northern Ireland specifically focuses upon early modern British expansion. I am interested in examining late medieval Irish life and the subsequent interactions between the Irish and the (mainly) English and Scots who settled in Ireland as part of the late sixteenth and early seventeenth-century processes of plantation. I do so in full recognition that this period and these interactions remain contested and constitute the root of the dichotomous historical memories that gave rise to the Troubles and which continue to structure everyday life. I believe that a better understanding of the complexities of the early modern period in Ireland, which includes a consideration of the entwined forces of capitalism and colonialism, can provoke and enhance understanding between today's two traditions and contribute to the construction of some form of shared, peaceful future. I am well aware that such a motivation appears to contradict my own critique of critical archaeology in terms of "useable pasts," and I often question my right to comment at all. While my strong family connections to the north of Ireland served as an influential part of my upbringing (and provided me with Irish citizenship), I did not grow up there. Instead, I inherited the prejudices of the twentieth-century postpartition émigré before I myself moved to Northern Ireland. My perspective has certainly evolved from what I learned as a child about the divisions between north and south and the divide between Protestant and Catholic, but my attitudes are inevitably influenced by all of the places I have lived: the USA, Northern Ireland, the Republic of Ireland, and England. I find balancing my responsibilities to the people of the past and of the present, from my position as both an outsider and insider, a constant and conscious challenge.

The Colonial Past in the Capitalist Present

"*Native American chief asks NUI Galway to return 'iconic' canoe.*" So ran the headline on the front page of the *Irish Times* on 28 March, 2009. The following story related the efforts of the St Mary's First Nation Wolastokwiyik (Maliseet) community of New Brunswick, Canada to reclaim a birch bark canoe, presented by their ancestors to the British Lieutenant governor Sir Howard Douglas in the early nineteenth century, from the collections of the National University of Ireland at Galway. Speaking for her community, Wolastokwiyik Chief Candace Paul framed the plea for the return of the canoe in terms of a shared history, noting that their ancestors suffered from "many of the same forms of oppression as the Irish people at the hands of colonialism" (Siggins 2009: 1).

In the sixteenth and early seventeenth century, a handful of English commentators found it politically and lyrically expedient to draw parallels between the "uncivilized" nature of Native North Americans and the Gaelic Irish, as part of a process of othering inherent to early modern British expansion. Their writings underpin the Maliseet claim and identification with the Irish experience. Scholarly support for such an equation is readily available in the broader literature on the Atlantic World. In an effort to broaden understandings of colonial North America, historians in the 1980s began focusing more explicitly upon the Atlantic contexts of colonial American life. From this base arose a set of historical assumptions about the commonalties between the colonial experience in British North America, and that of postmedieval Ireland. As expressed by historian Alison Games (2006: 683): "… colonial historians often think of Ireland as a formative place in shaping English plantations in America."

While England had maintained a degree of control over Ireland since the twelfth century, the Reformation, fear of Spain, and economic avarice encouraged the strengthening of England's grip on the island in the sixteenth century, manifested through the disestablishment of churches; the political courting of elites, both native and Old English (descendants of the twelfth-century Anglo Norman invaders); the imposition of new systems of landholding; experiments with plantation; and outright warfare. Ireland did not yield to English authority until the submission of the Ulster leader and Earl of Tyrone Hugh O'Neill in 1603, and his "flight" to the continent in 1607. The subsequent implementation of the Ulster Plantation has been viewed as analogous to New World colonization, and is implicated in the twentieth-century creation of Northern Ireland. The Ulster Plantation involved the granting of lands in counties Tyrone, Fermanagh, Armagh, and Derry/Londonderry to loyal servitors, British planters, "deserving" Irish, and the Church. Much of the newly created Co. Londonderry (carved out of the lands known as "O'Cahans Country" after the chief sept) was granted to the 12 premier London Companies in exchange for the financial support of the Plantation scheme. Development of the two principal Londonderry Plantation towns, Coleraine and Londonderry, was given to the Irish Society, made up of representatives from the individual London Companies. "Unofficial" plantation also took place in counties Antrim and Down. In total, perhaps 30,000 Protestants settled in Ireland as a direct result of all of the plantation schemes, a very small achievement considering that the overall population of the country in the middle of the seventeenth century was somewhere between 1.3 and 1.5 million. In 1641 Catholics still owned 59% of profitable land in Ireland. By the eighteenth century, that figure would drop to 22% following the 1641 Uprising, the Cromwellian conflicts of mid-century, and the Williamite War (Barnard 2004: 13, 29, 61). Despite historical memories of plantation, it is those later events that truly forged a divided Ireland.

British settlers in North America and Ulster struggled to implement idealized plans and to replicate familiar forms to meet their own needs and to ensure profitable commodities for the Crown and private investors. In these efforts, they acted not dissimilarly to those within England and Scotland also seeking to reformulate post-Reformation society. At the same time, local populations in each land devised their own strategies and responses to British expansion; strategies consistent with their own social and political structures and existing knowledge of the English. For the Irish, that knowledge had roots stretching back to the Mesolithic. Except at the very basic level of acknowledging agency and self-awareness on the part of native people in Ireland and the Americas, their responses, and their outcomes, are not easily equated.

Perceptions of the colonial past of Ireland and America as being similar are interlinked more by a belief in the civilizing of wild lands and wild people – an echo of sixteenth-century colonial rationalizations – than by any empirical evidence. Even a cursory examination of Gaelic society on the eve of Plantation calls into question any assertion of equivalency with the highly diverse native New World societies and their undeniably colonial encounters with the English. For example, the extensive economic ties between medieval Ireland and continental Europe are materially manifested in urban archaeological assemblages replete with French, Spanish, and Italian wares. Although the "ordinary" rural Irish of the late medieval period remain obscure in the archaeological record (O'Conor 2002), the Gaelic, Old English, and Scottish elite that held sway over their lives were intimately aware of their roles within European power struggles. Furthermore, the notion that Ireland served as a successful model of colonization ignores chronological realities. The attempted sixteenth-century plantations in Ireland failed miserably, while the Ulster Plantation was not launched until after the settlement of Jamestown. Notwithstanding the historical memories of Plantation, the Ulster Plantation can in no way be understood as having gone according to plan.

When we look at the macro scale relationship between Ireland and Britain up to the early twentieth century, we also have to take account of Ireland's structural role as a separate, if subordinate, kingdom rather than as a dependent colony. As expressed by Colin Rynne (2008: 3): "the social trajectories of Ireland's white and Roman Catholic 'natives' within the empire were very different from those of Britain's African and Asian colonies. Ireland had, after all, enjoyed an important trading partnership with Britain, with most of the profits remaining in Ireland. It was also a junior partner in British colonialism, supplying both goods and key personnel to Britain's overseas colonies. In other words, Ireland fulfilled roles within the British imperium that real colonies could never expect to, roles that issues of race and geography would always ensure they could not." From the perspective of economic historian Liam Kennedy (1996: 170), early twentieth-century Ireland enjoyed "much the same average living standards as countries like Spain, Norway, Finland, Italy. While lagging behind world leaders such as Britain and Germany, Ireland was comfortably ahead of Greece, Portugal and Hungary." While colonialism may characterize some of the mechanisms employed by the British to maintain hegemony over the kingdom of Ireland, colonialism itself, in the words of historian Stephen Howe (2000: 50), was not a "wholly willed phenomenon" that was carefully and consciously imposed upon Ireland and the Irish.

Questioning Ireland's historic status as a colony is not to deny the efficacy of employing colonialism as a lens to understand social relations. To return to issues of scale, I find it problematic to use the label of "colony" to describe the macroscale political and economic relationship between Britain and Ireland, while at the same time I find the insights of postcolonial theorists such as Homi Bhabha (1994) very helpful in considering the interactions of all the players on the "plantation stage", including Gaels, Old English, Scottish and English planters, continental traders, politicos, and religious figures. Notions of ambiguity and the acknowledgement that "new" forms of behavior and material culture can simultaneously challenge and reify ethnic and cultural boundaries provide a useful framework for interpreting the material records of plantation with promise for the present (my "useable" past?).

Regardless of whether or not early modern Ireland can be understood as a colony, many, like the Maliseet, find contemporary political strength in an assumed shared history between Ireland and native North America. At one level, this construction/ useable past constitutes a potent form of resistance to the inequities of colonial experiences. At another level, this equation reflects the continuing strength of mythic histories. In the case of the canoe, the mythic history arguably serves to right an historic wrong as the Maliseet draw strength from reclaiming objects of cultural patrimony. Yet, this object was originally created as a metaphor for the colonial relations between the Maliseet and the British. The Maliseet packaged a version of themselves up as a canoe and offered that to the British governor. Now, they reclaim that constructed self-image in the hopes that it reflects a past reality and indigenous identity. So should an accepted history be allowed to stand, if it is to the benefit of an historically disenfranchised community? Who loses if the good folks of NUI-Galway choose to position themselves as former victims of colonial overlords to broker good will with an indigenous community on the other side of the Atlantic, regardless of more complicated past actualities and present motivations? Should it matter that Irish Labour party president Michael D. Higgins gained political capital by personally intervening to ensure the repatriation of the canoe? As described by Galway geologist Kathryn Moore, the canoe "went from being a nuisance we wanted to get rid of to being something really precious, a symbol of national importance" (Boswell 2007). If our aim as historical archaeologists is to disentangle the historical intricacies of capitalism and colonialism in a range of locally rooted contexts then I do not believe we can divorce understandings of the contemporary exchange value of "symbols of national importance" from an exploration of their origins.

The Republic of Ireland is a self-defined postcolonial nation well-versed in employing "symbols of national importance" as exemplified by the centrality of heritage tourism in the national economy. Tourism is the third largest sector in the Irish economy, generating income in excess of €4.8 billion in 2008. Over 76% of the visitors come from overseas, including (in 2008) 983,000 from North America (Fáilte Ireland 2009). Irishness, and by extension versions of Irish history palatable to the Irish Diaspora, is recognized as a marketable commodity (Graham 2001). Northern Ireland Tourist Board chief executive Alan Clarke openly acknowledged the saleability of self in voicing his worries about staffing tourist attractions with non-Irish employees: "Irishness is a brand, if all the staff are from eastern Europe it dilutes the brand" (Douglas 2005). More tongue-in-cheek but no less apt is Terry Eagleton's (1999: 39) observation: "Ireland's other major export is itself...Irishness is the intoxicating liquor which the country is best at distilling. Consumed too freely, it produces more fantasies, hallucinations, false hopes, weepiness, bravado and phoney cheeriness than Bushmills ever did. The country is well on its way to becoming one enormous theme park, a kind of Celtic Disneyland with Queen Maeve standing in for Mickey Mouse."

A chief consumer of "Brand Ireland" is Irish America. Ireland as postcolony (e.g. Kiberd 1997) clearly suits the needs of nationalism, of tourism, and for an Irish-American imagined homeland that bolster notions of the American dream. The symbolic value of Irish ruins in reifying Irish American claims is evident in the American writer Michael Mays' (2005: 3) lament over the appearance of "weekend retreats springing up seemingly everywhere, standing side-by-side with, or replacing altogether, the Famine huts that had stood for a century-and-a-half as silent testimony and mute memorials to the hundreds of thousands who perished during the time of 'the great hunger'." While Diasporic visitors seek confirmation of their remembered histories through the testimony of abandoned landscapes, however, locals may instead seek renewal. Furthermore, the capacity of Ireland's recognized dependency on the tourist dollar to breed resentment should not be underestimated. Irish Americans who seek to claim and consume modern Ireland might do well to heed the caustic words of Irish writer George O'Brien: "These are our four green fields you're treading on with your seven-league cowboy boots. Tread softly, for you tread on our bullshit" (O'Brien 1991/1992: 42).

Commemoration, Excavation, Reconsideration?

The construction of Ireland as postcolony may be relatively unproblematic when one focuses only upon the Republic, where the strength of a nationalist narrative stresses the colonial character of the relationship with Britain and the triumph of early twentieth-century independence. Colonial equations are rather more problematic in Northern Ireland, where both contemporary communities (glossed as Catholic/nationalist, self-identified descendants of the Gaels; and Protestant/unionist, self-identified heirs of the Planters) view themselves as subaltern. Therefore, any contemporary consideration of the past must acknowledge that both traditions understand themselves as threatened minorities; unionists in the context of an overwhelmingly Catholic Ireland, nationalists in terms of their numbers within Ulster. Official approaches to a series of quadricentennial Ulster Plantation anniversaries serve to illustrate the challenges of public history.

In the USA, anniversaries are big business and serve as a tool to create unity through emphasizing the agreed historical metanarrative, the "continuum" from the earliest English-speaking colonial settlements striving for self-sufficiency, to the creation of an independent nation founded upon principles of democracy, to the shift to global economic domination in the twentieth century. The divergent character of historical memories of colonialism in the "Atlantic world" was neatly encapsulated in the contrast between two anniversaries in 2007; that of the 1607 English establishment of Jamestown and the 1607 Flight of the Earls of Tyrone and Tyrconnell and their followers from Rathmullan, Co. Donegal (Fig. 3.1). Jamestown anniversary events celebrated the achievements of Anglo-American colonial society through the presence of Queen Elizabeth II and the presentation of Jamestown's archaeology as the physical incarnation of the birth of American democracy. In Northern Ireland, anniversaries are never straightforward. There is no agreed history that unites the two traditions, because no one group's voice is any louder than the other. Thus, the anniversary of the Flight of the Earls was greeted with academic reflection but very muted public recognition. In contrast to the near deification of Jamestown's archaeology and its chief archaeologist, the ivy-choked Rathmullan Priory, the traditional departure point of the Gaelic lords, silently sinks into decay. Where a *seemingly*

Fig. 3.1 Rathmullan Priory, Co. Donegal

unambiguous Jamestown anchors received national memories of glorious deeds and imagined successes, the acknowledged symbolic ambiguity of Rathmullan Priory militates against such a simplistic presentation.

History as commodity is an inevitable part of most commemoration activities. Arguably, American scholars don't really need to be concerned about the commercialization of the colonial past, in contrast to the more deadly uses made of history in places such as Northern Ireland. But perhaps the inherent tension between nationalist and unionist versions of Irish history is more likely to yield a deeper consideration of historical realities than the largely uncontested and commodified narratives of colonial America. Certainly whatever political voice Virginia's Native people achieved in the run up to 2007 has inevitably receded as the anniversary passed. Unlike Northern Ireland, where divergent understandings of contested histories are held by two groups of roughly equivalent power, the power differential in addressing Virginia's contested colonial past is vastly unbalanced.

Despite the functioning of the Northern Ireland Assembly and the "normalization" of life since the signing of the Good Friday Agreement in 1998, the Troubles, which began in 1968 and claimed over 3700 lives, are not wholly resolved. On 4 November 2009, the Independent Monitoring Commission released its report on paramilitary activity in Northern Ireland between 1 March and 31 August 2009. In that period, there were three paramilitary murders committed by dissident Republicans; their targets two members of the British security forces and one police constable (Sapper Mark Quimsey, Sapper Patrick Azimkar, and PC Stephen Carroll), while the number of Loyalist assaults increased by 88%. According to the Commission, "the numbers of casualties of republican shootings (all the results of dissident attacks) and of loyalist assaults rose very sharply and were the highest for

Fig. 3.2 Contesting Plantation nomenclature: signage for the city of Derry/Londonderry

six years and four years respectively" (IMC 2009: 30). Further evidence for continuing conflict is found in the increasing number of "peace lines" being constructed to separate communities in conflict. The total stands at 88 in 2009, as opposed to only 29 in 1994 when the ceasefire was declared (McDonald 2009).

In the same week that the Independent Monitoring Commission issued its sobering report, I participated in a symposium organized by the Belfast City Council to discuss how to mark the four hundredth anniversary of the 1613 granting of Belfast's charter, an event associated with Plantation and thus inherently contentious. This symposium was followed by an event organized by the Coleraine-based Causeway Museum Service that involved tours and discussions about the archaeology of Plantation in north Co. Antrim and Co. Derry/Londonderry (Fig. 3.2). The City Council event featured a panel discussion following four talks; one on the challenges of teaching history in Northern Ireland, one about the process of commemorating Liverpool's eight hundredth anniversary, a presentation about the Jamestown commemoration from the perspective of the Virginia Indians, and my own talk on the archaeology of the Ulster Plantation. I considered the origins of Belfast as a medieval Gaelic stronghold (see MacDonald 2006; ÓBaoill 2006, 2007; O'Keeffe 2006), and focused upon what the archaeological and documentary records reveal about the ways that Plantation settlements actually functioned, as opposed to the ways they were intended to function. Such stories include clear evidence for the presence of Irish in Londonderry Plantation villages (in which they were officially barred from living), the intercultural sharing of drink in the Plantation's many illegal alehouses, and even the participation of Catholic Scots as settlers in the supposedly Protestant Plantation (see Horning 2001, 2004, 2009). The not-very subtle subtext of my presentation was the convoluted, complicated but – at every step of the way and like it or not – *shared* history of Plantation.

The event, opened by the Sinn Féin Deputy Lord Mayor and facilitated by a BBC presenter, was attended by a self-selected audience that nonetheless represented a cross-section of views. As I sat on the panel flanked by individuals I would rate as rather more actively engaged in the task of furthering peace in Northern Ireland than I as an archaeologist could ever claim to be (such as the chief executive of the Community Relations Council and the Head of the School of Education at Queen's University Belfast) I questioned my right to be present. While I firmly advocate an archaeology of the Plantation period that encourages engagement by and with the "two traditions," I recognize that archaeology is an unlikely tool for changing the world. The Belfast discussions were open and serious, but it was the follow-on 1613 event that most clearly demonstrated the potential of archaeology to play a not-in-consequential role in reenvisioning the future of Northern Ireland.

Approximately 30 members of the public joined museum professionals and archaeologists on a one and a half day tour of sites related to the Plantation, including the Plantation village at Dunluce established by the Scottish Catholic Randal MacDonnell currently under investigation by Colin Breen of the University of Ulster; the medieval priory and Plantation bawn at Dungiven (Brannon 1985); the Mercers' Company village of Movanagher where archaeology revealed a vernacular Irish style dwelling in the midst of the Plantation settlement (Horning 2001); the enigmatic Goodland/Ballyuchan Plantation settlement on the north coast of Co. Antrim likely associated with Catholic planters from Islay (Horning 2004); and Limavady, the site of a medieval O'Cahan castle and early seventeenth-century Plantation bawn.

The story of Limavady illustrates both the complexity of the Plantation process and the value of a multiscalar approach. Situated within the Roe Valley Country Park and thus readily accessible to the public, the site includes a later medieval O'Cahan tower house, demolished sometime in the eighteenth century, and of subsequent developments by an English servitor, Sir Thomas Phillips. A superficial reading could emphasize the destruction of the Gaelic world personified by the downfall of the O'Cahan chief, Donal Ballach O'Cahan, whose lands were seized and granted to Phillips, himself one of the architects of the Londonderry Plantation scheme and an early modern protocapitalist entrepreneur. Such a characterization would also resonate with Marx's understanding of the Ulster Plantation which he described as "Ulster having been taken from its Irish owners who at that time held the land in common, and handed over to Scotch Protestant military colonists....the whole agrarian history of Ireland is a series of confiscations of Irish land to be handed over to English settlers" (Marx to Jenny Longuet 24 February 1881, in *Marx and Engels on the Irish Question* [MEIQ] 1971: 326–320). That the site's Plantation history has disappeared from local memory (the site is referred to only as "O'Cahan's Rock") could be read as indicative of local resistance to the Plantation narrative and the twin forces of capitalism and colonialism.

A more interesting reading is possible. In 1602, Donal Ballach O'Cahan gave his allegiance to the English Crown in exchange for a knighthood and title to his lands, which, *contra* Marx, were not held in common. Gaelic society was firmly hierarchical, and O'Cahan, like other Gaelic lords, controlled the use of his lands and by extension the lives of his tenants. O'Cahan saw personal advantage in the English

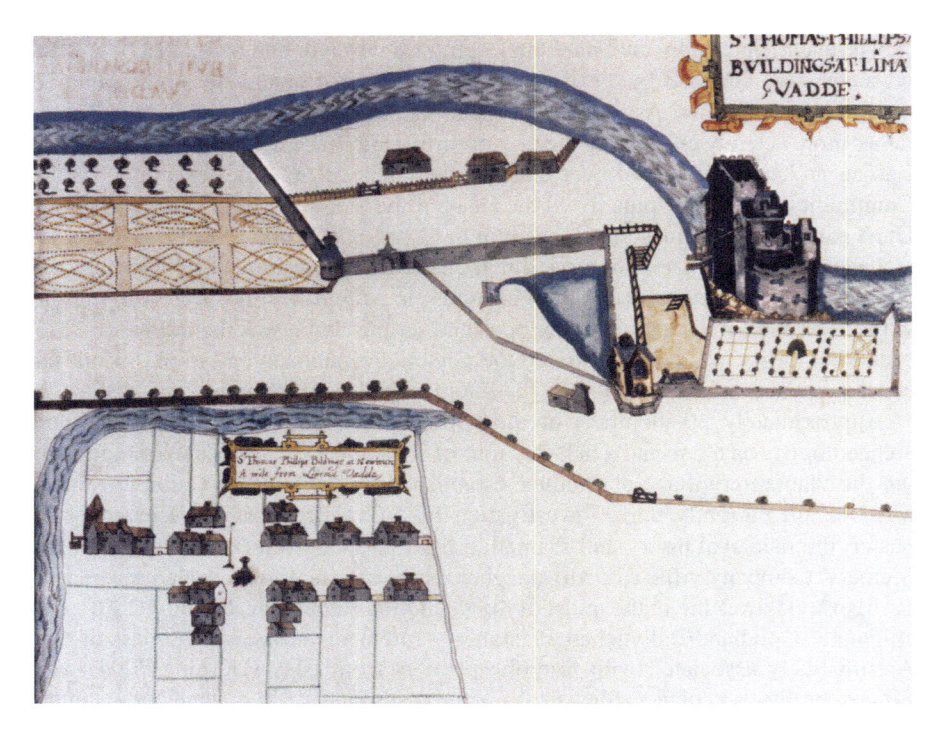

Fig. 3.3 1622 map by Thomas Raven depicting the castle and bawn at Limavady (*top*) and Newtown Limavady (*bottom*)

system of landholding, as the traditional Gaelic practice required him to pay tribute to Hugh O'Neill. O'Cahan's efforts to manipulate the English system failed, as he later fell under suspicion of treason. O'Cahan was arrested by Phillips in 1608 and ultimately imprisoned in the Tower of London, where his fellow prisoners included Sir Walter Raleigh and the Earl of Northumberland, Henry Percy. Never tried or convicted, O'Cahan died in the Tower. O'Cahan's forfeited "chief seat" at Limavady was granted to Sir Thomas Phillips (an English, not "Scotch" military man) in compensation for the loss of Phillips' lands at Coleraine, which were given to the Irish Society as part of the Londonderry Plantation scheme despite the fact that Phillips had, by his own account, "bought the abbey of Coleraine and employed all he had in the world on it" (Calendar of State Papers, Ireland [CSPI] 1606–1608: 280–281). The removal of Phillips from Coleraine, where he had built a manor house, fortifications, and planter dwellings, illustrates both the greater financial importance of the City of London and the expedient, rather than carefully constructed, character of Plantation.

Despite his losses, Phillips wasted little time developing his new lands (Fig. 3.3). At Limavady, Phillips reedified the castle, constructed a manor house with formal gardens, a fish pond to store salmon (a lucrative commodity) and constructed a new Plantation town, Newtown Limavady, a few miles away. This new town served as

Phillips' model for Londonderry Plantation settlements, with its cruciform plan, central market square, timber-framed "English" houses, custom-built inn, and gristmill. By contrast, disarray and incompletion characterized most of the Company settlements. Phillips complained vociferously to the Crown and the Companies about the dereliction of their duties and especially their complete failure to remove Irish tenants from their lands.

Phillips himself was not barred from retaining Irish tenants. Documents attest to the presence of Irish in Newtown Limavady, where resident Anthony Mahue relied on the translation skills of his maidservant "who well speaks and understands the Irish" (CSPI 1615–1625: 48). It is likely that the Irish who lived just outside the O'Cahan castle remained as tenants of Phillips. Without foreknowledge, it is debatable whether or not they saw their lives as radically changed by the presence of Phillips, rather than O'Cahan, in the castle. For that matter, neither O'Cahan nor Phillips could predict the outcome of their individual decisions. At a macro level, O'Cahan and Phillips could be viewed as victims of the über forces of capitalism and colonialism. O'Cahan died in the Tower of London, bereft of land and power; Phillips died bankrupt in London in 1636 having spent his money in suing the Companies. What of the fate of the nameless natives and settlers? Their stories seem to have been lost in the historical memories that prioritize dichotomous understandings of the Irish past. Assemblages from the site of the O'Cahan/Phillips castle and bawn include Irish hand-built cooking pot fragments, wheel-thrown, gravel tempered pottery from North Devon, and English and Dutch pipestem fragments, echoing assemblages from other Plantation sites and hinting at a significant degree of material exchange linked to material practices.

Some insight into the stories that lie behind those pots and pipes can be gleaned from considering drinking practices in the Ulster Plantation (Horning 2009). The sharing of alcoholic beverages was a key element in both Irish and English notions of hospitality, albeit governed by different rules, customs, and expectations that could easily, if unintentionally, be violated. This may explain the violence that erupted on the Mercers' Company lands in 1615, when four English men (including two leatherworkers, John Browne and John Williams) were assaulted and stabbed to death by nine woodkerne (Irish outlaws). Far from being a premeditated act, however, the attack occurred after the men and three of their Irish neighbors had spent several hours imbibing "beer, wine, and aqua vitae" together *with* the nine raiders in Browne's home (Canning 1616; Canny 2001: 435). Was this a drunken brawl sparked by a violation of custom or an ill-thought out comment? Whatever the impetus, such shared consumption of alcohol tells us a great deal about the intimacy of relations between the London Company settlers and the Irish whom they were supposed to be supplanting.

One theme that emerged strongly from both 1613 anniversary events is how little many people in Northern Ireland actually know about sixteenth- and seventeenth-century history, even those so interested as to sign up for a symposium or coach tour. The lack of understanding can be attributed in part to the past character of history teaching where Protestant schools employed English textbooks and Catholic schools relied on texts produced in the Republic. As expressed by one former

Loyalist paramilitary member, "In school I was told about the Tower of London but never Dunluce Castle; I heard mention of Stonehenge but never anything about Newgrange. I went through the Northern Ireland school system and came out knowing next to nothing about my own country, the whole focus was on **English** history" (anon., cited in Hall 2008: 7). The past unwillingness of schools to confront "local" histories could be seen to presuppose the subversive potential of those histories.

Tour participants were often surprised by what the archaeology had to say about places they had known all of their lives. Of the 26 who filled out comment sheets (11 self-identified as Protestant, 5 as Catholic and 10 declined to name a community affiliation), 22 agreed that the event had changed their perception of the Ulster Plantation. When asked "what one thing stands out in your memory that you will tell other people about?" one respondent stated "the hidden nature of the physical evidence and how it challenges our pre-conceived ideas," another noted that "we need to re-visit our understanding (pre-conceived ideas) about the whole process of the plantation", and a third remarked on "how by involving archaeologists they can exert such influence" (Causeway Museum Service 2009). With influence surely comes responsibility. However much I may question my own authority, my knowledge of Plantation-period archaeology places me in an influential position. Rather than questioning my right to comment, it would seem instead that I have a *responsibility* to comment. Sharing the convoluted history and ambiguous material evidence from these sites gave the participants a greater opportunity to decide for themselves what matters most about the events and human experiences of Plantation.

Concluding Thoughts

Issues of scale will always remain paramount to historical archaeology. For those of us engaged in comparative analysis, however, there is one overarching caution that must be acknowledged: To know the archaeology of inequality and oppression in one part of the modern world is *not* to know it in another, except in the most superficial of fashions. In the case of Northern Ireland, the ability of surprising insights to emerge from seemingly familiar landscapes is surely a more powerful tool of engagement than assertions equating "Irish peasants" with enslaved African Americans, an abstract equation as likely to confuse or alienate contemporary Northern Irish of both traditions as it would offend the descendants of those millions of Africans who endured the Middle Passage, the horrors of enslavement, and centuries of race-based discrimination. Lest I be misunderstood (and find myself back in the desert), I am not denying the validity of addressing the macroscale, those linkages between the north of Ireland and African America that are materially manifested in the eighteenth-century cotton and sugar warehouses of Belfast and the sherds of Irish-made pottery on southern American plantations, or memorialized in the role of the Irish Brigades in the American Civil War. Furthermore, I am fully cognizant that any local responses to parallels drawn between the Irish and African American experience would be framed in part by understandings of race and identity grounded in the nineteenth-century clash between the two diasporas in America (Ignatiev 1995; Orser 2007). My priority here is in engagement, and in exploring the capacity of Irish history itself to surprise.

On one level, Marx was clearly correct when he could see the salvation of the British laborer being facilitated through common cause with the Irish working class, just as a brighter future for Northern Ireland's working class can readily be envisioned in the crossing of the sectarian divide today. But Marx was wrong when he ultimately discounted the strength of locally rooted experiences and identities in their ability to trump class commonalties, just as class-based approaches to the Northern Ireland "problem" have failed to undermine the strength of historical memory through implying that community identities are invalid. The very real ambiguities of Irish history that gave pause to Marx, even when he himself grossly oversimplified that history, should not be "subdued" by overly prescriptive approaches to historical archaeology that employ the North American experience of colonialism and capitalism as the norm against which the experience of all other locales can be understood.

As we as historical archaeologists strive to disentangle the complicated weave of colonial identities, the character of colonial relations and entanglements, and the myriad ways in which individuals and groups negotiated structures of economic, social, and political inequality inherent to the capitalist world system we would do well to acknowledge the complexity of modern-day identities and historical memories and the ways in which archaeological practice and insight may interface with those memories. There would seem little point in studying the past if we are not prepared to engage, one way or another, with the political implications of historical revisionism. It seems to me that the best way to understand the contemporary uses and constructions of history is to actually analyze the past.

My interpretation of the archaeology of Plantation-period Ireland consciously questions today's dichotomous understanding through revealing the incomplete and chaotic nature of the Plantation process and highlighting the ambiguity in relations between natives and newcomers; intimate relations that could be close and congenial one moment and full of violence in another, as illustrated by the events that took place in Mrs. Browne's illicit alehouse. Acknowledging the existence of the violence and inequality alongside the evidence for syncretism and hybridity complicates the task of challenging historical memories, but is fundamentally more honest to the past and to the present than presenting past people as pawns of the twin forces of capitalism and colonialism, or as pawns to promote a contemporary agenda. It would seem that archaeologists can *exert influence* after all.

Acknowledgments I am grateful to Sarah Croucher and Lindsay Weiss for their patience, and especially for pointing me in new directions with their incisive and helpful comments; to Martin Hall for challenging me to be overt about my own positionality; and to Charles Orser for his continued support of and commitment to Irish historical archaeology. The following colleagues informed this essay far more than they may be aware (or may have wished!): Nick Brannon, Colin Breen, Colm Donnelly, Robert Heslip, Paul Logue, Thomas MacErlean, Danielle Moretti-Langholtz, Franc Myles, Ruairí Ó Baoill, Deirdre O'Sullivan, Helen Perry, Gemma Reid, Colin Rynne, Sarah Tarlow, and Buck Woodard.

References

Barnard, T. 2004 *The Kingdom of Ireland, 1641–1760*. Palgrave MacMillan, Basingstoke.

Bhabha, H. 1994 *The Location of Culture*. Routledge, London.

Boswell, Randy. 2007 Colonial Canoe Comes Home for a Refit. *Vancouver Sun* May 22. http://www.canada.com/vancouversun/news/story.html?id=76636c38-429c-4a22-8288-8ef0951f97b5#

Brannon, N. 1985 Archaeological excavations at Dungiven Priory and Bawn. *Benbradagh* 15: 15–18.

Canning, G. 1616 Letter . Guildhall Library MS 17,278, 15 January.

Canny, N. P. 2001 *Making Ireland British: 1580–1650*. Oxford University Press, Oxford.

Causeway Museum Service. 2009 1613–2013: Exploration of the Causeway Comment Sheet Evaluation.

Deetz, J. 1991 Introduction: Archaeological Evidence of Sixteenth- and Seventeenth-Century Encounters. In *Historical Archaeology in Global Perspective,* edited by Lisa Falk, pp. 1–9. Smithsonian Institution Press, Washington.

Douglas, Debra. 2005 Tourism Chief in Migrant Bust-Up. *Belfast Telegraph* 20 June. http://www.belfasttelegraph.co.uk/imported/tourism-chief-in-migrant-bustup-13712273.html

Eagleton, T. 1999 *The Truth about the Irish*. New Island Books, Dublin.

Fáilte Ireland. 2009 *Tourism Facts 2008*. http://www.failteireland.ie/getdoc/29adc07d-a264-4e64-875f-9fcd539037d7/Revised-Tourism-Facts-2008

Frazer, B. 1999 Common Recollections: Resisting Enclosure 'by agreement' in Seventeenth-Century England. *International Journal of Historical Archaeology* 3(2): 75–100.

Funari, P.P.A., S. Jones, and M. Hall. 1999 Introduction: Archaeology in History. In *Historical Archaeology: Back from the Edge*, edited by P.P.A. Funari, M. Hall, and S. Jones, pp. 1–20. Routledge, London.

Funari, P.P.A. 1999 Historical Archaeology from a World Perspective. In *Historical Archaeology: Back from the Edge* edited by P.P.A. Funari, M. Hall, and S. Jones, pp. 37–66. Routledge, London.

Games, A. 2006 Beyond the Atlantic: English Globetrotters and Transoceanic Connections. *William and Mary Quarterly* 63(4): 675–692.

Graham, C. 2001 *Deconstructing Ireland*. Edinburgh University Press, Edinburgh.

Hall, Martin. 2009 New Subjectivities: Capitalist, Colonial Subject and Archaeologist. Review of "Capitalism in Colonial Contexts." *Archaeologies* 5(1): 3–17.

Hall, Michael (ed). 2008 *Divided by History? A Grassroots Exploration*. Farset/Inishowen and Border Counties Initiative, Island Pamphlets No. 87, Belfast.

Harvey, D. 2001 Spaces of Capital: Towards a Critical Geography. Edinburgh University Press, Edinburgh.

Horning, A. 2001 Dwelling houses in the old Irish Barbarous Manner': Archaeological evidence for Gaelic Architecture in an Ulster Plantation village. In *Gaelic Ireland 1300–1650: Land, Lordship, and Settlement* edited by P. J. Duffy, D. Edwards, and E. FitzPatrick, pp. 375–396. Four Courts Press, Dublin.

Horning, A. 2004 Archaeological Explorations of Cultural Identity and Rural Economy in the North of Ireland: Goodland, Co. Antrim. *International Journal of Historical Archaeology* 8 (3): 199–216.

Horning, A. 2006 Archaeology, Conflict, and Contemporary Identity in the North of Ireland: Implications for theory and practice in comparative archaeologies of colonialism. *Archaeological Dialogues* 13(2): 183–199.

Horning, A. 2009 "The root of all vice and bestiality": exploring the cultural role of the alehouse in the Ulster Plantation' In *Plantation Ireland,* edited by J. Lyttleton and C. Rynne, pp.113-131. Four Courts Press, Dublin.

Howe, S. 2000 *Ireland and Empire: Colonial Legacies in Irish History and Culture*. Oxford University Press, Oxford.

Ignatiev, N. 1995 *How the Irish became White*. Routledge, New York.

Kennedy, L. 1996 *Colonialism, Religion, and Nationalism in Ireland.* Institute of Irish Studies, Queen's University Belfast, Belfast.

Kiberd, D. 1997 Modern Ireland: Postcolonial or European? In *Not on Any Map: Essays in Postcoloniality and Cultural Nationalism*, edited by S. Murray, pp. 81–100. University of Exeter Press, Exeter.

Lucas, G. 2006 Historical archaeology and Time. In *The Cambridge Companion to Historical Archaeology*, edited by D. Hicks and M. C. Beaudry, pp. 34–47. Cambridge University Press, Cambridge.

MacDonald, P. 2006 Medieval Belfast Considered. *Ulster Journal of Archaeology* 65: 29–48.

McDonald, H. 2009 Bridge over Troubles Water. *The Guardian* 29 July 2009: p5, SocietyGuardian. London. http://www.guardian.co.uk/society/2009/jul/29/northern-ireland-racism-sectarian-violence-duncan-morrow?INTCMP=SRCH

McGuire, R. 2006 Marxism and capitalism in historical archaeology. In *The Cambridge Companion to Historical Archaeology* edited by D. Hicks and M. C. Beaudry, pp.123-142. Cambridge University Press, Cambridge.

McGuire, R.H. and P. Reckner. 2005 Building a Working Class Archaeology: the Colorado Coal Field War Project. In *Industrial Archaeology: Future Directions,* edited by E.C. Casella and J. Symonds pp. 217–242. Springer, New York.

Marx, K. and F. Engels. 1988 *Marx and Engels Collected Works* vol. 43. Lawrence and Wishart, London.

Marx, K. and F. Engels. 1971 *Marx and Engels on the Irish Question.* Progress Publishers, Moscow.

Matthews, C., M. Leone, and K. Jordan. 2002 The Political Economy of Archaeological Cultures. *Journal of Social Archaeology* 2(1): 122.

Mays, M. 2005 Irish Identity in an Age of Globalisation. *Irish Studies Review* 13(1): 3–12.

Naipaul, V.S. 1967 *The Mimic Men.* André Deutsch, London.

Nassaney, M.S. and M.R. Abel. 2000 Urban Spaces, Labor Organization, and Social Control: Lessons from New England's Cutlery Industry. In *Lines that Divide: Historical Archaeologies of Race, Class, and Gender*, edited by J. Delle, S. Mrozowski, and R. Paynter, pp. 239–275. University of Tennessee Press, Knoxville.

Ó Baoill, R. 2007 Carrickfergus and Belfast. In *The Archaeology of Post-Medieval Ireland c. 1550–1750*, edited by A. Horning, R. ÓBaoill, C.Donnelly, and P. Logue, pp. 91–116. Wordwell, Bray.

Ó Baoill, R. 2006 The Urban Archaeology of Belfast: A Review of the Evidence. *Ulster Journal of Archaeology* 65: 8–19.

O'Brien, G. 1991/1992 Ireland 2000: A Very Short Story. *The Irish Review* 11: 40–46.

O'Conor, K. 2002 Housing in Later Medieval Gaelic Ireland. *Ruralia* 4: 197–206.

O'Keeffe, J. 2006 What Lies Beneath? Medieval Components in Belfast's Urban Development. *Ulster Journal of Archaeology* 65: 20–27.

Orser, C.E. 1999 Negotiating our 'Familiar Pasts.' In *The Familiar Past? Archaeologies of later historical Britain,* edited by Sarah Tarlow and Susie West, pp. 273–286. Routledge, London.

Orser, C.E. Jr. 2006 On Finding Focus. *Archaeological Dialogues* 13(2): 202–204.

Orser, C.E. Jr. 2007 *The Archaeology of Race and Racialization in Historic America.* University of Florida Press, Gainesville.

Orser, C.E. Jr. 2009 The Dialectics of Scale in Historical Archaeology. In *Crossing Paths or Sharing tracks? Future Directions in the Archaeological Study of post-1550 Britain and Ireland,* edited by Audrey Horning and Marilyn Palmer, pp. 1–17. Boydell and Brewer, Woodbridge, Suffolk.

Palus, M.M., M.P. Leone, and M.D. Cochran. 2006 Critical Archaeology: Politics Past and Present. In *Historical Archaeology*, edited by Martin Hall and Stephen W. Silliman, pp. 84–106. Blackwell, Oxford.

Rynne, C. 2008 Technological Change as a 'Colonial' Discourse: The Society of Friends in 19th-Century Ireland. *Industrial Archaeology Review* 30(1): 3–16.

Siggins, L. 2009 Native American chief asks NUI Galway to return 'iconic' canoe. *Irish Times*, 28 March 2009: p.1.

Tarlow, S. 2007 *The Archaeology of Improvement in Britain 1750–1850.* Cambridge University Press, Cambridge.

Thomas, J. 2000 Comment. *Current Anthropology* 40(1): 770.

Wilkie, L. and K. Bartoy. 2000 A Critical Archaeology Re-Visited. *Current Anthropology* 40(1), 747–777.

Chapter 4
Ethnicity and Periphery: The Archaeology of Identity in Russian America

Aron L. Crowell

Capitalism did not extend around the globe by an invisible hand; it was imposed in face-to-face encounters that drew European colonizers and indigenous populations into processes of confrontation, accommodation, and exchange (Wolf 1982). Textual and material transcripts of this discourse are the basis for an archaeology of the modern world, in Martin Hall's conception, from which he asks us to interpret "the richly textured, local manifestations of the exercise of power and resistance" (Hall 2000: 17–18). A focus on ethnicity emerges from this approach, foregrounding the peripheries of the capitalist world-system as places where social identities were contested and transformed (Crowell 1997a, b; Lightfoot 1995; Lightfoot and Martinez 1995; Stein 2002; Stein and Gil 2005; Orser 1996, 2009).

Russia's mercantile fur trade in the North Pacific and its century of colonial domination in Alaska (1740s to 1867) offer a uniquely "off-center" view of capitalist expansion and its situational entanglements. Russia possessed limited industry, infrastructure, and shipping capacity compared to the European countries that comprised the core of the world-system, and was merely part of its semiperiphery in Immanuel Wallerstein's view (1989: 141–142). From a Eurocentric perspective, Siberia and Alaska – the vast terrain of Russia's eastward conquests – were among the most remote and unknown regions of the Earth. Nonetheless, Russia's annexation of Alaska as its only overseas colony, with subsidiary outposts in California and the Kurile Islands, was an expansive capitalist enterprise, organized and administered through the government-chartered, privately owned Russian-American Company (RAC). Sustained by profitable Chinese and European markets for sea otters and other Alaskan furs, the RAC's venture entailed considerable investment, difficulty, and risk (Black 2004; Gibson 1976; Lightfoot 2003). Over several generations, its Russian-Siberian workforce became enmeshed with the Native

A.L. Crowell (✉)
Arctic Studies Center, National Museum of Natural History,
Smithsonian Institution, Washington, DC, USA
e-mail: Crowella@si.edu

S.K. Croucher and L. Weiss (eds.), *The Archaeology of Capitalism in Colonial Contexts*,
Contributions To Global Historical Archaeology, DOI 10.1007/978-1-4614-0192-6_4,
© Springer Science+Business Media, LLC 2011

societies of southern and western Alaska, a process characterized by extensive intermarriage, cultural interchange, and growth of a mixed-race Creole class (Black 1990; Crowell 1997a; Fedorova and Svetlana 1973; Fedorova and Svetlana 1975; Luehrmann 2008; Oleksa 1990). Russian rule ended in 1867, with purchase of the Alaska territory by USA.

Russian America offers both unique and comparative dimensions for global historical archaeology. The multiethnic social hierarchy of the colony and the process of creolization – primary concerns of the present paper – invite particular comparison to New Spain, La Florida, and Alta California (Deagan 1983; Ewen 2000, 2009; Lightfoot 2005b; Voss 2008a, b). Russian America's political economy took the form of what Grinev (1996, cited in Luehrmann 2008: 69–81) called "colonial politarianism," that is, the administrative control of indigenous kin-based production to extract key resources, backed by force and often with the assistance of suborned local leaders. The impetus for this mode of production can be identified at the level of the world-system; unlike Britain and France, Russia lacked capacity for a fully commoditized fur trade in the subarctic and by necessity perhaps as much as choice imposed a coerced labor regime that was close to slavery (Crowell 1997a: 10–16: Eccles 1988; Kardulias 1990; Wolf 1982: 158–194). At the same time, the RAC carried on a degree of commodity-based trade (glass, metal, and ceramic goods exchanged for furs) but employed this alternative primarily in geographically marginal areas where its control over local populations was weak (Crowell et al. 2008). The RAC's trade and administrative strategies instantiate a pattern of colonial practice that has been observed worldwide, in which strong "territorial" control is maintained in closely held entrepots, while more diffuse "hegemonic" dominance is exerted in outlying zones (Jordan 2009). As discussed here, cultural fusion between colonizers and colonized was amplified in the primary zone of Russian control but limited in the regions beyond.

Transcripts of Russian America exist as documentary records of the Russian-American Company, the Russian Orthodox Church, and international maritime expeditions (Black 2004; Gideon 1989; Kan 1999; Luehrmann 2008; Okun and Semen 1979; Tikhmenev 1978; Vancouver 1801); indigenous oral tradition (Dauenhauer et al. 2008); and archaeological remains of forts, work stations, and villages (Crowell 1997a, b, 2009; Knecht and Jordan 1985; Lightfoot 2003, 2005a, b; Lightfoot et al. 1998; McMahan and David 2002; Oswalt and Wendell 1980; Veltre and Douglas 1979; Veltre et al. 2001). The role of material evidence is multifaceted; in one register, Western-produced objects are signals of new relations of appropriated or commodified labor, of changing core–periphery relations in the global sense, and of the operation of local networks of supply and control. In another, objects and architecture express the complex interplay of ethnicity, status, and power that characterized Russian colonial society.

Contemporary Alaska Native communities are engaged in the revitalization of their cultures, history, and languages, a trend that articulates with the self-conscious revaluation of identity (Clifford 2004; Crowell 2004a; Worl 2010). A century and a half after the Russian withdrawal, the legacy of colonial incursion is still visible in blue Orthodox domes that float above scores of southern Alaskan villages from Kodiak to the Yukon River, and is perpetuated in Russian family names, loan words, foods, and customs such as Christmas season "starring" processions and New Year celebrations (Crowell et al. 2001). The comingling of Russian and indigenous blood and culture laid the foundation for a complexly layered contemporary ethnicity that echoes the "double consciousness" of indigenous Latin America (Gaitán-Ammann, Chap. 7: 151). Blended Native and Russian identities have been challenged and renegotiated over time, as when the American "one drop" racial classification system and discriminatory civil laws disenfranchised the Creoles along with those who were culturally and racially identifiable as Indians, Eskimos, or Aleuts (Leuhrmann 2008: 117–120). The English language, Protestant religion, and cultural Americanization were imposed by US policies, but with passage of the Alaska Native Claims Settlement Act in 1971, indigenous cultural identities began to be reemphasized (Pullar 2001). Ethnic discourse that originated in the colonial encounter thus continues to the present day, exemplified on Kodiak Island by the gradual shift of preferred autonym from "Aleuty" or "Alutiiq," conferred by Russian conquerors, to the original "Sugpiaq," meaning "real person" (plural, Sugpiat). It resonates with the discoveries of archaeology, now carried out through collaborations between Native communities and outside researchers (Crowell 2004b; Steffian 2001). Sugpiaq scholar Gordon Pullar noted one elder's expression of confusion upon viewing wooden masks, spruce-root baskets, and other precontact artifacts recovered at the Karluk site; she said, "I guess we really are Natives after all. I was always told we were Russians" (Pullar 1992: 183).

Russian Conquest and Colonialism

Russian expansion to Alaska began in 1743, following reports from the 1741 Bering–Chirikov expedition that sea otters, fur seals, and foxes were abundant in the newly discovered Near (Commander) Islands and Aleutian Islands. Dozens of small companies of frontiersmen (*promyshlenniki*), servicemen, and traders pushed eastward in small ships along the island chain, subjugating indigenous Unangax̂ communities and compelling them to harvest furs (Berkh 1974; Black 2004: 59–77; Fedorova and Svetlana 1975: 5–6; Fisher 1990; Liapunova 1987).

Grigorii Shelikhov's conquest of Kodiak Island in 1784 and his founding of a base at Three Saints Harbor opened up the Gulf of Alaska for exploitation, and marked the beginning of a more capital and labor-intensive phase of the Alaskan fur trade (Crowell 1997a; Fedorova and Svetlana 1973). Shelikhov and his main rival, the Lebedev-Lastochkin Company, established forts and *artels* (Native work camps) in the Kodiak archipelago, Cook Inlet, Prince William Sound, and southeast Alaska (*see* map, Fig. 4.1). In 1799, Russian tsar Paul I granted Shelikhov's corporate successors monopoly status as the quasi-governmental Russian-American Company. The maturing RAC expanded operations to Fort Ross in northern California (1812–1840) (Lightfoot et al. 1991), to the Kurile Islands north of Japan where Alaska Native hunters were transported in 1828 (Shubin 1990), to Bristol Bay in 1818 (VanStone 1967), to the Alaskan interior and northern coasts in the 1830s, where trading forts including Kolmakovskiy Redoubt were built (Arndt 1990; Oswalt and Wendell 1980), and briefly (1816–1817) to Fort Elisabeth in the

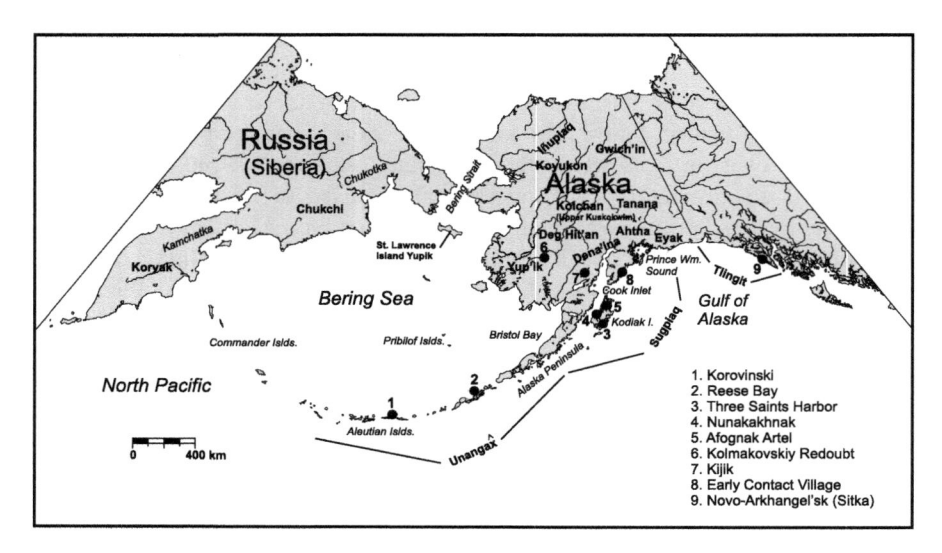

Fig. 4.1 The geography of Russian America, with locations, indigenous peoples, and archaeological sites discussed in the text

Hawaiian Islands (Mills 2002). Novo Arkhangel'sk (Sitka) in southeastern Alaska was the RAC's American capital after 1804. The Russian Orthodox Church, whose first missionaries arrived on Kodiak Island in 1794, was supported by the RAC but pressured it for reform, and Orthodox advocacy for amelioration of harsh labor conditions was a factor in the church's success in gaining Native converts (Oleksa 1992; Smith 1990).

From the beginning, the RAC experienced daunting problems in supplying Alaska with food and consumer goods. All imports from its western Siberian operational base at Irkutsk had to be barged and carted overland to the Pacific coast at Okhotsk, then shipped east in small vessels (Gibson 1976). In later years, the RAC augmented this supply route by buying goods from better-supplied British and American fur trade companies on the Northwest Coast, sending round-the-world voyages to Alaska via Cape Horn, growing agricultural crops at Fort Ross, and purchasing from the Hudson's Bay Company (Gibson 1976: 201–208; Tikhmenev 1978: 236). Nonetheless, colonial supply remained a difficult problem. The RAC also experienced strains in recruiting, transporting, and paying its personnel, with the result that Russian administrative staff and contract workers in Alaska – consisting almost entirely of men – averaged around 500 and never exceeded about 820 in any year (Fedorova and Svetlana 1973: 150–155).

In large part because of these difficulties the RAC was able to assert full colonial dominance only in a nuclear zone that included the Aleutian Islands, the Pacific coast of the Alaska Peninsula, and the Kodiak Island archipelago. This region, called "settled" or "dependent" in Russian colonial documents (Dmytryshyn et al. 1989: 470), was geographically closest to the RAC's Siberian ports and was uncontested by its North Pacific rivals – Britain, USA, and Spain. It was highly attractive because of rich fur resources and large Unangax̂ and Sugpiaq populations – combined, perhaps

25,000 at first contact – that could be subjugated as a labor force. Only Native men were capable of taking otters at sea, using traditional kayaks, darts, and arrows, and direct Russian hunting was never a viable option.

The Russian voyagers sometimes engaged in peaceful trade with Native groups but more often coerced them by brutal punishments, killings, and hostage-taking (Black 2004: 128–135; Gideon 1989: 69–71: Liapunova 1987). Communities were occasionally able to mount resistance and reprisals, but lacked firearms and were vulnerable because isolated on small islands and mountainous coasts. Defeated villages were put to work producing food as well as furs for private profit and government "tribute" (*iasak*).

Although *iasak* taxes were banned in 1788, they were replaced by a universal forced labor system. As formalized in the 1821 and 1844 RAC charters (Dmytryshyn et al. 1989: 362–363, 472–473), half of the able-bodied men between 18 and 50 years of age had to hunt for the company for limited periods (2 or 3 years), while other classes of the population were exempt, but in reality nearly all men, women, and children had to labor year-round at hunting, fishing, sewing clothing, and preparing food for the company. Native workers received nominal compensation consisting of small trade items (beads, tobacco, needles, finger-rings) or in-kind goods (tanned hides, bird-skin parkas) that they had produced themselves (Davydov 1977: 191–197; Gideon 1989: 61–69; Liapunova 1987; Okun 1979: 200). Salaries paid to Native workers starting in the 1820s were inadequate to buy even necessities (Dmytryshyn et al. 1989: xlvi-xlvii). Collaborating Native headmen (*toions*) received larger payments of cash, clothing, and other gifts in return for organizing village work crews and enforcing company rules.

The forced labor system led to hunger and hardship in Alaska Native communities because it undermined the ability of villages to accumulate their own food supplies for winter (Davydov 1977: 196; Gideon 1989: 70). Indigenous populations in the nuclear contact zone declined rapidly due to introduced disease, malnutrition, and social disruption, reaching a nadir of about 1,200 Unangax̂ and 3,500 Sugpiat after the smallpox epidemic of 1837–39 (Clark 1984; Lantis 1984). Although minor reforms and liberalized payments to workers were instituted in the 1820s and 1830s, Liapunova wrote about the Unangax̂ and Sugpiat that "…there were no sudden changes in their fate: they remained in a semiservile state in relation to the Russian-American Company" (1987: 142).

East and north of the zone of maximum Russian control was a large "semidependent" region where the RAC established scattered trading posts but did not attempt to enforce tribute collection or forced labor. In this free-trade zone, Native men and women were not forced to work, but instead received payments and were allowed to trade goods for their furs or labor. The inner boundaries of the region were somewhat ambiguous; for example, while the 1844 RAC charter claimed the Dena'ina of Cook Inlet and the Sugpiat of Prince William Sound and the Kenai Peninsula as dependent peoples, other Russian documents referred to these groups as semidependent (Fedorova and Svetlana 1975: 17; Okun and Semen 1979: 206; Znamenski 2003: 10–11). More distant Yup'ik, Iñupiaq, and Athabascan peoples were unambiguously included in the semidependent category, as were California Indian communities in the vicinity of Fort Ross (Lightfoot 2003: 22).

The Alaskan contact zone farthest to the east was the "independent" Tlingit region where the Native population at contact numbered 10,000–14,000 (Boyd 1990). The Tlingit were politically integrated through clan-based alliances and well armed with guns and cannons obtained from British and American trading vessels. They resisted Russian incursion, destroying the original Novo-Arkhangel'sk fort at Sitka in 1802 and the RAC's Yakutat post in 1805 and making other attacks on Russian settlements throughout the colonial period (Kan 1999). Although Novo-Arkhangelsk was rebuilt and expanded as the Pacific headquarters of the RAC, the Tlingit were never disarmed and Russian relations with them remained both fearful and dependent, in particular since trade with the local populace was the source of basic food supplies (Gibson 1987). Southeast Alaska initially possessed large sea otter populations and Novo-Arkhangel'sk served as a base for exploiting hunting grounds as far south as the Queen Charlotte Islands (Black 2004: 158).

Ethnicity in Russian America

Russian America has been characterized as a relatively open colonial society, marked by the advance of bicultural, biracial Creoles into social positions only somewhat below that of the colonial ruling class (Black 1990; Black 2004: 204–220; Luehrmann 2008). While "Creole" (a term borrowed from the Spanish *criollo*) was a specific legal status applied by the RAC exclusively to individuals of mixed Russian-Alaska Native parentage, a more general process of "creolization" or cultural synthesis (Gundacker 2000) may be seen in shifts of ethnic identity and daily practice across a broad middle spectrum of colonial society, both indigenous and Russian.

This trend lies at the heart of the present inquiry, for it illustrates the dynamic tensions of colonial societies in which hegemonic distinctions of class, race, and ethnicity were continually eroded by material, genetic, and cultural interchange. Native creolization is readily identifiable after the 1820s, when the hostilities of conquest were in the past and the harshest conditions of forced labor had been ameliorated, and it advanced to the greatest degree in the nuclear region where contact between Russian and Native populations was most intense and prolonged. Thus, in the Aleutian Islands and on Kodiak Island Creoles composed about 20% of the colonial population by the 1850s (Dmytryshyn et al. 1989: 505–506), while a large proportion of the populace that was not Creole in the official sense was bicultural, bilingual, and Orthodox (Oleksa 1990; Veniaminov 1984: 229–239). The Tlingit, on the other hand, maintained their primary *kwaan* (tribe) and clan identities, although Orthodox conversion became common by the 1830s (Grinev 2005; Kan 1999). There was little Tlingit-Russian intermarriage (Golovin 1979: 17). Other Alaska Native groups that were marginal to the Russian system, including the Yupiit, Iñupiat, Dena'ina, Ahtna, Deg Hit'an, and Koyukon, did not undergo transformative shifts in culture or identity, although many individuals converted to Orthodoxy (Ellanna and Balluta 1992: 58–68; VanStone 1967).

Creolization from the opposite direction may be perceived in the heavily Nativized lifeways of the *promyshlenniki* and other Russian workers, in the social bonds they formed though marriage to indigenous families and communities, and in the desire of many to reside permanently in the colony after their contracts were finished (Fedorova and Svetlana 1973: 154–160; 1975). Even as early as 1806, *promyshlenniki* were petitioning to remain in Alaska where they "had acquired houses and had married savages and begot children" (Nicolai Rezanov, quoted in Fedorova and Svetlana 1973: 155).

The process of creolization can be framed by a constructivist view of ethnicity (Barth 1969; Jenkins 1997; Thompson 1989). Ethnicity is understood as a dynamic social construct based on "shifting, situational, subjective identifications of self and others . . . rooted in ongoing daily practice and historical experience, but also subject to transformation and discontinuity" (Jones 1997: 13–14). Active identity construction contrasts with essentialist conceptions of social groups as bounded entities defined by persistent cultural, linguistic, and racial traits. Moreover, constructivist ethnicity is actor-defined, moving "from a focus on the biological to the social, and from the category to the boundary" (Meskell 2002: 286). Markers of inclusion and exclusion may be altered, strategically hidden, or emphasized to achieve social aims. Archaeologically, this process is visible through material practices – architecture, settlement organization, clothing, implements, and foodways – that play a role in the expression and reproduction of ethnic identities (e.g., Deagan 1983; Ewen 2000; Hodder 1982; Lightfoot et al. 1998; Voss 2008b). Creolization may thus be understood as purposeful boundary shifting, motivated by potential social and economic advantages.

Social position in Russian America was formally defined by the system of feudal estates (*sosloviye*) that ordained the rights and privileges of the Russian nobility, clergy, and commoners of many ranks, from merchants to serfs. The estate system was a state-sponsored essentialist model of society, incorporating fixed and inherited distinctions of ancestry, race, class, residence, and occupation. As applied in Russian America, it placed "honorable" Russian and European officials, merchants, military officers, and ship commanders at the apex of society (Fedorova and Svetlana 1973, 1975). Subordinate to this elite class were "semihonorable" *promyshlenniki*, clerks, navigators, and laborers, who were mostly Russian townsmen from central and western Siberia but included men of Native Siberian or mixed Russian-Siberian parentage. A third estate consisted of "colonial citizens," RAC employees who remained in America as permanent residents. The lowest estates were reserved for Native residents, categorized as either *inorodtsy* ("settled foreigners") or *inovertsy* ("unsettled foreigners") according to their controlled or independent status (Black 1990: 145).

Creoles were defined in the RAC's second charter (1821) as the offspring of Russian or Siberian men and Alaska Native women, occupying a middle stratum between Russian and indigenous estates. They had to be paid for their labor, were exempt from taxes, and received education at RAC expense (Black 1990; Dmytryshyn et al. 1989: 360–361, 468–470; Fedorova and Svetlana 1973: 206–215; Luehrmann 2008: 116–123). Historian Lydia Black suggested that the RAC's Creole policy was intended to compensate for the limited number of Russian personnel by building up a reliable and permanent labor pool of "men and women whose loyalty would be to both Alaskan land and Russian culture and political order" (Black 2004: 209). Russian unions with Alaska Native women were frequent and the total number of Creoles grew rapidly, from about 300 in 1821 (Dmytryshyn et al. 1989: 360) to almost 2000 in 1860 (Golovin 1979: 141). Many were educated in Alaska or Russia and became clergy, administrators, clerks, navigators, and artisans.

Michael Oleksa underlines aspirational and self-definitional aspects of Creole identity: "To be "Creole" came to mean that one had adopted certain Slavic-European attitudes and traits, had been trained to some extent in a Western-type school, and thereby qualified for a position in the middle or upper management of the colony. Creoles were not necessarily of mixed racial stock and did not necessarily abandon much of their heritage as Native Americans. They thought of themselves as having the best of two worlds, rather than as victims caught tragically between them" (Oleksa 1990: 188). RAC chief administrator P. N. Golovin, however, characterized the Creoles as a despised racial "caste," many born in the early years from unsanctioned unions with *promyshlenniki*: "Not only [do the Russians] look on them with great contempt, but the word "creole" is used as a pejorative. Even the Aleuts [i.e. Unangax̂ and Sugpiat] have no respect for the creoles, and say that they are lower than Aleuts because their mothers were immoral women" (Golovin 1979: 17–18). Fedorova (1975: 13–14) also argued that Creoles were not fully accepted in either Russian or Alaska Native communities. However, Zagoskin remarked that, "The greatest desire of every girl is to marry a Russian or perhaps a Creole, or in other words to marry out of the native condition into which she was born" (Zagoskin and Lavrentii 1967: 87).

Ethnicity and Material Culture

Russian American social identities were materially expressed in ways that could either enforce or erode the essentialist hierarchy of the official status system. Scarce imported goods served as symbols of Russian identity and power as well as connection to the motherland and the world-system, while Alaska Native goods, technologies, foods, and housing signified the primacy of local, indigenous identities (Crowell 1997a: 16–30). Thus, the officers and managers of the RAC used clothing, ceramics, and furniture that had been shipped from Russia, ate imported or agriculturally produced foods including liquor, bread, beef, pork, and garden vegetables, and occupied Russian-style wooden buildings with glass windows and brick stoves (Fedorova 1973: 215–242; Middleton 1996; Senkevitch 1987). This consumption pattern projected elite status, pure Russian/European ethnicity, and class alliance with the RAC (Shelikhov 1981: 43–44). By contrast, working-class employees could afford few imported goods, and especially during the early years of the colony they wore locally made fur and intestine clothing, ate wild fish and meat, and lived in earthen-walled houses that derived from indigenous designs (Svetlana 1973: 228–242). George Vancouver, observing Russian fur traders in Cook Inlet in 1794, wrote that they "appeared to be perfectly content to live after the manner of the Native Indians of the country; partaking with equal relish and appetite their gross and nauseous food, adopting the same fashion, and using the same materials for their apparel" (Vancouver 1801: 207). In addition to poverty, this Nativized material pattern may have projected weak class identification with RAC interests, social connections to local communities, and for some, indigenous Siberian heritage.

Creole consumption patterns were emulative of Russian models, and with the relative prosperity of later years Creoles adopted imported clothing and household goods, foods such as coffee, tea, sugar, and garden vegetables , and Russian-style or syncretic dwellings (Golovin 1979: 18–19). Creole workers and families frequently formed their own communities or residential areas, as at Afognak where they occupied the neighborhood known as "Russian Town," while Sugpiaq Native families resided in nearby "Aleut Town" (Luehrmann 2008: 42–44, 56–57). Creole material culture, diet, and residential patterns publicly projected a Russian ethnic orientation, reinforced by Russian language, education, and Orthodox religious practice.

Material patterns in Alaska Native communities were differentiated by the RAC's dual production strategy and by internal social stratification (Crowell and Luehrmann 2001; Lantis 1970; Townsend 1980). Creolization was most widespread in the forced labor zone but it was precisely in this region that the RAC expended the fewest imported commodities to pay Native hunters and workers. As a result, the material aspects of culture change and ethnic reorientation can be expected to lag behind the nonmaterial. Reverse conditions prevailed in the free-trade zone, where ethnic change occurred to a lesser degree but commodities flowed more freely.

In both areas, indigenous headmen and elite lineages enjoyed preferential access to imported commodities. Unangax̂ and Sugpiaq leaders were able to continue and even reinforce their traditional roles by assuming positions as RAC-appointed Native managers (*toions*) who oversaw fur and food production in their villages in exchange for sumptuary goods. The Orthodox missionary Gideon, on Kodiak Island in 1802–1803, listed "many beads" as among the possessions of one Sugpiaq "rich man" (Gideon 1989: 41). Such wealth was displayed and distributed at winter ceremonies to enhance the prestige of the host and retain the loyalty of supporting kin groups (Crowell 1992). Postcontact enhancement of indigenous elite status was especially notable in the uncontrolled zones, where the Tlingit, Dena'ina, and other groups acted as middlemen in the Russian, British, and American fur trades. Clan leaders accumulated blankets, dentalium shells, iron, copper, and other goods for prestige redistribution (DeLaguna 1972: 629–639; Kan 1999; Simeone 1995; Townsend 1975).

Material Expression in the Archaeological Record

The material patterning of ethnic identity and change, from architecture and spatial organization to artifact assemblages and food remains, has been investigated at numerous Alaska Native villages and Russian settlements. The selected examples that follow illustrate broad findings and trends.

Alaska Native Village Sites

Reese Bay, Unalaska Island, eastern Aleutian Islands (early 1700s – 1790). Unangax̂ people were living at Reese Bay when Russian traders first reached Unalaska Island in 1759, and stayed there until about 1790 (Veltre et al. 2001). Traditional bone and stone tools made up over 80% of the artifacts found in one of the large traditional longhouses. About 90% of the Russian-imported artifacts were glass beads, the balance consisting of curved and flat glass, iron nails, and metal scraps. The limited quantity and diversity of imported artifacts is typical of early contact period sites in the Aleutian Islands, where people were living under the forced labor system. Investigators identified a concentration of beads at the eastern end of the house where the lineage head and high-ranking families would have resided, suggesting preferential access to Russian goods.

Early Contact Village, Kenai Peninsula, Alaska (ca. 1790–1810). This site on the Kenai Peninsula represents early contact period indigenous adaptations in the free-trade zone. It was occupied for several years between about 1790 and 1810, possibly for opportunistic trade with the Russian fort at Voskresenskii (Crowell and Mann 1998; Crowell et al. 2008). Almost 80% of the artifacts from midden and pit house excavations were stone and bone forms (lance blades, arrow points, scrapers, fish hooks, harpoon points, etc.), mingled with Russian trade items that included glass beads, copper fragments, glass reworked into scrapers, nails, a hand-forged iron knife, and a 1748 Russian ½ kopeck coin (1/200 of a ruble). The beads, coin, and iron knife (highly valuable in this early context) suggest remunerative free trade with the Russians rather than forced labor. Abundant faunal remains (seal, sea lion, whale, murre, puffin, cod, halibut, shellfish) indicate an unconstricted subsistence pattern with no hint of the disruptions and shortages induced in the forced labor zone by diversion of hunters to the sea otter fleets.

Nunakakhnak, Kodiak Island (1840s). Nunakakhnak was a Sugpiaq resettlement village, occupied by refugees from the 1837 smallpox epidemic. A sod-walled house of traditional Sugpiaq design yielded over 1,000 shards of RAC-imported English whitewares and Chinese porcelain (Knecht and Jordan 1985). Several thousand glass beads along with metal axe heads, gunflints, musket balls, an Orthodox cross, woolen cloth, bottle glass, and assorted iron items were recovered. Few stone tools were present. By comparison, the slightly earlier Mysovskoe village on the east side of the island (abandoned by the 1830s) contained only 7% nonaboriginal items (Clark and Donald 1974). Nunakakhnak was located at the heart of the Russian zone of control and demonstrates a significant degree of creolization, materially expressed through Russian trade goods that had become more accessible due to the RAC's improved supply connections and labor reforms.

Kijik, Alaska Peninsula (ca. 1800–1906). Kijik was a large Dena'ina village at Lake Clark, inhabited during the Russian and early American territorial periods (Lynch and Alice 1982; VanStone et al. 1970). This area was strategically located along overland trade routes between Cook Inlet and Bristol Bay and never under effective Russian control, providing the opportunity for Dena'ina chiefs to engage in the fur trade as middlemen and to elevate themselves through the accumulation, display, and redistribution of trade goods (Townsend 1975). Two exceptionally large Kijik houses with multiple rooms contained large quantities of imported goods, suggesting that these were the homes of wealthy Dena'ina leaders (VanStone et al. 1970: 163). The total inventory of imported manufactures at the site was extensive and diverse and although originating in large part from Alaska Commercial Company trade after 1867 also reflects economic and social dynamics of free-trade zone interaction during the Russian period.

Russian Settlements

Three Saints Harbor, Kodiak Island (1784–ca. 1820). Three Saints Harbor was one of the earliest Russian settlements and the unofficial capital of the colony from 1784 to 1793. Residential zones at the site corresponded to class-ethnic divisions (Crowell 1997a, b). Company officers lived at the west end of the site in log cabins with gardens, a bread oven, warehouses, a smithy, and bathhouse nearby, all signifying Russian elite consumption. The main structure was a combined manager's residence and headquarters, described by contemporary observers as a sizeable wooden building with planked floors, glass windows, brick/clay heating stove, and rich furnishings (Olson 2002; Sauer 1802: 173; Shelikhov 1981: 44–45). Excavation revealed a rock foundation, collapsed chimney, stored trade goods, and bones from domestic animals (cattle, pigs, goats) and local game. Russian and Siberian workers lived in humbler quarters at the eastern end of the settlement, where an earthen-walled barracks of Aleutian Islands – Siberian design was excavated and found to contain metal knives, gun flints, lead shot, glass beads, rings and other *promyshlenniki* tools of the trade. Bones of sea mammals, birds, and fish were present, but no domestic animals. Sugpiaq stone tools and pottery in the dwelling could have been used by the men themselves or by coresident Sugpiaq women. The building and its contents typify the ethnic pattern of Russian-Siberian workers, with its blend of imported and indigenous elements. A separate *artel* for Suqpiaq hunters and their families, located about one km away, represented a third ethnic occupation zone. The differentiated architecture and spatial segregation of managers, workers, and Native hunters at Three Saints Harbor is a general characteristic of Russian colonial sites.

Korovinski, Atka Island, western Aleutian Islands (1820–1870s). The RAC artel at Korovinski was established in the 1820s after the Unangax̂ population of the Aleutian Islands precipitously declined, and some residents were forcibly resettled there from survivor communities (Veltre 1979: 72–139). Personnel included Russians, Creoles, and Unangax̂ men and women, whose production activities focused on sea otter hunting, fox trapping, gardening, and stock raising. Buildings included a store, school, church, warehouses, and dwellings for RAC employees and Native families. Unangax̂ oral histories recalled that Native workers had a meager diet of dried fish, birds, potatoes, turnips, flour, tea, and sugar, and that their foreign possessions included knives and axes (Bergsland 1959). Unangax̂ houses at the site were earthen *barabaras*, small compared to the precontact longhouses, with ground-level entrances and windows that were covered with translucent skin; window glass was a privilege of *toions* and *baidarshchiks* (Veltre 1979: 202–205). Excavation of a barracks for Russian or Creole employees produced transfer-printed whitewares, window and bottle glass, rifle cartridges, nails, beads, buttons, fabric, shoes, and miscellaneous metal tools and scraps, along with a few indigenous stone tools.

Afognak Artel (Katenai), Kodiak Island archipelago (before 1803–1830s). Artels were production stations in the forced labor system, where Russian overseers (*baidarshschiks*) and employees supervised Native hunters and female workers (Fedorova and Svetlana 1973: 198–203). Activities at Katenai included hunting, whaling, production of dried fish, and raising cattle (Woodhouse-Beyer 1999, 2001). Separate dwellings were provided for the *baidarshchik*, Russian employees, and Suqpiaq families, each with architecture and household goods suitable to the colonial estate of the inhabitants. The *biadarshchik's* log cabin had wooden floors, a stove, brick chimney, and glazed windows; Russian workers lived in a simple earthen-walled pit-house and Suqpiaq worker families occupied two sod-walled longhouses. Imported goods were diverse and abundant in the *biadarshchik* cabin and far less so in the Russian worker and Suqpiaq dwellings. Teacups and saucers found in the latter reflect the adoption of Russian tea customs, incorporated by Alaska Native peoples as a ceremony of hospitality (Jackson 1991). Katenai was a microcosm of relations of production in the forced labor zone, reflecting close contact and cultural exchange between Russian and Native personnel. Although Russian-headed and Creole families resided in nearby Afognak Village by the late nineteenth century (Harvey 1991; Huggins 1981), there is no documentary evidence of Creole occupation at Katenai, which was occupied before this estate became numerous.

Kolmakovskiy Redoubt, interior Alaska (1841–1917). Kolmakovskiy Redoubt was built in 1841 to facilitate commodity-based free trade with "semidependent" Yup'ik, Deg Hit'an, Kolchan, and other interior peoples (Oswalt 1980). The manager was Creole, and employees included Creole men with their Yup'ik wives. A *qasgiq* (traditional Yup'ik men's house) was constructed for visiting Native fur traders. Class-ethnic scaling was evident in the architectural appointments of the dwellings: the manager's cabin had planked floors and an iron stove; the Creole barracks had a wooden floor and was heated with a Russian-style clay and stone oven; and the *qasgiq* had a dirt floor and open fire-pit. Imported trade items including glass beads, English transfer-print ceramics, and metal goods were found in all of the dwellings

(Jackson 1991; Oswalt 1980: 114–147). Locally made skin boots, sleds, boats, fishing equipment, hunting weapons, birch bark baskets, grass mats, and spruce bowls (well preserved in the frozen ground) were also found in all three, indicating considerable dependence on local technologies and food supplies. Wendell Oswalt concluded that Kolmakovskiy Redoubt was so remote that "not only was the company unable to ensure its employees a dependable supply of nonlocal foods, but the quantity of trade goods remained limited" (Oswalt 1980: 42).

Novo-Arkhangel'sk, southeast Alaska (1804–1867). Novo-Arkhangel'sk was built in 1799, destroyed by the Tlingit in 1802, and then rebuilt as the Russian colonial capital. The town was a hub of colonial industry from shipbuilding to lumbering, milling, and munitions manufacture (Senkevitch 1987). Located in the free-trade zone of southeast Alaska, Novo Arkhangel'sk had few indigenous residents or workers until a Tlingit settlement was built outside its stockade in 1821. Excavations at Castle Hill uncovered a complex of Russian period features that included workers' residences and an 1830s metalwork shop. About 300,000 artifacts were collected, reflecting a diversity and abundance of goods that was extraordinary in comparison with earlier settlements (McMahan 2002). Artifact classes included kitchen items, architectural elements, bottles, firearms, tools, clothing, tobacco pipes, personal ornaments, game pieces, and children's toys. Russian dependence on Tlingit food supplies and trade was represented by cedar bark cordage and baskets for food storage. It appears that the frontier consumption pattern typical of Russian-Siberian *promyshlenniki* was transformed at Novo Arkhangel'sk by time (relatively late in the colonial period) and by location in the well-supplied Russian American capital.

Fort Ross, northern California coast (1812–1840). Fort Ross was built on the northern California coast in 1812 for sea otter hunting and agricultural production. As at other RAC outposts, spatial organization reflected the company's ingrained class and ethnic consciousness (Lightfoot 2005a, b; Lightfoot et al. 1991; Martinez 1997). The Russian manager's dwelling was located inside the palisade, which also enclosed a warehouse, company store, chapel, and kitchen. A "Russian Village" was located just outside the walls, where Russian and Creole employees and their families lived in plank houses with gardens. Alaska Native hunters, mostly Sugpiaq men transported from Kodiak Island, lived in earthen-walled pit houses outside the fort with Kashaya Pomo, Miwok, and Southern Pomo wives and their children. Household middens at the Alaska Native village were tested to examine how Sugpiaq men and California Native women projected their cultural identities in mixed ethnic households (Lightfoot et al. 1998). Analysis revealed that food preparation, cooking, waste disposal, and domestic artifacts followed Pomo and Miwok patterns, while Sugpiaq culture was reflected in men's hunting tools and by the spatial arrangement of the settlement as a whole. Assemblages were dominated by indigenous tool types but included glass beads, metal scraps, and broken fragments of glass and ceramics that were used as raw materials for tools and ornaments. Some domestic fauna (pigs and sheep) were consumed in addition to abalone, mussels, deer, sea lion, seal, sea birds, and fish, indicating access to these "Russian" foods.

Archaeological Interpretation

In one analytical dimension, Russian American archaeological sites provide a quantitative baseline for the colony's gradual maturation and integration into the world-system. The meagerness of early Russian colonial supply is evident in pre-1820s components discussed above, including Reese Bay, Three Saints Harbor, and the Early Contact Village, while diversification of global sources and better connections to the European core are evident in 1830s assemblages at Afognak, Fort Ross, and most impressively Novo-Arkhangel'sk, the colonial capital. After 1839, an alliance between the RAC and Hudson's Bay Company brought in larger quantities of the British and European ceramics, glassware, and beads, found at such sites as Korovinski and Nunakakhnak.

Increased imports coincided with, and may have encouraged, the liberalization of RAC labor policies, so that Alaska Native hunters began receiving more goods as well as modest payments in coin or colonial scrip, redeemable at company stores (Pierce 1990). The RAC's efforts to develop and reward a growing Creole work-force also relied on its ability to provide desired consumer commodities including clothing, tea, ceramic wares, and metal tools. Nonetheless, colonial supply during even the late Russian colonial period appears weak by comparison with the post-1867 American phase, when the Alaska Commercial Company and other US firms imported large quantities of factory-made goods to Alaskan fur trading posts. Large and diverse assemblages of American-made wool and cotton clothing, shoes, rifles, canned food, bottled condiments and alcohol, metal cookware and tools, and large ceramic inventories are typical of sites such as the late component at Kijik (see above) and the Denton site (1860s – early 1900s) on the Kenai Peninsula (Crowell and Mann 1998: 110–112; Crowell et al. 2008: 247).

As a register of cultural change and ethnic process, archaeological data both augment and challenge the historical record. Certainly, they offer a more compre-hensive view of the colony's subordinate social groups, including working-class Russians, Creoles, and Alaska Natives, whose lives were only marginally inscribed in colonial documents. For example, the Alaska Native Village at Fort Ross is not shown in nineteenth century drawings of the settlement, and RAC managers recorded little about the families who lived there (Lightfoot et al. 1991). Similarly, the hundreds of Russian and Alaska Native workers who resided at Three Saints Harbor and at nearby Three Saints *artel* are barely mentioned in Russian and Spanish reports, which focus on the activities, dwellings, and lifeways of Shelikhov and other company managers. Alaska Native villages such as Reese Bay, Nunakakhnak, and scores of others can be investigated today as archaeological locations but as living villages received scant attention in colonial documents.

Archaeology is positioned to generate unique insights into social and cultural change among these overlooked strata of colonial society, where creolization unfolded through the daily interaction of men and women, colonizers and indigenes. Golovin, Veniaminov and other writers of the colonial era described patterns of Russian-Native intermarriage and discussed the growth and social position of the official Creole population, but tended to cast creole identity within the narrow, racially defined mold of the estate system. To some extent, modern historians have been seduced by this essentialist view, enforcing the impression that the RAC's hierarchical classification described and contained social reality. The perspective developed here is that creolization was a far broader ethnic process that arose from shifting self-identification and social contention among both Alaska Natives and lower class Russians, and that the material world – accessible through archaeology – was one of its important expressive dimensions.

Ethnicity so understood comes into view at Three Saints Harbor, where Russian-Siberian men were already by the 1780s living with Sugpiaq women and relying on Sugpiaq foods and tools. At the Nunakakhnak resettlement village, residents wore woolen clothing and in at least one instance an Orthodox cross, although they appear to have been non-Creole refugees from nearby Sugpiaq villages (Luehrmann 2008: 39–40). At Afognak artel, the non-Creole Sugpiaq residents were drinking tea from imported ceramic cups, adopting a Russian social ceremony and its implements as their own. In the Aleutian Islands, traditional longhouses like those occupied at Reese Bay in the late eighteenth century gave way within a few generations to Russian-influenced single family homes with ground-level doorways and gut-covered windows, like those at Korovinski.

The material language of ethnicity was strongly on display in the built environments of Russian settlements such as Fort Ross, Three Saints Harbor, Novo-Arkangelskh, and Kolmakovskiy, modeled as a projection of colonial power and ideal social order. Spatially, these outposts were maps of social distance, in which residences for the honorable estate were centrally placed, flanked by separate and increasingly distant dwellings or neighborhoods for Russians, Creoles, and Alaska Natives. Indigenous workers and their families were often situated in separate *artels*, not least because rebellion was feared even after decades of oppressive control (Luehrmann 2008: 44–45). The ethnic-status grading of architecture included such distinctions such as wood vs. earthen construction; planked vs. dirt floors; metal or shingled vs. thatched roofs; brick heating stoves vs. pit hearths; and glass vs. mica or skin-covered windows.

For the indigenous elite in southern Alaskan societies, interaction with Russian invaders tended to reinforce traditional roles as clan leaders, warriors, traders, and alliance makers. Even the provision of hostages to Grigorii Shelikhov and other Russian strongmen was a traditional pattern for settling conflicts with military opponents (Davydov 1977: 106; De Laguna 1972: 521; Emmons 1991: 351–358; Gideon 1989: 44; Shelikhov 1981: 89). It is notable that most of the foreign goods that Native leaders obtained from the Russians had prestige rather than utilitarian values from the outset, and were then repurposed as social prestations.

Conclusion

The archaeology of Russian America, as presented here, is an attempt at synthesis on several scales, including core–periphery dynamics of Russia and its colony in the context of the world-system; relations of production and commodification in the colony as a whole; ethnic hierarchy and interaction among diverse communities and social levels; and domestic life in many settings, with its material systems of social meaning. This kind of "plying backwards and forwards between the local and the global," as Martin Hall expressed it (Hall 2000: 18), is fundamental to an archaeology of the modern world; and it is moreover a way of discovering parallels between the colonial projects of different nations, and of comparing the social dynamics of different capitalist settings. Among the studies presented in this volume, any number of analogs with Russian America may be identified. For example, under Omani colonial rule in Zanzibar the use and circulation of ceramic bowls made in Europe and imported by Indian traders reinforced local hierarchies of power and subordination, but at the same time contributed to a sense of identity that was shared by planters and the enslaved (Croucher, Chap. 8). In Spanish New Grenada, imported ceramic vessels were "objects of distinction" used by urban elites, commodities that were being incorporated into "powerful, hybrid materialities" (Gaitán-Ammann, Chap. 7). Every instance discussed in this essay and throughout the volume reinforces our understanding that capitalism has one history, but also many histories, and that archaeology must keep all levels in view.

References

Arndt, Katherine L. 1990 Russian Exploration and Trade in Alaska's Interior. In *Russian America: The Forgotten Frontier*, edited by Barbara Sweetland Smith and Redmond J. Barnett, pp. 95–107. Washington State Historical Society, Tacoma.

Barth, Frederik. 1969 *Ethnic Groups and Boundaries: The Social Organization of Social Difference*. Universitetsforlaget, Oslo.

Bergsland, Knut. 1959 Aleut Dialects of Atka and Attu. *Transactions of the American Philosophical Society* 49(3):1–128.

Berkh, Vasilli Nikolaevich. 1974 *A Chronological History of the Discovery of the Aleutian Islands, or the Exploits of the Russian Merchants*. Translated by Dmitri Krenov, edited by Richard A. Pierce. The Limestone Press, Kingston, Ontario.

Black, Lydia T. 1990 Creoles in Russian America. *Pacifica* 2(2):142–155.

Black, Lydia T. 2004 *Russians in Alaska 1732–1867*. University of Alaska Press, Fairbanks.

Boyd, Robert T. 1990 Demographic History, 1774–1874. In *Handbook of North American Indians*, Vol. 7, *Northwest Coast*, edited by Wayne Suttles, pp. 135–148. Smithsonian Institution, Washington, DC.

Clark, Donald W. 1974 *Koniag Prehistory: Archaeological Investigations at Late Prehistoric Sites on Kodiak Island, Alaska*. Tubinger Monographien zur Urgeschichte, Band 1. Kolhammer, Stuttgart.

Clark, Donald W. 1984 Pacific Eskimo: Historical Ethnography. In *Handbook of North American Indians*, Vol. 5, *Arctic*, edited by David Damas, pp. 185–197. Smithsonian Institution, Washington, DC.

Clifford, James. 2004 Looking Several Ways: Anthropology and Native Heritage in Alaska. *Current Anthropology* 45(4):5–30.

Crowell, Aron L. 1992 Postcontact Koniag Ceremonialism on Kodiak Island and the Alaska Peninsula: Evidence from the Fisher Collection. *Arctic Anthropology* 29(1):18–37.

Crowell, Aron L. 1997a *Archaeology and the Capitalist World System: A Study from Russian America*. Plenum Press, New York.

Crowell, Aron L. 1997b Russians in Alaska, 1784: Foundations of Colonial Society at Three Saints Harbor, Kodiak Island. *Kroeber Anthropological Society Papers 81*. University of California Press, Berkeley.

Crowell, Aron L. 2004a Terms of Engagement: The Collaborative Representation of Alutiiq Identity. *Études/Inuit/Studies* 28(1):9–36.

Crowell, Aron L. 2004b Connecting with the Past: The Kenai Fjords Oral History and Archaeology Project. *Alaska Park Science* 3(1):33–38.

Crowell, Aron L. 2009 Russian Colonization of Alaska and the Northwest Coast. In *Archaeology in America*, Vol. 4, *West Coast and Arctic/Subarctic*, edited by Francis P. McManamon, pp. 282–286. Greenwood Press, Westport CT and London.

Crowell, Aron L. and Sonja Luehrmann. 2001 Alutiiq Culture: Views from Archaeology, Anthropology, and History. In *Looking Both Ways: Heritage and Identity of the Alutiiq People*, edited by Aron L. Crowell, Amy F. Steffian, and Gordon Pullar, pp. 21–72. University of Alaska Press, Fairbanks.

Crowell, Aron L. and Daniel H. Mann. 1998 *Archaeology and Coastal Dynamics of Kenai Fjords National Park, Alaska*. National Park Service, Alaska Region, Anchorage.

Crowell, Aron L., Amy F. Steffian, and Gordon L. Pullar (editors). 2001 *Looking Both Ways: Heritage and Identity of the Alutiiq People*. University of Alaska Press, Fairbanks.

Crowell, Aron L., David R. Yesner, Rita Eagle, and Diane K. Hanson. 2008 An Historic Alutiiq Village on the Outer Kenai Coast: Subsistence and Trade in the Early Russian Contact Period. *Alaska Journal of Anthropology* 6(1–2):225–252.

Dauenhauer, Nora Marks, Richard Dauenhauer, and Lydia T. Black (editors). 2008 Anóoshi lingit aaní ká: *Russians in Tlingit America: The Battles of Sitka, 1802 and 1804*. University of Washington Press, Seattle.

Davydov, Gavriil Ivanovich. 1977 *Two Voyages to Russian America, 1802–1807*. Translated by Colin Bearne, edited by Richard A. Pierce. The Limestone Press, Kingston, Ontario.

Deagan, Kathleen. 1983 *Spanish St. Augustine: The Archaeology of a Colonial Creole Community*. Academic Press, New York.

DeLaguna, Frederica. 1972 *Under Mount Saint Elias: The History and Culture of the Yakutat Tlingit*. Smithsonian Contributions to Anthropology 7. Smithsonian Institution, Washington, D.C.

Dmytryshyn, Basil, E.A.P. Crownhart-Vaughan, and Thomas Vaughan (eds). 1989 *To Siberia and Russian America: Three Centuries of Russian Eastward Expansion*, Vol. 3, *The Russian American Colonies 1798–1867*. Oregon Historical Press, Portland.

Eccles, W. J. 1988 The Fur Trade in the Colonial Northeast. In *Handbook of North American Indians*, Vol. 4, *History of Indian-White Relations*, edited by William E. Washburn, pp. 324–334. Smithsonian Institution, Washington, DC.

Ellanna, Linda J. and Andrew Balluta. 1992 *Nuvendaltin Quht'ana: The People of Nondalton*. Smithsonian Institution Press, Washington, DC.

Emmons, George Thornton. 1991 *The Tlingit Indians*. Douglas and McIntyre and American Museum of Natural History, Vancouver and New York.

Ewen, Charles R. 2000 From Colonist to Creole: Archaeological Patterns of Spanish Colonization in the New World. *Historical Archaeology* 34(3):36–45.

Ewen, Charles R. 2009 The Archaeology of La Florida. In *International Handbook of Historical Archaeology*, edited by Teresita Majewski and David Gamister, pp. 383–398. Springer, New York.

Fedorova, Svetlana G. 1973 *The Russian Population in Alaska and California, Late 18th Century – 1867*. Translated and edited by Richard A. Pierce and Alton S. Donnelly. The Limestone Press, Kingston, Ontario.

Fedorova, Svetlana G. 1975 Ethnic Processes in Russian America. Translated by Antoinette Shalkop. *Occasional Paper* No. 1, Anchorage Historical and Fine Arts Museum.

Fisher, Raymond H. 1990 Finding America. In *Russian America: The Forgotten Frontier*, edited by Barbara Sweetland Smith and Redmond J. Barnett, pp. 17–32. Washington State Historical Society, Tacoma.

Gibson, James R. 1976 *Imperial Russia in Frontier America: The Changing Geography of Supply of Russian America, 1784–1867*. Oxford University Press, New York.

Gibson, James R. 1987 Russian Dependence upon the Natives of Alaska. In *Russia's American Colony*, edited by S. Frederick Starr, pp. 77–104. Duke University Press, Durham.

Gideon. 1989 *The Round the World Voyage of Hieromonk Gideon, 1803–1809*. Translated by Lydia T. Black, edited by Richard A. Pierce. The Limestone Press, Kingston, Ontario.

Golovin, Pavel Nikolaevich. 1979 *The End of Russian America: Captain P. N. Golovin's Last Report 1862*. Translated and edited by Basil Dmytryshyn and E.A.P. Crownhart-Vaughan. Oregon Historical Society, Portland.

Grinev, Andrei Val'Terovich. 2005 *The Tlingit Indians in Russian America, 1741–1867*. Translated by Richard L. Bland and Katerina G. Solovjova. University of Nebraska Press, Lincoln.

Gundacker, Grey. 2000 Creolization, Complexity, and Time. *Historical Archaeology* 34(3):124–133.

Hall, Martin. 2000 *Archaeology and the Modern World: Colonial Transcripts in South Africa and the Chesapeake*. Routledge, London.

Harvey, Lola. 1991 *Derevnia's Daughters: Saga of an Alaskan Village*. Sunflower University Press, Manhattan, KA.

Hodder, Ian. 1982 *Symbols in Action*. Cambridge University Press, Cambridge UK.

Huggins, Eli L. 1981 *Kodiak and Afognak Life, 1868–1870*. Edited by Richard A. Pierce. The Limestone Press, Kingston, Ontario.

Jackson, Louise M. 1991 Nineteenth Century British Ceramics: A Key to Cultural Dynamics in Southwestern Alaska. Ph.D. dissertation, University of California, Los Angeles.

Jenkins, Richard. 1997 *Rethinking Ethnicity: Arguments and Explorations*. Sage, London.

Jones, Siân. 1997 *The Archaeology of Ethnicity: Constructing Identities in the Past and Present*. Routledge, London.

Jordan, Kurt A. 2009 Colonies, Colonialism, and Cultural Entanglement: The Archaeology of Postcolumbian Intercultural Relations. In *International Handbook of Historical Archaeology*, edited by Teresita Majewski and David Gamister, pp. 31–49. Springer, New York.

Kan, Sergei. 1999 *Memory Eternal: Tlingit Culture and Russian Orthodox Christianity through Two Centuries*. University of Washington Press, Seattle.

Kardulias, P. Nick. 1990 Fur Production as a Specialized Activity in a World System: Indians in the North American Fur Trade. *American Indian Culture and Research Journal* 14(1):25–60.

Knecht, Richard A. and Richard H. Jordan. 1985 Nunakakhnak: An Historic Period Koniag Village in Karluk, Kodiak Island, Alaska. *Arctic Anthropology* 22(2):17–35.

Lantis, Margaret. 1970 The Aleut Social System, 1750 to 1810, from Early Historical Sources. In *Ethnohistory in Southwestern Alaska and the Southern Yukon: Method and Content*, edited by Robert Ackerman, pp. 139–301. The University Press of Kentucky, Lexington.

Lantis, Margaret. 1984 Aleut. In *Handbook of North American Indians*, Vol. 5, *Arctic*, edited by David Damas, pp. 1161–184. Smithsonian Institution, Washington, DC.

Liapunova, Rosa G. 1987 Relations with the Natives of Russian America. In *Russia's American Colony*, edited by S. Frederick Starr, pp. 105–143. Duke University Press, Durham.

Lightfoot, Kent G. 1995 Culture Contact Studies: Redefining the Relationship between Prehistoric and Historical Archaeology. *American Antiquity* 60(2):199–217.

Lightfoot, Kent G. 2003 Russian Colonization: The Implications of Mercantile Colonial Practices in the North Pacific. *Historical Archaeology* 37(4):14–28.

Lightfoot, Kent G. 2005a The Archaeology of Colonization: California in Cross-Cultural Perspective. In *The Archaeology of Colonial Encounters: Comparative Perspectives*, edited by Gil Stein, pp. 207–237. School of American Research Press, Santa Fe.

Lightfoot, Kent G. 2005b *Indians, Missionaries, and Merchants: The Legacy of Colonial Encounters on the California Frontiers*. University of California Press, Berkeley.

Lightfoot, Kent, Thomas A. Wake, and Ann M. Schiff. 1991 *The Archaeology and Ethnohistory of Fort Ross, California*. Vol. 1. Contributions of the University of California Research Facility No. 49. University of California, Berkeley.

Lightfoot, Kent G. and Antoinette Martinez. 1995 Frontiers and Boundaries in Archaeological Perspective. *Annual Review of Anthropology* 24:471–492.

Lightfoot, Kent G., Antoinette Martinez, and Ann M. Schiff. 1998 Daily Practice and Material Culture in Pluralistic Social Settings: An Archaeological Study of Culture Change and Persistence from Fort Ross, California. *American Antiquity* 63(2):199–222.

Luehrmann, Sonja. 2008 *Alutiiq Villages under Russian and U.S. Rule*. University of Alaska Press, Fairbanks.

Lynch, Alice J. 1982 *Qizhjeh: The Historic Tanaina Village of Kijik and the Kijik Archeological District*. Anthropology and Historic Preservation, Cooperative Park Studies Unit, University of Alaska, Fairbanks.

Martinez, Antoinette. 1997 *View from the Ridge: Kashaya Pomo in a Russian-American Company Context*. Kroeber Anthropological Association Papers 81:141–156.

McMahan, J. David (ed.). 2002 *Archaeological Data Recovery at Baranof Castle State Historical Site, Sitka, Alaska: Final Report of Investigations (ADOT & PF Project No. 71817/TEA-000-3[43])*. Alaska Office of History and Archaeology Report No. 84. Alaska Office of History and Archaeology, Anchorage.

Meskell, Lynn. 2002 The Intersections of Identity and Politics in Archaeology. *Annual Review of Anthropology* 31:279–301.

Middleton, John. 1996 *Clothing in Russian America: A New Look*. The Limestone Press, Kingston, Ontario.

Mills, Peter R. 2002 *Hawai'i's Russian Adventure: A New Look at Old History*. University of Hawai'i Press, Honolulu.

Okun, Semen B. 1979 *The Russian-American Company*. Edited by B. D. Grekov, translated by Carl Ginsburg. Octagon Books, New York.

Oleksa, Michael J. 1990 The Creoles and Their Contributions to the Development of Alaska. In *Russian America: The Forgotten Frontier*, edited by Barbara Sweetland Smith and Redmond J. Barnett, pp. 185–196. Washington State Historical Society, Tacoma.

Oleksa, Michael J. 1992 *Orthodox Alaska: A Theology of Mission*. St. Vladimir's Seminary Press, Crestwood, NJ.

Olson, Wallace M. 2002 *Through Spanish Eyes: The Spanish Voyages to Alaska, 1774–1792*. Heritage Research, Auke Bay, Alaska.

Orser, Charles E. Jr. 1996 *A Historical Archaeology of the Modern World*. Plenum Press, New York.

Orser, Charles E. Jr. 2009 World-Systems Theory, Networks, and Modern-World Archaeology. In *International Handbook of Historical Archaeology*, edited by T. Majewski and D. Gamister, pp. 253–268. Springer, New York.

Oswalt, Wendell H. 1980 *Kolmakovskiy Redoubt: The Ethnoarchaeology of a Russian Fort in Alaska*. Monumenta Archaeologica 8, The Institute of Archaeology, University of California, Los Angeles.

Pierce, Richard A. 1990 The Russian-American Company Currency. In *Russian America: The Forgotten Frontier*, edited by Barbara Sweetland Smith and Redmond J. Barnett, pp. 145–154. Washington State Historical Society, Tacoma.

Pullar, Gordon L. 1992 Ethnic Identity, Cultural Pride, and Generations of Baggage: A Personal Experience. Arctic Anthropology 29(2):182–209.

Pullar, Gordon L. 2001 Contemporary Alutiiq Identity. In *Looking Both Ways: Heritage and Identity of the Alutiiq People*, edited by Aron L. Crowell, Amy F. Steffian, and Gordon L. Pullar, pp. 73–98. University of Alaska Press, Fairbanks.

Sauer, Martin. 1802 *An Account of a Geographical and Astronomical Expedition to the Northern Parts of Russia*. A. Strahan, London.

Senkevitch, Anatole Jr. 1987 The Early Architecture and Settlements of Russian America. . In *Russia's American Colony*, edited by S. Frederick Starr, pp. 147–195. Duke University Press, Durham.

Shelikhov, Grigoriil. 1981 *A Voyage to America, 1783–1786*. Translated by Marina Ramsay; edited by Richard A. Pierce. The Limestone Press, Kingston, Ontario.

Shubin, Valery O. 1990 Russian Settlements in the Kurile Islands in the 18th and 19th Centuries. In *Russia in North America: Proceedings of the Second International Conference on Russian America, Sitka, Alaska, August 19–22, 1987*, edited by Richard A. Pierce, pp. 425–450. The Limestone Press, Kingston, Ontario.

Simeone, William E. 1995 *Rifles, Blankets, and Beads: Identity, History, and the Northern Athapaskan Potlatch*. University of Oklahoma Press, Norman and London.

Smith, Barbara Sweetland. 1990 Russia's Cultural Legacy in Alaska: The Orthodox Mission. In *Russian America: The Forgotten Frontier*, edited by Barbara Sweetland Smith and Redmond J. Barnett, pp. 245–253. Washington State Historical Society, Tacoma.

Steffian, Amy F. 2001 Cúmilalhet – "Our Ancestors." In *Looking Both Ways: Heritage and Identity of the Alutiiq People*, edited by Aron L. Crowell, Amy F. Steffian, and Gordon L. Pullar, pp. 99–136. University of Alaska Press, Fairbanks, AK.

Stein, Gil J. 2002 From Passive Periphery to Active Agents: Emerging Perspectives in the Archaeology of Interregional Interaction. *American Anthropologist* 104(3):903–916.

Stein, Gil J. 2005 The Comparative Archaeology of Colonial Encounters. In *The Archaeology of Colonial Encounters: Comparative Perspectives*, edited by Gil J, Stein, pp. 3–30. School of American Research Press, Santa Fe.

Thompson, Richard H. 1989 *Theories of Ethnicity: A Critical Appraisal*. Greenwood Press, New York.

Tikhmenev, Petr Aleksandrovich. 1978 *A History of the Russian-American Company*. Translated and edited by Richard A. Pierce and Alton S. Connelly. University of Washington Press, Seattle.

Townsend, Joan. 1975 Mercantilism and Societal Change: An Ethnohistoric Examination of Some Essential Variables. *Ethnohistory* 20:21–32.

Townsend, Joan. 1980 Ranked Societies of the Alaskan Pacific Rim. In *Alaska Native Culture and History*, edited by Yoshinobu Kotani and William B. Workman, pp. 123–156. Senri Ethnological Series No. 4. National Museum of Ethnology, Osaka.

Vancouver, George. 1801 *A Voyage of Discovery to the North Pacific Ocean and Round the World*. 6 vols. John Stockdale, London.

VanStone, James W. 1967 *Eskimos of the Nushagak River: An Ethnographic History*. University of Washington Press, Seattle.

VanStone, James W. and Joan B. Townsend. 1970 *Kijik: An Historic Tanaina Indian Settlement*. Fieldiana Anthropology Vol. 59. Field Museum of Natural History, Chicago.

Veltre, Douglas W. 1979 Korovinski: The Ethnohistorical Archaeology of an Aleut and Russian Settlement on Atka Island, Alaska. Ph.D. dissertation, Department of Anthropology, University of Connecticutt, Storrs.

Veltre, Douglas W. and Allen P. McCartney. 2001 Ethnohistorical Archaeology at the Reese Bay Site, Unalaska Island. In Don E. Dumond, ed. *Archaeology in the Aleut Zone of Alaska: Some Recent Research*. University of Oregon Anthropological Papers No. 58, pp. 87–104. Eugene.

Veniaminov, Ivan. 1984 *Notes on the Islands of the Unalaska District*. Translated by Lydia T. Black and R. H. Geoghegan. Edited by Richard A. Pierce. The Limestone Press, Kingston, Ontario.

Voss, Barbara L. 2008a Gender, Race, and Labor in the Archaeology of the Spanish Colonial Americas. *Current Anthropology* 49(5):861–893.

Voss, Barbara L. 2008b *The Archaeology of Ethnogenesis: Race and Sexuality in Colonial San Francisco*. University of California Press, Berkeley.

Wallerstein, Immanuel. 1989 *The Modern World-System III: The Second Era of Great Expansion of the Capitalist World-Economy, 1730–1840s*. Academic Press, New York.

Wolf, Eric R. 1982 *Europe and the People without History*. University of California Press, Berkeley.

Woodhouse-Beyer, Katherine. 1999 Artels and Identities: Gender, Power, and Russian America. In *Manifesting Power: Gender and the Interpretation of Power in Archaeology*, edited by T. Sweely, pp. 129–154. Routledge, London.

Woodhouse-Beyer, Katherine. 2001 Gender Relations and Socio-Economic Change in Russian America: An Archaeological Study of the Kodiak Archipelago, Alaska, 1741–1867 A.D. Ph.D. dissertation, Department of Anthropology, Brown University.

Worl, Rosita. 2010 The First Peoples of Alaska: A Path to Self-Determination. *In Living Our Cultures, Sharing Our Heritage: The First Peoples of Alaska*, edited by Aron L. Crowell, Rosita Worl, Paul C. Ongtooguk, and Dawn D. Biddison, pp. 36–43. Smithsonian Books, Washington, DC.

Zagoskin, Lavrentii A. 1967 *Lieutenant Zagoskin's Travels in Russian America, 1842–1844: The First Ethnographic and Geographic Investigations on the Yukon and Kuskokwim Valleys*. Edited by Henry N. Michael. Published for the Arctic Institute of North America by the University of Toronto Press, Toronto.

Znamenski, Andrei A. 2003 *Through Orthodox Eyes: Russian Missionary Narratives of Travels to the Dena'ina and Ahtna, 1850s-1930s*. Translated by Andrei A. Znamenski. University of Alaska Press, Fairbanks.

Chapter 5
Building Farmsteads in the Desert: Capitalism, Colonialism, and the Transformation of Rural Landscapes in Late Ottoman Period Transjordan

Lynda Carroll

In the second half of the nineteenth century, merchant settlers from Palestine crossed the Jordan River and moved east into the Balqa' region of the Transjordan. Under a new Ottoman land tenure system, these settlers acquired land and invested in large-scale agricultural production, and constructed a series of large farmstead complexes, transforming the cultural and physical landscape of Transjordan's rural countryside. Many Bedu tribes that had previously used the landscape mainly for pastureland were drawn into this new economy as laborers, and their pastures were turned into large farms.

While the development of large farmsteads in Transjordan and the Middle East is part of the process of capitalist expansion into the rural countryside, the intersection of capitalist investment with the empire's changing administrative policies were part of a new colonial discourse; during the nineteenth century, the Ottoman state attempted to redefine its relationship to nomadic groups and embraced the ideologies of colonialism in its efforts to settle its Bedu subjects and turn pastureland into agricultural spaces.

Archaeological approaches to changing settlement in late Ottoman period Transjordan, however, move beyond a view that global structures were simply imposed on tribal groups. Instead, Bedu use of landscapes – both hidden and visible – helped them negotiate their everyday lived conditions, by creating their own challenges to the structures of state, capitalism and colonialism.

The Archaeology of Ottoman Transjordan

The Ottoman Empire was one of the Great Powers of the early modern period; at its height during the sixteenth century, it controlled much of the Middle East, North Africa and the Balkans. In 1516, the Ottoman Empire gained control of Transjordan,

L. Carroll (✉)
Public Archaeology Facility, Binghamton University, Binghamton, NY, USA
e-mail: carroll.palmer@gmail.com

S.K. Croucher and L. Weiss (eds.), *The Archaeology of Capitalism in Colonial Contexts*,
Contributions To Global Historical Archaeology, DOI 10.1007/978-1-4614-0192-6_5,
© Springer Science+Business Media, LLC 2011

Fig. 5.1 The perennial spring of *Ain Hisban*, photographed by Phillips in 1867 (Courtesy of the Palestine Exploration Fund Photo Archive, London)

and held it as a frontier province until 1918. At the time of its conquest, the Transjordan was well populated, with sizable villages and towns. However, during the seventeenth century, many of these settlements were abandoned, especially in central and southern regions. Historians and archaeologists have provided a number of reasons for this population dispersal, including fear of conscription and a way to avoid Ottoman taxation (e.g., Amiran 1953: 78; Hütteroth and Abdulfattah 1977: 55–67; Khammash 1986: 11; Walker 1999). Dispersal also followed large-scale migrations of nomadic and seminomadic tribes from the Arabian Peninsula into Transjordan a century before. The seventeenth through mid-nineteenth centuries are, therefore, considered a period of "nomadization" accompanied by a general decline in agriculture (e.g., Abujaber 1989; Fischbach 2000; Hütteroth and Abdulfattah 1977; Johns 1994; LaBianca 1990, 2000; Lewis 1987; Rogan 1999: 90; Walker 1999).

Although some of the tribal groups were large, numbering thousands of people, the archaeological record for land use in the Ottoman period is limited. While some of this limited evidence is related to research goals of archaeologists working in the region, it is also the case that material remains of mobile groups are relatively difficult to detect archaeologically; tents were the primary source of shelter for mobile Bedu, and fewer ceramics are attributed to this period. Nevertheless, pastoralist Bedu groups sometimes engaged in limited cultivation and made seasonal use of sites and other fixed spaces in the landscape; the lines between settlement and abandonment are – more often than not – blurred (e.g., Bernard and Wendrich 2008; Bernbeck 2008; Cribb 1991).

McQuitty (2005) has argued that archaeological evidence exists for the seventeenth through nineteenth centuries in Transjordan, and it includes a wide variety of previously unconsidered spaces throughout the landscape (see also LaBianca 1990; Walker 1999: 215). Tents were often used in conjunction with a wide variety of features, such as small structures for storage; cisterns and springs (Fig. 5.1); terraces; small garden plots; fieldstone enclosures for animals; and caves used for habitation, storage, and shelter for livestock. Walker (1999) has also included Bedu cemetery sites, handmade painted pottery, and isolated farmsteads that were seasonally used.

By recognizing these spaces in the Ottoman landscape, not only does a clearer picture of Bedu land use in the Ottoman period emerge, but it also provides a starting point to understand the shift in settlement that occurred in the second half of the nineteenth century, during the late Ottoman period. Beginning in the mid-nineteenth century, merchants from Palestine moved east, and began to construct large farmsteads (AbuJaber 1989) – sometimes also called *Qasrs*. This movement brought about new relationships between the Ottoman state, its Bedu subjects, and merchant capitalists, including new relationships linked to global capitalism, as well as new policies to control the frontiers by using models of colonialism to settle its nomadic subjects.

Ottoman Archaeology as Global Historical Archaeology

Archaeology of the Ottoman Empire stems from a wide variety of disciplinary and theoretical backgrounds (Baram and Carroll 2000: 15–25; see also Baram 2009: 649–650). However, Baram and Carroll (2000: 16–18) argue that Ottoman archaeology can contribute to the goals of global historical archaeology, which is generally defined as a global approach to the archaeology of the modern period (Orser 1996). By shedding light on the development of the modern Middle East through material remains and physical evidence, Ottoman archaeology as global historical archaeology "opens an avenue to study the intersection of internal colonialism, foreign imperialism and local agency in a global, comparative context" (Baram 2009: 651).

According to Johnson (1999: 28), capitalism and European colonialism are the themes that comprise a master narrative in global historical archaeology. The field, however, is fragmenting (Johnson 1999) as historical archaeologists increasingly recognize the dangers of using global structures like capitalism and European colonialism as universalizing constructs to define the modern period. So, while there is potential for understanding the materiality of the recent past of the Middle East through global historical archaeology, there is a danger that Ottoman archaeology could be constructed as just one more study of how the West materialized itself in yet another non-Western setting, whether through so-called capitalist penetration or through colonial encounters.

Postcolonial archaeologies have challenged the essentialized, Eurocentric views of the past and provide counterdiscourse that emanates from subaltern voices, through the hidden transcripts (Hall 2000; see also Given 2004: 10–12) that can be interpreted through archaeological evidence, and tell different stories than the state, colonial powers, or Eurocentric observers. Thus, the contribution of a "postcolonial historical archaeology of capitalism" (Croucher and Weiss, Chap. 1) is in its multivocality, its ability to provide alternative stories about the past, and its emphasis on particularisms in the face of the global structures of capitalism and colonialism (e.g., Funari et al. 1999: 43; Gosden 2001, 1999: 1 79–205; Hall 2000; Johnson 1999: 35; Schmidt and Walz 2007).

The potential for a postcolonial approach to the archaeology of the Ottoman Empire is clear, as it allows for new discourses to help explore the daily lives of Ottoman subjects who lived under the shadow of the state. However, postcolonial scholars have largely ignored the Ottoman Empire (Deringil 2003: 313–316). Even the foundational postcolonial text, *Orientalism* (Said 1978) – which argued that western scholarship has imagined and essentialized the East as backward and stagnant – makes little reference to the Ottoman Empire (Deringil 2003: 313). As a major non-Western sovereign state, the Ottoman case is epiphenomenal: it was not Eastern enough, not Muslim enough, and not enough of an "other." The Ottoman Empire, therefore, "fell between the cracks" of postcolonial studies (Deringil 2003: 315). A postcolonial archaeology, therefore, provides voice not only to the people who lived under the Ottoman state but also, ironically, to the Ottoman state itself. Ottoman archaeology allows for new discourses to help explore local interactions between state and subjects, as they both engaged in and challenged processes of capitalism and colonialism.

The Ottoman Empire and the Tanzimat

For centuries, the frontier regions of the Ottoman Empire had been left in the hand of local leaders. As Kasaba (2009) argues, the mobility of nomadic groups was sometimes seen as an advantage to the state; tribal leaders could maintain order more effectively than garrisons of armies or appointed administrators because they were more closely connected to local networks and other tribal groups. By accommodating and enlisting the support of local tribal leaders, their mobility became a way for the central government to maintain connections with the empire without extensive garrisoning or the placement of administrators. In Transjordan, this relationship was relatively successful throughout the seventeenth and eighteenth centuries, as tribal groups maintained sufficient control over the rural countryside. However, as the eighteenth century came to a close, this relationship was about to change.

The Ottoman Empire of the late eighteenth century was – like its contemporaries, Hapsburg Austria and Romanov Russia – in a "struggle for survival in a world where it no longer made the rules" (Deringil 2003: 322). Ottoman leaders and intellectuals alike grew concerned that the state was in trouble; the empire was burdened with debt, and experienced an increasing number of major military defeats (such as the loss of the Crimea in the Russo-Turkish War of 1768). One of the state's many concerns was that its territories were in danger of being divided up and parceled out to European colonial powers. In particular, frontier regions were at risk since they had relatively loose ties to the Ottoman central authority.

As the global balance of power tipped in favor of European states, the Ottomans began to reorganize the empire based on models that appeared to work for Europe. Beginning in 1839 C.E., the state set in motion a series of reforms based on Enlightenment ideals, and were linked to discourses of progress and modernity.

This period was called the *Tanzimat*, or "reorganization" period. During the *Tanzimat*, the Ottoman state embarked on a path of modernization, set into motion a series of new laws and policies, and aimed at the reorganization of social and economic life. Under the *Tanzimat*, life, honor, and property rights were guaranteed to all of its subject populations. The state also aimed at creating more equitable forms of taxation and made investments in infrastructure and education. The goal was *Ottomanization* of the empire, to bring civilization to its subjects. However, these efforts were more difficult to implement in the frontier provinces than in the center.

In the Arab provinces, the state used primitivist tropes to target Bedu. The state argued that "progress" could only be accomplished by transforming its so-called "primitive" populations into productive subjects of the state (Deringil 1998, 2003; Green 2005). As Deringil (2003: 342) argues, when faced with the expansion of European states, the Ottomans "rejected the subaltern role that the West seemed intent on making them adopt, but they could only do this by inviting (to put it euphemistically) 'their own' subalterns into history."

Nomads became the focus of this new policy, as the state made efforts to settle tribes and control their migrations. Ottoman intellectuals and administrators outlined steps to uplift the "noble savage," through a vast investment of resources for education, construction projects, and directly reconnecting with local leaders once again. The state's efforts to settle Bedu was amplified by conveying its efforts with new meaning; while the Ottoman state had historically made concessions for pastoralism (Kasaba 2009), nomadic pastoralism was redefined as antithetical to being modern, and counter to the Ottoman projects of modernity and Ottomanization (Deringil 2003: 318–329).

In many frontier provinces, the economy was defined primarily by pastoralism. Thus, the Ottoman state began the process of turning "unproductive" pastures into agricultural fields by implementing new land tenure system that encouraged private landholdings (e.g., Baram 2007, 2009; Carroll 2008). The labor for the new rural economy could effectively be achieved by transforming Bedu into a settled peasantry. The mechanics involved "sending settlers out to lands where people still live in a state of nomadism and savagery, developing those areas, and causing them to become a market for its own goods" (İzzed 1890). In addition, by encouraging the production of wealth, the state assumed that merchants, elites, and local leaders would repay the state for these concessions and work in favor of the center. Transforming the frontiers into productive land would accomplish the state's goal to bring a new order to the frontiers. Investors would protect their own investments at the local level (Deringil 2003: 322).

In practice, the *Tanzimat* brought capitalist logic and colonial models to many Ottoman subjects, as the state tried to reestablished economic and political control. The state wanted to redefine how it would use its existing possessions in an expanding global capitalist economy – through policies that supported capitalist investments and created a form of Ottoman colonialism (Deringil 1998, 2003; Green 2005).

Ultimately, Ottoman merchants were encouraged to exploit pastureland and to use the land for new sources of raw materials and produce exports for global and imperial markets (e.g., Kasaba 1988, 2009; Pamuk 1987). The state envisioned these areas as being ready for capitalist investment, and its population – once settled – could become a source of cheap labor.

The Ottoman Land Code and Bedu Registrations

During the *Tanzimat*, the Ottomans embarked on its own version settler colonialism. Key to this process was the restructuring of the Ottoman land tenure system, known as the Land Code of 1858. The goals of the Land Code included protecting landed peasants by codifying private ownership of land, and encourage settlement over mobility. Ottoman subjects were, therefore, required to register their use of land with the state, or lose their land-use rights. In addition to encouraging private land-holdings, the Land Code stressed the concept of abstracted spatial measurements and boundaries of land.

However, this new land tenure system was counter to traditional land use patterns of Bedu tribes. Prior to the *Tanzimat*, land use patterns in Transjordan were based on tribal membership, or measured in terms of productive activities or spaces, such as the amount of space that could be ploughed by a team of oxen or land necessary to support livestock. After the Land Code was implemented, space and land were parceled out into divisible, bounded, and abstract spatial units, and then registered to individuals (e.g., Fischbach 2000: 35; Palmer 1999).

Large tracts of land were in demand, and the potential to register land that was considered unused appealed to settlers, merchants, and urban capitalists. Grain and other produce were in high demand on the global market, and would generate wealth for individual investors (see Mundy 1996 and Palmer 1999 for examples from Northern Jordan). The demand for grain on the market made the large tracts of undeveloped land prime targets for capitalist investment. Throughout the Ottoman world, so-called "unproductive" areas became contested areas in the process of turning them into highly productive agricultural spaces (see Baram 2007 for an example in the Levant).

While the Land Code offered some protections to agricultural peasantry, the goal of agricultural production often conflicted with how much of the rural landscape was actually used – as pastureland. Faced with the possibility of losing their claims to pastures, Bedu registered tribal lands, usually in a tribal leader's name. In some cases, Bedu who registered land made agreements with merchant-farmers who would farm sections of the registered land. Under these agreements, a portion of the agricultural yield would revert back to the tribes. In return, tribal groups would provide protection of merchant's capital investment and sometimes provide the labor (Lewis 1987: 129).

This relationship between settlers and Bedu also attracted merchants to Transjordan. Urban merchant families from Palestine, in particular, saw agriculture and land acquisition in a seemingly desolate and abandoned landscape as an economic venture (Rogan 1992: 240, 1994: 51). As a result, former pastureland was converted to farms (Rogan 1999: 89). Agriculture proved to be profitable, as Transjordan became part of a breadbasket of the empire, and abroad.

By the late nineteenth century, large farmsteads became the primary model for extracting profit from private landholdings. Ultimately, redefined property boundaries, and the influx of capitalist investors, transformed the provinces into a new source of agricultural products, supplied by cheap Bedu labor.

As agricultural production encroached on traditional pastureland, Bedu groups turned to a combination of transhumant and settled life. Some took to farming, which could be profitable in favorable years. Others hired themselves out seasonally as agricultural workers when labor was needed, either for cash or for shares in the produce. Grain agriculture became the foundation of this new economic system, and demand for cash to purchase seeds, tools, draft animals, and other provisions necessary for settled life increased. However, cash was increasingly difficult to come by. With newfound investments in the region, the Ottoman state increased its administrative presence, leading to increased taxation (Abujaber 1989: 83–84). In addition, extracting tribute from settled populations – which had been a source of cash for tribal groups – became more difficult with the increased presence of the state. In a context where cash to pay both taxes and debt was scarce, and access to its acquisition through raiding and tribute was further limited, some tribal groups mortgaged off or sold the lands they had registered.

Case Study: Qasr Hisban

Just on the edge of the village of Hisban, located in the Balqa' region of Jordan, and part of the Madaba Plains (Fig. 5.2), a farmhouse complex overlooks the valley walls of the Wadi Hisban. *Qasr Hisban* (also known as *Beyt Nabulsi*) consists of a two-story farmhouse and associated buildings that overlook agricultural fields, and a series of habitation caves and stone corrals scattered throughout the wadi (e.g., Ahmad et al. 2001; Carroll 2008; Carroll et al 2006; Fenner and LaBianca 2004; LaBianca 1990; Russell 1989; Walker and LaBianca 2003). *Qasr Hisban* is just one example of the large farmsteads that appeared in the Balqa' during the late Ottoman period (see for other examples Abujaber 1989; LaBianca 1990).

The area around Hisban was desirable due to a natural spring, cisterns, and the presence of numerous caves, which were used for storage, shelter, and keeping animal herds (LaBianca 1990, 2000). During the early nineteenth century, the area around Hisban was repeatedly visited by the Ajarma and the Adwan tribes during their movements through the region; the Adwan was the larger tribe of the two, and its political alliances cast a larger shadow over a wider area (Russell 1989: 31; see also Prag 1990).

During the second half of the nineteenth century, members of the Ajarma tribe began to intensify its use of Hisban – both as pastoralists and limited cultivators. But in 1881, the Ajarma tribe registered Hisban and the surrounding region with the Ottoman state (Lewis 1987: 127–128). A small farmhouse, built at Hisban using material from nearby ruins, was registered to a local Ajarma strongman. The Adwan accepted Ajarma registration of the land as part of a political alliance, since the two tribes were allied against the larger and more powerful Beni Sahkr tribe (Conder 1892: 322, Russell 1989: 32).

The Ajarma began to cultivate limited crops, such as figs and olives, most likely for local consumption and trade. Demand for agricultural products was

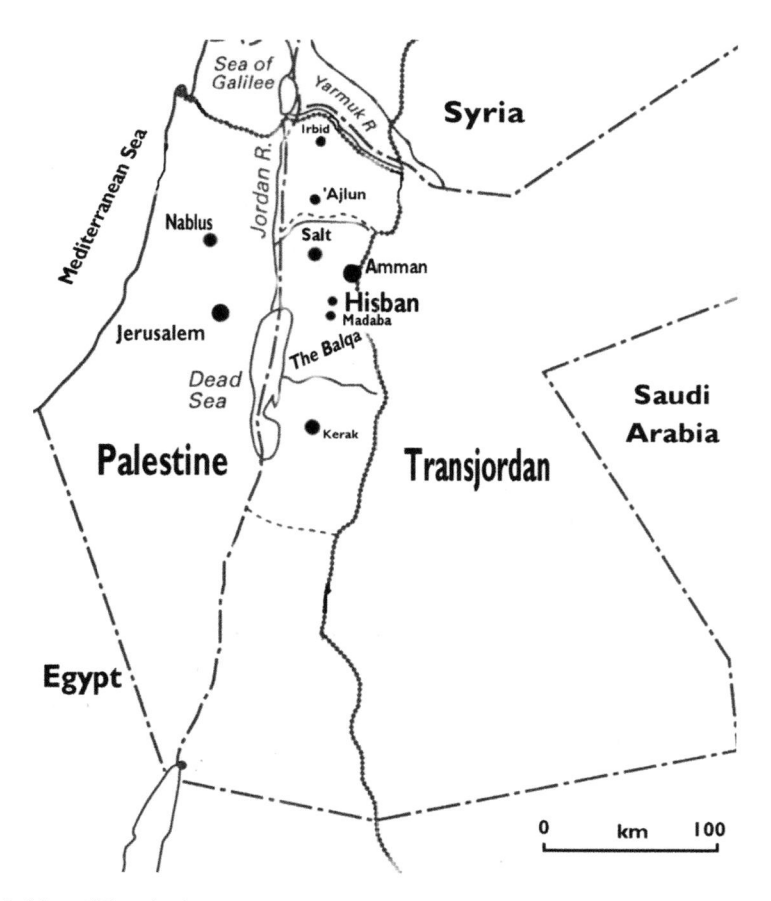

Fig. 5.2 Map of Transjordan

high in the mid-nineteenth century, and migrations of settlers into towns such as al-Salt also created a high demand for produce and livestock. The Ajarma tried to capitalize on this new economic situation and borrowed money from a merchant family from Nablus, which had moved to al-Salt. The Nabulsi family often engaged in money lending with local tribes (e.g., al-Nimr 1938: 87; Kana'an 1993), but the Ajarma gradually fell into increasing debt, were plunged into cycles of credit and indebtedness, and were obliged to sell the land at Hisban to the Nabulsi family (Russell 1989).

As the new landowners, the Nabulsis turned their attention to large scale rain-fed agriculture. They also expanded the farmhouse (Ferch et al. 1989: 31–33). Within a decade, the complex was transformed from a small domestic space with associated storage spaces into a farmhouse complex. A two-story building was constructed on the site; the structure has both domestic and storage

Fig. 5.3 The nineteenth-century farmhouse structure (*Beyt Nabulsi*) at Hisban. Domestic space, including a guesthouse, is located above storage rooms. (Courtesy of the author)

space, and includes a guesthouse (*madafa*) and large, dome-vaulted storerooms (Fig. 5.3). The complex is characterized by urban construction styles and included stables, storage rooms, and smaller single-room structures used as domestic spaces for workers (Fig. 5.4). Its dome vaulted buildings, made out of cut quarried stone, resemble the historic Ottoman houses found in large cities and towns on the West Bank of the Jordan River, such as Nablus and Jerusalem. Based on architectural details, such as roof construction, window style, and the general house plan, the farm complex was mainly pieced together in stages, mainly between 1882 and 1890 (Salt Development Corporation 1990; Fenner and LaBianca 2004).

Over the next two decades, the landscape at Hisban was significantly transformed, as the Nabulsis continued to invest in the complex and add to it. But the Nabulsi family did not live in the farmstead for the majority of the year. Instead, they maintained their primary residence in al-Salt and visited *Beyt Nabulsi* mainly around harvest times. In effect, the Nabulsis became absentee landlords.

At the same time, the Nabulsis hired Ajarma tribesmen to work the fields. The operations of the farm employed and housed dozens of workers and their families, and the single room structures for Bedu laborers point to the capitalist relations brought to Hisban. The Ajarma went from short term visits in a seasonal migratory cycle, to living a relatively settled life centered at the farmstead complex. And although pastoralism continued to be part of the economy – and remains so even through the present day – it was no longer the primary component.

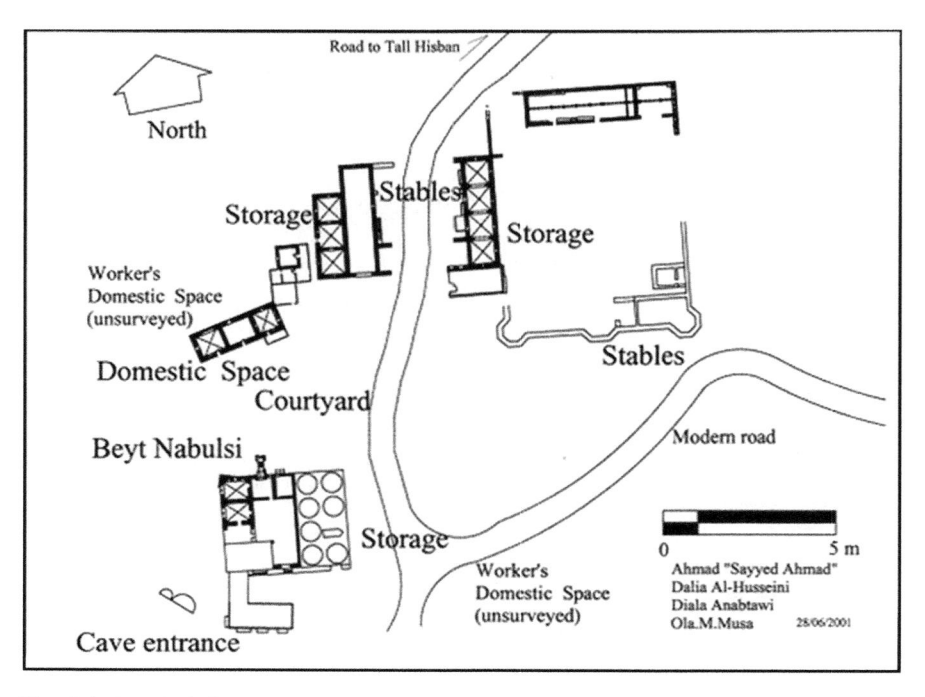

Fig. 5.4 *Beyt Nabulsi* and the nineteenth-century farmstead complex at Hisban (Courtesy of Madaba Plains Project, Tall Hisban Expedition)

Parallel Landscapes of Resistance: Caves and Guesthouses

The model of changing settlement, and the construction of large farms, has been thus far been constructed based on top-down models of change, initiation from the policies of the state through colonial attitudes, or as the result of capitalist exploitation through the investments of merchant settlers. Throughout this discourse, Bedu remain largely passive recipients of both of these global structures. However, at *Qasr Hisban,* the natural and built landscapes provide an alternative story.

At Hisban, Ajarma used both hidden spaces – through the use of caves throughout the adjacent valleys – and the architecture of *Beyt Nabulsi* itself, to create their own challenges to the structures of state, capitalism and colonialism. These spaces helped them negotiate their everyday lived conditions in the Ottoman frontier.

In *The Archaeology of the Colonized*, Given (2004) presents a range of archaeological examples for understanding the experiences of people living under the control of colonial powers. The landscape, in particular, plays a role in his examination of how people interact with the state (Given 2004: 138). In one of his examples, also based in the Ottoman Empire, Given examines the use of clandestine agricultural production areas to understand how people evaded Ottoman tax collectors; although this example focuses on sixteenth century Cyprus, he argues that the location of threshing floors outside of the view of state officials gave Ottoman subjects the ability to circumvent the state's policies of extracting taxes on agricultural produce (Given 2004: 116).

In Transjordan, caves dot the landscape of Transjordan. Throughout the Ottoman period, caves were used for storage, for housing animals, and even as domestic spaces. These were often used as permanent features of the landscape around which tribal migrations were tethered to, through the course of their cyclical migrations. In addition, they were used as part of a landscape used to resist the state. Much like the threshing floors of Cyprus described by Given (2004), caves in Transjordan often became clandestine spaces, to provide activity areas that remained outside of the view of the state.

The mobility of Bedu, especially before the *Tanzimat*, made it easy to circumvent state monitoring efforts. The use of caves, along with their ability to move camp, was part of a strategy used to underrepresent produce, hide taxable livestock, or even hide potential conscripts. More importantly, moving through the landscape but using caves to obscure that activity meant that the state could not fully concentrate its efforts to settle their Bedu subjects.

There are hundreds of caves of varying shapes and sizes located within a few miles of Hisban, and a large percentage have been surveyed over the past 30 years by the Hisban team of the Madaba Plains Project (see LaBianca 1990, 2000; Walker and LaBianca 2003). Although there are many caves scattered throughout the area, one cave located just to the south of the two story farmhouse structure at Hisban is of special note (Fig. 5.5). This cave contains several activity areas, including a corral for animals, and a large subterranean structure inside, which was most probably an old cistern repurposed as a storage installation. This feature was connected to the farmhouse itself, and the only entrance into the structure is located from above, from inside the building. The subterranean structure was used as a grain silo and was part of the official storage space of the complex.

However, local ethnographic accounts consistently describe caves as a space where tribal groups hid goods and produce (and sometimes themselves!) specifically from Ottoman officials and tax collectors (Oestgaard et al. 2003: 460; see also Chaudoir and Habash, n.d.; LaBianca 1990). The use and modification of natural caves provided spaces to hide and underreport produce to those they were indebted to – the state, or even to absentee landlords. The continued use of caves in the region of *Qasr Hisban* points to resistance to state policies, as the Ajarma continued to maintain traditional modes of production.

Resistance to oppression is multifaceted, however. As Given argues (2004: 164) this may include "open rebellion, operating a hidden economy, and maintaining your self-respect." This last possibility – that the changes in the landscape at *Qasr Hisban* point toward the displacement of Bedu – may also be seen in new light, as an attempts to negotiate their positions within a new global capitalist economy, and decide with whom they wanted to make those negotiations (Kasaba 2009). At Hisban, the Ajarma entered into global economic networks through their interactions with the Nabulsi family.

Bedu had, throughout the period, been suppliers of goods for the Ottoman state, such as dairy and meat, wool products, and carpets. However, as tribes began to tap

into global trade networks that could be more profitable, they moved away from existing imperial trade networks (Kasaba 2009). Instead, they worked with the urban merchant class, who also offered the opportunities to engage in global networks of exchange. Tribal groups began to expand on new political and economic opportunities independently, and outside of the state's control, as they facilitated the production and flow of goods and services for an expanding global market (Kasaba 2009).

While it is possible that Bedu might have used caves to circumvent taxes and the state, it is clear that they dealt directly with the merchant settlers who were able to link them to expanding trade networks in urban centers at al-Salt and beyond. The Ajarma had little choice in this process of cycles of indebtedness. But the use of the farmstead complex itself could be used to their advantage, as an important social space. The *Qasr* was used as a space not only to forge relationships with a visiting landlord but also to serve as a local political center.

Although Nabulsi was the landlord and therefore the legal and legitimized owner of *Qasr Hisban*, he maintained the family residence in al-Salt. Therefore, it was the Ajarma who would – more often than Nabulsi – use this space. This was an important strategy to maintain local standing, as local leaders, merchants, Bedu, and *fellahin* would all gather in these complexes.

According to Abujaber (1989), farmstead complexes in the Balqa' became seats of local power for tribal leaders, and places to negotiate the politics of daily life. Hospitality often involved dedicated spaces such as the *madafa*, or guesthouses. In Transjordan, the guesthouse was (and continues to be) an important space, specifically used to provide an arena for receiving guests, conducting business, and making political negotiations (e.g., AbuJaber 1989: 158–159; Antoun 2000; Bell 1907, 1914; Carroll 2004, 2005; McQuitty 2004). The guesthouse can be a separate structure, used specifically for its intended purpose of extending hospitality.

Qasr Hisban, however, did not have a specific guesthouse like larger complexes, villages, and towns did. Instead, the domestic spaces were multifunctional, although the top floor of *Beyt Nabulsi* is still referred to as the *madafa* even today – even though it no longer functions as such. Still, *Qasr Hisban* provided a new arena to conduct business and host visitors; even in the face of large scale forces of colonialism and capitalism, local politics were played out in these settings, and the new built environment provided a spatial context for tribal cooperation and political negotiations.

Conclusions

Capitalist investment in agriculture, and a state policy that encouraged private ownership of land, led to major changes in the landscape of Transjordan, specifically with the construction of large farmstead complexes. The transition from a predominantly pastoral economy to one that included intensive agriculture within a capitalist context helped the Ottoman state in its long-term attempt to settle its nomadic population.

While the *Tanzimat* opened up the frontier for investment, how that transformed the lives of Bedu took on local meanings. The imposition of the Land Code of 1858 and the creation of private landholding; intensive agricultural production; and the changing attitudes toward mobile populations during the *Tanzimat* all brought a series of shifting social relations between landowners, the state, and Bedu.

The dynamics that played out at *Qasr Hisban* illustrates how the Ajarma dealt with two processes that were closing in on their world on a daily basis – specifically colonial definitions of civilization and progress, and capitalist investment, alienation, and potential displacement from pastureland. Yet, even as the Bedu faced these global processes, they utilized features of the natural and built landscape to their advantage at the local level.

Acknowledgments Archaeological survey for this study was supported by the 2001 Tall Hisban investigations of the Madaba Plains Project Consortium. This work would not be possible without the continued support and dialogues I have enjoyed over the years with Bethany Walker (Missouri State University) and Sten LaBianca (Andrews University), and the hard work of their many team members, especially Lean Fakhouri (University of Jordan) and her team who conducted the architectural study of *Beyt Nabulsi during* the 2001 field season. I am also grateful to Sarah Croucher and Lindsay Weiss for inviting me to contribute to this volume, and for their comments and suggestions. This work has benefited from all of their help, while all omissions and errors are the author's alone.

References

Abujaber, Raouf S. 1989 *Pioneers Over Jordan: The Frontier of Settlement in Transjordan, 1850–1914*. I.B. Tauris and Co. Ltd., London.

Ahmad, Ahmad S., Dalia al-Huseini, Diala 'Anbatawi, and Ola Musa. 2001 *Mabani Qaryat Hisban*. Manuscript on file, Madaba Plains Project, Hesban Expedition, Horn Archaeological Museum, Andrews University, Berrien Springs.

Al-Nimr. 1938 *Tarikh Jabal Nablus wa al-Balqa'* Volume I.

Amiran, D.H.K. 1953 The Pattern of Settlement in Palestine. *Israel Exploration Journal* 3(2): 65–78.

Antoun, Richard. 2000 Civil Society, Tribal Process and Change in Jordan. *International Journal of Middle East Studies* 32(4): 441–463

Baram, Uzi. 2007 Images of the Holy Land: The David Roberts Paintings as Artifacts of 1830s Palestine. *Historical Archaeology* 41(2): 108–119.

Baram, Uzi. 2009 Above and Beyond Ancient Mounds: The Archaeology of the Modern Periods in the Middle East and Eastern Mediterranean. In *International Handbook of Historical Archaeology*, edited by Teresita Majewski and David Gaimster, pp. 647–662. Springer, New York.

Baram, Uzi and Carroll, Lynda (editors). 2000 *A Historical Archaeology of the Ottoman Empire: Breaking New Grounds*. Kluwer Academic/Plenum Press, New York.

Bell, Gertrude L. 1914 *The Diaries of Gertrude Bell, 1868–1926*. Electronic document, http://www.gerty.ncl.ac.uk/, accessed March 25, 2010. Robinson Library, University of Newcastle.

Bell, Gertrude L. 1907 *Syria, the Desert & the Sown*. E.P. Dutton and Co., New York.

Bernard, Hans and Wendrich, Willeke. 2008 *Archaeology of Mobility: Old World and New World Nomadism*. Cotsen Institute of Archaeology, Los Angeles, CA.

Bernbeck, Reinhard. 2008 An Archaeology of Multisited Communities. In *Archaeology of Mobility: Old World and New World Nomadism*, edited by Hans Bernard, Hans and Willeke Wendrich, pp. 43–77. Cotsen Institute of Archaeology, Los Angeles, CA.

Carroll, Lynda. 2008 Sowing the Seeds of Modernity on the Ottoman Frontier: Agricultural Investment and the Formation of Large Farms in Nineteenth-Century Transjordan. *Archaeologies: Journal of the World Archaeological Congress* 4(2): 233–249.

Carroll, Lynda. 2005 *An Archaeology of Hospitality: Travelers, Tribes and Fortified Farmsteads in Late Ottoman Period Transjordan*. Paper presented at the joint Conference on Historical and Underwater Archaeology and Society for Post-Medieval Archaeology, York, England.

Carroll, Lynda. 2004 *Political Economy of Fortified Farmsteads in Late Ottoman Period Transjordan*. Paper presented at the Annual Meeting of the American Schools of Oriental Research, San Antonio.

Carroll, Lynda, Adam Fenner and Øystein S. LaBianca, 2006 The Ottoman *Qasr* at Hisban: Architecture, Reform and New Social Relations. *Near Eastern Archaeology* 69(3–4): 138–145.

Chaudoir, David and Khaled Habash. n.d. *History of the Qasr, and its Caves, in Hisban*. Unpublished report on file with the Madaba Plains Project – Hisban Excavations, Andrews University, Berrien Springs, Michigan.

Conder, C.R. 1892 *Heth and Moab: Explorations in Syria in 1881 and 1882*. Watt, London.

Cribb, Roger. 1991 *Nomads in Archaeology*. Cambridge University Press, Cambridge.

Deringil, Selim. 2003 "They Live in a State of Nomadism and Savagery": The Late Ottoman Empire and the Post-Colonial Debate. *Society for Comparative Study of Society and History* 45(3): 311–342.

Deringil, Selim. 1998 *The Well-Protected Domains: Ideology and the Legitimation of Power in the Ottoman Empire 1876–1909*. I.B. Tauris & Co Ltd, London.

Ferch, A.R., M. B. Russell, and W. K. Vyhmeister. 1989 *Hisban 3: Historical Foudations: Studies of Literary References to Hisban and Vicinity*. Andrews University Press, Berrien Springs.

Fenner, Adam and Øystein S. LaBianca. 2004 *Was Hisban a Throne Village during Ottoman Period times?* Paper presented at the Annual Meeting of the American Schools of Oriental Research, San Antonio.

Fischbach, Michael. 2000 *State Society & Land in Jordan*. Brill Academic Publishers, Leiden.

Funari, Pedro Paulo A., Martin Hall, and Siân Jones (editors). 1999 *Historical Archaeology: Back From the Edge*. Routledge, London.

Given, Michael. 2004 *The Archaeology of the Colonized*. Routledge, London.

Gosden, Chris. 2001 'Postcolonial Archaeology: Issues of Culture, Identity, and Knowledge.' In *Archaeological Theory Today*, edited by Ian Hodder, pp. 241–261. Polity Press, Cambridge, MA.

Gosden, Chris. 1999 *Anthropology and Archaeology: A Changing Relationship*. Routledge, New York.

Green, Molly. 2005 The Ottoman Experience. *Dædalus* Spring 2005: 88–99.

Hall, Martin. 2000 *Archaeology and the Modern World: Colonial Transcripts in South Africa and the Chesapeake*. Routledge, London.

Hütteroth, W. and K. Abdulfattah. 1977 *Historical Geography of Palestine, Transjordan and Southern Syria in the Late 16th Century*. Erlangen: Selbstverlag der Frankischen Geographischen Gesellschaft in Kommission bei Palm und Enke.

İzzed, Mehmed. 1890 *Yeni Afrika*. Interpreter for the Imperial Palace. P. 2.

Johns, Jeremy. 1994 The Longue Durée: State and Settlement Strategies in Southern Transjordan Across the Islamic Centuries. In *Village, Steppe and State: The Social Origins of Modern Jordan*, edited by Eugene L. Rogan and T. Tell, pp. 1–13. British Academic Press, London.

Johnson, Matthew. 1999 Rethinking Historical Archaeology. In *Historical Archaeology: Back From the Edge*, edited by Pedro Paulo Funari, Martin Hall, and Siân Jones, pp. 23–36. Routledge, London.

Kana'an, R. 1993 *Patronage and Style in Mercantile Residential Architecture of Ottoman Bilad Al-Sham: The Nablus Region in the Nineteenth Century*. Unpublished Master's Thesis, Oxford University, UK.

Kasaba, Reşat. 2009 *A Moveable Empire: Ottoman Nomads, Migrants, and Refugees*. University of Washington Press, Seattle.

Kasaba, Reşat. 1988 *The Ottoman Empire and the World Economy: The Nineteenth Century*. State University of New York Press, Albany.

Khammash, A. 1986 *Notes on Village Architecture in Jordan*. University of South Western Louisiana Press, Lafayette.

LaBianca, Øystein. S. 1990 *Sedentarization and Nomadization: Food System Cycles at Hisban and Vicinity in Transjordan*. Hisban 1. Institute of Archaeology and Andrews University Press, Berrien Springs.

LaBianca, Øystein. S. 2000 Daily Life in the Shadow of Empire: A Food Systems Approach to the Archaeology of the Ottoman Empire. In *A Historical Archaeology of the Ottoman Empire: Breaking New Ground*, edited by Uzi Baram and Lynda Carroll, pp. 203–218. Plenum Press, New York.

Lewis, N. 1987 *Nomads and Settlers in Syria and Jordan 1800–1980*. Cambridge University Press, Cambridge.

McQuitty, Allison. 2004 The Architecture of Hospitality: A *madâfâh* in Northern Jordan. In *From handaxe to Khan : essays presented to Peder Mortensen on the occasion of his 70th birthday*, edited by Kjeld von Folsach, Henrik Thrane & Ingolf Thuesen, pp. 255–264. Arhaus University Press, Denmark.

McQuitty, Allison. 2005 The Rural Landscape of Jordan in the seventh-nineteenth centuries AD: the Kerak Plateau. *Antiquity* 79: 327–338.

Mundy, Martha. 1996 *'Qada'* 'Ajlun in the Late nineteenth Century: Interpreting the Region from the Ottoman Land Registers. *Levant* 28: 77–98.

Oestgaard, Terje, Lynda Carroll and Øystein S. LaBianca. 2003 Field G. In The Islamic Qusur of Tall Hisban: Preliminary Report on the 1998 and 2001 Seasons, edited by Bethany Walker and Øystein LaBianca. *ADAJ – The Annual of the Department of Antiquities, Jordan.* 47: 443–471.

Orser, Charles E. Jr. 1996 *A Historical Archaeology of the Modern World*. Plenum Press, New York.

Palmer, Carol. 1999 Whose Land is it Anyway? An historical examination of land tenure and agriculture in Northern Jordan. In *The Prehistory of Food: Appetites for Change*, edited by Chris Gosden and J. Hather, pp. 288–305. Routledge, London.

Pamuk, Şevket. 1987 *The Ottoman Empire and European Capitalism 1820–1913: Trade, Investment and Production*. Cambridge University Press, Cambridge.

Prag, Kay. 1990 A Walk in the Wadi Hesban. *Palestine Exploration Quarterly pp. 48–61*

Rogan, Eugene L. 1999 *Frontiers of the State in the Late Ottoman Empire: Transjordan, 1850–1921*. Cambridge University Press, Cambridge.

Rogan, Eugene L. 1994 Bringing the State Back: The Limits of Ottoman Rule in Jordan, 1840–1910, in *Village, Steppe and State: The Social Origins of Modern Jordan*, edited by Eugene L. Rogan and Tariq Tell, pp. 32–57. British Academic Press, London.

Rogan, Eugene L. 1992 Moneylending and Capital Flows from Nablus, Damascus, and Jerusalem to Qada al-Salt in the Last Decades of Ottoman Rule. In *The Syrian Land in the 18th and 19th Century*, edited by Thomas Philipp. Berliner Islamstudien, Bd. 5: Franz Steiner Verlag, Stuttgart.

Russell, Malcolm. 1989 Hisban During the Arab Period: A.D. 635 to the Present. In *Hisban 3: Historical Foundations: Studies of Literary References to Hisban and Vicinity*, edited by Larry Geraty and L. G. Running, pp. 25–35. Andrews University Press, Berrien Springs.

Said, Edward. 1978 *Orientalism*. Vintage Books, New York.

Salt Development Corporation. 1990 *Salt: A Plan for Action*. Vol. 1. June.

Schmidt, Peter R. and Jonathan R.Walz. 2007 Re-Representing African Pasts through Historical Archaeology. *American Antiquity* 72(1): 53–70.

Walker, Bethany J. 1999 Militarization to Nomadization: The Middle and Late Islamic Periods. *Near Eastern Archaeology* 62(4): 202–232.

Walker, Bethany J. and Øystein S. LaBianca. 2003 The Islamic Qusūr of Tall Hisbān: Preliminary Report on the 1998 and 2001 Seasons. *ADAJ Annual of the Department of Antiquities, Jordan* 47: 443–471.

Chapter 6
Uneven Topographies: Archaeology of Plantations and Caribbean Slave Economies

Mark W. Hauser

Introduction

Thirty five years of archaeological examinations in former British West Indian colonies have revealed that there is a substantial material record of slavery between from the mid-seventeenth century up until the second quarter of the nineteenth century. This material record is manifest in documents written about colonial enterprises by metropolitan administrators, the landscapes envisioned and produced by settlers in the colonies, and the everyday forms of material culture that comprise the archaeological record of plantation life. Capitalism, modernity, and race have provided the primary narratives to frame the discussion of this material record. While these grand narratives are important for understanding the Caribbean colonial experience and the expression of social relations through material remains, ultimately they relegate the totality of Caribbean life to a by-product of rather monolithically conceived forces unleashed in the metropole, instead of understanding the complexities that may have shaped everyday life in colonial Jamaica. Indeed, individuals in colonial Jamaica inhabited and fashioned their selves in worlds that were shaped by multiple and complex forces that are not adequately addressed in studies focused on tracing the workings of rather monolithically conceived models of capitalism and modernity. Such studies also tend to privilege contemporary concerns – such as mapping the development of twentieth century capitalism and modernity with their concomitant forms of inequality – and don't pay enough attention to the needs, interests, and concerns that may have been most important in the everyday lives of the enslaved in colonial Jamaica.

This is not to dismiss the importance of the analytical categories these studies bring to bear. Certainly, looking at commodities and the ways in which social relations can be defined through their production, circulation, and ultimate consumption is important.

M.W. Hauser (✉)
Department of Anthropology, Northwestern University, Chicago, IL, USA
e-mail: mark-hauser@northwestern.edu

S.K. Croucher and L. Weiss (eds.), *The Archaeology of Capitalism in Colonial Contexts*, 121
Contributions To Global Historical Archaeology, DOI 10.1007/978-1-4614-0192-6_6,
© Springer Science+Business Media, LLC 2011

Wealth was accumulated through the alienation of individuals from their labor. Similarly, ideas of progress were important in framing best practices of colonial settlement and eighteenth century agrarian economics. The following questions must be asked though: Did the enslaved laborers, as subjects of capitalism and conscripts to modernity, (1) accumulate wealth and deploy labor in ways anticipated by mercantile logics established in the metropole and (2) view progress in the same way as European thinkers and metropolitan administrators? While the second question is difficult to infer from the archaeological record, the first question can be approached through a detailed analysis of the ways in which people made a living off land they did not own.

In fact, the record shows a diversity of practices that are not easily aggregated into such monolithic models of capitalist development and modernity. There was in fact a tremendous diversity of social, cultural, economic practices in colonial Jamaica, and colonial/postcolonial models, or models of capitalism/modernity, only capture a part of that diversity. Archaeology, with its attention to diverse material traces as opposed to imperial records, is central to capturing and analyzing this diversity. Landscapes, architecture, and artifacts for us to expand and play with our scales of analysis introduces other kinds of sources that help us read against the grain and show how geographically disparate worlds are connected through material relationships.

In this chapter, I show how the archaeology of slavery in the Caribbean sheds light on these kinds of diverse practices. In the first section, I discuss the ways in which the categories of analysis introduced by capitalism and modernity are useful at least in terms of understanding parts of the archaeological record. These analyses rely largely on categories established through the documentary record housed in imperial archives. They reveal insights into colonial attitudes to efficiency and power and reveal anxieties about colonial subjects and the internal contradictions of slave society. In the second section, I show how those material things, born of colonial life, allow a certain reading against the grain. While commodities are important, they are not configured only through rules established in metropolitan Europe.

Metropolitan Archives and Colonies

Bernard Cohn suggested that the imperial point of view was a "view from the boat" and enabled a body of scholarship arguing that ideology could indeed be a form of practice (1980). Indeed, such insights generated a vast body of postcolonial scholarship analyzing the very foundations of capitalism and modernity through interrogations of the interrelated concepts of race and labor. Here, the mapping of imperial prescriptions and everyday practice become a mechanism of moving anthropology beyond a method and theory of ahistorical practice. The Caribbean plantation colony was built out of the material processes of slavery and markets and has drawn scholars wishing to interrogate the very foundations of some of modernity's dominant ideologies: capitalism and racism. While the Caribbean plantation colony was at industrial capitalism's doorstep, its administrators had to account for diversity in economic networks in which the colony's planters and enslaved participated. Variations on the themes initially drawn by Eric Williams in *Capitalism and Slavery* (1961) have led many to argue that such colonies were capitalism's "first least-camouflaged expression" (Blackburn 1997a: 554) and its enslaved inhabitants, the world's "first conscripts to modernity" (Scott 2003). Likewise, many have argued that regimentation of trade through treaties, legal statutes, and precedent shaped colonial subjects through the kinds of economic interaction prescribed.

Much of this work has been carried out through the extensive analysis of materials archived in metropolitan and postcolonial centers. These have included the quotidian accounts of overseers and planters managing labor, balancing books, and marking transactions; the use of representational texts such as landscapes and maps to discern the placemaking of the Caribbean plantations as both a site of labor and exploitation and as part of a larger scenic economy, and legal codes as a way to get at those governing practices that attempted to mediate between imperial prescriptions of parliamentarians and financiers and the day-to-day realities of colonial administration. Although they have limitations, these have proved incredibly useful artifacts of shared practice in understanding the colonial Caribbean.

Perhaps one of the most enduring ideological dimensions to have emerged from slavery was the institutionalization of difference based on phenotypic characteristics. While some have argued that there is a European prehistory to the kind of racialization that emerged during the late seventeenth and early eighteenth century (Davis 1966, 1997; Sweet 1997), many agree that the idea of race was born out of the material practices of European colonialism and chattel slavery. If we turn to the Spanish speaking world, mixed racial categories – noted famously in the Mexican *casta* paintings – represented metropolitan reactions to choices made by colonial subjects. Perhaps there is more than a little truth in Eric Williams' observation that "slavery was not born of racism: rather, racism was the consequence of slavery" (1944: 7) where surveillance, alienation, and classification became regimes that enabled the plantation economies of the Caribbean to work (Blackburn 1997b).

In Jamaica, we are limited in our ability to discuss the ramifications of promulgated codes, architectural space, and material practice in the seventeenth century due to a paucity of archaeological sites with discrete components. While ongoing projects are seeking to discern in greater detail the material life of plantations (Galle Jillian 2010), for the most part our understanding of colonial Jamaica/plantation society comes from the settlements of Port Royal and Seville Estate. The attraction of the "sunken city" in Port Royal has fostered a considerable amount of archaeological research into the early colonial period, ranging from amateur investigations focused on the "pirate port" to intensive and systematic investigations seeking to recover and re-create the seventeenth-century port city landscape. Most notable is the multiyear project conducted by Donny Hamilton of Texas A&M University and the Institute for Nautical Archaeology, which resulted in a number of articles focusing on the merchants and craft producers of Port Royal, as well as a number of theses and dissertations specializing in specific sets of material culture (see Armstrong and Hauser 2009).

In the case of Seville, we have a more ready comparison with the Virginia case described above. Doug Armstrong highlights in his discussion of Seville Plantation (1992, 1998, 1999; Armstrong and Kelly 2000) that the owners of the English estate, the Hemmings family, had already established their sugar plantation in St. Ann's Bay by the time the earthquake struck. The organization of the estate was similar to those idealized settlements of the eighteenth century where the laborer's village, the time keeper's house, and the estate owner's house were all separated by space and organized in a way that betrays, to a certain extent, the efficiencies required for sugar cultivation. While race is potentially a factor in understanding the organization of the estate, the difference in intensity and magnitude of the kind of slavery taking place in Jamaica requires a shifting of our definition of race.

In legislative terms, early codes do evoke categories that we consider racialized today. Attempts at regulating market activities by enslaved laborers can be seen as early as the seventeenth century:

> … some little disturbance … had happened at Passage Fort on Saturday night last with the Negroes at this Market which if not prevented might in time grow. …Upon consideration whereof the Board being of Opinion that the liberty given to Negroes to give a Market at the River Mouth and Passage Fort every Saturday had been an Occasion of that disturbance. (Council of Jamaica 1678)

These "little" disturbances highlight a general disorder that many elites perceived as a product of the informal economic activities of the enslaved. Ultimately, the enslaved were never trusted with property. In 1662 and 1678, laws attempted to abate the practice of stealing imported consumables and selling them back in the street markets.

During the eighteenth century, this reaction to the sale of stolen items is iterated and reiterated in a succession of codes concerning peddling, including laws passed by the Assembly in 1711, 1730, 1735 (Jamaica 1743), 1749 (Jamaica 1786), 1786, 1788, and 1793 (Jamaica 1793). In essence, these laws permit "Mulattoe, Indian, or Negro" (Jamaica 1738a, b) to hawk "provisions, fruits, and other enumerated articles" (Long [1774] 1970), "provided the persons have a Ticket from the Master or Owner of such Goods" (Jamaica 1738a, b: 294), "in which Ticket is to be expressed their Name, from whence, and whither going" (Leslie 1740), and "upon complaint and conviction before a justice, to be whipped by order of such justice" (Long [1774] 1970).

In these laws, we see not only a circumscription of economic activity among the enslaved, but also an identification of opposition between formal and informal markets: those run by property-owning (renting) white merchants who must pay taxes, and those (implied as people of African extraction) who are not subjected to the same demands. In the preamble of Act 106 of the 1735 code, we see these politics play out proscriptions based on race:

> Whereas divers Mulattoes, Indians, and Negroes, have of late been frequently employed in hawking and selling, from Place to Place, all Manner of Goods, Wares, and Merchandize which are commonly used and sold in this island; which Practice tends to manifest Prejudice of Trade, and great Discouragement of House-keepers, who are subject to Parochial Duties, Taxes, and Rents for their Houses: be it therefore enacted … That no Mulattoe, Indian, or

Negro whatsoever, shall hawk, or carry about to sell, from Place to Place, or shall sell in any open Street or Market, any sort of Goods, Wares, or Merchandize whatsoever. (Jamaica 1738a, b: 223)

The non-European participants are seen as parasitic to the overall economic well-being of the island, even though it is well known, or at least generally understood, that the division in economic activity is not so rigid and, as I have argued elsewhere (Hauser 2008), such activities were central to the plantation economy.

Market sellers, who did not have to pay taxes or rent, were seen as predatory. In the minds of colonial writers such as Edward Long, Brian Edwards, and William Beckford, they seditiously profited from the hard work of poor white settlers and dependents who played by the rules. By championing the cause of settlers and dependents, administrators successfully embedded and imbued the market with connotations of illegality and conspiracy. Indeed, many administrators blamed factors, planters, and slaves. Describing the differences between merchants and peddlers, Patrick Browne states:

The Merchants import their own goods, and run the risque of the markets; but generally turn to pedlars in the disposal of them; the business was, indeed, beneficial while they could supply the neighboring markets ... and the next class [pedlars] is entirely engrossed by the factors, who generally import such commodities as are commonly wanted at a plantation. (Browne [1759] 1789: 24)

In this case, hardworking merchants are undermined by the collusion of wholesalers and peddlers who cornered the market on imported commodities and imposed inflated prices on settlers and dependents.

What becomes paramount to understanding these statements about the enslaved are issues of political economy, social transformations, and local responses to global colonialism and capitalism. Discourses articulating the inferior nature or character of the enslaved provided a solution to the problem of labor management. Such discourses made it easier to make decisions on where to house the enslaved, what to feed them, and how to manage the product of the labor in ways that would maximize capital accumulation and boost the position, wealth, and control of European powers. Creating an other, to rephrase Williams, is a consequence of European capitalism, and most especially of its economic centerpiece – the colonial plantation.

Planters, through the apparatus of colonial government, manipulation of organized living and working space, and some economic maneuvering, vied to control and discipline the everyday life of the laborers. While in Great Britain merchants were disciplining the consumption of sugar by processing it in ways to make it more appealing for the nascent working class, planters were disciplining enslaved laborers to create the raw materials of its production (Mintz 1985). As such the plantation, conceived of generally as an institution and specifically as a site of production, was the center of power through which populations in these hinterlands were both directly and indirectly controlled. This control was both economic and social and provided the structure through which to understand the history of peoples in the Caribbean. Perhaps because of a tendency to simplify peoples and economies in what Elsa Goviea calls the slave society (Goviea 1965, 1970), and also because of the desire to make explicit the underlying inequality of the colonial system built on slavery, versions of the "Pure Plantation Model" (Best 1998, see discussion in conclusion) emphasize the repressive economic control over people. At the macroeconomic scale, one cannot overstate the implications of such a regional, if not global, system. Laws were written to proscribe against acts that might endanger the slave regime (Goviea 1970; Patterson 1969).

Capitalism taken as an accumulation of wealth or as the frames in which labor is developed and deployed has material implications for the colonial landscapes of Jamaica. Barry Higman's work on plats (manuscript estate plans) between 1750 and 1880 in Jamaica is one of the earliest attempts to engage these concepts through the physicality of the plantation (1986a, b, 1987, 1988). These plats were in themselves mechanisms through which colonial regimes surveilled and controlled agro-industrial production (1986a). Higman noted that the organization of plantation space varied depending on region, sources of power (wind, water, or cattle mills) and commodity (1986b, 1987, 1988). Indeed, while notable differences exist in the patterns of coffee and sugar estate layouts (1986b: 73), a unifying and significant factor in the industrial layout of the sugar estate (1986a: 17) and coffee estates (1986b: 76) was an economy of movement (1986a: 17), thus placing these specific localities within larger capitalist regimes of production. Probably the most well-documented study of the ways in which European colonialism and capitalism became inscribed on the landscape comes from James Delle's work on Blue Mountain coffee plantations in Jamaica (1998, 1999, 2000a, b, 2001, 2002). In this study, Delle sets out to define the ways in which European ideologies interwoven in emergent capitalism were inscribed on these colonial landscapes. Arguing against approaches in economic history in which economic efficiency was the primary measure of analysis (Higman 1986a, b, 1987, 1988), Delle joins a series of scholars in demonstrating the ways in which European capitalism regimented the daily lives of colonial subjects (1998, 1999, 2000a).

While assemblages at Seville plantation highlight the accumulation of material wealth among the enslaved (described later in the paper) an examination of the utilization of space over time reveals an accretion of different strategies. Seville estate is located about 1 km west of St. Ann's Bay on Jamaica's north coast. It is located on the major coastal road that connects Ocho Rios with Montego Bay. In the eighteenth century, it would have been approximately 61 miles from Spanish Town. Like plantations described by Higman, it was also a sugar estate and was initially organized to maximize the economic efficiency of the plantation. The great house rests on the top of a hill leading up into the mountains and has a commanding view of St. Ann's Bay. The plantation is located near a stream that provided fresh water to the plantation and the fields, and power to the sugar works. Seville was first owned by Richard Hemming in 1670, and it was continually occupied up until the 1890s. Maps of the plantation, which date between 1721 and 1791, show significant changes in the spatial layout of the plantation. The early enslaved village existed southeast of the planter's residence. The 1791 map shows a new location for the village. By tracing shifts in household and village arrangements between the 1670s and the late nineteenth century, showing how house placement and architecture were "governed by the choices and actions of African Jamaican residents," rather than solely by the plantation owner (Armstrong and Kelly 2000).

While economic historians and examinations of space have demonstrated the saliency of labor and identity in understanding archaeological contexts associated with plantation slavery, archaeological analysis has demonstrated one must seek a broader suite of analogs than contemporary Europe to decipher the archaeological record.

Colonies as the Archives of Empires

In 1687 Hans Sloane, the noted British physician and naturalist whose collections formed the basis of the British Museum, spent 15 months in English Jamaica. In his account, he reports:

> On these Red Hills, four Miles from Town [Guanoboa], lived Mr. Barnes a Carpenter. … Half a Mile from his Plantation, 10 years ago, he found a Cave in which lay a human Body's Bones … the rest of the Cave was fill'd with Pots or Urns, wherein were Bones of Men and Children, the Pots were Oval, large, of redish dirty colour… The Negroes had remov'd most of these Pots to boil their Meat in. (Sloane 1707–1725, Volume 1:25)

Sloane was referring to pottery made several centuries earlier by the indigenous Taino who had been decimated under Spanish rule before the English occupied Jamaica in 1655 (Sauer 1966; Taylor 1965). Sloane visited Jamaica only 32 years after the English established their presence on the island. While in the context of the entire document, the above account could be read as a curiosity like the flora and fauna presented in subsequent chapters of his Natural History, at its most functional reading, this account seems to indicate that there was a demand for cooking pots by enslaved laborers. Specifically, it points to what may have been lacking in the infrastructures accounted and planned for in the imperial designs for plantation colonies. To feed their slaves, Jamaican planters allocated provision grounds in the mountainous areas where the enslaved were compelled to grow their own food (Delle 1998), but contemporary documents are relatively silent about the arrangements made by planters for provisioning enslaved laborers with cooking vessels (c.f. Meyers 1999). Is it possible that planters did not anticipate the need for cooking vessels?

Answering this question not only addresses this singular reading of Hans Sloane but also speaks to broader concerns of the ways in which colonies and subjects are managed and accounted for. Colonies are the archives (*sensu* Trouillot 1995) of empire in that they depositories of imperial knowledge, explicitly and implicitly organized in ways that betray relations of power, and are subject to differential preservation, which ultimately shapes the narratives of their unfolding. For many Caribbean colonies, these narratives inevitably return to the plantation as the ideological and material embodiment of society. This is not to define the history of colonial subjects only through the lens of slavery and establish the foundations of Caribbean society through the varied *Code Noirs* of different islands. Rather, it is to argue that we must not examine historical forces ahistorically, and seek out the larger contexts in which the particularities of what has been called modernity emerge. If colonies are the archives of empire, then archaeology gets at those most interesting bits of the archives, the little forgotten scraps of stuff at the bottom of the archive chest, and sometimes the artifacts that cannot be filed away into the neat categories created by the grand narratives produced about imperial regimes. Analysis of these kinds of archives require asking questions framed out of similar categories of analysis, but introduces interesting methodological questions: How do we establish economic participation – what did the majority of the population consume, make, and trade?

A Focus on Consumption

There is a particular theorizing of slavery as social death – slavery robbed people of social technologies, and stripped people of the cultural capacity to organize, manage and lead (Patterson 1982). The devastation of slavery did not create enduring cultures of poverty, corruption and crime. The archaeology of domestic contexts in plantation societies can be helpful in understanding these activities. While some elements such as plantation layout tend to be circumscribed to particular plantations, the archaeological assemblages in houseyards in plantation villages and tenements and servants quarters in the city tend to be constituted of a similar combination of goods made in Europe, North America, and locally. Such goods can constitute idioms of material expression that were refashioned either through alteration or assemblage into ways unexpected by those who organized their production (Fennell 2003, 2007a, b; Franklin and Fesler 1999; Leone and Fry 1999; Ogundiran and Falola 2007; Ruppel et al. 2003; Wilkie 1997, 2000). Here, rather than assuming the middle passage as a rupture in systems of knowledge and ways of doing things, it highlights that the eliding of cultural content is something that needs to be archaeologically demonstrated.

In the eighteenth century, many of the items that would have been documented in the home and houseyard of an enslaved laborer would have been of local production (Anonymous 1797; Armstrong 1990; Higman 1976; McDonald 1993). The imported goods present become difficult to use in tracing the extent of the markets because while records do document ports of entry, they are often not detailed enough to illustrate flow through the internal markets. These include items such as glass, refined earthenware, and metal objects. An additional ambiguity is introduced. While I do believe that many imported goods were purchased by enslaved laborers through the internal market system, there is evidence of planters gifting goods. Therefore, there would always be doubt about how an enslaved person acquired a specific imported good. At Seville Estate, in St Ann's bay Jamaica, discarded fragments from enslaved laborer house areas associated with the second half of the eighteenth century included domestic utensils such as ceramic tableware, ceramics used for storage and cooking, glass bottles, glassware/stemwares and iron cooking pots. They also included items of adornment such as buttons and beads, along with items associated with drug use and health. Comparing broad differences in the ways that materials were used can help us interpret different conditions of enslaved life in each of the contexts (Table 6.1)

Table 6.1 Proportion of a selection of recovered archaeological artifacts from House Area 16 (Digital Archaeological Archive of Comparative Slavery)

		Seville	
Cooking/storage	Local coarse earthenware	98	8.00%
	Spanish colonial	172	14.10%
	Iberian storage	2	0.20%
	Iron cooking pot	4	0.30%
	Glass bottles	28	2.30%
	Total	304	24.90%
Tableware	Slipware	50	4.10%
	Tin-glazed earthenware	178	14.60%
	Cream-colored ware	527	43.10%
	Slip dip stoneware	8	0.70%
	Porcelain	30	2.50%
	Glassware	9	0.70%
	Total	802	65.60%
Clothing and adornment	Buttons	19	1.60%
	Buckles	5	0.40%
	Beads	27	2.20%
	Total	51	4.20%
Drug/medicine	Tobacco	16	1.30%
	Pharmaceutical bottles	17	1.40%
	Total	33	2.70%

Of these materials, ceramics are an excellent unit of observation in the analysis of economic networks and idioms of social solidarity. First, ceramics are far less susceptible to the destructive processes that create archaeological sites. Second, 30 years of archaeological practice on plantation sites in the Caribbean has demonstrated that ceramics both local and imported are the most ubiquitous class of material in an archaeological assemblage (Handler and Lange 1978; Armstrong 1990; Deagan 2002; Howson 1990). Finally, there is variability in shape, form, and decoration of ceramics which enable one to track changes in time and space (social or geographic) (Skowronek 1987, 1992). Locally manufactured ceramics made by peoples (probably women) of African extraction have the added advantage that they can be used to reconstruct local trade in ways that are not possible with the European-made materials.

A Focus on Production

It is important to establish the independent production of peoples of African extraction in slave colonies such as Jamaica because it establishes that cultural capacities were not striped in the middle passage, and reveals the creativity of people confined by slavery, and the extension of definitions of labor during slavery. Here I focus on ceramics called *yabbas* to reveal not only the creative and productive capacities of the enslaved, but also the complex networks and social relations they enabled in colonial Jamaica.

In Jamaica the term "yabba" refers to several types of ceramics. *Yabbas* are a local coarse earthenware that people made as early as 1655 and continued to manufacture with different recipes in shaped in modified forms to the present day. They can be either glazed or slipped and the common attribute is that they are handmade (as opposed to wheel thrown) and are of local manufacture. Indeed, yabba type pottery can be made into a pot, a Spanish jar, a monkey jar, or a yabba. The form yabba refers to a large restricted-orifice, direct-rim bowl used to cook stews, rice, and fried foods. These ceramics were used by people of African descent, made by people of African descent, and most importantly sold in the internal markets of Jamaica (see Hauser 2008; Hauser and DeCorse 2003 for review of studies on this pottery).

Two contemporary descriptions exist for *yabbas*. In research conducted for his master's thesis, Roderick Ebanks interviewed, and documented pottery manufactured by, Ma Lou, Ms. Louisa Jones. The industry responsible for production of Jamaican pottery today is concentrated in family compounds and organized around female members of the family (Ebanks 1984). Ma Lou passed away in 1992, and her daughter, Munchie, took up her trade. Moira Vincentelli (2004) has recently interviewed and recorded the production of pottery by Munchie, Marlene Roden. Munchie learned the trade from her mother, a transmission of knowledge that seems to be rooted in kinship ties focused on matrifocal house yards (Ebanks 1984: 3; Vincentelli 2004: 125).

Archaeological excavations of sites occupied in eighteenth centuries have recovered numerous *yabba*-type pottery in three varieties based on differences in manufacture, surface treatment, and decoration. These include a variety that was coil made, fired in an open pit, and treated with a red slip and polished with a burnishing stone (Fig. 6.2). The second variety was coil made, treated with a lead glaze on the interior and fired in a kiln (Fig. 6.1). The third variety was formed from a slab, it remained untreated and fired at a relatively low temperature (Fig. 6.3). Our knowledge of pottery production in Jamaica during the eighteenth and nineteenth century is dependent on numerous complementary sources. These source include (1) contemporary travel accounts with brief mentions of ceramic manufacture, clays used by potters, or laws intended to either facilitate or proscribe independent production among the enslaved; (2) inference from ceramic sherds recovered from archaeological deposits that date to the eighteenth and nineteenth century and finally (3) by analogical reasoning, the documentation and scholarship of museologists and anthropologists in the twentieth and twenty-first centuries.

There are some references in published accounts from the eighteenth and nineteenth century identifying the presence of the ceramic and discussing its manufacture and use (Sloane 1707–1725; Long [1774] 1970; Edwards 1793; Anonymous 1797). While it is generally understood that such texts, used in isolation, are a flawed resource for the reconstruction of Jamaican society, they have been valuable sources of information to archaeologists in framing questions and isolating potential features (Armstrong 1990, 1990; Delle 1998, forthcoming; Reeves 1997). These accounts are incredibly useful in helping identify particular kinds of ceramics we find in

Fig. 6.1 Slipped and/or burnished water jar with handle. Yabba from the Marx Collection, Port Royal, Jamaica. Photograph by author

archaeological assemblages, and determining the way they were used. Jillian Galle of Monticello is now expanding on this research including nineteenth century sites.

It is, however, not very useful in identifying where or how the ceramics were made. For that, highly detailed and specific kinds of analysis are required to retrieve information often overlooked by contemporary writers. In my research, a combination of physical analysis and chemical analysis through ceramic petrography and INAA helped reveal the kinds of repeated gestures associated with ceramic production, and the potential places where it was produced Jillian Galle of Monticello is now expanding on this research including nineteenth century sites.

The results of the archaeological analysis of eighteenth century I conducted can be summarized as follows. First, petrographic studies indicate only a limited number of production locales for *yabbas*. Given the systems of control and the relative dearth of documentary evidence pertaining to their production these ordinary objects

Fig. 6.2 Glazed yabba with handle. Yabba from the Marx Collection, Port Royal, Jamaica.
Photograph by Author

Fig. 6.3 Untreated yabba with punctuated decoration. Yabba from the Marx Collection, Port
Royal, Jamaica. Photograph by Author

were produced with a relatively extraordinary intensity in this 100 year time period. Second, archaeological analysis indicates that all households had access to *yabbas* from all production locales indicating an Island wide system of exchange of *yabbas*. Given the ubiquity of this form of material culture in contexts associated with enslaved laborers, free persons and local administrators, it seems not only that the logicians of the colony never thought carefully about how food was going to be prepared, but also that this need was met locally – most likely through the productive capacities and ingenuity of enslaved and free women of African descent. Finally combining archaeological and ethnographic analysis allowed the probable delineation of three production locales. The fact that we identified three recipes allows us to infer a certain density of interaction centered everyday exchanges organized by free and enslaved people of African extraction. Ultimately, this shows the extent of everyday exchanges and their role in providing spaces for communication and exchange beyond the control of the planter.

A Focus on Circulation

The pots did not remain confined to the matrifocal household but became embedded in broader networks of exchange. They were exchanged, purchased, traded, and consumed over wide distances. Here, compositional analysis proved instrumental in showing (if only partially) the extent of these commercial activities. The clay pots moved, but not of themselves. They did so in fields of social relations. Street marketers were responsible for making the crucial link between the producers and the ultimate consumers of this pottery. In 1929 Mary Beckwith wrote, "Earthen bowls, hand-turned and covered with a rude glaze, are always to be had in the Kingston market" (Beckwith 1929, 47). In the early twentieth century, it appears that Lebanese and Syrian immigrants began to control the retail commerce in Jamaica (Nicholas 1986, pg. 55–56). Indeed in oral histories captured by Jerome and Henia Handler,

> If a woman was good at making yabbah she might produce several dozen a day. They were given to people to sell in town, "mostly Syrian", who would carry them down and make "100 percent profit". A small yabbah about five inches high, 8 inches across were sold to the seller at a shilling a dozen. The seller would sell them for 2 pence or threpence a piece.

Because of these accounts we have a clear discussion of the ways that this particular ceramic was sold at least in the twentieth century. Such ethnographic accounts (written between 100 and 150 years after emancipation) demonstrate that goods produced for local circulations are as iconic a commodity as those shipped across oceans. Here we have a commodity that is tradition-bound, matrifocal in production, and geared towards profit on twentieth century street markets. There is nothing alternative about the purchasing of the product – it was one of many items open to purchase for the twentieth century woman in search of a cooking vessel.

What interested me about these markets is the infrastructure it provided. First they provided the infrastructure that enabled planters to have enslaved Africans use their own labor to feed and fend for themselves. Second they created the infrastructure through which the loosely linked network of higglers and markets not only circulated goods, but also perhaps information. The markets provided a space for information to be passed, solidarities to be built, and social action to be orchestrated. What follows are two examples – first an examination of the circulation of goods within a plantation colony, followed by an examination of circulation between colonies.

Market activity undertaken by higglers embodied the local economy, in that the trade was one of island-produced goods and the islands' shores circumscribed the flow of the commodities. The higglers themselves were also local, in that they had mastered the various physical and economic geographies of Jamaica. They could move seamlessly between plantation and city and between provision ground and market. This mobility allowed the higglers to develop an expertise in the various demands and supplies for local produce on the island – a knowledge not shared by the planter. In a sense, they were a very localized version of what Mary Helms has described as "long distance specialists of various sorts who make it their business to go away and return with tangible and intangible rewards" (Helms 1988: 3). For the enslaved, circumscribed by the obligations of laboring on plantation grounds 6 days a week, the distances traversed by higglers were great. Conversely, for the planters who did not know the provision ground trails or the unwritten rules of the informal trade, the higglers' knowledge was equally "esoteric." Such knowledge made a higgler a potentially dangerous sort of person who could control the market and pass information outside the gaze of the planter.

When Adam Smith wrote The Wealth of Nations, he argued that higgling (the bargaining of prices up) and haggling (the bargaining of prices down) were two elements in a homeostatic system that results in the imperfect valuation of commodities and labor:

> In exchanging indeed the different productions of different sorts of labour for one another, some allowance is commonly made for both. It is adjusted, however, not by any accurate measure, but by the higgling and bargaining of the market, according to that sort of rough equality which, though not exact, is sufficient for carrying on the business of common life. (Smith [1776] 1994: 1.5.5)

In the absence of haggling, or bargaining the price down, a monopoly on the part of sellers is complete. Because of their mastery of the interstitial spaces of Jamaica, and their ability to move between and beyond the bounded localities of Jamaica, higglers, at least from the perspective of the planter, were able to create an imbalanced hold on the market for island produce.

Implicit in the definition of higgler is an opprobrium in which the actors have mastered "the 'art of bargaining' in the absence of competition" (Brown 1994: 66). The term, derived from the older form, to haggle, has been in use in the English language at least since the seventeenth century. In 1797, Thomas Sheridan's dictionary, *A Complete Dictionary of the English Language*, defined a Higgler as "One who sells provisions by retail". According to the *Oxford English Dictionary*, early in its use, connotations of the word included the linking of urban populations with hinterland goods (see DeFoe 1895 [1756]: 140) and the "forestalling" of those goods for a captive set of consumers (see Ellis 1744: 70; Henry Fielding's *Tom Jones* 1791: 168). Today, the term is considered a Jamaican one, at least in Jamaica (see Cassidy and LePage 1967: 225), and indeed was in common usage when Sidney Mintz (1955), Sidney Mintz and Douglas Hall (1970), as well as Margaret Katzin (1959a, b, 1960), wrote their initial articles describing the origins and practice of the internal market system. In the eighteenth century, however, it does not seem to be a term used to class this specific group of itinerant country peddlers linking the provision grounds with the city markets. In the eighteenth century, a variety of terms are used, including hawkers, peddlers, and forestallers (Jamaica 1735). It is not until the very end of the eighteenth century and the early nineteenth century that higgler is used to describe this petite bourgeoisie (Kingston Ordinances 1803 cited in Simmonds 2004: 289).

There is a reconfiguration of the sites of production and of consumption here. The towns, Kingston and Spanishtown, were sites of economic and political authority for the planters, their representatives, and merchants. Drawing an analogy with Watson's and Smith's work in Bridge Port, sites of cosmopolitan consumption sat in sumptuary competition with metropolitan Europe (2009). Plantations as places where sugar cane and coffee were grown and processed fueled that consumption with the money from its profits. The transactional schema follows a classic schema from plantation to metropole to colonial town. Value is assigned, at least in theory in metropole. However, when we refocus our gaze on the movement of *yabbas* and other local goods, we see the roles reversed. The town becomes the site of production and the plantation a site of consumption. We should therefore try and elicit the kinds of social relations that enabled capital accumulation and growth, and yet are hidden or ignored in the grand narratives on empire, capitalism, and modernity.

Discussion

In the introduction I framed two questions; how well did the local economy articulate with imperial visions, and did the enslaved see progress in the same way as European thinkers and administrators? Jamaica, as a plantation colony in the seventeenth century, as envisioned in London, or practiced on the grounds of sugar estates, was remarkably different than the early nineteenth century Jamaica described by scholars of slavery (Higman 1998; Craton and Walvin 1970). By the turn of the eighteenth century, colonial codes had accounted for the manufacture and sale of marketable goods by enslaved laborers (Jamaica 1735) and narrative accounts document that selling such local goods had become common practice by the turn of the nineteenth century (Anonymous 1797; Edwards 1793: 125; Higman 1976; McDonald 1993: 28; Stewart: 1823). These goods were part of a system referred to and written extensively about called an internal market system. Rather than being a dual, informal or alternative economic schema, it was part of a larger economic process- just enabled by conditions intensely local to colonial Jamaica. This intensity was unexpected by imperial visions but enabled the formation of subjects within the empire.

One could look to Edward Long and contemporary writer to imagine how ideas of progress were tied up with slavery. An advocate for the cause of slavery in the British West Indies, Long argued that "In general they [Africans] are void of genius, and seem almost incapable of making any progress in civility or science" (1774). Abolitionists, while opposed to slavery, did not dismiss the importance of progress. Adam Smith, in arguing against slavery said,

> But, as the profit and success of the cultivation which is carried on by means of cattle, depend very much upon the good management of those cattle, so the profit and success of that which is carried on by slaves must depend equally upon the good management of those slaves; and in the good management of their slaves the French planters, I think it is generally allowed, are superior to the English. The law, so far as it gives some weak protection to the slave against the violence of his master, is likely to be better executed in a colony where the government is in a great measure arbitrary than in one where it is altogether free.

Since the French ran their plantations, he thought, with greater respect to the private property and rights of the enslaved, colonies such as San Domingue were more profitable for the mother country, and progressive in their politics.

Of course, the enslaved inhabitants of San Domingue had a different idea of progress. The 1789 Haitian revolution was not the first slave insurrection; it was only the most successful. The debates surrounding the ideological anticipations and material causes for the rebellion are many. People point to the social infrastructures of enslaved life and the economically polarized nature of life in the *Ancien Régime*. Many interpretations hinge on the failure of the colonial apparatus, but some of the more salient look to the rebellion as just a Caribbean expression of modernity. Joining the American Revolution and the French Revolution, it has been argued to be another expression of the enlightenment (CLR James 1963). As such, for enslaved laborers it marked a steady sign of progress and envisioned a Caribbean modernity.

To call the Hatian revolution an alternate modernity like the market systems through which it was organized is to set it aside, making it a footnote of history. But as Sidney Mintz's argued "slaves who plotted armed revolts in the marketplaces had first to produce for the market, and to gain permission to carry their produce there" (Mintz 1971: 321). We as retrievers of a certain past are, therefore, trapped by a particular problem space (*sensu* David Scott 2004a) established during the colonial order we wish to explode. In the analysis of inequality, archaeologists have sought out contexts of study where relations of power conditioned and structured by bureaucratic, economic and political elites limit possibilities and the actions of nonelites as inferred from the material record transgress those very limitations. As such, inequality's analysis has left us with a particular problematic where the scholar attempts to create a real and empirical history at the same time destabilizing narratives that leave blank the spaces between archival texts (Scott 2004b). While the focus on the material world allows us to explode such problem spaces we must be careful not to assign too much value to democratic nature of material culture or the emancipatory potential of their interpretation. Rather the material world insists on an attachment to context whereby canon and resistance are neither monolithic nor freestanding.

Conclusion

Many scholars have shown a direct link between the development of capitalism in Britain and northern Europe and the explosion of chattel slavery in the West Indies and the southeast USA (Dunn 1972; Genovese 1972; Goveia 1965, 1980; Mintz 1985; Tomich 1994; Trouliot 1992; Williams 1970, 1994). Certainly, while many of the studies demonstrate the accumulation of wealth in metropolitan centers, what is of principal importance is labor, its alienation and mobility. Some have argued that the best way to understand this relationship is through the plantation system, whereby the economic, and therefore to some extent social, histories of the peripheries can be written through an understanding of the unequal trade between metropoles and their hinterlands (Stern 1988). The "Pure Plantation Model" model states that the Caribbean was a tightly articulated appendage of metropole economies that have undergone little structural change over the past 400 years (Best and Levitt 1967; Best 1998). However, local structures were not merely functional units, but were partially bounded entities with their own logic through which people could make sense of the slave regime and/or the markets they fed.

It is has been argued that in the postconquest period, the Caribbean was a laboratory of European modernity in which emergent empires experimented with strategies of production, methods of distribution, and technologies of control. These technologies include the manipulation and production of space through cartography, the racialization and (class)ification of colonized and Diaspora peoples, and a series of legislative mechanisms that dictated trading relationships in efforts to make colonial control complete. While certainly a story that Europe told itself [revolving on Trouillot's (2003)] "North Atlantic universals"], "modernity" was not a homogeneous historical force, but an ambiguous assemblage of local traditions and trajectories, different projects of political, economic, and technological expansion, uneven accounts of modernization and their local engagements with its threats and promises. Economic practice was no different. Such an uneven topography enabled exceptions to be established, and lines to be drawn between the urban and the rural, the modern and the folk, and the subject of agronomists and the topic of anthropologists.

In the context of the boom-bust cycles that plague the plantation landscape such networks better situated the enslaved to reproduce the cultural and symbolic forms of everyday life and a acted as a locus of community formation. Insights from the particularities of slave societies allow us to speculate about the implication, I stress how everyday interactions and practices shaped and were shaped by cultural landscape and how the localities in which people live, work, and interact are central to social solidarity and processes of social reproduction.

References

Anonymous. 1797 Characteristic traits of the Creolian and African Negroes in Jamaica. In *Columbia Magazine III*.

Armstrong, D. V. 1990 *The Old Village and the Great House: An Archaeological and Historical Examination of Drax Hall Plantation, St. Ann's Bay, Jamaica*. Urbana: University of Illinois Press.

Armstrong, D. V. 1991 The Afro-Jamaican community at Drax Hall. *Jamaica Journal* 24(1): 3–8.

Armstrong, D. V. 1992. African-Jamaican housing at Seville: A study of spatial transformation.

Armstrong, D. V. 1998. Cultural transformation within enslaved labor communities in the Caribbean. In *Studies in Culture Contact: Interaction, Culture Change, and Archaeology*, edited by J. G. Cusick, pp. 378–401. Southern Illinois University Center for Archaeological Investigations, Carbondale.

Armstrong, D. V. 1999. Archaeology and ethnohistory of the Caribbean plantation. In *"I, too, am America": Archaeological Studies of African-American Life*, edited by T. A. Singleton, pp. 173–92. University Press of Virginia, Charlottesville.

Armstrong, D., and K. G. Kelly. 2000. Settlement patterns and the origins of African Jamaican society: Seville Plantation, St. Ann's Bay, *Jamaica. Ethnohistory* 7(2): 369–947.

Armstrong, D. V. and Hauser, M. W. 2009 A Sea of Diversity: Historical Archaeology in the Caribbean. *International Handbook of Historical Archaeology*, edited by T. Majewski and D. Gaimster, pp. 583–612. Springer: New York.

Beckwith, M. W. 1929 *Black Roadways: A Study of Jamaican Folk Life*. The University of North Carolina Press, Chapel Hill.

Best, L. 1998 Outlines of a Model of Pure Plantation Economy (After twenty-five years). *Marronage* 1: 27–40.

Best, Lloyd and Levvit, K. 1967 *Externally Propelled Growth in the Caribbean: Selected Essays*, mimeo. McGill Centre for Developing Area Studies, McGill University, Montreal.

Blackburn, R. 1997a *The Making of New World Slavery: From the Baroque to the Modern 1492–1800*. Verso, London.

Blackburn, R. 1997b The Old World Background to European Colonial Slavery *William and Mary Quarterly* (1): 65–102.

Brown, V. 1994 Higgling: The Language of Markets in Economic Discourse. In *Higgling: Transactors and Their Markets in the History of Economics*, edited by M.S. Morgan, pp. 66–93. Durham and London: Duke University Press.

Browne, P. [1759] 1789. *The Civil and Natural History of Jamaica*. B. White and Son.

Cassidy, F. G., and R. Le Page, London. [1967] 1980. Dictionary of Jamaican English. Cambridge University Press, Cambridge.

Council of Jamaica. 1678. Council Minutes. Volume 2, Folio 159v, 8 (August). Jamaica Archives and Records Department.

Craton, M., and J. Walvin. 1970. A Jamaican Plantation: The History of Worthy Park, 1670–1970. University of Toronto Press, Toronto.

Davis, D.B. 1966 *The Problem of Slavery in Western Culture*. Cornell University Press, Ithaca.

Davis, D.B. 1997 Constructing Race: A Reflection. *William and Mary Quarterly* LIV(1): 7–18.

Deagan, K. 2002 *Artifacts of the Spanish Colonies of Florida and the Caribbean, 1500–1800*. Vol. 2, Portable Personal Possessions. Smithsonian Institution, Washington, D.C.

Dunn, R. S. 1972. *Sugar and Slaves: The Rise of the Planter Class in the English West Indies, 1624–1713*. Published for the Institute of Early American History and Culture at Williamsburg, VA, by the University of North Carolina Press, Chapel Hill.

DeFoe, D. [1756] 1895. *Journal of the Year of the Plague*. Longmans, New York:

Delle, J. A. 1998 *An Archaeology of Social Space: Analyzing Coffee Plantations in Jamaica's Blue Mountains*. Plenum Press, New York.

Delle, J. A. 1999 The landscapes of class negotiation on coffee plantations in the Blue Mountains of Jamaica, 1797–1850. *Historical Archaeology* 33(1): 136–58.

Delle, J. A. 2000a The material and cognitive dimensions of creolization in nineteenth-century Jamaica. *Historical Archaeology* 34(3): 56–72.

Delle, J. A. 2000b. Gender, power and space: Negotiating social relations under slavery on coffee plantations in Jamaica, 1790–1834. In *Lines That Divide: Historical Archaeologies of Race, Class and Gender*, edited by J. A. Delle, S. A. Mrozowski, and R. Paynter, pp. 168–203. University of Tennessee Press, Knoxville.

Delle, J. A. 2001. Race, missionaries, and the struggle to free Jamaica. In *Race and the Archaeology of Identity*, edited by C. E. Orser, pp. 177–95. University of Utah Press, Salt Lake City:

Delle, J. A. 2002. Power and landscape: Spatial dynamics in early-nineteenth-century Jamaica. In *The Dynamics of Power*, edited by M. O'Donovan, pp. 341–61. Center for Archaeological Investigations, Occasional Paper No. 30. Southern Illinois University, Carbondale.

Delle, J. A. 2009 The Governor and the Enslaved: An Archaeology of Colonial Modernity at Marshall's Pen, Jamaica. *International Journal of Historical Archaeology* 13(4): 488–512.

Ebanks, R. 1984. Ma Lou, an Afro Jamaican pottery tradition. *Jamaica Journal* 17: 31–37.

Edwards, B. 1793, 1972 *The History, Civil and Commercial, of the British Colonies in the West Indies*. Research library of colonial Americana; 2. Arno Press, New York.

Ellis, W. 1744. *The Timber-Tree Improved*. Printed for, and sold by T. Osborne and M. Cooper.

Fennell, C. C. 2003 Group identity, individual creativity, and symbolic generation in a BaKongo diaspora. *International Journal of Historical Archaeology* 7: 1–31.

Fennell, C. C. 2007a *Crossroads and Cosmologies: Diasporas and Ethnogenesis in the New World*. University Press of Florida, Gainesville.

Fennell, C. C. 2007b BaKongo identity and symbolic expressions in the Americas. In *Archaeology of Atlantic Africa and the African Diaspora*, edited by Ogundiran, A., and Falola, T., pp 199–232. Indiana University Press, Bloomington.

Fielding, H. 1791. *The History of Tom Jones: A Foundling*. Printed for J. L. Legrand.

Franklin, M., and Fesler, G. 1999. The exploration of ethnicity and the historical archaeological record. In *Historical Archaeology, Identity Formation, and the Interpretation of Ethnicity*, edited by M. Franklin and G. Fesler, pp1–10. Colonial Williamsburg Foundation, Williamsburg.

Galle, J. 2010 Costly Signaling and Gendered Social Strategies among Slaves in the Eighteenth-Century Chesapeake. *American Antiquity* 75(1): 19–43.

Genovese, E. 1972 *Roll Jordan Roll: The World the Slaves Made*, New York: Vintage.

Goveia, E. V. 1965. *Slave Society in the British Leeward Islands at the End of the Eighteenth Century*. Caribbean series 8. Yale University Press, New Haven.

Goveia, E. V. 1970 *The West Indian Slave laws of the Eighteenth Century*. Cave Hill Campus Barbados: University of West Indies.

Goveia, E. V. 1980. *A Study on the Historiography of the British West Indies to the End of the Nineteenth Century*. Howard University Press, Washington, D.C.

Handler, J. S. and F. Lange. 1978 *Plantation Slavery in Barbados: An Archaeological and Historical Investigation*. Harvard University Press, Cambridge, MA.

Hauser, M. 2008 *The Archaeology of Black Markets, Local Ceramics and Economies in Eighteenth Century Jamaica*. University Press, Florida, Gainesville.

Hauser, M. and C. R. DeCorse. 2003 Low-Fired Earthenwares in the African Diaspora: Problems and Prospects. *International Journal of Historical Archaeology* 7(1): 67–98.

Helms, M. 1988 *Ulysses' Sail: An Ethnographic Odyssey of Power, Knowledge, and Geographical Distance*. Princeton University Press, Princeton.

Higman, B. W. 1976. (Editor) *Characteristic Traits of the Creolian and African Negroes in Jamaica*. Caldwell Press Originally Published by an anonymous author in Columbian Magazine or Monthly Miscellany, April–Oct., 1797. Kingston, Jamaica: William Smith Publisher.

Higman, B. W. 1986a. Plantation Maps as Sources for the Study of West Indian Ethnohistory. In *Ethnohistory: A Researcher's Guide,* edited by D. Wiedman, pp. 107–36. Studies in Third World Societies, Publication No. 35. Department of Anthropology, College of William and Mary, Williamsburg.

Higman, B. W. 1986b. Jamaican Coffee Plantations, 1780–1860: A Cartographic Analysis. *Caribbean Geography* 2: 73–91.

Higman, B. W. 1987. The spatial economy of Jamaican sugar plantations: Cartographic evidence from the 18th and 19th centuries. *Journal of Historical Geography* 13(1): 17–19.

Higman, B. W. 1988. *Jamaica Surveyed: Plantation Maps and Plans of the Eighteenth and Nineteenth Centuries.* Institute of Jamaica Publications, Jamaica and San Francisco.

Higman, B. W. 1998. *Montpelier, Jamaica: A Plantation Community in Slavery and Freedom, 1739–1912.* The Press, University of the West Indies, Mona, Jamaica.

Howson, J. 1990 Social Relations and Material Culture: A Critique of the Archaeology of Plantation Slavery. *Historical Archaeology* 23: 78–91.

James, C.L.R. 1963. *Black Jacobins: Toussaint L'Ouverture and the San Domingo Revolution.* 2nd ed. revised from 1963. Vintage, New York.

Jamaica. 1735. Acts of Assembly, passed in the island of Jamaica; from 1681, to 1734, inclusive.

Jamaica. 1738. Acts of Assembly, passed in the island of Jamaica; from 1681, to 1737, inclusive. London,

Jamaica. 1738 [1739]. In Eighteenth Century Online, St Jago de la Vega.

Jamaica. 1743. Acts of Assembly, passed in the Island of Jamaica; from 1681, to 1737, Inclusive.

Jamaica. 1786. An Abridgment of the Laws of Jamaica: comprehending the subject-matter of each Act and clause, … To which is prefixed, by way of index, a table …. In Eighteenth Century Collections Online, Kingston, Jamaica.

Jamaica. 1793. An Abridgment of the Laws of Jamaica; Being an alphabetical digest of all the public Acts of Assembly now in force, from the thirty-second year of King Charles II. to the thirty-second year of … George III. Inclusive, as published in two volumes… Eighteenth-Century Collections Online. St. Jago de la Vega, Jamaica.

Katzin, M. F. 1959a. Community organization in rural Jamaica. *Social and Economic Studies* 8(4): 424–429

Katzin, M. F. 1959b. The Jamaican country higgler. *Social and Economic Studies* 8(4): 421–40.

Katzin, M. F. 1960. The business of higglering in Jamaica. *Social and Economic Studies* 9(3): 297–331.

Leslie, C. 1740. A New and Exact account of Jamaica, wherein the ancient and present state of that colony, its importance to Great Britain, laws, trade, manners and religion, together with the most remarkable and curious animals, plants, trees, &c. are described: with a particular account of the sacrifices, libations, &c. at this day in use among the negroes.… 3rd ed. R. Fleming, Edinburgh.

Leone, M. P., and G. Fry. 1999. Conjuring in the big house kitchen: An interpretation of African American belief systems based on the uses of archaeology and folklore sources. *Journal of American Folklore* 112: 372–403.

Long, E. [1774] 1970. The history of Jamaica; or, General survey of the ancient and modern state of that island: with reflections on its situations, settlements, inhabitants, climate, products, commerce, laws, and government. New, with a new introduction by George Metcalf. Cass library of West Indian studies, No. 12, F. Cass, London.

McDonald, R. A. 1993 *The economy and material culture of slaves: goods and chattels on the sugar plantations of Jamaica and Louisiana.* Baton Rouge: Louisiana State University Press.

Meyers, A. D. 1999. West African tradition in the decoration of colonial Jamaican folk pottery. *Journal of Historical Archaeology* 3(4): 201–24.

Mintz, S. W. 1955. The Jamaican internal marketing pattern. *Social and Economic Studies* 4: 95–103.

Mintz, Sidney. 1971 Men, Women, and Trade. *Comparative Studies in Society and History* 13(3): 247–269.

Mintz, S. W. 1985. *Sweetness and Power: The place of sugar in modern history.* Viking, New York.

Mintz, S. W., and D. Hall. [1970] 1991. The origins of the Jamaican internal marketing system. In *Caribbean Slave Society and Economy: A Student Reader*, edited by V. Shepherd, pp. 319–34. New Press, New York.

Nicholas, D. 1986 The "Syrians" of Jamaica. *Jamaican Historical Review* 15: 50–62.

Ogundiran, A., and T. Falola. 2007. Pathways in the archaeology of transatlantic Africa. In *Archaeology of Atlantic Africa and the African Diaspora*, edited by A. Ogundiran and T. Falola, pp. 3–48. Indiana University Press, Bloomington.

Patterson, Orlando. 1969 *The sociology of slavery; an analysis of the origins, development, and structure of Negro slave society in Jamaica*. Rutherford [N.J.]: Fairleigh Dickinson University Press.

Patterson, Orlando. 1982 *Slavery and Social Death: A Comparative Study*. Cambridge, MA: Harvard University Press.

Reeves, M. 1997 "By Their Own Labor": Enslaved Africans' Survival Strategies on Two Jamaican Plantations. Ph.D. Dissertation, Syracuse University.

Ruppel, T., J. Neuwirth, M. Leone and G. Fry. 2003. Hidden in view: African spiritual spaces in North American landscapes. *Antiquity* 77: 321–335.

Sauer, Carl. 1966 The Early Spanish Main. Berkely: University of California Press.

Sweet, J.H. 1997 The Iberian Roots of American Racist Thought. *William and Mary Quarterly LIV* (1): 143–166.

Scott, David. 2003 Political rationalities of the Jamaican modern. *Small Axe* 14: 1–22.

Scott, David. 2004a. Modernity that predated the modern: Sidney Mintz's Caribbean. *History Workshop Journal* 58: 191–210.

Scott, David. 2004b *Conscripts of Modernity: The Tragedy of Colonial Enlightenment*. Duke University Press, Durham.

Simmonds, L. E. 2004 The Afro-Jamaican and Internal Marketing Systems: Kingston, 1780–1834. In *Jamaica in Slavery and Freedom: history, heritage and culture*, edited by K. Monteith, pp. 274–290. Kingston, Jamaica: University of West Indies Press.

Skowronek, Russell K. 1987 Ceramics and Commerce: The 1554 flota Revisited. *Historical Archaeology* 21(2): 101111.

Skowronek, Russell K. 1992 Empire and Ceramics: The Changing Role of Illicit Trade in Spanish America. *Historical Archaeology* 26(1): 109–118

Sloane, H. S. 1707–1725. *A voyage to the islands Madera, Barbados, Nieves, S. Christophers and Jamaica, with the natural history of the herbs and trees, four-footed beasts, fishes, birds, insects, reptiles, &c. of the last of those islands; to which is prefix'd an introduction, wherein is an account of the inhabitants, air, waters, diseases, trade, &c. of that place, with some relations concerning the neighbouring continent, and islands of America. Illustrated with figures of the things described, which have not been heretofore engraved; in large copper-plates as big as the life*. Printed by B. M. for the author, London.

Smith, A. 1776 1994 *An Inquiry into the Nature and Causes of the Wealth of Nations*. Modern Library, New York.

Stern, Steven. 1988 Feudalism, Capitalism and the World-system in the Perspective of Latin America and the Caribbean. *American Historical Review* 93: 829–872.

Stewart, James. 1823 A View of the Past and Present State of the Island of Jamaica. London: Oliver and Boyd, Tweeddale-House.

Taylor, S.A.G. 1965 *The Western Design: An Account of Cromwell's Expedition to the Caribbean*. Kingston: Institute of Jamaica.

Tomich, D. 1994 Small Islands, Large Comparisons. *Social Science History* 18(3): 339–58.

Trouillot, M-R. 1995. *Silencing the Past: Power and the Production of History*. Beacon Press, Boston.

Trouillot, M-R. 1992 The Caribbean Region: An Open Frontier in Anthropological Theory. *Annual Review of Anthropology* 21: 19–42.

Trouillot, M-R. 2003 *Global Transformations: Anthropology and the Modern World*. Palgrave Macmillan, New York.

Vincentelli, M. 2004. *Women Potters: Transforming Traditions*. Rutgers University Press, New Brunswick.

Watson, K. and F. Smith. 2009 Urbanity, Sociability, and Commercial Exchange in the Barbados Sugar Trade: A Comparative Colonial Archaeological Perspective on Bridgetown, Barbados in the Seventeenth Century. *International Journal of Historical Archaeology* 13(1): 63–79.

Williams, Eric. 1970 *From Columbus to Castro: The History of the Caribbean*. Vintage Books, New York.

Williams, Eric. 1961 *Capitalism & Slavery.* Russell & Russell, New York.

Williams, Eric Eustace. 1994 *Capitalism and Slavery.* Chapel Hill: University of North Carolina Press.

Wilkie, L. A. 1997. Secret and sacred: Contextualizing the artifacts of African-American magic and religion. *Historical Archaeology* 31(4): 81–106.

Wilkie, L. A. 2000. *Creating Freedom: Material Culture and African American Identity at Oakley Plantation, Louisiana, 1840–1950.* Louisiana State University Press, Baton Rouge.

Chapter 7
A Life on Broken China: Figuring Senses of Capitalism in Late Nineteenth-Century Bogotá

Felipe Gaitán-Ammann

In the first two decades of the nineteenth-century, emancipation movements sweeping across the Spanish colonial empire were blissfully welcomed throughout the Western, modern world. For liberal thinkers and capitalist spirits alike, the Wars of Independence breaking out throughout Spanish America signified the advent of a long awaited time of freedom, one that would bring about progress and prosperity to all those formerly colonized people who so desperately wanted to embrace the civilized lifestyle of European, capitalist bourgeoisies. Like most early Latin-American nations, the republic of New Granada, roughly corresponding to the present-day Colombia,[1] stumbled and lingered in its transition toward a capitalist system, as if it had been doomed to forever lag behind the economic blooming of the Northern metropoles set on the fast track to financial modernization and industrialization. The underdevelopment of Latin-American states vis-à-vis their North American counterparts and European past parent-states was for long a most popular, yet persistently unresolved topic of research in the social sciences (Weaver 1976; Allahar 1990; Clark et al. 1994) until, with the rise of postcolonial postures in the late twentieth century, the problem of the economic stagnation of former Spanish colonies in the New World was rephrased in less deterministic terms attempting to assess, but not necessarily to explain the genealogy of Latin America's unfavorable position in the exploitative social and economic global order coming about with the emergence of the capitalist model of production.

---

[1] The official denomination for the territory corresponding to the present-day Republic of Colombia changed several times throughout the nineteenth century, making it historically inaccurate to use only one name to refer to that geographical and political entity over the 1800s. In this chapter, to avoid confusions, I use the term "New Granada" to designate a succession of at least six republican states that were created after the fall of the Spanish empire in what was formerly known as the New Kingdom of Granada (1550–1717), or the Viceroyalty of New Granada (1717–1819). The last of these states was established in 1886, permanently adopting the name "Republic of Colombia."

F. Gaitán-Ammann (✉)
Department of Anthropology, Columbia University, New York, NY, USA
e-mail: fg2112@columbia.edu

S.K. Croucher and L. Weiss (eds.), *The Archaeology of Capitalism in Colonial Contexts*, 143
Contributions To Global Historical Archaeology, DOI 10.1007/978-1-4614-0192-6_7,
© Springer Science+Business Media, LLC 2011

This chapter aims at demonstrating that a historical archaeology of the modern world (*sensu* Orser 1996; Hall 2000a, b) may still have some light to shed on the understanding of the atypical development of capitalist relations in early republican Latin America. By casting an archaeological glance into some consumption patterns prevailing in late-nineteenth-century Bogotá, the first city of New Granada and perhaps one of the most isolated of all republican capitals in the region (Martínez 2001: 45), I describe the local process of modernization, not just as a simple case of economic failure, but rather as a powerful expression of the hybrid cultural nature characterizing social and economic formations in the Spanish colonial and postcolonial world (García-Canclini 2001). Within the context of recent theorizations emerging in the field of Latin-American cultural studies as to the particular role that pervading colonial structures played in the way Latin-American nations experienced the development of a capitalist world system, I uncover the fascinating life story of Leonidas Posada Gaviria, a long-forgotten crockery merchant from late-nineteenth-century Bogotá who made a fortune by supplying to the modernized needs and gentrified tastes of his fellow citizens (Gaitán Ammann 2005a). Posada Gaviria's successful journey toward social recognition is revealing in the sense that it did not evolve into a self-reproducing model of capitalist accumulation, even though it took place at a time when New Granada, known by then as the United States of Colombia (1863–1886), was experiencing the most radically liberal period of its modern history. Instead of consolidating his status as a modern, transnational capitalist, Leonidas Posada Gaviria's entrepreneurial project served him to establish himself as a local landowner, providing him with the means to purchase large farming estates in the outskirts of Bogotá, within which he could arguably maintain premodern relations of production with the local peasant population. The point of this chapter is, thus, that Leonidas Posada Gaviria's story may be a reflection of the hybrid forms of capitalism occurring in republican New Granada, in which benefits obtained from the rise of bourgeois consumerism were ultimately reinvested in the maintenance of premodern relations of production. Ultimately, by invoking the memory of Leonidas Posada Gaviria, this chapter exemplifies the ambiguous relationship that rising Latin-American bourgeoisies held with capitalism and modern values, and provides us with an original insight into the social lives of hundreds of other individuals in the confines of Western civilization who cunningly manipulated the strings of consumption and exchange to partake in the strengthening of modern, capitalist world-systems (*pace* Frank 1991).

Modernity, Coloniality, and Capitalism

Centuries of unequal exchange created a chain of subordination and lead to the division of the planet into developed and underdeveloped regions. (Mielants 2007: 45)

It is, perhaps, a commonplace to state that the appearance of capitalist structures in early republican societies of Latin America cannot be dissociated from other, closely interrelated historical phenomena, such as the rise and fall of the Spanish empire, and the creation and modernization of republican nation-states in its former colonial territories. In Latin America as elsewhere, the fundamental categories of colonialism and capitalism are constructed one upon the other, and their implementation into the social discourse of modernity cannot operate but within the framework of the unequal social, economic, and geopolitical order of the modern world. It is precisely this system of stubbornly colonial power relations embedded in the unequal, modern order created by the capitalist model of production that the chapters in this volume seek to interrogate. Not surprisingly, it could be argued that, in the last few years, anthropological debates focusing on the historical trajectories of the colonialism-capitalism relationship have remained much more active in what Immanuel Wallerstein (1987) described as the peripheries of the West, while they appear to have gradually gone out of intellectual fashion in the core of the modern world. For example, it is clear that, because Latin-American identities, as varied as they may be, are so closely tied to the region's colonial experience, scholarship in the area has retained an enduring interest in issues of colonialism and capitalism, remaining on the cutting edge of the academic critique of classical, yet still influential theories such as Wallerstein's world-systems analysis, that seem to be totally out of touch with perceived realities in postcolonial Europe and North America (e.g., Bradshaw et al. 1996). Especially within the field of Latin American cultural studies (see Humar 2009), complex understandings of the region's peripheral role in the making of the modern world have contributed to the development of new versions of the past in which local social actors, like Leonidas Posada Gaviria, are identified as key elements in the process of the formation of capitalist world-systems. From this perspective, Latin America can be portrayed as a historical, geographical, and cultural construct, within which notions of colonialism, capitalism, and modernity are granted specific meanings. It is for this reason that, to fully recognize the contributions that a case study set in late-nineteenth-century New Granada can make to a historical archaeology of the modern world, it is necessary to start by discussing the genealogy of these particular meanings, and the way in which local understandings of colonialism and capitalism have been used in Latin-American thought to endorse strongly politicized ideas as to the historical uniqueness of the whole region.

In the late 1980s, the return to democratic regimes in countries such as Chile and Argentina created a quite favorable intellectual environment for the reopening of a critical debate: that of Latin-American essential *difference* (Humar 2009: 380) – a shared cultural condition derived from centuries of colonization and ethnic mixing that made societies from the former Spanish colonies fundamentally distinct from all others. This vague and homogenizing understanding of Latin America as a distinctive cultural, historical, and territorial collectivity congregating the crumbles of the Spanish colonial project was, by the end of the twentieth century, also buttressed by the intellectual turmoil entailed by the remembrance of the fifth centenary of the European invasion to the New World (Stern 1992; Annino 1996). Indeed, the critical commemoration of the 1492 Columbian endeavor spurred even further the efficacy of amorphous notions such as *hybridity* and *difference* (Mignolo 2000a; García-Canclini 2001; cf. Bhabha 1985), empowering them as central, transnational elements of a potent Latin-American creation myth that has ever since rarely been disputed.

One could hardly think of a more accurate description of Latin-American inherent cultural difference and hybridity than the one Simón Bolívar captured on

September 12, 1815, in his celebrated Letter from Jamaica: "We are, moreover, neither Indian nor European, but a species midway between the legitimate proprietors of this country and the Spanish usurpers. In short, though Americans by birth we derive our rights from Europe, and we have to assert these rights against the rights of the natives, and at the same time we must defend ourselves against the invaders. This places us in a most extraordinary and involved situation" (Bertrand 1951: na). In a much less expectant and indulgent tone than General Bolívar, Walter Mignolo (2000b) has recently drawn on the seminal work of African-American scholar W.E.B. Du Bois (1990 [1904]) to critique the indolent, hybrid double-conscience characterizing Latin-American cultural and economic elites from the times of the Libertador to the present. According to Mignolo, among many others, former Spanish colonies in the New World have, since the Wars of Independence, based their national projects on a rejection of the political dominance of Europe over their territories, but certainly not on the negation of their inherited, civilized European spirit. It is precisely through that European spirit, something that Wallerstein once termed the Western geoculture (Wallerstein 1991a, 1995), that Latin-American nations have remained forcibly appended to the West, a factitious geographical space that represents a perfect reification of the powerful ascendant that Europe has managed to maintain over its bygone colonial Empire (Mignolo and Walter 2000b: 64).

Nothing could be more ambiguous than the cultural status of early – and, to some extent, current – Latin-American bourgeoisies, immersed in a pervasive geoculture that is blind to the intrinsic, colonial condition of the New World. Throughout the nineteenth and early twentieth centuries, hegemonic groups such as the ones Leonidas Posada Gaviria frequented and served, experienced modernity through persistently premodern social structures, and perceived themselves as the heirs of the civilizing – i.e., Christianizing – mission inaugurated four hundred years earlier by the Spanish conquistadors (Castro-Gómez 2004). This first stage in the colonization of local ideas was, as Colombian philosopher Santiago Castro-Gómez argues, articulated in the nineteenth century to a second modernizing and civilizing phase, in which the enlightened thinking of the French revolution (cf. Wallerstein 1991b) was used to justify the dominance of Western Europe over the rest of the globe, and to inspire modern discourses of exclusion that underpinned the construction of the nation-state in young Latin-American republics. As Castro-Gomez convincingly posits, local republican elites in Latin America were also successful in assimilating modernizing discourses of enlightenment to one of the main pillars of Spanish colonial society – the notion of *pureza de sangre* or purity of blood[2] (Fayard 1979: 205),

---

[2] A primary sociocultural legacy from Medieval Spain, the concept of "purity of blood," was first popularized in times of the Spanish Reconquista (eighth to fifteenth centuries AD), when access to many civil rights were reserved to individuals who could prove that they came from long-established Christian lineages that had not been contaminated by either Jewish or Moorish blood. Above all, and mainly in plebeian spheres, the notion of "pureza de sangre" served as a social filter to limit social mobility. In colonial contexts, it became the basis for the establishment of a complex system of *mestizo* castes resulting from the recurrent practice of miscegenation in Spanish colonial society.

around which other instruments of domination, based on subjective and material perceptions such as skin color, religious practices and etiquette codes, were subsequently constructed (Pardo Rojas 2006: 243). This dual, insidious process of modernization *and* colonization of the Latin-American psyche, of its intimate sensitivities and bodily regimes, is an important component of what Aníbal Quijano (2000) has referred to as the coloniality of power.

Both an instrument and an incentive of modern western expansionism, capitalism is certainly the most important link bringing together the coloniality of power and the basic principle of modernity. In particular, the understanding of the capitalist world-system as an essentially fluid historical formation originating well beyond the first decades of the sixteenth century (Abu-Lughod 1989) is vital to the recognition of coloniality as a continuing process that Latin America still endures today as part of its experience of modernity. It is, thus, indispensable for our comprehension of the historical trajectory of Latin America, as a constitutive – if peripheral – element of the West, to analyze the twin issues of modernity and coloniality not only from a longue-durée perspective but also in the light of the historical development of mature capitalist relations in the New World.

In an open challenge to one of Immanuel Wallerstein's fundamental premises, stubbornly situating the origins of capitalism in sixteenth-century Western Europe (Mielants 2007: 12), André Gunder Frank, among others, has convincingly demonstrated that a world encompassing political and economic system of exchange was already well established long before 1500 and far beyond the geographical borders of Europe (Frank 1991: 171; Frank and Gills 1993). Frank's attempt to prove the chronologically fluid and geographically unspecific nature of the historical process resulting in the axial division of the planet in developed and underdeveloped regions (Mielants 2007: 45) is not, in itself, a groundbreaking proposition, since it had already been considered in some of the earliest, classic works devoted to the study of modern capitalism (e.g., Sée 1968). Frank's posture is, however, still important in supporting our reading of Latin-American transition toward modernity as occurring in a *longue-durée* continuum, along which capitalist and precapitalist relations coexist in a state of mutual dependency. This being said, it should be noted that, more often than not, social scientists have found it difficult to conceive the movement toward a full-fledged capitalist system in terms of continuums rather than in those of transitions, perhaps because of the tendency that, since the time of classical Marxism, scholars in economic history have had to analyze social change in terms of well-defined shifts in economic modes of production (Mielants 2007: 11). By contrast, in defense of his continuist perspective on the process of formation of the modern world-system (*pace* Wallerstein 1991c), Frank has gone as far as proposing the suppression of the seminal notion of *transition* of the capitalist epistemological repertoire, largely because of the clearly Eurocentric connotation the term entails. This radical move toward a more fluid understanding of the rise of capitalism in the West, however, also results into the blurring of spatial and temporal referents that, as we have seen, are crucial to our understanding of the intimate connection existing between colonialism, capitalism, and modernity in the New World.

From a more balanced perspective, Wallerstein has argued that it is important to describe the transition toward a capitalist world-economy not solely in terms of a shift in modes of production, but also in those of the emergence of a structured world market-system allowing for the continuous circulation of ideas, peoples, and things at a global level. Ultimately, according to Wallerstein, it is through those fluid market-systems that capitalist peripheries, in Latin America or elsewhere in the modern world, can be incorporated to the capitalist world-economy, not only through their consumption of manufactured goods imported from the core but also through the peripheral development of productive activities regulated from that core, and over which peripheries themselves have little direct control (e.g., Martínez Vergne 1992).

In a typically postcolonial critique of the core–periphery notion popularized by Wallerstein, Walter Mignolo, among many other advocates of the modernity–coloniality school of thought (see Mignolo 2008), observed, not so long ago, that world-system theories tended to naturalize the subaltern role of peripheries by explaining the rise of capitalism as an essentially Western European occurrence (Mignolo 2000b: 57). Still, it is also true that, at least since the late 1960s, the world-systems approach has promoted a critical rethinking of underdevelopment theories, and an understanding of peripheral dependency not as an expression of peripheries' deprival of viable means of production, but as a consequence of their positioning in an international system of exchange that is itself dependant on a large-scale, trade-connected, axial division of labor. Modern capitalism may, thus, not be considered a uniquely European construct, but it is no less part of the excluding cultural, political, and philosophical complex of modernity (Castro-Gómez 2004). Indeed, there can be no modernity without capitalism, nor can capitalism in the peripheries of the modern world be detached from that ontological state of colonial subjugation Quijano has described as the coloniality of power.

Ascending to the Olympus

In the last few years, in the lead of influential contemporary thinkers such as Mignolo, Quijano, García-Canclini, and Castro-Gómez, historical examples of the contradictory double-conscience characterizing Latin-American modern societies have been widely explored in Colombian scholarship (e.g., Martínez 2001; Cunin 2003; Castro-Gómez 2004). However, when it comes to analyzing the processes of assimilation of republican New Granada into the capitalist world-system of the late nineteenth century, traditional versions of Colombian history still pervade in scholarly spheres, typically consisting of comprehensive assessments of the causes and consequences of the country's limited access to modern, industrial modes of production (e.g., Nieto Arteta 1975; McGreevey 1982; Bushnell 1996). Most of these versions, unfortunately, neglect to address problems that are crucial to the understanding of the colonial nature of Latin-American modernity, such as the gradual transformation of practices of consumption at the local level. In order to get a better sense of the extent to which modern entrepreneurs such as Leonidas Posada Gaviria could participate in that transformation process through a keen interpretation of the material and symbolic needs of newly constituted republican bourgeoisies in New Granada, it important to describe in some detail the political, economic, and social environment in which their capitalist projects were carried out.

The second half of the nineteenth century in what is nowadays Colombia has often been caricatured as an era of unleashed freedom, a time in which radical liberal elites strove to implement the most novel systems of republican governance in a country that had not even succeeded in constituting itself as a nation (Bushnell 1996). Yet what Colombian historiography has traditionally defined as a stage of general liberal hegemony, starting around 1849 and reaching its climax in 1863, was far from being a politically homogeneous time. Rather, this period would be better characterized as a moment of chronic social instability, marked by constant and profound political reformations, sanguinary civil wars, and frequent popular upheavals (Delpar 1971).

The 1850s also inaugurated an economic age in which New Granada was particularly sensitive to the ups and downs in the prices of tropical exports on international markets so that successive bonanzas in the international trade of gold, tobacco, cinchona bark, and indigo dye only contributed to spread the false idea that the country had finally been set on the path of prosperity (Nieto Arteta 1975; McGreevey 1982; Tirado Mejía 1988). The political leaders of New Granada, mostly composed of traditional land-owning upper classes (Delpar 1971: 251), undoubtedly benefited from the forcible integration of their young, peripheral republic to the modern, capitalist world-system. Regardless of their particular political postures, republican elites all seemed eager to experiment with the basic principles of the free trade and, more often than not, were ready to reach a general consensus as regards to the best policy to adopt to develop and modernize the national economy.

Interestingly enough, political frictions as to the degree to which liberal ideologies were to guide the process of construction of a nation-state did not emerge only between members of the traditional Liberal and Conservative parties. As Helen Delpar pointed out several decades ago, the period of liberal hegemony in the early republic of New Granada was mostly a time of intraparty disagreement, fiercely opposing two factions of liberal politicians (Delpar 1971: 253). On the one hand, the so-called Independents – or *Draconianos* – were partisans of applying moderate liberal changes to the national project, since they realized that New Granada was still largely unprepared to undertake a drastic renovation of its social, political, and economic structures. On the other hand, the extravagant and impatient Radicals, locally nicknamed *Gólgotas,* were committed to policies of extreme anticlericalism, federalism, and laissez-faire, and promoted an immediate transformation of New Granada into a utopian model of the European liberal state (Tirado Mejía 1997).

From the 1850s and well into the 1880s, these two liberal wings alternately gained the political support of the Conservative opposition and of some key, politically influent popular sectors, such as urban artisans and merchants. In particular, the period comprised between 1863 and 1886 corresponded to the move of the Radical faction to the front of the political scene and, quite predictably, to the taking of liberal experimentation to formerly unthinkable limits (Rodríguez Piñeres 1986). The succession of ultraliberal, ultrafederalist regimes that would be known later on as the *Olimpo Radical* – or Radical Olympus – however, proved to be a major political failure. The development of strong regional loyalties, largely as a consequence of the country's enormous ethnic, social and economic diversity, interfered with the consolidation of stable, political allegiances at the national level (Palacios and Safford 2002). Anticlerical tendencies that came along with the rise of liberalism since the 1850s also reached a peak during the Radical Olympus, which contributed to the weakening of the traditionally fragile institutional bases of the Church (Martínez 2001: 367). As a result, Catholicism itself was not an effective factor of national unity, but rather was a major target in the political struggle dividing not only the two traditional parties but also the two intraparty factions of the liberal camp. Not surprisingly, conservative opponents to the Radical government, of which Leonidas Posada Gaviria was presumably part, presented themselves as the only legitimate standard-bearers of Catholic faith (Delpar 1971: 251), the central, moral axis around which, following the downfall of the radical project in the 1880s, the modern Colombian state would be constructed upon the regenerating principles of authority and order.

There is a general agreement among historians that, in New Granada, the liberal reforms of the 1850s marked a definitive rupture with the political institutions inherited from the colonial period. Yet it also often argued that the liberal state that emerged from those reforms was never strong enough to achieve a radical transformation of the local social order (Palacios 2001: 22). As a result, on the eve of the twentieth century, the country was still stranded in complex social struggles that were still, in many ways, premodern in nature. In early republican New Granada, social conflicts did not oppose rebellious working classes to an incipient capitalist bourgeoisie (Palacios 2001: 23). Rather, they confronted traditional oligarchies with popular urban sectors, such as artisans and small traders, who permanently contested the symbolic frontiers beyond which the upper classes intended to perpetuate their political and cultural hegemony. Interestingly enough, money was never an indispensable requisite to be admitted in local elites, and economic capital did not grant to whoever possessed it direct access to social distinction. As Palacios keenly observes, to be and remain on top of society, local elites needed to demonstrate the capacity to express their political views and to inflame public opinion (Palacios 2001: 14). Social status was, therefore, a question of rhetoric as much as it was a matter of appearance.

The history of the second political generation of New Granada – the one that replaced the heroes of the Independence and faded out at by the turn of the century – is the history of the hardships of the construction of a modern nation-state in the post-colonial world. As Martinez posits, Latin-American political discourse was born under the sign of cosmopolitanism: it reflected European ideals of modernity that republican travelers to the Old World had brought back from their civilizing journeys and dreamt to reproduce in their own land (Martínez 2001). By the late nineteenth century, however, strongly nationalist postures emerge, probably as part of a legitimatization strategy aiming at promoting the adoption of simplified, essentialized national identities that could be effectively used as political propaganda. Yet nationalism, conceived as an open rejection to any foreign influence in the nation-state construction project, was never much more than a discourse on local grounds, one that tended to coexist freely with an increasing number of actual institutional imports from European republican models (Kalmanovitz 2001). Nationalism, thus, seems to have been used as a mere instrument to conceal a more complex reality: the incapacity or unwillingness of local elites to develop identity discourses in which they would not appear as inevitable social actors mediating between the national state and the European universe of civilization (Martínez 2001: 38).

Few concrete evidences of the materialization of this European dream in Republican New Granada could be more evocative than the fabulous endeavor of the *Fábrica de Loza Bogotana* – the Pottery Manufacturing Company of Bogotá, one of the first industrial societies through which New Granadean entrepreneurs manifested their engagement with the modernization of local modes of production (Therrien 2007, 2008). First founded around 1835, the Bogotá pottery was equipped with the latest English technology in the fabrication of industrial, refined earthenwares; it began to function regularly as two British technicians arrived in the city to run it. In time, the quality of the pottery fired in the Bogotá kilns became so good that it can be difficult nowadays to see the difference between the local production and regular transfer printed ceramics imported from Britain throughout the nineteenth century (Therrien et al. 2002: 32). In the long run, however, the pottery was not competitive enough to rival the British – and probably American – supply; its production gradually tapered off and definitely stopped in the early twentieth century.

When he visited Bogotá by the mid-nineteenth century, North American traveler Isaac Holton was so impressed by this unusual, local example of industrial entrepreneurship that he dedicated a few lines in his travel journal to the *Fábrica de Loza Bogotana*:

> In the southeast corner of the city, or just out of it, is one establishment, however, that does credit to Granadean perseverance and talent. It is the pottery of Don Nicolas Leiva. To understand the difficulties he has contended with, you must know something of native character, and especially its aversion to steady labor. In entire provinces you cannot find one man who has ever wrought faithfully all the working days of an entire month and yet this potter would do credit to the United States. Among the uncommon articles made here are porcelain mortars and pestles, and those Venetian shades that exhibit soft and delicate figures by transmitted light. (Holton 1857: 268)

One can easily fantasize about the nature of the delicate figures Isaac Holton saw gleaming on the Venetian porcelain shades fired at the *Fábrica de Loza Bogotana*, and wonder if these fancy creations could actually constitute today an efficacious embodiment of the pervasive tendency of Latin-American bourgeoisies to alternate praise and blame vis-à-vis their former European colonizers which, as we have seen, Mignolo refers to in terms of a typical double-consciousness. Indeed, domestic-made ceramics were often decorated with motives quite distinct from the ones used on the wares produced in Europe for the European market. In a fascinating example of a European material rhetoric pronounced with a unique, foreign accent, some of the pieces fired in the pottery showed bucolic renderings of local scenes, images of the beautiful landscapes of the Bogotá plain, representations of Indians and peasants wrapped up in striped woolen ponchos, and even, as an unquestionable evidence of the industrious nature of Granadean people, pictures of the kilns, and shops of the *Fábrica de Loza* itself.

Further, in a quite tangible instance of its nationalist vocation, the Bogotá pottery also produced delicate tricolor teacups commemorating the glorious memory of General Bolívar, the Libertador (Gaitán and Lobo Guerrero 2006).

However, in their tortuous quest for an elusive identity that could assist them in the process of construction of the nation of their dreams, local elites consistently ended up drawing on practical, cosmopolitan models. Trapped in their self-attributed role of modernizing mediators, dominant classes reflect their social insecurities in the contradictory choices they make in the practice. The last years of the Radical period, the time in which Leonidas Posada Gaviria initiated his great voyage toward success, are thus the moment when the dichotomy between a nationalist effort to construct a modern state, and a cosmopolitan desire to experience modernity in the flesh can be felt more strongly in Colombian history. Not surprisingly, these years of the late nineteenth century are characterized by a climate of extreme political social and economic instability in which capitalist enterprises seem condemned to failure, largely because the classic Marxist configuration of class struggle is jumbled up and unable to reproduce itself in local conditions.

Tracking Back the Merchant's Mark

Since the formation and consolidation of historical archaeology as a scholarly discipline in the second half of the twentieth century, few researchers in the field have overlooked the fact that the emergence of capitalism is one of the principal focal points of material culture studies interrogating the social life of objects within the ever-expanding limits of the modern world (Paynter et al. 1999; Hall 2000a, b; Johnson 1996; Leone 1995). Historical archaeology has, thus, frequently been dubbed an archaeology of capitalism, a material history of the gradual, yet inexorable spreading-out of Western geoculture all over the globe. As Charles Orser stated, no so long ago, capitalism stands high among the haunts of historical archaeology – those closely interrelated "historical processes that underlie all historical archaeological research whether or not the archaeologist realizes it" (Orser 1996).

This being said, in the same way that the two first sections of this essay do not seek to trace a comprehensive genealogy of the capitalist experience, neither in the broad context of Latin America nor in the specific one of late-nineteenth-century New Granada, the remaining portion of this chapter does not aim at generating an all-encompassing archaeological definition of the processes through which rational, capital-producing, and commodity-consuming individuals (Gilje 1996) contributed to transform the material course of social life in the New World. Rather, my attempt here is to demonstrate that particular practices of consumption can be observed archaeologically and used to identify the presence of richly textured capitalist traits within an altogether peripheral and precapitalistic urban society such as the one living in Bogotá under the Radical Olympus. In doing so, I also highlight the unique capacity of historical archaeology to stand at the confluence of the private and the public spheres, right in the spot of the coloniality of power where the materiality of domestic practices becomes a reification of intricate national politics of modernization.

Fig. 7.1 Outdoor corridor in the Quinta de Bolívar. Courtesy of the Casa Museo Quinta de Bolívar, Ministerio de Cultura, Bogotá, Colombia

In the summer of 1999, during the restoration of what used to be Latin-American transnational hero Simón Bolívar's country house in Bogotá – *the Quinta de Bolívar* – a team of workmen accidentally stumbled upon the walls of an old cistern buried in the backyard of the villa (Gaitán Ammann 2005a; see Fig. 7.1). The stone-lined pool, presumably built in the early nineteenth century to store up the crystal-clear waters cascading from the moors that overlooked the capital city of New Granada, had been turned into a domestic dump by the late 1800s. Not surprisingly, this unglamorous architectural feature had never been reported in any description of the house dating back to its days of glory, and it was soon forgotten after it was filled and covered in domestic refuse (see Fig. 7.2).

From an archaeological standpoint, it was the first time that a sealed deposit dating to the late republican period was located and considered of cultural interest in Colombia, obviously because of the grand historical figure to which the materials in it were initially thought to be associated.[3] Mixed together with the colorful debris of coarse lead-glazed earthenwares, medicine flasks, wine bottles, piles of faunal

---

[3] In 1999, historical archaeology was still not well established as an anthropological discipline in Colombia. Consequently, the importance of the trash deposit in Bolívar estate was not immediately identified at the time it was discovered. A significant portion of the deposit was destroyed by workmen participating in the restoration of the house, and only its lower layers were excavated by professional archaeologists. However, because archaeologists in charge were not familiar with the depositional characteristics of historical sites, they did not apply a proper methodology to recover the cultural material in the cistern. Moreover, photographs and detailed records of the excavation were never produced or went missing before they could be analyzed. Therefore, the interpretation of the process of formation of the deposit was based on the labels found on unwashed bags of archaeological materials and on cross-mending sherds found in the collection.

Fig. 7.2 Backyard cistern at the Quinta de Bolívar. Bogotá, Colombia

remains, and the first archaeological toothbrush excavated in Colombia (see Gaitán Ammann 2005b), numerous remnants of white cups and plates were unearthed from the cistern.[4] Between 1999 and 2000, the typology and stylistic characteristics of these whiteware fragments were analyzed in detail, based on the information available for North American urban contexts of the same period (e.g., Miller 1991, Fitts 1999, Wall 1999), since no local data comparable to those recovered at Bolívar estate existed in Colombia at that time.[5] The merging of this new archaeological information and the ample archival data already existing about one of the greatest historical landmarks in the city of Bogotá (e.g., Valderrama 1998) strongly suggested that most of the whiteware sherds found in the cistern corresponded to a plain ironstone tableware[6] used on the table of the Uribes, a prominent bourgeois family who had owned Bolívar villa between 1870 and 1878 (Gaitán Ammann 2003).

A great deal of literature exists in historical archaeology as to the paramount role that tableware played in the process of shaping the modern self (e.g., Yamin 2000;

---

[4] About 1,112 ceramic fragments were recovered in the deposit in Bolívar estate. Of these, about 10% corresponded to undecorated porcelain, and 17.5% to plain whiteware. About 42% of those whiteware fragments could be classified as ironstone (for an exhaustive description and analysis of all the artifacts found in the cistern, see Gaitán Ammann 2005a).

[5] Archaeological data available for the late republican period in Bogotá have increased significantly in the last few years, mainly thanks to the development of some rescue archaeology projects within the historical district of the city (e.g., Gaitán et al. 2007). However, a consistent pool of ceramics data is still unavailable for the area, principally because of the lack of unity in ceramic typologies.

[6] Fitts (1999: 50) indicates that to be considered a tableware set, an assemblage must contain at least three different vessel forms in the same pattern.

Wall 1991; Brighton 2001). Especially for urban, middle-class contexts in North America, visible patterns in the consumption of tea or dinner sets have often been employed to evaluate the pace at which the materiality of dining rituals changed in the past in accordance with the rise of the purchasing power of salaried workers caught in the web of capitalist relations. The number and nature of the cups and plates assignable to a determined household in a particular time has traditionally been used as an almost unequivocal gauge to assess its social and economic standing, (Miller 1980, 1991) and the cultural practices to which these artifacts are normally linked have long been recognized as powerful bodily codes through which individualistic ideals, advocated by modernized western societies, can be played out in private, domestic spheres (Fitts 1999; Reckner and Brighton 1999; Majewski and Schiffer 2001).

The archaeological cups and plates excavated at Bolívar house were all impeccably plain and white, a trait that has also been found in contexts associated to puritan North American middle classes (cf. Reckner and Brighton 1999). Although it could be argued that this interesting similarity may be related to the limited availability of fine dining items in late nineteenth century Bogotá, there are good reasons to think that this pattern actually responded to a deliberate choice by Republican consumers, one that, perhaps, satisfied local high-classes' need for civilized and civilizing novelties and, at the same time, proclaimed the domestic, selective asceticism (*sensu* Bourdieu 1979) that, manifestly, local elites deemed the most perfect application of their traditional Catholic values. Whereas it is not really surprising to encounter consistent evidence for the use of a fine English ironstone dinner set in an affluent, high-class milieu of nineteenth century Bogotá, such as the patrician country house which had once been home to the author of the Letter from Jamaica, the absolute simplicity of the Uribes' dining materialities begs further thinking.[7] Would it be possible that, through their ascetic sense of domesticity, dominant groups in republican Bogotá were participating in the globalization of a discourse of temperance also popularized among Catholic working classes in late-nineteenth-century New York (Brighton 2001: 25)? If so, there is little doubt that the reasons explaining the implementation of such a discourse of moral superiority among elites in the peripheries of the modern world would be quite different from those justifying its use by middle classes in one of the main capitalist cores of the West. Yet in both cases, a religiously loaded taste for domestic plainness was certainly used as a strategy of social differentiation, contributing to the maintenance of the status quo in socially unstable contexts. Whereas American working classes could use the rhetoric of temperance to distinguish themselves both from the vices of the lower classes and from the sumptuary excesses of the upper ones (Reckner and Brighton 1999: 67), historical evidence clearly indicates that republican elites in the capital of New Granada were more than comfortable spending fortunes on simple materialities imported from the civilized West which, given the tremendous geographical isolation of the city of Bogotá well into the twentieth century, could effectively vouch for their dominant

---

[7]Isolated data from archaeological deposits related to working-class sectors in Republican Bogotá suggests that these groups were much more likely to consume colorful transfer-printed ceramics than their elite counterpart (Therrien et al. 2004; Gaitán et al. 2007). More data is presently needed to test this hypothesis.

Fig. 7.3 The backside of a J&G Meakin saucer with Leonidas Posada Gaviria's printed mark. Collection of the Casa Museo Quinta de Bolívar, Ministerio de Cultura, Bogotá, Colombia

position in their country's social, political and economic life.[8] It was, thus, certainly not without a touch of contempt that our friend Isaac Holton observed, back in 1857:

> I have thought that in New York there was a propensity to retrench in necessaries and spend too much in show. That failing is no less here. (Holton 1857)

Interestingly enough, as the remains of the Uribes' immaculate dinnerware were refitted and analyzed, a unique trademark was observed on at least four specimens in the assemblage. All of a sudden, overlaying the imprint of the well-known J&G Meakin Pottery of Hanley, England, a sober transfer-printed mark reading BOGOTA evoked the long-forgotten life story of Leonidas Posada Gaviria – a merchant of fine English crockery – who in the times of the Radical Olympus supplied the city's upper classes with modern objects of distinction specifically fired in England for the purpose of being consumed in the confines of the modern world (see Fig. 7.3). Born in 1848 in a coal-mining region of North Western New Granada, Posada Gaviria was among the many rural migrants who, by the second half of the nineteenth century, had left their hometowns to try their luck in Bogotá, probably enticed by widely circulating liberal propaganda espousing the virtues of modernity and of free trade. Although not much can be said of his early years as a migrant or as a trader, we

---

[8] More often than not, local elites justified their prominent social standing through their inherent capacity to behave according to Western, civilized canons. Travelers' accounts, etiquette codes, and humorous vignettes describing bourgeois social life in late-nineteenth-century Bogotá all contain compelling examples as to the way in which the capacity to abide by civilized manners was considered inherent to white race and Catholic religion, a posture that was obviously inherited from colonial times (see Gaitán Ammann 2005b).

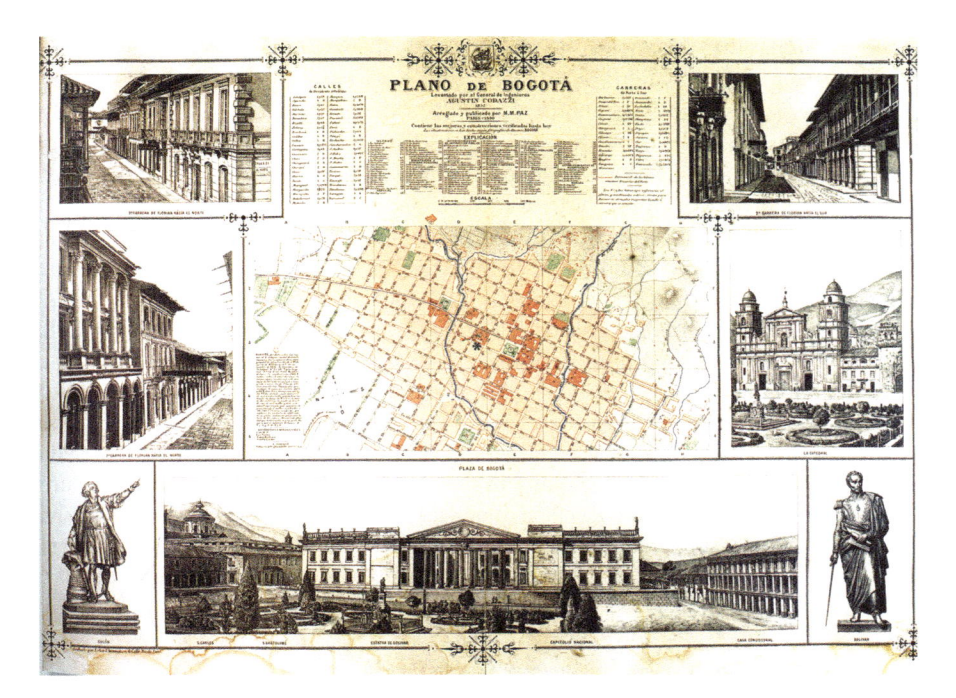

Fig. 7.4 A 1852 map of the city of Bogotá drawn by Agustín Codazzi, edited and published in 1890 by M.M. Paz. A black star indicates the location of Leonidas Posada Gaviria's shop on the 2a Calle de Florián, which is also represented on the top and middle-left etchings framing the map. Courtesy of the Museo de la Independencia, Casa del Florero, Ministerio de Cultura, Bogotá, Colombia

know that, by the end of the 1870s, Posada Gaviria owned his own glass and dinnerware shop in the most elegant commercial street in the city, the Calle de Florián, for which he had ordered plain ironstone dinner sets matching the tastes of a local bourgeoisie craving an exclusive access to modern fabrications (Fig. 7.4).

By stimulating novel consumerist practices in a traditional social context openly hostile to the democratization of refinement, Posada Gaviria was, in fact, just profiting from one among many commercial opportunities that the extremely liberal commercial policies of the period offered to those wishing to partake in the worldwide networks of capitalist exchange. I can truly think of no better embodiment of Posada Gaviria's social ascension than the simple trademark he had appended to the dishes he sold which, all at once, identified his merchandise, kindled his pride, and reified his success as a modern individual, as a thriving entrepreneur, and as a full-fledged citizen of the capital city of New Granada.

Leonidas Posada Gaviria seemed to have everything in hand to consecrate himself as a model of the self-made, capitalist, bourgeois man in the early postcolonial world-system. However, notarial records indicate that, as his business flourished, supplying the needs of a nascent bourgeoisie eager to emulate cosmopolitan fashions,

Posada Gaviria did not reinvest the surplus cash he was making in expanding his trading industry. On the contrary, he was buying large extensions of the best farming land available around Bogotá. On February 26, 1886, as New Granada was moving back to a conservative, centralist and presidential system relying on traditional Catholic values, Leonidas Posada advertised in a local newspaper[9] for someone to take over his crockery store, by then located on the first floor of his residence in the Plaza de Santander, the most exclusive neighborhood in town. Around that time, Posada Gaviria was also committed to the creation of the first almshouse for the elderly in town, a noble activity which, nonetheless, also betrayed his political ambitions. Indeed, Leonidas Posada Gaviria was well aware that only through his consecration as a worthy politician would he be able to attain the highest possible rank in republican society. In no time, then, our former crockery merchant was publicly listed among the Conservative candidates to the National Assembly. By the 1890s, the Almanac and Commercial Guide to Bogotá had stopped listing Posada Gaviria among the main traders in town and, interestingly enough, placed him among the principal landowners and ranchers in the Bogotá region. Finally, the nineteenth century surely came to a glorious end for Leonidas Posada Gaviria when, in 1899, he, the man who knew how much his name was worth on the backside of a white plate, took office as the Mayor of the republican city of Bogotá.

Capitalist Dualities

The republic of New Granada, like all young Latin-American nations, came into the world on deeply troubled grounds, marred by centuries of colonial rule that had left a long-lasting imprint in every thread of their postcolonial social and economic fabric. The logics of exploitive, unequal exchange had stealthily conquered the Spanish colonies in the New World well before the concept of modern capitalism had been established in industrial societies. For over 300 years, people, ideas and things traveling in galleon fleets, slave vessels and interloper ships had actively contributed to weave a complex network of exchange across the Atlantic, creating conditions of material dependency between the Old and the New World that could simply not be suspended by the brusque dissolution of the colonial bond linking America to Spain. Thus, many social structures directly inherited from colonial times survived the chaotic voyage Spanish America made toward modernity, determining the different ways in which mature capitalist relations would be socially constructed and reproduced at the local level. Following the achievement of their political independence, Latin-American republics would face decades of social, political and financial instability as they figured out how to walk the path of self-determination in a growingly globalized world. Undecided on the best way to justify their claim for autonomy while still mimicking the civilized manners of a mother-

---

[9] Diario de Cundinamarca, Bogotá, February 26, 1886.

land they had just disowned, new Latin-American countries also constituted a most fertile and coveted terrain on which the sprouts of a full-fledged capitalist system could take roots and grow. It is, no doubt, with much of a modern entrepreneurial vision, and more than just a touch of cynicism that Lord Canning, Chancellor of Great Britain observed in 1824:

> Spanish America is free, and if we do not mismanage our affairs, she is English. (As quoted in Kaumann 1951: 178)

Indeed, modern capitalism took roots and grew in free Spanish America and, in fact, it is now widely recognized that most societies bearing the legacy of Spanish colonial rule did not lay in complete isolation from the socioeconomic developments radically transforming lifestyles in the Atlantic world since the early sixteenth century. In most cases, Spanish colonial provinces and young Latin-American republics took a constituent part in the mercantilist ventures allowing the seed of capitalism to germinate in regions that would later become the main centers of industrial production and worldwide economic growth. Yet, what this chapter aims at highlighting through the archaeological rediscovery of the life-story of a self-made crockery merchant in republican Bogotá is that in this early postcolonial world afflicted since its political independence by a social and cultural condition of colonialism and dependency, the logics of modernity were inevitably transformed. This transformation or hybridization process can be observed in the historical and archaeological evidence discussed here. For example, the use that both Leonidas Posada Gaviria and the Uribe family made of plain English ironstone dinnerware illustrates the way in which certain modern practices, materialized through the consumption of specific, long-distance traveling goods often slipped off their ideal cultural pathways when they were enacted in peripheral and socially unstable contexts such as early postcolonial Latin America (Gaitán Ammann 2005b). More often than not, in these frontier contexts, mass-produced artifacts were transformed into rare objects of distinction (*sensu* Bourdieu 1979), which, despite their wide availability at a global level, did not contribute to a process of simplification of the social codes guiding local material consumption (cf. Shackel 1993; Mullins 2004; Palus 2005; see Gaitán Ammann 2005a). Rather, when experienced in the periphery of the capitalist world, manufactured goods objectifying modern senses of the self left the door open for powerful, hybrid materialities (Meskell 2004) to bloom up out of trivial, industrial artifacts such as cups and dishes, unexpectedly ascending to the category of precious and symbolically laden modern things.

Similarly, as Leonidas Posada Gaviria's life unfolds before our eyes, the city of Bogotá reveals to us as a complex heterotopic space (Foucault 1966; Hall 2000a, b) in which politically decolonized agents succeeded in manipulating the strings of the capitalist system so as to reproduce conditions of coloniality through precapitalist forms of inequality and social interaction. In that sense, the case study I propose in this chapter tangentially addresses a most intriguing and recurrent theme in the scholarly literature concerned with the rise of capitalist world-systems: the seemingly slow and flawed implementation of a primary core of capitalist values and features – such as the emergence of an individualist urban working class underpinning active processes of industrialization – within the former Spanish colonial territories.

In recent times, theses explaining the capitalistic stagnation of Latin America in terms of its historical dependency on the European metropoles have been convincingly discredited by studies uncovering the extraeconomic factors keeping local entrepreneurships trapped in webs of coercive, feudal-like relations of production (Stern 1988). Cases such as Leonidas Posada Gaviria's put these sociocultural factors in the foreground by suggesting, for example, that the progression of capitalism in nascent Latin-American nations may have been determined by a duality between peripheral, yet dynamic urban centers openly engaged in the capitalist experience, and retrograde rural zones either controlled or simply disregarded by these rising urban centers. Within these peripheral urban centers, the transition toward capitalism went hand in hand with the consolidation of traditional modes of social differentiation. Often relying on the exclusive access to distinctive instances of material culture such as the ones Posada Gaviria sold, these modes of social differentiation proved central to the maintenance of a stubbornly colonial social order, openly resisting many liberal and democratic views commended by radical republican ideals. Finally, as the life-story of Leonidas Posada Gaviria shows, even though Republican times brought about a gentrification process throughout a politically decolonized New Granada, for most local entrepreneurs, the implementation of new chains of production and exploitation did not rely on the formation of a modern type of individual, which may have served as the basis for the construction of a true capitalist working class. Rather, this rising gentrified class channeled its wealth in ways that reinforced the coloniality of power, thus keeping early postcolonial societies stranded in the periphery of the capitalist world, despite the fact that, from the standpoint of material consumption, they were wholly immersed in the global modern order.

Acknowledgments I would like to thank Sarah Croucher and Lindsay Weiss for inviting me to take part in the 2008 SHA session of which this volume derives. I am very much grateful for their unfailing patience, keen observations, and constant encouragement throughout this project. Thanks also to Daniel Castro and all the staff at the Casa Museo Quinta de Bolívar, in Bogotá, Colombia, for all their support during the research which, more than a decade ago, allowed me to amass the data I use in this chapter. Heather Atherton, Martin Hall, Zoad Humar, and María Lucía Vidart also provided important comments and suggestions on earlier drafts of this essay. Any lack of clarity or error in the arguments I expose here are, of course, my entire responsibility.

References

Abu-Lughod, Janet L. 1989 *Before European Hegemony. The World System A.D. 1250–1350.* Oxford University Press, New York.
Allahar, Antón L. 1990 The Evolution of the Latin American Bourgeoisie: An Historical-Comparative Study. *International Journal of Comparative Sociology* 31 (3–4):222–236.
Annino, Antonio (editor). 1996 *La invención del quinto Centenario: Antología* México, D.F: Instituto Nacional de Antropología e Historia.
Bertrand, Lewis. 1951 *Selected Writings of Bolívar* The Colonial Press Inc, New York.
Bhabha, Homi. 1985 Signs taken for wonders: questions of ambivalence and authority under a tree outside Delhi, May 1917. *In* Europe and its Others. Proceedings of the Essex Conference on the

Sociology of Literature. F. Berker, P. Hulme, M. Iversen, and D. Loxley, eds. Pp. 89–106. Colchester: University of Essex.

Bourdieu, Pierre. 1979 *La Distinction. Critique sociale du jugement.* Les Éditions de Minuit, Paris.

Bradshaw, York W., and Michael Wallace. 1996 *Global Inequalities.* Pine Forge Press, Thousand Oaks, CA.

Brighton, Stephen. 2001 Prices that Suit the Times: Shopping For Ceramics At The Five Points. *Historical Archaeology* 35 (3):16–30.

Bushnell, David. 1996 *Colombia, una nación a pesar de sí misma: de los tiempos precolombinos a nuestros días.* Planeta, Bogotá.

Castro-Gómez, Santiago. 2004 *La hybris del punto cero. Ciencia, raza e ilustración en la Nueva Granada (1750–1816).* Pontificia Universidad Javeriana; Instituto Pensar, Bogotá.

Clark, Christopher, Daniel Vickers, Stephen Aron, Nancy Grey Osterud, and Michael Merrill. 1994 The Transition to Capitalism in America: A Panel Discussion *The History Teacher* 27 (3): 263–288.

Cunin, Elizabeth. 2003 *Identidades a Flor de Piel: Lo "negro" entre apariencias y pertenencias: categorias raciales y mestizaje en* Cartagena. Instituto Colombiano de Antropologia e Historia, Universdad de los Andes, Instituto Francés de Estudios Andinos, Observatorio del Caribe Colombian, Bogotá.

Delpar, Helen. 1971 Aspects of Liberal Factionalism in Colombia, 1875–1885 *The Hispanic American Historical Review* 51 (2):250–274.

Du Bois, W.E.B. 1990 [1904] *The Souls of Black Folk.* Vintage Books, New York.

Fayard, Janine. 1979 *Les membres du Conseil de Castille à l'époque moderne (1621–1746).* Librairie Droz, Genève.

Fitts, Robert K. 1999 The Archaeology of Middle-Class Domesticity and Gentility in Brooklyn. *Historical Archaeology* 33 (1):39–62.

Foucault, Michel. 1966 *Les mots et les choses: Une archéologie des sciences humaines.*

Frank, Andre Gunder. 1991 Transitional Ideological Modes: Feudalism, Capitalism, Socialism *Critique of Anthropology* 11 (2):171–188.

Frank, Andre Gunder, and Barry K. Gills (editors). 1993 *The World System. Five hundred years or five thousand?* Routledge, London.

Gaitán Ammann, Felipe. 2003 Recordando a los Uribe: Memorias de higiene y de templanza en la Bogotá del Olimpo Radical. *Revista de Antropología y Arqueología* 13 (1):125–146.

Gaitán Ammann, Felipe. 2005a Expresiones de Modernidad en la Quinta de Bolívar: Arqueología de la alta burguesía bogotana en tiempos del Olimpo Radical (1870–1880).

Gaitán Ammann, Felipe. 2005b With a Hint of Paris in the Mouth: Fetishized Toothsbrushes or the Sensuous Experience of Modernity in Late 19th Century Bogotá. *In* Archaeologies of Materiality. L. Meskell, ed. Pp. 71–95. Oxford: Blackwell.

Gaitán, Felipe, and Jimena Lobo Guerrero. 2006 Cuentos de la basura: Arqueología de lo sucio y de lo limpio en la Bogotá republicana. Unpublished report. Fundación de Investigaciones Arqueológicas Nacionales; Banco de la República, Bogotá.

Gaitán, Felipe, Jimena Lobo Guerrero, and Elena Uprimny. 2007 Rescate del patrimonio arqueológico de Bogotá. Excavaciones en la Casa Saravia. Unpublished report. Fundación de Investigaciones Arqueológicas Nacionales; Banco de la República, Bogotá.

García-Canclini, Néstor. 2001 *Culturas híbridas: estrategias para entrar y salir de la modernidad.* D.F: Grijalbo, México.

Gilje, Paul A. 1996 The Rise of Capitalism in the Early Republic *Journal of the Early Republic* 16 (2), Special Issue on Capitalism in the Early Republic: 159–181.

Hall, M. 2000 *Archaeology and the Modern World: Colonial Transcripts in South Africa and the Chesapeake.* Routledge, New York.

Holton, Isaac. 1857 *New Granada: twenty months in the Andes.* Harper & Brothers, New York.

Humar, Zoad. 2009 Rutas biográficas e historias de los estudios culturales en Colombia. Entrevista a Santiago Castro-Gómez. *Tabula Rasa* 10:377–391.

Johnson, M. 1996 *An Archaeology of Capitalism*. Blackwell, Oxford.

Kalmanovitz, Salomón. 2001 *Las instituciones y el desarrollo económico en Colombia*. Norma, Bogotá.

Kaumann, W.W. 1951 *British Policy and the Independence of Latin America, 1804 –1828* Yale University Press, New Haven.

Leone, Mark. 1995 A Historical Archaeology of Capitalism. *American Anthropologist* 97:251–68.

Majewski, Teresita and Michael Brian Schiffer. 2001 Beyond consumption: Towords an archaeology of consumerism. *In* Archaeologies of the Contemporary past. V. Buchli and G. Lucas, eds. Pp. 26–50. London and New York: Routledge.

Martínez, Frédéric. 2001 *El nacionalismo cosmopolita: la referencia europea en la construcción nacional en Colombia, 1845–1900*. Banco de la República; Instituto Francés de Estudios Andinos, Bogotá.

Martínez Vergne, Teresita. 1992 *Capitalism in colonial Puerto Rico: Central San Vicente in the late nineteenth century*. University Press of Florida, Gainesville.

McGreevey, William Paul. 1982 *Historia económica de Colombia 1845–1930*. Ediciones Tercer Mundo, Bogotá.

Meskell, Lynn M. 2004 *Material Biographies: Object Worlds from Ancient Egypt and Beyond*. Berg, London.

Mielants, Eric. 2007 *The origins of capitalism and the "Rise of the West."* Temple University Press, Philadelphia.

Mignolo, Walter D. 2000a Introduction: From Cross-Genealogies and Subaltern Knowledges to Nepantla. *Nepantla: Views from South* 1 (1):1–8.

Mignolo, Walter D. 2000b La colonialidad a lo largo y a lo ancho: el hemisferio occidental en el horizonte colonial de la modernidad *In* La colonialidad del saber : eurocentrismo y ciencias sociales : perspectivas latinoamericanas E. Lander, ed. Pp. 55–86. Buenos Aires: CLACSO.

Mignolo, Walter D. 2008 Preamble: The Historical Foundation of Modernity/Coloniality and the Emergence of Decolonial Thinking. *In* A Companion to Latin American Literature and Culture. S. Castro-Klaren, ed. Pp. 12–52. Malden, MA: Blackwell.

Miller, George. 1980 Classification and Economic Scaling of 19th C Ceramics. *Historical Archaeology* 14:1–40.

Miller, George. 1991 A revised Set of CC Index Values for Classification and Ecoomic Scaling of English Ceramics from 1787–1880. *Historical Archaeology* 25 (1):1–25.

Mullins, Paul R. 2004 Ideology, Power, and Capitalism: The Historical Archaeology of Consumption. *In* A Companion to Social Archaeology. L. Meskell and R. Preucel, eds. Pp. 195–211. Oxford: Blackwell.

Nieto Arteta, Luis Eduardo. 1975 *Economía y cultura en la historia de Colombia*. Viento del Pueblo, Bogotá.

Orser, C. E. Jr. 1996 *A Historical Archaeology of the Modern World*. Plenum, New York.

Palacios, Marco. 2001 Prólogo. *In* El nacionalismo cosmopolita : la referencia europea en la construcción nacional en Colombia, 1845–1900. F.d.r. Martínez, ed. Pp. 13–25. Bogotá: Banco de la República; Instituto Francés de Estudios Andinos.

Palacios, Marco, and Frank Safford. 2002 *Colombia: Fragmented Land, Divided Society*. Oxford University Press, New York.

Palus, Matthew. 2005 Building an Architecture of Power: Electricity in Annapolis, Maryland in the 19th and 20th Centuries *In* Archaeologies of Materiality. L. Meskell, ed. Pp. 162–189. Oxford: Blackwell.

Pardo Rojas, Mauricio. 2006 La hybris del punto cero. Ciencia, raza e ilustración en la Nueva Granada (1750–1816). Santiago Castro-Gomez. Reseña. *Tabula Rasa* 4:339–346.

Paynter, Robert, Mark Leone, and Parker Potter (editors). 1999 *Historical Archaeologies of Capitalism*. Kluwer Academic Press, New York.

Quijano, Aníbal. 2000 Colonailidad del poder, eurocentrismo y América Latina. In *La colonialidad del saber: eurocentrismo y ciencias sociales. Perspectivas latinoamericanas.*, edited by E. Lander. CLACSO, Consejo Latinoamericano de Ciencias Sociales, Buenos Aires.

Reckner, Paul, and Stephen A Brighton. 1999 "Free From all Vicious Habits": Archaeological Perspectives on Class Conflict and the Rhetoric of Temperance. *Historical Archaeology* 33 (1): 63–86.

Rodríguez Piñeres, Eduardo. 1986 *El olimpo radical*. Editorial Incunables, Bogotá.

Sée, Henri Eugène. 1968 *Modern capitalism, its origin and evolution*. A.M. Kelley, New York.

Shackel, Paul. 1993 *Personal Discpiline and Material Culture: An Archaeology of Annapolis, Maryland, 1619–1870*. University of Tennessee, Knoxville.

Stern, Steve J. 1988 Feudalism, Capitalism, and the World-System in the Perspective of Latin America and the Caribbean *The American Historical Review* Vol. 93 (4):829–872.

Stern, Steve J. 1992 Paradigms of Conquest: History, Historiography, and Politics. *Journal of Latin American Studies* 4 Quincentenary Supplement: 1–34.

Therrien, Monika. 2007 *De fábrica a barrio: urbanización y urbanidad en la Fábrica de Loza Bogotana*. Pontificia Universidad Javeriana, Bogotá.

Therrien, Monika. 2008 Patrimonio y arqueología industrial: investigación vs. protección? Políticas del patrimonio industrial en Colombia. *Apuntes: Revista de Estudios sobre Patrimonio Cultural* 21 (1):44–61.

Therrien, Monika, Elena Uprimny, Jimena Lobo Guerrero, María Fernanda Salamanca, Felipe Gaitán, and Marta Fandiño. 2002 *Catálogo de cerámica colonial y republicana de la Nueva Granada: producción local y materiales foráneos (costa caribe, altiplano cundiboyacens-Colombia)*. FIAN, Banco de la República, Bogotá.

Therrien, Monika, Felipe Gaitán, and Jimena Lobo Guerrero. 2004 Civilidad y policía en la Santafé colonial, siglos XVI y XVII – unpublished report, Fundación de Investigaciones Arqueológicas Nacionales – Banco de la República, Bogotá.

Tirado Mejía, Alvaro. 1988 *Introducción a la historia económica de Colombia*. El Ancora, Bogotá.

Tirado Mejía, Alvaro. 1997 Colombia: siglo y medio de bipartidismo. La República Conservadora: Mundo. (AT). In *Colombia hoy, perspectivas hacia el siglo XXI*, edited by J. O. Melo, Pp. 97–189. Tercer Mundo, Bogotá.

Valderrama, Flor Marina. 1998 Quinta de Bolívar. Historia. Unpublished manuscript. Casa Museo Quinta de Bolívar, Bogotá.

Wall, Diana DiZerega. 1991 Sacred Dinners and Secular Teas: Constructing Domesticity in Mid-19th Century New York. *Historical Archaeology* 25 (4):69–81.

Wall, Diana DiZerega. 1999 Examine Gender, Class, and Ethnicity in 19th Century New York City. *Historical Archaeology* 33 (1):102–117.

Wallerstein, Immanuel. 1987 World-Systems Analysis. In *Social Theory Today*, edited by A. Giddens and J. H. Turner. Polity Press, Cambridge.

Wallerstein, Immanuel. 1991a *Geopolitics and Geoculture. Essays on the Changing World-System* Cambridge University Press, Cambridge.

Wallerstein, Immanuel. 1991b *Unthinking the Social Sciences. The Limits of Nineteenth-Century Paradigms*. Polity Press, Cambridge.

Wallerstein, Immanuel. 1991c World System versus World-Systems: A critique. *Critique of Anthropology* 11 (2):189–194.

Wallerstein, Immanuel. 1995 *After Liberalism*. The New Press, New York.

Weaver, Frederick Stirton. 1976 American Underdevelopment: An Interpretive Essay on Historical Change. *Latin American Perspectives: Dependency Theory and Dimensions of Imperialism* 3 (4):17–53.

Yamin, Rebecca (editor). 2000 *Tales of Five Points: Working Class Life in 19th Century New York*. Volume II, A Narrative History and Archaeology of Block 160. John Milner Associates, Inc., West Chester, PA.

Chapter 8
Exchange Values: Commodities, Colonialism, and Identity on Nineteenth Century Zanzibar

Sarah K. Croucher

Introduction

Picture brightly painted ceramic bowls. These are large bowls – too large for an individual serving. Hard white earthenware forms their bodies, with a clear glaze overlying painted and printed decoration. Bright pink, blue, and sometimes black bands around the edges, in varying thicknesses; sometimes large floral patterns bedeck the interior of the bowls, pink and blue petals, stamped sponge-printed repeating flowers, and leafy green foliage (see Fig. 8.1). Flip the bowls over, as surely no user would have done during the course of a meal, and sometimes a maker's mark, locating the piece as manufactured in the Netherlands or Great Britain, will be your reward. For despite the fact that these ceramics are found in Zanzibari houses, curio stores, and in sherd form spread across farmers' fields, no East African manufacturer is represented by the marks (see Fig. 8.2).[1] It is these ceramics – mostly in bowl form, but with the odd teacup, platter, and saucer, that form the material examined within this chapter.

The narrative takes, in part, a traditional archaeological form, presenting the proportions of sherds found across different clove plantation sites on nineteenth century Zanzibar. In doing so, an archaeological context which is firmly capitalist and colonial is established. Capitalist through the context of plantations producing a mono-crop (cloves) for a global market during the nineteenth century; and in tracing findings of a mass produced ceramic, manufactured as a commodity and sold for cash to plantation residents. All of the material discussed in this chapter took place

---

[1] Locally produced ceramics of Zanzibar formed the majority of the assemblage from the archaeological investigations discussed in this chapter. Their usual form was open "carinated cooking pots" regularly decorated with arc decorations and occasional burnishing and red paint (Croucher 2006; Croucher and Wynne-Jones 2006).

S.K. Croucher (✉)
Assistant Professor of Anthropology, Archaeology, and Feminist,
Gender & Sexuality Studies, Wesleyan University, Middletown, CT, USA
e-mail: scroucher@wesleyan.edu

S.K. Croucher and L. Weiss (eds.), *The Archaeology of Capitalism in Colonial Contexts*, 165
Contributions To Global Historical Archaeology, DOI 10.1007/978-1-4614-0192-6_8,
© Springer Science+Business Media, LLC 2011

Fig. 8.1 Ceramics in a Zanzibar curio shop, 2006

within the context of Omani colonialism – the majority of clove plantation owners were Omani colonists, and the Omani Sultanate controlled the islands. Such a background provides the colonial context, albeit not the European colonial context we are most used to as historical archaeologists, but still one in which colonial rule coexisted with capitalist practice. Within this field, I am taking capitalism to mean the form of intense agricultural production and the increasing inability for Zanzibaris to procure the basic necessities of life without involvement in a cash economy, as was the case by the late-nineteenth century on Zanzibar (Bose 2006; Pearson 1998; Sheriff 1987). Capitalism is a complex concept, with widespread debates as to periodization and meaning within a range of social sciences, and it could be argued that the lack of industrial production on Zanzibar in the nineteenth century means that this was only an incipient capitalist economy and society (Goody 2004; Harvey 2010; Wolf 1997 [1982]). This chapter is specifically concerned with the discourse about the multiplicity of capitalism*s* within the field of historical archaeology as it is usually constituted by US-based scholars. Within historical archaeology, an understanding of a very broad definition of capitalism which includes plantation agriculture within a global economic system has become a near-universal definition of the field (Delle 1998; Orser 1996). As the place of Africans seems so often troubled within these global narratives of capitalism (Lane 2007; Prestholdt 2008; Schmidt and Walz 2007) I wish to interrogate how we might address the potential multiplicity of social systems if we are to retain this large-scale definition of capitalism within our field as a heuristic device allowing for meaningful comparative discourse. This argument moves forward beyond a semantic or methodological debate about the term "historical archaeology" as utilized within the African context and instead considers the core concepts at the heart of the discipline (capitalism and colonialism),

Fig. 8.2 *Top*, white earthenware teacup base with maker's mark, painted floral decoration. *Bottom*, base sherd of European imported ceramic, showing makers mark (Societie Ceramique, Maastricht, made in Holland)

attempting to question and broaden these so that they apply to the later historical archaeology of Africa within a postcolonial theoretical framework.

At the micro-level, with specific regard to Zanzibari, East African, and Indian Ocean historical analysis, I am interested in the manner in which exchange took place within plantations. Although these were cash purchased commodities, by juxtaposing archaeological data and oral histories, I argue that social relations were also embedded in the exchange of goods within nineteenth century Zanzibari plantation culture. In so doing I take a familiar path of drawing out the complexities of commodity exchange, noting the manner in which a *partial* "gift" economy – which emphasizes reciprocal social obligations (Mauss 1990 [1950]: 3) – was in operation between plantation residents, often in relation to circulating some of the most highly commoditized goods. Through this exploration the manner in which the colonial context of Zanzibar shaped a particular cultural iteration of commodity exchange for plantation residents will become clear.

At a macro-level, these brightly decorated ceramics, all of which were manufactured many thousands of miles away in Europe, provide a useful material form for applying a "commodity chain" analysis to mass produced goods on nineteenth century Zanzibar. Such approaches are now widespread in a number of disciplines, including geography, history, and anthropology (Brewer and Trentman 2006; Clarence-Smith and Topik 2003; Hansen 2000; Jackson 2004; Marcus 1995; Mintz 1985; van den Bersselaar 2007; Walsh 2010). Their premise is that commodities in a globalizing world can only be fully analyzed through tracing their meanings through production and various exchanges, taking note of the cultural contexts within each step (Crang et al. 2003; Jackson 1999; Tsing 2005). These "chains" also echo what Appadurai (1986: 27) called "ecumenes"; the entirety of networks between producers and consumers of commodities. This has the advantage of being focused on no sole context of production, exchange, or consumption. It offers instead a means of tying together all of these into a single frame of analysis. As anthropology as a field increasingly grapples with how to analyze global connections at a meaningful local scale (Marcus 1995), this approach links together various contexts through the flow of materials and cultural translation which occur within commodity chains.

Within historical archaeology, debates have been intensifying on how to frame the global relations within which the subjects of our studies were enmeshed. Some have attempted to make a clear geographical linkage between sites: for example, a field of Atlantic historical archaeology has emerged, in which relations of trade, forced-, and voluntary-migration played out between Europe, North, and South America (DeCorse 2001; Hall 2000; Hicks 2005; Ogundiran and Falola 2007; Orser 1996; Richard 2009, 2010, Chap. 9; Singleton 1995, 2005; Stahl 2007). Grappling with these global questions is vital in order to attempt to interpret the particular contexts we study and the manner in which global relations were understood by past subjects. But it is vital we focus a critical postcolonial gaze upon broader discourse in our own subject. Historical archaeology risks essentializing capitalism within the West in an uncritical manner (Carrier 1992: 205). Concomitantly, sometimes insidiously within the work of those focused exclusively on the West is the manner in which cultural Others (in this case Zanzibaris on the "periphery" of global capitalism) are often used as uncritical foils to our constructs of Western capitalism (Richard 2010; van Dommelen 2010: 38), in the process creating both as monolithic cultural types.

By exploring the commodity chain of nineteenth century imported ceramics on Zanzibar, it is possible to do more than simply explore a narrow case study exchange relations on Zanzibar. Beyond this, we begin to see the various scales of capitalism in operation, and the manner in which agency and cultural practice are able to traverse global relations through the very medium of commodity chains, even if this be diffuse, and sometimes without the intent of individual subjects. Commodity chain analysis presents a clear methodology for archaeology since it is possible to trace the relations and meanings of material culture in various contexts with a combination of artifactual and historical data. It is also an important analysis in providing us with a means to further engage with the global meanings of capitalism in the nineteenth century, a subject of relevance to *all* historical archaeologists of this period, wherever their context of research.

Contextualizing Capitalism: Plantations on Nineteenth Century Zanzibar

Zanzibar during the 1800s was a major entrepôt for trade from the intensifying caravan trade which transported ivory and enslaved Africans from mainland East and Central Africa[2] (Rockel 2006; Pearson 1998; Sheriff 1995a). Politically the islands of Zanzibar,[3] along with a strip of land along the East African coast, were at this time under the control of the Omani sultanate. The importance of Zanzibar was, until the mid-nineteenth century, based largely on mercantilism, with ivory fetching a high price and with a ready market for enslaved labor across the Indian Ocean region and beyond (Sheriff 1987). From the 1810s however, a new crop began to be planted on the islands, closely associated with the Omani elite – the clove tree. This spice required specialized environmental conditions for growth which were found across much of the islands (see Fig. 8.3). This environmental factor, combined with availability of land and slave labor on Zanzibar (another push was a shrinking market for enslaved persons elsewhere, as the British and other colonial powers attempted to abolish the slave trade during the nineteenth century) made for the rapid expansion of plantations across Zanzibar, with Pemba becoming a preferred location for new plantations from the mid nineteenth century onwards (Cooper 1977, 1979; Sheriff 1987).

Cloves were a highly marketable commodity. Spices had long been a mainstay of global commodity trade (Crofton 1936; Dalby 2002), and continued to command a high price into the nineteenth century, even as the price of cloves fluctuated according to the glut of production produced by Zanzibar into global markets. Plantation agriculture is thought to have been influenced greatly by knowledge of European plantations in the Indian Ocean region, brought to Zanzibar by its cosmopolitan population who were traveling widely in the region (Cooper 1977; Prestholdt 2008;

---

[2] The Swahili cities of the East African coast have been shown to be participants in inter-regional trade across the Indian Ocean from at least the ninth century AD (see Horton 1996; LaViolette and Fleisher 2005; Juma 2004 for comprehensive archaeological discussions). Swahili towns were linked into wide Indian Ocean regional trading networks which spread from East Africa, through the Middle East, India, and across to China. This network, termed by Michael Pearson (1998: 36) the "Afarasian Sea" had a truly global scope from the close of the fifteenth century with the entry of the Portuguese into Indian Ocean trade. However, important European trade may be to the later history discussed in this chapter, it is important to note that this grew out of a long established mercantile system, and scholars of this region have been keen to point out the long-term historical build up to nineteenth century mercantile trade (Pearson 2006; Sheriff 2010).

[3] In this chapter, I refer to the two islands by their proper names; Unguja, the southern of the two main Zanzibari islands is that usually referred to as Zanzibar, and Pemba, the northern portion of the political entity which forms Zanzibar. The term Zanzibar is used to refer to the islands as a whole or to the urban center of Zanzibar on Unguja.

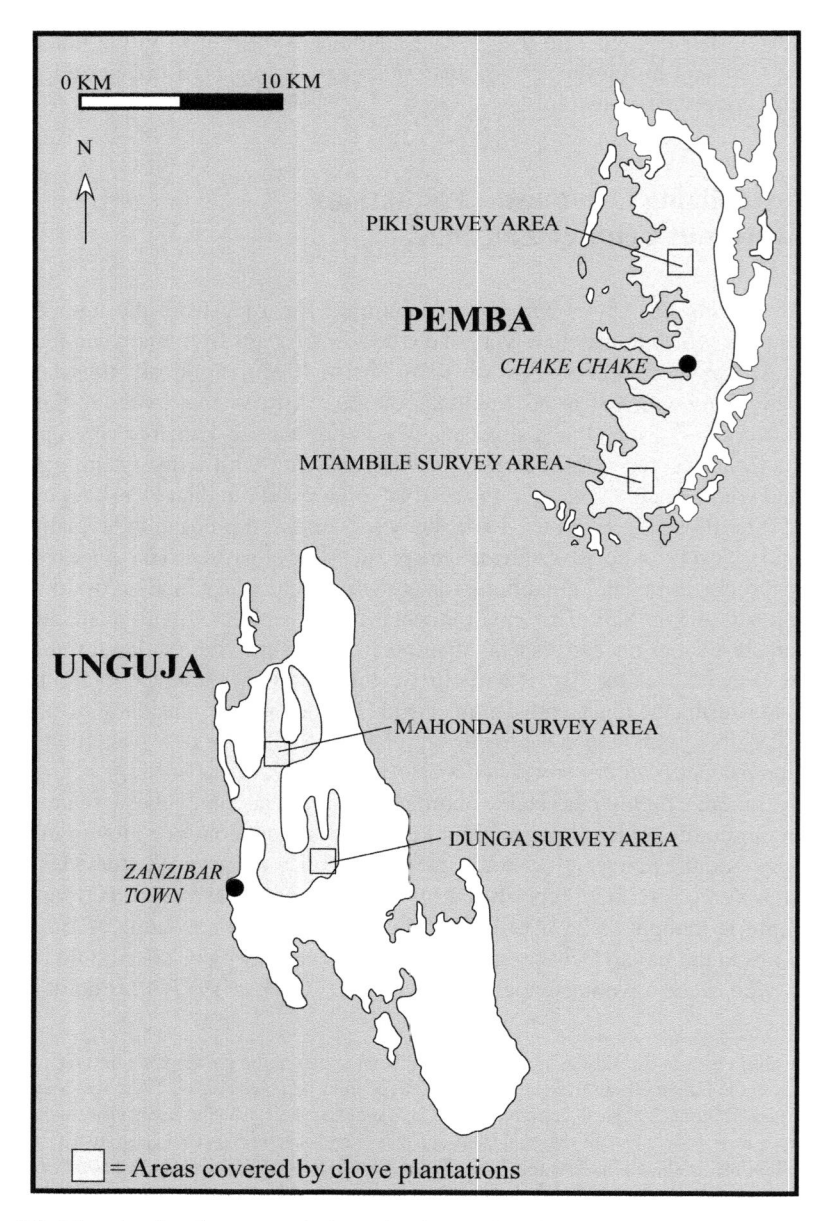

Fig. 8.3 Map showing the extent of clove planting on Zanzibar, and the location of the survey areas for the ZCPS03

Sheriff 1987). Archaeological evidence demonstrates close similarities and divergences with the more widely known forms of European plantations (for archaeological studies of these see, for instance, Delle 1998). Zanzibari planter's homes appear to have followed a spatial ordering which drew heavily on pre-existing Omani and Swahili spatial norms, particularly in architectural style and in the gendering of space. In these homes would have lived plantation owners, their wives, concubines, children, and those of the enslaved population who may have worked closely within the household. Outside of these homes, spaced out into the wider plantation landscape would have been the home of enslaved field laborers. Excavations have also shown that new spaces such as clove drying floors for monitoring work on the plantation, which appear to be tailored to regimes of labor mirroring those seen in plantations in the Americas, were also built into the landscape of nineteenth century plantations. Such spaces provided a clear area in which we can see that spatial practices were not simply those of prior cultural convention but were instead shaped by new economic models (Croucher 2006, 2007, in preparation).

On the basis of mono-crop plantations which fed into a global commodity market, it would seem easy to characterize Zanzibar as fully participant in global capitalism of the nineteenth century. Yet the fact that this was run by colonial rule and capitalist subjects entirely within an Islamic, African, and Arabic cultural context seems to prevent the full realization of this image. Implicit within many of our writings about global capitalism in the nineteenth century is the idea that capitalism is a European institution and culture, with non-European cultures as only ever being peripheral to global capitalism (e.g., Wallerstein 1976; for further discussion of core and periphery models in historical archaeology see Crowell, Chap. 4; Gaitán-Amman, Chap. 7). A key issue of this chapter is therefore an interrogation of whether we can view the culture of clove plantations on Zanzibar during the nineteenth century as being fully part of capitalism, or whether the Islamic and East African context made these plantations only peripheral to the wider globalization of capitalist social relations at this time.

Building further upon this issue is how we might fit nineteenth century Zanzibar within broader historical archaeological discourse of colonialism and capitalist modernities, linking to the analysis of global capitalism via commodity chains. In the clearest iteration of "African historical archaeology/ies" (Reid and Lane 2004; Schmidt 2006; Schmidt and Walz 2007), we might argue that the situation on Zanzibar is something apart from the mainstream of USA/European historical archaeology, with African subjects placed at the center of our analysis not fitting with larger ideas articulated by the canon of historical archaeology (which are most usually cited as Deetz 1996; Orser 1996). As I have outlined in my narration of nineteenth century Zanzibari history, however, the situation is not so clear. It is easy to see that we can identify Omani colonialism as in many ways fitting many of the patterns of contemporaneous European colonial rule, particularly in developing new areas for plantation agriculture to feed into global markets. The increasing use of enslaved Africans simply as agricultural labor during the nineteenth century also marked a move into the conceptualization of slavery as a means of gaining the labor necessary to produce cash crops. This replaced slavery as a way of increasing a client base and gaining higher social prestige – although the two systems were not antithetical and a mixture of understandings of enslavement were in play in nineteenth century Zanzibari society. Even though the majority of Zanzibari residents were Swahili, Arab, African, or Indian, it is important to recognize the influence of a growing undercurrent of European dominated global capitalism on the islands (Pearson 1998: 162). Historical archaeological analysis of plantations on Zanzibar must, therefore, be aware of all of these elements and a sophisticated study must attempt to identify and analyze the various strands of social, economic, and political action being played out in material realms.

Taking Notice of Ceramics

Turning back to material culture, outside of the archaeological realm, my fieldwork on Zanzibar was characterized by frequent introductions to late-nineteenth and early-twentieth centuries mass produced ceramics from Europe. It is, of course, with hindsight that I placed together these different moments, but the contemporary context of these ceramics – now cast into roles as heirlooms, antiques, and museum pieces – adds an important dimension to understanding the social role of these objects in the past. My first realization that these might be culturally important came from my landlady in the city of Zanzibar. I had been working at the Zanzibar archives and lodging locally. I would eat with my landlady and her daughters every evening, sitting on a large mat in the front room to share dishes. All of the dishes for the daily meals were kept in a sideboard in this room with some dishes used every day and others only used now and then, mostly when we ate special meals. One platter in particular was never removed during my stay. Just before my survey fieldwork was due to begin, my landlady engaged me in conversation about this platter. It was her best – a treasured family heirloom and used only for very special meals she told me. But on Pemba, people had plenty of big platters like this, and sometimes sold them. If I was offered one at a reasonable price, could I buy it on her behalf and bring it back?

No one offered a platter for sale, but I did see more of these dishes on Pemba. One day when my field crew and I were undertaking survey fieldwork, a man whom we had met earlier when asking about sites suddenly reappeared with a sack. Inside were some things that he wanted to show us, family heirlooms passed down to him from his grandmother (Fig. 8.4). At the time I was most interested in the wooden pot he had that was filled with paper jewelry. The bright colored ear decorations were something some interviewees had told us had been commonly used by poorer women in the past on Zanzibar, but of course we never found any on archaeological sites. The platter was interesting – a large rectangular willow pattern platter with the common blue and white design printed across the entirety of the vessel. But it had no maker's mark on the bottom, just a smooth surface of white glazed earthenware. I guessed it could date from anytime from the late-nineteenth century into the twentieth century, and thought little more of it until later when a sherd of a nearly identical platter was recovered from excavations at a clove plantation site (Fig. 8.5).

Returning to those brightly colored bowls, the material at the center of my analysis comes from archaeological survey data drawn from the Zanzibar Clove Plantation Survey 2003 (hereafter ZCPS2003, see Fig. 8.3 for a map of survey areas) and from excavations at the plantation site of Mgoli on Pemba, located in the Piki survey area. The combination of this data provides a between materials found on different

Fig. 8.4 Heirlooms on the road: a willow pattern platter and wooden boxes containing jewelry (this photograph was taken with full consent that it be published in sources that would be circulated and read internationally and on Zanzibar)

nineteenth century clove plantation sites on Zanzibar and a more detailed interrogation of materials found at a single site.[4]

Drawing out contextual archaeological data from one site, at the earliest excavated contexts at Mgoli imported commodities, including non-ceramics such as glass, beads, and metals, figured as a fairly small proportion of the overall assemblage; just 11.4%. Out of this assemblage mass produced ceramics made up only 6% overall and a little over half of the nonlocally produced goods.[5] When taken as a percentage only of the ceramic assemblage, mass produced imports from the mid-nineteenth century made up 7%.

---

[4] Survey data are drawn from the Zanzibar Clove Plantation Survey 2003. This consisted of purposive surface survey conducted at four different areas on Unguja and Pemba (see Fig. 8.3 for a map showing these areas). No subsurface testing was conducted, and the visibility of artifacts at different sites did vary upon the level of recent digging for purposes of farming. However, imported ceramics were found to be readily visible. For the purpose of analysis, material here is largely considered in terms of the presence and/or absence on different sites. Proportions of different materials at sites with this survey data offer extremely tentative evidence, since they were collected in a nonsystematic manner. Proportions of material presented from excavation data, all of which derives from excavations at Mgoli, Pemba in 2004, are based on 100% collection and sieving and can therefore be taken as valid proportional data.

[5] Particular contexts were drawn out for analysis from the material at Mgoli as a whole. Where mid-nineteenth century material is discussed, these contexts are from Trench C, numbered 3005 and 3009. Where late-nineteenth/early-twentieth century material is mentioned, contexts were analyzed from Trench D, numbered 4007 and 4008. Overall numbers for the site of Mgoli refer to material from all contexts. Percentages provided here are calculated by count.

Fig. 8.5 Four conjoining rim sherds of a black transfer printed willow pattern platter, recovered from Mgoli, Trench C

Later material from the late-nineteenth/early-twentieth century showed a small increase in the number of imported ceramics. Figures were skewed by a large dump of metal refuse such as rusted can pieces, so the proportion of mass produced imported ceramic sherds made up just 5% of the assemblage in these later contexts, but a significantly larger 11% when taken only as a percentage of ceramics. These data appear to support the idea that commodified goods – here in the form of mass produced ceramics – were becoming increasingly common at the close of the nineteenth century, although they still formed a minority of wares in comparison to locally made dishes.

If the ceramic sherds from Zanzibar discussed here were laid alongside assemblages excavated by the majority of other historical archaeologists, many clear differences would immediately be apparent. The first would be in the design of many of the vessels. The decoration of mass produced imported vessels fell mostly into two clear categories: transfer printed or hand painted and/or sponge print decoration.[6]

---

[6] Less than 4% of mass produced ceramics excavated from Mgoli overall had a design falling outside of these two categories. Full details of these materials can be found in Croucher (2006) Chapter 7 and Appendix D. By far the most common decorative form on transfer printed vessels was willow pattern, found on several "platter" sherds – these would have been from large, flat, rectangular serving plates, still used today for special occasions. The proportion of transfer printed ceramics fell over the course of the nineteenth century, comprising 40% of imported sherds in earlier analyzed contexts and dropping to just 9% in later contexts. Painted and sponge designs were most common overall, forming 38% of the imports from the site of Mgoli overall, 43% from mid-nineteenth century contexts, and 19% of those from late-nineteenth century/early-twentieth century contexts, where numbers of decorated ceramics had dropped significantly.

Bright colored lines and sponge printing dominated the most common bowl forms of material.[7] The brightly painted and/or sponge decorated wares that formed the majority of imports used by are little discussed in the majority of historical archaeological literature. In most European and American contexts, they are found in much lower numbers in comparison to decorative styles such as transfer prints, flow blues, and other styles of designs, if they are even found at all (Miller 1980, 1991). Their use in European and American contexts tended to be limited to very cheaply produced cut-sponge decorated earthenwares, used only in poor households, and often differing in form – e.g. mugs and small individual bowls – than those found in Zanzibar (e.g., Brooks 2003: 125).

This leads neatly to the second major difference visible between Zanzibari material and that from other regions of the world studied by historical archaeologists: the forms of the ceramics. Large bowl forms predominated on Zanzibar – as is clear from the ceramics curated through time and now on sale in curio shops – with teacups, small plates, and large platters following in frequency.[8] Comparison of these frequencies of forms to other East African contexts is impossible, since no data exist for these, although it has been noted that such brightly colored large bowls are the common form of imports at later sites (Fleisher personal communication; Horton personal communication). Zanzibari material does have clear contrasts with mass produced ceramics from other areas of the world where historical archaeologists work. In Cape Town, South Africa, for instance, predominant forms of nineteenth century ceramics were tablewares, predominantly plates used for individual servings of meals at a table (Malan and Klose 2003: 202; Weiss 2009, Chap. 10). Since many trade routes ran from Europe around South Africa (although the opening of the Suez Canal in 1869 did change this pattern) we might expect that trade goods sent along these routes would be similar. The South African ceramic signature, however, although not identical, had far clearer parallels with British, Australian, and North American contexts, where

---

[7]Drawing on excavated material painted and sponge designs was most common when the assemblage is taken as a whole, forming 38% of the imports from the site of Mgoli overall, 43% from mid-nineteenth century contexts and, 19% of those from late-nineteenth century/early-twentieth century contexts, where numbers of decorated ceramics had dropped significantly. By far the most common decorative form on transfer printed vessels was willow pattern, found on several platter sherds – these would have been from large, flat, rectangular serving plates, still used today for special occasions. The proportion of transfer printed ceramics fell over the course of the nineteenth century, comprising 40% of imported sherds in earlier analyzed contexts and dropping to just 9% in later contexts.

[8]Bowls were most common in mid-nineteenth century contexts, where they accounted for 61% of diagnostic mass produced sherds, a further 29% of diagnostic imports were teacups, with a few further sherds of large platters. Numbers were significantly different for late-nineteenth century/early-twentieth century material, where only 4% of diagnostic mass produced sherds were bowl forms, with a much higher 57% of sherds being recognizable teacup forms. While this seems to signal a shift toward more common use of teacups, the overall percentages of material from the site where 40% of diagnostic mass produced ceramic sherds were bowl forms and 37% were teacups, seems to suggest that when a wider range of data is available for this period, we may not see such dramatic differences. Clearly the ceramics surviving today testify to the importance of bowls, as do oral histories. But teacups may have had a wider usage in daily life, and been viewed as more of a utilitarian form than bowls. If more were available and their daily frequency of use was higher, teacups may also have been more liable to breakage, therefore presenting more sherds in the archaeological record.

plates and bowls used to serve individual placements at tables were common during the eighteenth and nineteenth centuries (for some examples, see Brooks 1997; Brooks and Connah 2007; Leone 1999; Shackel and Palus 2006; Wall 1999).

Another contrast in ceramic assemblages between East Africa and regions studied by the majority of historical archaeologists would be that produced imported ceramics were only a small proportion of vessels utilized at mealtimes on Zanzibar. They made up just 4% of the overall ceramic assemblage from the site of Mgoli ($n = 11,090$) across all periods from the mid-nineteenth century into the twentieth century.[9] Such small numbers perhaps make them easy to ignore as an important artifact category with which to examine nineteenth century plantation society on Zanzibar. Thus, we could bookmark them as a useful dating tool, note their presence, and move on to analyze the majority locally produced wares. But the ubiquity of their use stood out: drawing upon survey data, 85% of recorded ceramic sherds were mass produced European imports, and imported ceramics were visible on the majority of sites recorded.[10] Only a single site from the 64 recorded had only locally produced ceramics with a complete absence of visible imported ceramics, and this site (recorded as SC34, see Croucher 2006: 385 for site details) was one which we were told had been the location of a village inhabited by enslaved plantation workers. Therefore, the low percentage of their overall proportions at the site of Mgoli must be contrasted with their widespread presence on clove plantation sites.

What then could these different factors mean? Non-local ceramics were rare by their low percentages in the Mgoli site assemblage – and it is worth noting that this related to the home of a wealthy plantation owner. Yet survey data indicated that mass produced ceramics had apparently been used at many different types of settlement, including those inhabited by enslaved workers (see Croucher 2004, 2007, for full

---

[9]Ceramics in total made up 76% of the entire assemblage by artifact count ($n = 14,602$). The remainder of the ceramic assemblage was made up of majority locally produced wares (93%) and non-mass produced imports (3%) – the majority of this latter category being "Indian" water pots (mitungi), which may have been produced locally (see Croucher 2006: Appendix E for details).

[10]Using quantitative data from this survey evidence is problematic. Since only purposive surface survey was carried out (for a discussion of full survey methodology and results see Croucher 2004), it is impossible to say that these data are a representative sample of material from all nineteenth century clove plantations across the four survey regions from which data were collected. Of 64 sites recorded on the survey, 86% (55 sites) had imported ceramics visible, compared to a slightly lower 75% (48 sites) with local ceramics visible on the surface, with many sites having both. The reasons for this distribution seem unclear, although they are explored in more detail further on in this chapter. In interpreting them it may be worth noting that the majority of survey sites, although by no means all, were those associated with plantation owners. Over three-quarters (76%) of all sites recorded had no stone remains visible on the surface. This means that despite the higher correlation with plantation owners, the majority of these sites related to people who likely did not have the economic means available to build a stone house (see Croucher 2006, in preparation for further discussion of the relationship between architectural styles on Zanzibar and social standing, as well as Myers 1996, 1997). A slight skewing of the data may have been caused by the visibility of ceramic remains in a tropical landscape context. On sites with dense undergrowth, locally produced wears which lack the reflective qualities of glazed imports may have been harder to pick out visually. Nevertheless, thorough visual examination was undertaken at each site recorded and so this is likely to cause only very minor differences in the recorded artifacts.

analysis of site types across the landscape). The use of mass produced ceramics on nineteenth century Zanzibar also seemed to represent a particular taste in commodity purchases, particularly through the brightly painted and printed bowls and the platters, differing from that found in most historical archaeological contexts. Thus, the commodity supply of ceramics to Zanzibar was not simply the overflow of that to the nearest European colonial settlements, but appears to represent the desires of nineteenth century consumers on Zanzibar and particular patterns of use which show the manner in which commodity exchange was incorporated into the cultural context of clove plantations. It is to these factors that I now wish to turn in my discussions.

Wealth and Reciprocity on Zanzibar

If mass produced ceramics formed only a small part of the assemblage of mid-nineteenth century plantation household wares, growing to a slightly larger proportion by the beginning of the twentieth century it is possible to hypothesize that they were potentially expensive goods and were available on a limited basis which grew over time. This pattern does not seem unexpected, and can be compared with work on commodity consumption in other capitalist contexts. As the use of commodities grew in other parts of the world, a "consumer culture" grew, in which social status was increasingly demonstrated through the consumption of material goods, particularly within North America (see Sassatelli 2007: Chapter 2 for an overview; Mullins 1999: 1). Debates range about the nature and spread of consumer culture, but for the purpose of this chapter it can be summarized that subjects – now consumers – are understood to increasingly express their subjectivities through commodities, usually mass produced, and bought through alienated cash exchanges (Douglas and Isherwood 1996 [1979]: 38; Foster 2008: 11; Miller 1995). Within historical archaeology, interpretation of assemblages from periods in which the consumption of commodities was increasing has been dominated by a straightforward cost-value index approach, in which the amount and expense of goods within an assemblage was assumed to allow for comparative analysis of the level of wealth of a household represented (Brooks and Connah 2007; Henry 1991; Miller 1980).[11] Processes of

---

[11] Debates within historical archaeology are now moving beyond a straightforward equation of the cost of goods and the status of a household, including some of those cited previously. Many of the more recent debates within historical archaeology about the nature of consumer goods within households stem from the work of Mullins (1999, 2004; see also Cook et al. 1996). Studies have shown that households may buy goods that exceed expectations based on their income, particularly when these are readily available in urban situations (Brighton 2001). However, underlying all of these discussions is a general assumption that the consumption of commodities is based upon consumers acquiring goods in an attempt to present symbolic messages – most often relating to class or economic status – to their immediate neighbors and acquaintances. The end result may be more nuanced than a direct correlation between economic wherewithal of a household and their material possessions, but where differences occur, these are most usually in the form of poorer households attempting to apportion larger amounts of their income to consumer goods in order to present the façade of a higher status than might otherwise be accorded by their social standing and economic means.

commodification were certainly taking place within nineteenth century Zanzibar, fuelled by the capitalism of caravan trading and plantations (Prestholdt 2004). Owning imported goods in nineteenth century East Africa could indeed function as symbolic markers of wealth, particularly when these were symbolic of elite coastal identities (Glassman 1995: 50; New 1875: 416).

From the growth of imported ceramics at sites over time (see also Pawlowicz 2009 for comparable data from survey on the southern Tanzanian coast) it is possible to conclude that an intensification of commodification was occurring on nineteenth century Zanzibar; increasingly mass produced goods and other products could be bought for cash and these we might expect would be understood to be symbolic of the wealth and/or status of a household, the two clearly being connected. But the mass produced ceramic data does not seem to straightforwardly conform to this general pattern, because sherds had such a wide distribution across different plantation sites. To interpret this pattern, we must delve a little deeper into the evidence surrounding processes of commodification on Zanzibar at this time. Oral histories, recorded in conjunction with the ZCPS03 and excavations at Mgoli shed some insights into how we might begin to see the particular form of consumer culture as it began to exist on nineteenth century Zanzibar.[12]

Some interviewees said that imported ceramics were used every day, particularly the smaller plates and teacups, although the households with the smallest available cash resources may have kept imported ceramics solely for use on special occasions.[13] Comments in these interviews led to the conjecture that in the past the level of *everyday* use of imported ceramics depended very much upon the economic status of households, and that if somebody could afford to buy imported goods then there were no impediments to buying them, whether they be a rich plantation owner or an ex-slave. In commenting on imported ceramic use during their childhoods, one interviewee, who remembered imported ceramics "all having very nice flowers" said that ceramics were used every day by her family in the past, but did note that some people had "extra" dishes that they kept only for guests, while another said that in his household only local ceramics had been used every day, although adding that the "strength [of imported ceramics] and the kinds of decorations on them depended on your money," suggesting that finances were the only impediment to using items such as European made teacups in daily dining. Another added that "owning ceramics depended on money, anyone who had money could buy them"

[12] Interview transcripts can be found in Croucher (2006), Appendices A and K. Specific references are provided to these transcripts where appropriate. These interviews were conducted between 2003 and 2005. Although interview subjects were usually older, most of their recollections can be expected not to fall before the 1940s, and most spoke about the period prior to independent rule. This is obviously *not* the same time period as the plantation archaeology data, which runs from the nineteenth through to the early-twentieth century. However, these provide a heuristic tool to begin to think about the social structures of Zanzibari society which may have been similar 50 years or more before these recollections are based.

[13] Croucher (2006: Appendix K), interviews 1, 5, 8, and 9.

and another that the use of imported ceramics "was just a matter of having money to buy them. After the clove harvest some people kept money to buy cups and other ceramics." This latter comment suggested that in the early-twentieth century, as clove harvesting became organized via wage labor, ceramics were one of the important investments of cash wages.[14]

In contrast to this daily use, larger plates and platters and certain cups might be kept only for use at special occasions, particularly weddings, even in richer households where these goods could most easily be replaced in the case of breakage. The same interviewee who commented that as he was growing up had only local ceramics in his household said that they had owned "big serving plates" used for guests and when village families – as many as 10 to 15 gathering at once – would eat together during Ramadan, or that would always be bought out for the use of visitors to their home. He added that when families had special dishes such as these, sometimes they would wrap them in *kangas* (a local printed cloth worn by women) and hide them under the bed when they were not in use.[15] This special use was significant as weddings were important occasions for the negotiation of identities via demonstrating full participation in coastal Islamic cultural norms, and special "Zanzibari" foods, consisting of large plates of biryani or pilau – made from the "luxury grain" rice (Cooper 1977: 64) – were always served to guests at a wedding. Large platters for serving guests were reserved "just for rice; pilau or biryani" and pilau was eaten by another interviewee in the past only "during wedding days, or when somebody rich had died".[16] Cementing the correct foods to be served was the manner in which these foods were to be served; on imported ceramic dishes. It is in such moments requiring particular conventions of etiquette that the widespread distribution of imported ceramics may begin to make sense. For if dishes, platters, or even teacups were needed in order to maintain the requirements of entertaining guests, neighbors would customarily assist those in need. One interviewee told us that "if any cup had lost its handle then they [her family and neighbors in the past] would never give it to guests. They would rather borrow another cup from a neighbor." Further comments stressed this point, with one woman saying that "Local families couldn't afford ceramics so they would just borrow them from neighbors for special occasions" although they would only use local ceramics on a daily basis, and another that "For a wedding neighbors would come and borrow extra plates from you." So although those who could afford it might buy extra plates in preparation for a wedding and invest in ceramics for daily use, if this was not financially possible extra dishes could be borrowed from neighbors for the use of serving guests. Such loans might also occur to the poorest households if they had guests for other meals and required imported dishes or teacups to serve their visitors.[17]

---

[14]Croucher (2006: Appendix K), interviews 1 and 9.

[15]Croucher (2006: Appendix K), interviews 4 and 9.

[16]Croucher (2006: Appendix K), interview 4.

[17]Croucher (2006: Appendix K), interviews 1, 4, and 8.

Understandings of neighborliness, which were a crucial part of Zanzibari society (Myers 1994: 204), were thus cemented through the reciprocal obligations of lending goods to those in need. This is evidenced by the widespread distribution of imported European mass produced ceramic sherds which since these show no differentiation between sites according to the economic means of the sites inhabitants. These social norms of reciprocity, which could in part have worked to cement social unity and community cohesion (Sahlins 1972: 188), would also have served to highlight wealth disparities and unequal relations. Poorer neighbors were indebted to those richer via the loan of goods, and it could be conjectured further that this may have been deepened in some cases if those borrowing expensive imported ceramics broke or damaged goods which were only temporarily in their possession.

Such relations can be understood through shifting our focus on exchange from envisaging capitalist societies, such as nineteenth century Zanzibar, as being engaged only in commodity exchanges. Economic anthropologists have looked at the range of transactions that occur as objects move from one person or group to another. Even within the USA, where we might assume that society is very deeply immersed in commodity culture, the lines between gift and commodity can be blurry (Herrman 1997; Thomas 1991). The movement of mass produced ceramics through non-commodified loans into relations which help to build up the social network of Zanzibar whilst these goods were still recognized as being at a state of readiness for commodity candidacy (Appadurai 1986: 13) is no unusual thing. Within anthropology, it is now almost axiomatic to place the social understandings of gifts and commodities on a sliding scale of meanings, rather than as two contrasting forms of exchange which never exist within the same cultural system. In an examination of mass produced ceramic use on nineteenth century Zanzibar, we see a particular iteration along this scale. This is perhaps more linked to African systems of valuation where importance may be placed in social relations and obligations as a form of wealth, rather than wealth simply inhering in amassing cash or particular objects (Graeber 2001; Guyer 1993; Guyer and Belinga 1995; Piot 1999). This system of valuation may have related to networks of patronage and clientage on Zanzibar, which were also intertwined with the social positions of enslaved workers (Cooper 1977; Glassman 1995). Thus, the distribution of commodities through purchase would largely have served to demonstrate wealth and status differences, even as the actual ability to be able to *use* commodities may not have depended on monetary wealth. Buying and owning mass produced commodities would have been a means of easily displaying status through the regular use of imported ceramics at mealtimes, and through setting up obligations from those who were socially indebted through their requirement to borrow an object. Commodities were commodities, in that they were bought for cash and had limited availability dependent on economic means. But commodities could also be temporary gifts and had gift candidacy (to borrow Appadurai's (1986) phrase on commodities) understood at this time not directly from their cash value, but through their place in social obligations and networks.

Trading Identity

To this point, the role of mass produced ceramics appears to have reflected and reinforced social bonds between groups of plantation residents, bridging between plantation owners, enslaved laborers, and others living upon plantation sites. As has been argued above, this system of exchange managed to create a sense of shared identity through reciprocity, whilst also still emphasizing economic difference and ties of dependency. If plantation owners were expected to lend to enslaved laborers as seems to be evidenced via sherd distributions across sites, this would seem to suggest one arena in which notions of enslavement as clientage was in operation (Cooper 1977). All those on plantations shared in a common cultural understanding that these dishes, platters, and teacups should be used at particular social occasions. But nineteenth century Zanzibari residents did not have a singular homogenous identity. Outside of clove plantation society – which largely consisted of plantation owners, enslaved workers, and those who had formerly been enslaved, along with some indigenous Swahili involved in owning or working on plantations (and it should be noted that the lines between these groups were not always clear) – were groups who were recognized as having identities which were distinctly *not* Zanzibari. These people, it may be expected, would not have participated in the same reciprocal relations outlined above. Exchange was, however, a crucial part in the mediation of these identities. For from both formal interviews and informal conversations it became clear than when most Zanzibaris spoke of "traders" in the past, the term implied an Indian ethnic identity. One person remembered that in the past (during the rule of the penultimate Sultan of Zanzibar thus definitely predating 1963) "In Wete, Chake, Mtambile, and Mkoani [the largest towns on Pemba], there was a lot of Indian traders with big shops." Imported ceramics were said to have been imported such by Indian shopkeepers in multiple interviews. Several also commented on the different eating habits of Indians, which they had largely heard about by rumor. For instance, one commented she "had heard that with Indians everyone [when eating] had their own plate," although she had never actually seen this practice herself. In contrast "Arabs ate like other Pembans all from the same dish." Foodstuffs of Indians, in contrast to other Zanzibaris/Pembans/Arabs (labeled by ethnonym as such in interviews) were also rumored to be different, with one person having heard that "Indians mixed rice with peas, green beans, or lentils" but there "was no difference between the ways Arabs and Pembans ate."[18]

Indian immigrants were widespread around the region at this time, and were deeply involved in Indian Ocean capitalism (Bose 2006: 78). Within nineteenth century Zanzibar, Indian immigrants mostly resided in urban areas (Clark and Horton 1985: 20; Sheriff 1995b). Although they lived in close proximity and shared regular social interaction with other Zanzibari residents, a sense of Indian identity developed which was clearly differentiated from many other social groups on Zanzibar in the ethnic politics of the islands. Indians were commonly viewed to be

---

[18]Croucher (2006: Appendix K), interviews 1 and 7.

rich (an image for which they suffered in the 1964 revolution) and as the nineteenth century progressed they increasingly had financial stakes in plantations via provisioning mortgages (Sheriff 1987: 106, 204). Thus, they were perceived as being a community apart, not only in some of their social practices, but also through their relationship to capital and their seemingly heavier involvement in trading.

Their sale of goods to plantation residents, even though this was often on a small scale, seems to have heightened the perception of ethnic difference between Zanzibaris – a category consisting of the plantation owners, their children, slaves, and free workers involved on plantations – and Indians. Few Indians resident on Zanzibar were Muslims, and it has been argued that Indians often also built slightly different house forms than their Arab and Swahili neighbors (Sheriff 1995b: 19, 21), these public differences would have been added in to those identified at a level of daily practice in eating habits. It is in the act of exchange, however, that we see this difference expressed at an interpersonal level, through which subjects were able to articulate their distinctions from one another. Even in capitalist society we can still follow the argument that "Exchange relations seem to be the substance of social life" (Thomas 1991: 7) since the "Evaluations of entities, people, groups, and relationships" are still emerging at the moment of a cash transaction (ibid). We tend not to think of exchange as the most important moment of analysis when thinking about capitalism. But the act of shopping for commodified goods is socially important in societies where commodity exchanges take place. As Appadurai (1986: 14) pointed out in his seminal work on commodity analysis, it is in the act of exchange itself that commodities are truly commodities as they are recognized for their role in an alienated cash transaction. Even where subjects are fully immersed within a context of consumer culture having the opportunity to participate in commodity exchanges may be restricted by discriminatory practices, thus turning the act of commodity exchange into a charged social moment (Chin 2001; Mullins 1999).

The perception of Indians as controlling the monetary economy of Zanzibar through trade and mortgages may also have been an aspect which created some tension between Indians and other Zanzibaris. The purchase of mass produced imports from a distinct social group may have stood in stark contrast for plantation residents to those exchange relations shared with their closer neighbors with whom they may have been involved in reciprocal exchange of dishes – even if this heightened recognition of social hierarchies – and in other exchanges such as small-scale purchase or gifts of locally made ceramics. Commodity exchanges were not only for mass produced ceramics; gold, silver and beaded jewelry were also most commonly purchased from strangers in town, generally alluded to be Indians or *not* regular Zanzibaris.[19] Because of the way in which Indian traders stood outside of the regular life of plantations, identified as Other we can imagine them as "strangers" to plantation residents (Thomas 1991: 22). While they might not have been unknown to plantation residents, they were not involved in the intimate social relations that produced shared community cohesiveness. Presenting cash to buy a mass produced

---

[19]Croucher (2006: Appendix K), interviews 5, 6, 8, and 9.

commodity may therefore has been a significant moment in dis-identification between plantation residents and traders, and simultaneously a moment in which broadly shared identification through non-commodity exchange was heightened between plantation residents, cementing some of the ideas of a new kind of common Zanzibari identity from which Indian immigrants were excluded.

Global Capitalist Relations

> The managers who facilitate this process can tell us: To produce a commodity is the work of the translator, the diplomat, and the power-crazed magician. (Tsing 2005: 52)

I have chosen this quotation to open this final discussion section on the ceramics found on Zanzibar since it emphasizes that commodity production is no straightforward process. Production is a vital part in understanding the complexities of commodity chains, for the output of this must be somehow attuned to the desires and needs of consumer. Mass produced ceramics were increasingly adopted in daily practices for Zanzibaris over time, as their ubiquitous use today also demonstrates. But there is nothing inevitable about the adoption of commodities. Indeed, increasing numbers of studies show the complexities of the subtle cultural choices that underlie the manner in which commodities come to be used widely, selectively, or rejected within specific contexts (for African examples, Burke 1996; Hansen 2000; Holtzman 2003; Richard 2010; Stahl 2002; Thornton 1998: 52). There is no pattern which can predict the desirability of particular commodities, nor whether they will be adopted in commodity form, "domesticated" into particular local uses, or modified into alternative spheres of exchange (Prestholdt 2008; Thomas 1991). Studying the manner in which commodities are desirable, and the shifts in manufacture which attempted to improve the desirability of mass manufactured goods provides an analytical tool for studying the fine grain of relationships for those who are broadly linked on a global scale through capitalism within particular cultural contexts, and to examine the effects of the extension of capitalist trade on the "cores" of production themselves. For we know that the hegemony of Euro-American culture is not a simple one way street – time and time again it has been shown just how much "the rest" have impacted on the very creation of "the west" (Carrier 1992; Clifford 1997; Marcus 1995) and recent studies have begun to highlight the multidirectional flow of cultural information via commodity use in colonial periods (Norton 2008).

As presented above, the imported ceramics from Zanzibar are significantly different from those of Europe, America, or European colonial areas such as South Africa and Australia. But as well as the collections from Zanzibar, ceramics of this design and style have been found in Namibia (Kinahan 2000) and by collectors from India, Sri Lanka, Malaysia, Burma (Myanmar), and Indonesia (Kelly 1994, 1999a, b), as well as exhibiting design similarities with some of the wares which are found in South African contexts (Klose and Malan 2000; Malan and Klose 2003). Although the stylistic canon of cut-sponge printing to produce brightly colored designs was first used on earthenwares in the early nineteenth century to manufacture cheap goods for local

Fig. 8.6 Avenue Ceramique, Maastricht, The Netherlands. The naming of this street shows the marking of industrial heritage into the landscape of this Dutch city

markets, later in the nineteenth century the technique, along with the painting of bright bands and flowers, spread to the production of specific wares for export markets. Several potteries in Britain and the Netherlands began to manufacture such wares specifically for the Asian market (Cruickshank 1982; Kelly 1999a: 182–183).

The acceptance, or not, of mass produced wares from Europe was likely predicated on preexisting patterns of taste in the new markets to which they were taken (Schneider 1987: 441; Stahl 2002: 841). The local cuisine of Zanzibar, where rice and sauce based dishes were eaten in a fairly communal style with diners sharing food from the same dishes,[20] helped shape which ceramics were desirable in local markets where the kinds of individual place settings found in most historical archaeological contexts would have been unsuitable for existing practices. The consumption patterns on Zanzibar, whilst representing local styles of cuisine, were also tied to wider Indian Ocean consumption patterns of rice based dishes. These loosely shared practices of cuisine within Asian and the Indian Ocean region fed back to the potteries of Scotland and the Netherlands. This resulted in the manufacture of wares in designs and styles thought likely to be acceptable to Asian and Indian Ocean markets (Kelly 2006). At these sites of production (Fig. 8.6), it could be argued that potters may have developed ideas about their difference to those far away consumers of the ceramics they produced. Whereas on Zanzibar difference may have been articulated at an interpersonal level via commodities, between Europe and East Africa differences may have been partly understood through the lens of material culture with no face-to-face interaction. The variance in shape and design to the

---

[20] Such practices are widespread. A contemporary nineteenth century description of the mealtimes of the elite is provided in *Memoirs of an Arabian Princess* (Reute 1998[1886]). Details were also provided in oral historical interviews (Croucher 2006: Appendix K, interviews 4, 5, and 7).

Fig. 8.7 Dutch ceramic manufacturer's maker's mark, along with non-Anglicized script for a local Indian Ocean market

ceramics used within their own homes, and the foreign scripts sometimes used in the manufacture of maker's marks for some export wares (Fig. 8.7) may have been a lens for pottery workers to imagine their European cultural homogeneity vis-à-vis far off populations in Africa and Asia. Their sense of difference to these populations may not have been one in which they were aware of actual cultural practices, but the real material linkages between consumers on Zanzibar, pastoralists living in the !Khusib Delta area, Namibia (Kinahan 2000: 74–75), and others throughout the Indian Ocean region (Kelly 2006) was indeed a nebulous linkage of communities whom, unbeknownst to one another, participated in broadly shared practices of taste in the selection of their brightly decorated dishes.

Conclusions: The Complexities of Capitalism

When reflecting on the varied histories of mass produced ceramics on Zanzibari plantations, the cultural fluidity of the adoption of capitalism becomes apparent. This is not simply a case study of a one way economic relationship between a European colonial power and a colonized culture increasingly bowing to pressure to purchase commodities from their oppressors. By taking over markets for imported ceramics – and indeed expanding these markets – we do see the British and Dutch enacting their economic might as European colonial powers usurping the previous networks of ceramic sales that had crisscrossed the Indian Ocean.[21] But to take these over was a complex process, and embedded many within the ecumene of the commodity. This network of producers, exporters and importers, merchants, and consumers, was a multidirectional web of cultural communication. Ideas about identities were, in part, created through actions seen and unseen of producers, sellers, buyers, and users. In all of these cases, the commodity candidacy of the mass produced wares was never in doubt. Yet concomitantly this network also passed into an almost gift-like aspect of economics on Zanzibar, where reciprocal relations between people were also passed through the sharing of bowls, platters, and teacups at moments when correct cultural practice required.

In seeing the complexity of capitalism on Zanzibar, it is impossible to adopt any simple evolutionary type approach to understanding the manner in which capitalist practices and meanings pass into colonized societies. As Tsing (2005: 76) has pointed out, capitalism is heterogeneous: "Capitalist forms and processes are continually made and unmade; if we offer singular predictions we allow ourselves to be caught by them as ideologies." This point, a counter-argument to evolutionary accounts of capitalism, resonates with studies such as Thomas (1991) and Piot (1999) as they study the mutability of capitalisms entanglement within colonial cultural relations. The main point I would stress from this brief study of one type of artifact, is that it is impossible to slot capitalist relations into any single "type" of capitalism. We cannot say that colonial powers on Zanzibar were merchant capitalists and therefore place all cultural iterations of capitalism as analogous to those of seventeenth century European merchants (cf. Pearson 1998; Sheriff 1987). Likewise, we cannot take the dominant mode of capitalism in Europe at the time as the "core" of capitalism, and dismiss cultural practices embedded within capitalist modes on Zanzibar as simply a reaction in a "periphery," where capitalism is an external force and unchanged by Zanzibari practices (cf. Wallerstein 1976).

The cultural exchanges which traversed the commodity chain are perhaps as important to note as the economic relations, since it is in these that we see the particularities of the manner in which understandings of capitalism on Zanzibar were shaped by the particular cultural context of the islands and the way in which the practices of Zanzibaris were also integral to the shaping of the wider capitalist world. There are many ways in which we could frame this complexity. One term which has gained widespread usage recently is Tsing's (2005) idea of "frictions"; Thomas' (1991) use of the word entanglement also works well within the Zanzibari context, providing an explanatory frame for the multiple directions of communication that passed through various persons and cultural groups via commodities. Entanglement

---

[21] Ceramics have a long (pre)history of trade around the Indian Ocean. Early imports are attested from the site of Kilwa dated back to at least the eighth Century CE (Horton 1996), details of further long-term trends in imported ceramics can be found for Unguja in Juma (2004), for Pemba in Fleisher (2003), and for the Kilwa region in Wynne-Jones (2005).

perhaps stops short of the depth of these relations however. As Piot (1999) notes for the Kabre in Togo, it is in part the very relationship of capitalism and colonialism to cultures that has produced what may at first seem to be cultural practices antithetical to capitalism, particularly within exchange relations. Seeing a "friction" between the requirements of enslavement and the need for client/patron relations to establish high social standing for nineteenth century Zanzibaris, against the dominant capitalist mode of production and the purchase of increasing amounts of mass produced goods, it is possible to speculate that perhaps the relations of reciprocity in some publicly used commoditized goods were a novel social practice. This may have been entirely created in the nexus of these two different cultural systems. As increasing amounts of archaeological work is carried out which examines the poorer sections of Swahili society prior to the seventeenth century (Fleisher 2003; Wynne-Jones 2005, 2006), potential exists to compare whether access to imported goods was differentiated along the same social variables as during later historical moments for East African coastal cultures. This question is a complex one, and requires more work (but see Croucher in preparation), yet it opens us up to thinking about whether reciprocal relations are here a fossilized practice of "pre-capitalist" culture in the Western Indian Ocean/East Africa, or whether they are in fact a product of modernity itself – truly a form of capitalism within a colonial context.

Acknowledgments Funding for the fieldwork discussed in this chapter was provided by the Arts and Humanities Research Council UK, the Emslie Horniman fund of the Royal Anthropological Institute, the British Institute in Eastern Africa, and a Zochonis Special Enterprise Award from the University of Manchester. Fieldwork on Zanzibar was carried out under research permit ZRP/98 granted via the Department of Archives, Museums, and Antiquities (DAMA), Zanzibar. Work on this chapter was completed at Wesleyan University and the School for Advanced Research (SAR). I would particularly like to thank Mr Hamad Omar, head of DAMA, along with many other staff and Zanzibari residents too numerous to mention here. Oral history interviews cited in the text were carried out in translation with Hajj Mohammed Hajj, whose friendship and generosity have contributed so much to my work on the islands. Several people read and commented on this chapter, including my current colleagues at the SAR, for whose critical insights I am extremely grateful. Lindsay Weiss also commented on this chapter, and is an ever unfailing source of inspiration, support, and friendship.

References

Appadurai, Arjun. 1986 Introduction: Commodities and the Politics of Value. In *The Social Life of Things: Commodities in Cultural Perspective*, edited by A. Appadurai, pp. 3–63. Cambridge University Press, Cambridge, UK.

Bose, Sugata. 2006 *A Hundred Horizons: The Indian Ocean in the Age of Global Empire.* Harvard University Press, Cambridge, MA.

Brewer, John, and Frank Trentman. 2006 Introduction: Space, Time and Value in Consuming Cultures. In *Consuming Cultures, Global Perspectives: Historical Trajectories, Transnational Exchanges,* edited by J. Brewer and F. Trentman, pp. 1–17. Berg, New York.

Brighton, Stephen A. 2001 Prices that Suit the Times: Shopping for Ceramics at the Five Points. *Historical Archaeology* 35(3):16–30.

Brooks, Alasdair. 1997 Beyond the Fringe: Transfer-Printed Ceramics and the Internalization of Celtic Myth. *International Journal of Historical Archaeology* 1(1):39–55.

Brooks, Alasdair. 2003 Crossing Offa's Dyke: British Ideologies and Late Eighteenth- and Nineteenth-century ceramics in Wales. In *Archaeologies of the British: Explorations of Identity in Great Britain and its Colonies 1600–1945,* edited by S. Lawrence, pp. 119–137. Routledge, London.

Brooks, Alasdair, and Graham Connah. 2007 A Hierarchy of Servitude: Ceramics at Lake Innes Estate, New South Wales. *Antiquity* 81(311):133–147.

Burke, Timothy. 1996 *Lifebuoy Men, Lux Women: Commodification, Consumption, and Cleanliness in Modern Zimbabwe.* Leicester University Press, London.

Carrier, James G. 1992 Occidentalism: The World Turned Upside Down. *American Ethnologist* 19(2):195–212.

Chin, Elizabeth. 2001 *Purchasing Power: Black Kids and American Culture.* University of Minnesota Press, Minneapolis.

Clark, Catherine, and Mark Horton. 1985 *Zanzibar Archaeological Survey 1984/5.* Ministry of Information, Culture, and Sport, Zanzibar.

Clarence-Smith, William Gervase, and Steven Topik (editors). 2003 *The Global Coffee Economy in Africa, Asia, and Latin America, 1500–1989.* Cambridge University Press, New York.

Clifford, James. 1997 *Routes: Travel and Translation in the Late Twentieth Century.* Harvard University Press, Cambridge, MA.

Cook, Lauren J., Rebecca Yamin, and John P. McCarthy. 1996 Shopping as Meaningful Action: Toward a Redefinition of Consumption in Historical Archaeology. *Historical Archaeology* 30(4):50–65.

Cooper, Frederick. 1977 *Plantation Slavery on the East Coast of Africa.* Yale University Press, New Haven.

Cooper, Frederick. 1979 The Problem of Slavery in African Studies. *The Journal of African History* 20(1):103–125.

Crang, Philip, Claire Dwyer, and Peter Jackson. 2003 Transnationalism and the Spaces of Commodity Culture. *Progress in Human Geography* 27(4):438–456.

Crofton, R. H. 1936 *A Pageant of the Spice Islands.* John Bale, Sons and Danielsson Ltd, London.

Croucher, Sarah K. 2004 Zanzibar Clove Plantation Survey 2003: Some Preliminary Findings. *Nyame Akuma* 62:65–69.

Croucher, Sarah K. 2006 *Plantations on Zanzibar: An Archaeological Approach to Complex Identities.* PhD thesis, School of Arts, Histories and Cultures, The University of Manchester.

Croucher, Sarah K. 2007 Facing Many Ways: Approaches to the Archaeological Landscapes of the East African Coast. In *Envisioning Landscape: Situations and Standpoints in Archaeology and Heritage,* edited by D. Hicks, L. McAtackney, and G. Fairclough, pp. 55–74. One World Archaeology, Left Coast Press, Walnut Creek, CA.

Croucher, Sarah K. in prep *Capitalism and Cloves: A Critique of Historical Archaeology.* New York: Springer.

Croucher, Sarah K. and Stephanie Wynne-Jones. 2006 People, Not Pots: Locally Produced Ceramics and Identity on the 19th Century East African Coast. *International Journal of African Historical Studies* 39(1):107–124.

Cruickshank, Graeme. 1982 *Scottish Spongeware.* Scottish Pottery Society, Aberdeen.

Dalby, Andrew. 2002 *Dangerous Tastes: The Story of Spices.* University of California Press, Berkeley and Los Angeles.

DeCorse, Christopher R. 2001 *An Archaeology of Elmina: Africans and Europeans on the Gold Coast, 1400–1900.* Smithsonian Institution Press, Washington, DC.

Deetz, James. 1996 *In Small Things Forgotten: An Archaeology of Early American Life.* Anchor Books, New York.

Delle, James A. 1998 *An Archaeology of Social Space: Analyzing Coffee Plantations in Jamaica's Blue Mountains.* Pleunum Press, New York.

Douglas, Mary, and Baron Isherwood. 1996 [1979] *The World of Goods: Towards an Anthropology of Consumption.* Routledge, London.

Fleisher, Jeffrey. 2003 *Viewing Stonetowns from the Countryside: An Archaeological Approach to Swahili Regions, AD 800 – 1500.* PhD thesis, Department of Anthropology, University of Virginia.

Foster, Robert J. 2008 Coca-*Globalization: Following Soft Drinks from New York to New Guinea.* Palgrave MacMillian, New York.

Glassman, Jonathon. 1995 *Feasts and Riot: Revelry, Rebellion and Popular Consciousness on The Swahili Coast, 1856–1888.* James Currey, London.

Goody, Jack. 2004 *Capitalism and Modernity: The Great Debate.* Polity, Malden, MA.

Graeber, David. 2001 *Toward an Anthropological Theory of Value: The False Coin of Our Own Dreams.* Palgrave, New York.

Guyer, Jane I. 1993 Wealth in People and Self-Realization in Equatorial Africa. *Man (New Series)* 28(2):243–265.

Guyer, Jane I., and Samuel M. Eno Belinga. 1995 Wealth in People as Wealth in Knowledge: Accumulation and Composition in Equatorial Africa. *Journal of African History* 36(1):91–120.

Hall, Martin. 2000 *Archaeology and the Modern World: Colonial Transcripts in South Africa and the Chesapeake.* Routledge, New York.

Hansen, Karen Tranberg. 2000 *Salaula: The World of Secondhand Clothing and Zambia.* The University of Chicago Press, Chicago.

Harvey, David. 2010 *A Companion to Marx's Capital.* Verso, London and New York.

Henry, Susan L. 1991 Consumers, Commodities, and Choices: A General Model of Consumer Behavior. *Historical Archaeology* 25(2):3–14.

Herrman, Gretchen M. 1997 Gift or Commodity: What Changes Hands in the U.S. Garage Sale? *American Ethnologist* 24(4):910–930.

Hicks, Dan. 2005 "Places for Thinking" from Annapolis to Bristol: Situations and Symmetries in "World Historical Archaeologies". *World Archaeology* 37(3):373–391.

Holtzman, Jon D. 2003 In a Cup of Tea: Commodities and History among Samburu Pastoralists in Northern Kenya. *American Ethnologist* 30(1):136–155.

Horton, Mark. 1996 *Shanga: The Archaeology of a Muslim Trading Community on the Coast of East Africa.* British Institute in Eastern Africa, London.

Jackson, Peter. 1999 Commodity Cultures: The Traffic in Things. *Transactions of the Institute of British Geographers* 24(1):95–108.

Jackson, Peter. 2004 Local Consumption Cultures in a Globalizing World. *Transactions of the Institute of British Geographers* 29 (1):165–178.

Juma, Abdurahman. 2004 *Unguja Ukuu on Zanzibar: An Archaeological Study of Early Urbanism.* Department of Archaeology and Ancient History, Uppsala University, Uppsala.

Kelly, Henry E. 1994 The Export Trade of J & M. P. Bell & Co. and other Scottish Potteries. *Scottish Pottery Historical Review* 16:49–47.

Kelly, Henry E. 1999 *Scottish Ceramics.* Schiffer, Atglen.

Kelly, Henry E. 1999 *Scottish Sponge Printed Pottery.* The Lomonside Press, Glasgow.

Kelly, Henry E. 2006 *The Glasgow Pottery of J. & M. P. Bell and Co.* Electronic document, www. bellsglasgowpottery.com, accessed September 15, 2010.

Kinahan, Jill. 2000 *Cattle for Beads.* Uppsala: Uppsala University, Sweden/Namibia Archaeological Trust.

Klose, Jane, and Antonia Malan. 2000 The Ceramic Signature of the Cape in the Nineteenth Century, with Particular Reference to the Tennant Street Site, Cape Town. *South African Archaeological Bulletin* 55:49–59.

Lane, Paul J. 2007 Wither Historical Archaeology in Africa? *The Review of Archaeology* 28:1–24.

LaViolette, Adria, and Jeffrey B. Fleisher 2005 The Archaeology of Sub-Saharan Urbanism: Cities and their Countrysides. In *African Archaeology: A Critical Introduction*, edited by A.B. Stahl, pp. 327–352. Blackwell Studies in Global Archaeology. Malden, MA: Blackwell.

Leone, Mark P. 1999 Ceramics from Annapolis, Maryland: A Measure of Time Routines and Work Discipline. In *Historical Archaeologies of Capitalism,* edited by M.P. Leone and P.B.J. Potter, pp. 195–216. Kluwer Academic/Plenum, New York.

Malan, Antonia, and Jane Klose. 2003 Nineteenth-Century Ceramics in Cape Town, South Africa. In *Archaeologies of the British: Explorations of Identity in Great Britain and its Colonies, 1600–1945,* edited by S. Lawrence, pp. 191–210. Routledge, New York.

Marcus, George E. 1995 Ethnography in/of the World System: The Emergence of Multi-Sited Ethnography. *Annual Review of Anthropology* 24:95–117.

Mauss, Marcel. 1990 [1950] *The Gift: The Form and Reason for Exchange in Archaic Societies.* Translated by W.D. Halls. W.W. Norton, New York.

Miller, Daniel. 1995 Consumption and Commodities. *Annual Review of Anthropology* 24:141–161.

Miller, George L. 1980 Classification and Economic Scaling of 19th Century Ceramics. *Historical Archaeology* 14:1–40.

Miller, George L. 1991 A Revised Set of CC Index Values for Classification and Economic Scaling of English Ceramics from 1787 to 1880. *Historical Archaeology* 25(1):1–25.

Mintz, Sidney W. 1985 *Sweetness and Power: The Place of Sugar in Modern History.* Penguin Books, New York.

Mullins, Paul R. 1999 *Race and Affluence: An Archaeology of African America and Consumer Culture.* Kluwer Academic/Plenum Publishers, New York.

Mullins, Paul R. 2004 Consuming Aspirations: Bric-a-Brac and the Politics of Victorian Materialism in West Oakland. In *Putting the "There" There: Historical Archaeologies of West Oakland,* edited by M. Praetzellis and A. Praetzellis, pp. 85–115. Sonoma State University, Anthropological Studies Center, Rohnert Park, CA.

Myers, Garth Andrew. 1994 Eurocentrism and African Urbanisation: The case of Zanzibar's other side. *Antipode* 26(3):195–215.

Myers, Garth Andrew. 1996 Naming and Placing the Other: Power and the Urban Landscape in Zanzibar. *Tijdschrift voor Economische en Sociale Geografie* 87(3):237–246.

Myers, Garth Andrew. 1997 Sticks and Stones: Colonialism and Zanzibari Housing. *Africa* 67(2):252–272.

New, Charles. 1875 Journey from the Pangani, Via Usambara, to Mombasa. *Journal of the Royal Geographical Society of London* 45:414–420.

Norton, Marcy. 2008 *Sacred Gifts, Profane Pleasures: A History of Tobacco and Chocolate in the Atlantic World.* Cornell University Press, Ithaca, NY.

Ogundiran, Akinwumi, and Toyin Falola. 2007 Pathways in the Archaeology of Transatlantic Africa. In *Archaeology of Atlantic Africa and the African Diaspora,* edited by A. Ogundiran and T. Falola, pp. 3–45. Indiana University Press, Bloomington and Indianapolis.

Orser, Charles E. Jr. 1996 *A Historical Archaeology of the Modern World.* Plennum, New York.

Pawlowicz, Matthew. 2009 Archaeological Exploration of the Mikindani Region of the Southern Tanzanian Coast. *Nyame Akuma* 72:41–51.

Pearson, Michael N. 1998 *Port Cities and Intruders: The Swahili Coast, India, and Portugal in the Early Modern Era.* The Johns Hopkins University Press, Baltimore.

Pearson, Michael N. 2006 Littoral Society: The Concept and the Problems. *Journal of World History* 17(4):353–373.

Piot, Charles. 1999 *Remotely Global: Village Modernity in West Africa.* The University of Chicago Press, Chicago.

Prestholdt, Jeremy. 2004 On the Global Repercussions of East African Consumerism. *American Historical Review* 109(3):755–781.

Prestholdt, Jeremy. 2008 *Domesticating the World: African Consumerism and the Genealogies of Globalization.* University of California Press, Berkeley and Los Angeles.

Reid, Andrew, and Paul J. Lane. 2004 African Historical Archaeologies: An Introductory Consideration of Scope and Potential. In *African Historical Archaeologies,* edited by A.M. Reid and P.J. Lane, pp. 1–32. Kluwer Academic/Plenum Publishers, New York.

Richard, François G. 2009 Historical and Dialectical Perspectives on the Archaeology of Complexity in the Siin-Saalum (Senegal): Back to the Future? *African Archaeological Review* 26(2):75–135.

Richard, François G. 2010 Recharting Atlantic Encounters. Object Trajectories and Histories of Value in the Siin (Senegal) and Senegambia. *Archaeological Dialogues* 17(1):1–27.

Rockel, Stephen J. 2006 *Carriers of Culture: Labor on the Road in Nineteenth-Century East Africa.* NH: Heinemann, Portsmouth.

Sahlins, Marshall. 1972 *Stone Age Economics.* Tavistock Publications, London.

Sassatelli, Roberta. 2007 *Consumer Culture: History, Theory and Politics.* Sage Publications, Los Angeles and London.

Schmidt, Peter R. 2006 *Historical Archaeology in Africa: Representation, Social Memory and Oral Traditions.* AltaMira Press, Lanham, MD.

Schmidt, Peter R., and Jonathan R. Walz. 2007 Re-Representing African Pasts through Historical Archaeology. *American Antiquity* 72(1):53–70.

Schneider, Jane. 1987 The Anthropology of Cloth. *Annual Review of Anthropology* 16:409–448.

Shackel, Paul A., and Matthew M. Palus. 2006 The Gilded Age and Working-Class Industrial Communities. *American Anthropologist* 108(4):828–841.

Sheriff, Abdul. 1987 *Slaves, Spices and Ivory in Zanzibar.* Ohio University Press, Athens.

Sheriff, Abdul. 1995a Introduction. In *The History and Conservation of Zanzibar Stone Town,* edited by A. Sheriff, pp. 1–7. Ohio University Press (in Association with the Department of Archives, Museums and Antiquities, Zanzibar), Athens.

Sheriff, Abdul. 1995b An Outline History of Zanzibar Stone Town. In *The History and Conservation of Zanzibar Stone Town,* edited by A. Sheriff, pp. 8–29. Ohio University Press (in Association with the Department of Archives, Museums and Antiquities, Zanzibar), Athens.

Sheriff, Abdul. 2010 *Dhow Cultures of the Indian Ocean.* Hurst & Company/Zanzibar Indian Ocean Research Institute, London/Zanzibar.

Singleton, Theresa A. 1995 The Archaeology of Slavery in North America. *Annual Review of Anthropology* 24:119–140.

Singleton, Theresa A. 2005 Before the Revolution: Archaeology and the African Diaspora on the Atlantic Seaboard. In *North American Archaeology,* edited by T.R. Pauketat and D.D. Loren, pp. 319–336. Blackwell, Malden, MA.

Stahl, Ann Brower. 2002 Colonial Entanglements and the Practices of Taste: An Alternative to Logocentric Approaches. *American Anthropologist* 104(3):827–845.

Stahl, Ann Brower. 2007 Entangled Lives: The Archaeology of Daily Life in the gold Coast Hinterlands, AD 1400–1900. In *Archaeology of Atlantic Africa and the African Diaspora,* edited by A. Ogundiran and T. Faloda, pp. 49–76. Indiana University Press, Bloominton and Indiana.

Thomas, Nicholas. 1991 *Entangled Objects: Exchange, Material Culture, and Colonialism in the Pacific.* Harvard University Press, Cambridge, MA.

Thornton, John. 1998 [1992] *Africa and Africans in the Making of the Atlantic World, 1400–1800.* Cambridge University Press, New York.

Tsing, Anna L. 2005 *Friction: An Ethnography of Global Connection.* Princeton University Press, Princeton.

van den Bersselaar, Dmitri. 2007 *The King of Drinks: Schnapps Gin from Modernity to Tradition.* Brill, Leiden.

van Dommelen, Peter. 2010 Complex histories, comment on Richard, Recharting Atlantic encounters. *Archaeological Dialogues* 17(1):37–41.

Wall, Diana di Zerega. 1999 Examining Gender, Class and Ethnicity in Nineteenth-Century New York. *Historical Archaeology* 33(1):102–117.

Wallerstein, Immanuel. 1976 *The Modern World-System: Capitalist Agriculture and the Origins of the European World-Economy in the Sixteenth Century.* Academic Press, New York.

Walsh, Andrew. 2010 The Commodification of Fetishes: Telling the difference between natural and synthetic sapphires. *American Ethnologist* 37(1):98–114.

Weiss, Lindsay Moira. 2009 *Fictive Capital and Economies of Desire: A Case Study of Illegal Diamond Buying and Apartheid Landscapes in 19th century Southern Africa.* PhD thesis, Graduate School of Arts and Sciences, Columbia University.

Wolf, Eric R. 1997 [1982] *Europe and the People Without History.* 2nd Edition. University of California Press, Berkeley and Los Angeles.

Wynne-Jones, Stephanie. 2005 *Urbanisation at Kilwa, Tanzania, AD800 – 1400.* PhD thesis, Archaeology, University of Cambridge.

Wynne-Jones, Stephanie 2006 *Creating Urban Communities at Kilwa Kisiwani, Tanzania, AD 800–1300.* Antiquity 81(312):368–380.

Chapter 9
"In [Them] We Will Find Very Desirable Tributaries for Our Commerce": Cash Crops, Commodities, and Subjectivities in Siin (Senegal) During the Colonial Era

François G. Richard

Formations of Colonial Capitalism: From Totalities to Assemblages

Why should historical archaeologists "at large" be interested in the material past of colonial French West Africa? One answer might invoke the fact that, over the past decade, the discipline has become increasingly concerned with the study of colonial modernity worldwide. This pursuit has primarily focused on recovering the faded existence of colonized peoples confined to the margins of recorded history, in an effort to complicate narratives of the past painted in broad regional or global strokes. By this account, the shifting patterns of action, acquiescence, and resistance crafted by the subject populations of French West Africa contribute valuable empirical materials to the wide tapestry of indigenous experiences that archaeology has so effectively documented and which illustrate the dynamic nature, implicit tensions, and intrinsic variability of colonial lifeworlds over time and space (e.g., Hall 2000; Dawdy 2008; Silliman 2005; Voss 2008).

The fact that this essay – the substantive portions of which examine the rationalities and uncertainties of colonial economy and governance in the Siin province (Senegal) – is the only chapter in this volume dealing with French imperialism and one of the three contributions on continental Africa may outline other elements of answer. First, despite a growing number of archaeological studies on African colonial worlds and despite the relative lateness of formal colonization on the continent (one of whose manifestations is a wealth of ethnographic and oral archives directly germane to the study of colonialism), Africa has not centrally featured in disciplinary conversations about colonial histories, processes, and materialities. Second, while archaeological research is shedding widening light on French imperial ventures in the Americas (Dawdy 2008; Kelly 2009), the archaeological history of French colonialism and capitalism in Africa has only begun to be written.

F.G. Richard (✉)
Department of Anthropology, University of Chicago, Chicago, IL, USA
e-mail: fgrichard@uchicago.edu

S.K. Croucher and L. Weiss (eds.), *The Archaeology of Capitalism in Colonial Contexts*, 193
Contributions To Global Historical Archaeology, DOI 10.1007/978-1-4614-0192-6_9,
© Springer Science+Business Media, LLC 2011

If the relative invisibility of French colonial Africa in historical archaeology is surely a matter of empirical poverty, it also indexes a certain structural unevenness in the geography of discourse and scholarship on colonialism and capitalism. As collective contributions to this volume testify, the archaeological study of colonial encounters *has* dramatically expanded its spatial compass over the past few years, and case studies now stretch around the globe from Alaska (Crowell, Chap. 4) to Australia (Paterson, Chap. 11), spanning a variety of national, imperial, territorial, and cultural configurations. Having recognized this, Kelly's (2009) recent observations about the Caribbean – that the material history of the region has often been written in relation to the *English* colonial world at the expense of a more complex mosaic of local colonial cultures, some quite singular in their expressions – nevertheless seem broadly applicable to the historical archaeology of colonialism. Because a disproportionate amount of research has taken place in settings occupied by people of British extraction and because of epochal developments in British manufacturing, production, and distribution that resulted in the global diffusion of mass-produced material culture in the second half of the eighteenth century, archaeology's colonial geographies often implicitly evoke the British imperial world as their primary context of reference (though the very robust body of work that is developing on the California mission system is rapidly promoting the Spanish empire as a complementary theater of analysis). In related fashion, archaeologies of capitalism have more often than not examined its Anglo-American variety, which is sometimes seen as a metonymic expression of capital as a historical and social formation (Delle et al. 2000; Johnson 1996; Leone and Potter 1999; McGuire and Paynter 1991; but see papers in Hamilakis and Duke 2007). A turn to French colonial Africa (and, by extension, other understudied imperial geographies), then, offers the proverbial decentering gesture, which can help to unsettle certain archaeological assumptions or expectations about the nature of colonial relations and power geometries; by pointing to commonalities and dissonances in the orchestration of colonial life over time across imperial dominions, such gestures have the potential to "make strange" and thus illuminate all the power fields under consideration.[1] To use an African example, for instance, British and French colonial Africa are often contrasted on the basis of different styles and regimes of governance, the former being associated with the so-called indirect rule and the latter with direct rule. As the case study presented in this essay reveals, however, this distinction is largely specious in that although the French administration gradually shifted over time from a posture of "governing at a distance" to a more capillary, makeshift form of governmentality (Conklin 1997: 6–7; also Cooper 1996), the colonial state was at all times beholden to local indigenous institutions, authorities, intermediaries, and elites for the exercise and enforcement of rule (Lawrance et al. 2006). Likewise,

---

[1] As examined elsewhere (Richard n.d.), this decentering move can be applied within imperial formations as well. For instance, the presence of different artifactual assemblages and archaeological patterns in eighteenth- to nineteenth-century French occupations in Louisiana, Guadeloupe, and Gorée speak to the possibility that different configurations of subjectivity, sociality, and placemaking were in existence in various parts of the French imperial world.

as I hope to argue below, capitalism as a historical mode of political economy is always mediated through local circumstances, institutions, and ideas, and French conceptions of "markets" and commerce, profitability, civility, and morality, and their relationship to political control did not always mirror the economic positions and practices espoused in various parts of the British empire. In other words, despite convergences and "family resemblances" speaking to shared concerns, realities, and philosophies of colonial imposition,[2] modern imperial formations – whether rooted in Britain, Spain, France, Portugal, Germany, Russia, or Japan – ultimately coagulated around different doctrines and ideologies of rule, different economic policies, as well as vastly variable cultural and political terrains *within* their territories (e.g., Pagden 1995). Capturing "coloniality" as a historical object, thus, demands an attentive eye to departures, permutations, and fluctuations across imperial lines, if only to reveal that variability and unpredictability are two of the most enduring attributes of "the colonial moment" and forms which it has historically adopted.

Recent efforts of archaeology to study global encounters at the nexus of (material) culture, capitalism, and colonialism follow in the well-trodden tracks of a set of perspectives pioneered in the fields of historical anthropology and postcolonial thinking. Starting in the 1980s and coming to full maturity the following decade, infused with the writings of Michel Foucault, cultural Marxism, and post-structuralism, this scholarship has worked to expand and rethink narratives of the left and the right regarding the incorporation of world populations into a common, if highly uneven, history of global exchange (Cohn 1996; Comaroff and Comaroff 1992; Cooper and Stoler 1997; Dirks 1992; Stoler 1995a, b; Taussig 1987; Thomas 1994). Part of this corrective work has endeavored to nuance a certain Marxist canon that has accorded preeminence to the implacable unfolding of capital's laws of development and its transformative hold on people caught in the eddies of the world economy. In the process of conversing with these strands of thought, postcolonial literature has also engaged a number of Marxist theses about the history of capital and colony in an effort to complicate classic scenarios merging the motions/motivations of capitalism to the class interests of the Bourgeois state, as well as analyses of imperialism and capitalist growth of Lenin and Rosa Luxemburg. On the other side of the political spectrum, anthropological histories have also challenged liberal and modernist orthodoxies chronicling the forward march, progressive agencies, and promises of free market exchange (Cooper 1993).

Collectively, these studies have forged a structure of feeling and conceptual foundation for historical analyses of the intersections among colonial sovereignty, imperial economies, and global markets. Anthropologies of colonialism have succeeded in tempering the certainties of earlier intellectual annals and substituting in their stead a more sobering commitment to the contingency and historicity of culture, power, and political economy. In lieu of previous tendencies to portray colonialism, imperialism, and capitalism as total systems organized by recurring sets of principles,

---

[2] Some of these family resemblances can be traced to very concrete historical processes of knowledge diffusion and construction. In effect, as shown in Stoler et al. (2007), social planners often looked "beyond the nation" to other colonial empires for inspiration regarding effective technologies of rule, development programs, and blueprints of population management (also Morgan 2009).

dynamics, and directions, the outcome has been a fragmentation of these totalities, which have been unhooked from a common trajectory of causation and determination and replaced by careful examinations of the discrepant contexts, agents, and structures framing the exercise of governance, passage of capital, and construction of colonial worlds and identities.

To take some of the relevant operative terms, for instance, the use of "the colony" (or "coloniality"), "empire," or "the postcolony" in the paradigmatic singular – as if describing an epochal "condition" or discursive formation, a Platonic idea or neo-Kantian form – has come under increasing scholarly criticism (Cooper 2004, 2005; Weate 2003). While recognizing the convenience of these terms as shorthands, pointing to broad commonalities in structures of power and lived existence, critics have noted the historical and sociological underspecification they convey, as well as a certain flattening of experience which ironically runs the risk of airbrushing the cluster of agencies, strategies, and histories that exceed their narrative frame.[3] Instead, recent scholarship has encouraged the need to examine colonies and empires as "sociohistorical formations," that are contingent configurations of political, economic, and cultural practices whose expressions must be thoroughly situated in time and space. As such, colonies and empires are not "things," but "polities of dislocation, processes of dispersion, appropriation, and displacement" working through people, milieux, and categories; they are not "steady states, but states of becoming, (polities) in states of solution and constant formation" (Stoler et al. 2007: 8–9; cf. Calhoun et al. 2006). Such critical analytic, in turn, is tailored to the recuperation of the plurality of forms, stakes, agendas, and experiences that constituted colonial worlds and which shaped the process of their making and unmaking. Of course, a similar critique can be leveled at the idea of "the colonial state," which is a subspecies of the state abstraction and creates a singular political object masking the empty foundations of sovereignty (Bartelson 2001), where there was in actuality an assemblage of practices, interests, rationalities, and institutions (Barry et al. 1996; Comaroff 1998; Moore 2005).[4]

A final critical category, both in the context of this volume and studies of colonial experience, is that of "capitalism." As is now well-recognized (e.g., Blim 2000; Sahlins 1994), there are, of course, different "moments" and configurations of capitalism – mercantile, industrial, corporate, (neo)liberal, financial, etc. … – though different epochal structures and logics of capitalism interweave with local economic institutions, political regimes, and cultural imaginations to achieve particular forms on the ground. As astutely remarked by Chakrabarty (2008: Chap. 2) in his close rereading of Marx's (1973) *Grundrisse*, while the historical move-

---

[3]Similar arguments have been extended to the use of "colonial governmentality" or "colonial modernity" declined in the singular, which both paper over the precise operations and mechanism involved in the construction of different ways of being and feeling in colonial settings (Cooper 2005).

[4]In this optic, I should indicate that when, in the course of the case study, I occasionally reference "colony" or "colonial state" in the singular, those abbreviations refer to the specific context of French Senegal – which does not mean that they cannot speak to a broader set of colonial dynamics.

ment of capital is propelled by its own structural logics (its inner *being*), capitalism always encounters antecedent histories that are rarely subsumed in full, as its agents, forces, and appendages work to create the conditions of its social reproduction. Its omnivorous and universalizing obsessions notwithstanding, capital does not simply exhaust difference and otherness. It can tolerate or even encourage their presence, leaving the possibility for the makers of these other histories to resist, ignore, or accommodate the logic of capital's workings. These other histories, in other words, whose traces anthropologists and archaeologists hope to retrieve, are both constitutive of capitalism and constantly interrupt its totalizing drives. Taking the emancipatory possibilities watermarking Marx's analyses to greater deconstructive lengths Gidwani (2008) has proposed to open the category of capitalism to question. He argues that the ceaseless interruption, alteration, and reinforcement of capitalism's motives – a compulsive pursuit of profit, accumulation for its own sake, and the exponential genesis of surplus value – by a variety of other logics challenge the ontology of capital as a (shape-shifting) totality animated by a series of unifying logics or laws. Instead, he proposes that

> Even though capitalist production dominates the universe of human (and nonhuman) activities, these activities are not reducible to – *not mere expressions of* – capital. Instead, we are forced to confront a "complex whole" *where production activity oriented to profit-making for accumulation interdigitates with other value-creating or normative practices.* Moreover, we encounter a dense circuitry of humans and nonhumans that capitalist value must traverse in the garb of product, commodity, and money in order to be affirmed. (Gidwani 2008: xxiv, original emphasis)

I find Gidwani's reformulation particularly compelling for two reasons: first, because it aims to explicitly address the convolutions of capitalism in agrarian societies (in Gujarat) in ways that are particularly germane for the rural communities that made up the vast majority of France's imperial subjects in Africa and second, because it converges with previously discussed efforts to rethink the critical categories of global history along an analytic of assemblages: to view them no longer as totalities, but as contingent formations of elements sutured together into the appearance of *dei ex machina*: "the colony," "the colonial state," and "capitalism" (see also Callon 1992, and Çaliskan and Callon 2009, for different but similarly minded analyses of "markets" and "economy").

Combining these different inspirations, I approach the question of colonial capitalism in Senegal by heeding Gidwani's search for intersecting regimes of value and the "dense circuitry" of people, spaces, and things channeling the various incarnations which capital can take. At the same time, my analysis *also* seeks to examine how processes of value creation and circulation articulated with, and were given shape by, other colonial assemblages involving different arrangements of political rule, social practices, and ideologies of development (Coronil 2001). One salient element of this relationship is that, instead of portraying French colonial capitalism as a smoothly functioning whole, the analysis points to disjunctures (both latent and realized) between the interests of merchant capital and those of colonial governance (Marseille 1984; also Boone 1992). Additionally, it highlights the role of political institutions and legal conventions in delimiting and constraining the freedom of markets and operations of capital (also Chakrabarty 2008: 51–52, 56–57). Interestingly, it is at the seams between politics and commerce that new forms of economic life emerge in starkest light and where the strategies of different colonial actors can be most clearly observed. It is also in the interplay of these articulations suturing different repertoires of practices and relations that colonial capitalism acquired shape, enduring but unstable, combining and recombining into new precipitates as its constitutive elements shifted over time.

Before these general remarks and turning to colonial past of Senegal, I should perhaps confess that my evocation of historical anthropology earlier in this introduction was not entirely innocent. As it stands, much of the analysis presented in this chapter is stitched together from ethnographic and documentary accounts, with archaeological sources featuring more marginally in the picture. As already alluded above, this analytical strategy is in part dictated by the rudimentary nature of the archaeological record in Siin, where rich material assemblages recovered from definable contexts are largely absent. With the exceptions of two sites (Joral and Pecc Waagaan), where small-scale excavations and limited testing were conducted, the bulk of the archaeological evidence for the colonial period comes in the form of surface assemblages collected at over 90 residential sites featuring late nineteenth–twentieth-century components. This empirical evidence limits archaeological observations to a very general level of argument and description. Having said this, the methodological choice underpinning this chapter is not solely a product of necessity, but also hails from conviction: a sentiment that historical archaeology is never so effective as when it is conceived as a form of historical anthropology, one where the contexts for the investigation of past materialities and cultural experiences are defined in the systematic triangulation between/within *different* evidential archives, regardless of their medium (Stahl 2001).[5] Surely, archaeological narratives can provide compelling alternatives to accounts crafted from nonmaterial sources, but in the absence of such self-standing narratives, archaeological sensibilities and attention to the minutiae of object worlds can still provoke new ways of engaging historical and ethnographic documents (e.g., Dawdy 2008; Hall 2000; Voss 2008). This means that texts can be read "archaeologically" with an eye for objects and material mediations that might have escaped the purview of earlier readers mining them for other information. This also suggests that archaeological patterns, even if they are not richly informative, can nevertheless productively mesh with more evocative textual evidence, with the twinned aims of pushing historical sources in new empirical directions while bringing archaeological ones into thicker registers of interpretation.

This somewhat long parenthesis into theory and methodology, thus, returns us to the question with which we opened this chapter, with further possibility for widening

---

[5]Certainly, the recent and sophisticated forays spearheaded by literary studies scholars associated with the journal *Critical Inquiry* into the analysis of materiality underscore the capacity of textual interpretation to enhance our understanding of the relationships binding people and things (e.g., Brown 2004a, b).

its readership. Beyond the substantive analysis of Siin's grapplings with France's ideology of empire and the deepening penetration of market forces, historical archaeologists may find interest in (1) the proposal for a dissolution of the various totalities that have dominated the study of the modern world system, (2) the suggestion that "colony," "capital," and "empire" be examined as contingent and intersecting formations made up of shifting assemblages of agents, relations, and representations, and (3) the proposed alloying of historical anthropology and archaeology. Having closed this prefatory circle, at least momentarily, it is now time to open the floor to Senegal.

Mise-en-Valeur: Logics and Aesthetics of Colonial Capitalism in French West Africa

In the late 1850s, on the eve of formal colonization, French officials were gazing upon the land of Senegal, their eyes filled with promise. Some 40 years prior, from its coastal enclaves, the nascent French colony had embarked on a project of *mise-en-valeur* ("putting to use"): a program of agricultural colonization focused on ameliorating cultivable land and exploiting available resources animated by the pursuit of realization of African soils' agricultural value through development (Hardy 1921; Monteilhet 1916). The escalation of political hostility generated by these measures led to the prompt abortion of the agricultural project, but the idea of *mise-en-valeur* never really expired and continued to stimulate France's imperial ambitions (Aldrich 2002). In effect, the decades leading up to colonial conquest saw the emergence of peanut cash cropping, and by the time of the first military expeditions, the lowly peanut had begun to bind African communities to French commercial interests while offering a foundation for the affirmation of French interventions in regional politics (Klein 1968; Mbodj and Becker 1999).

By the end of the 1880s, military "pacification" and muscular diplomacy had demarcated a nominally secure and stable territory, opening a new economic frontier, where French commercial energies would expand and thrive. The military and political costs of the colony would be validated and recouped through the economic returns obtained on the access to raw materials. As the official rhetoric went, natural and agricultural resources would be obtained in exchange for metropolitan goods and shipped to France, where they would be transformed into commodities and then circulated back to colonial consumer markets. The economic value accrued at each step in the process of transformation would not only help colonial government to pay for itself, but would also bring revenues into metropolitan coffers (Faidherbe 1889).[6] Seeking to limit capital investment and maximize revenues, colonial

---

[6]See Marseille (1984) for a trenchant discussion of the flaws in French colonial ideology, and incompatibilities between tricolor colonialism and capitalism (also Cooper 1993).

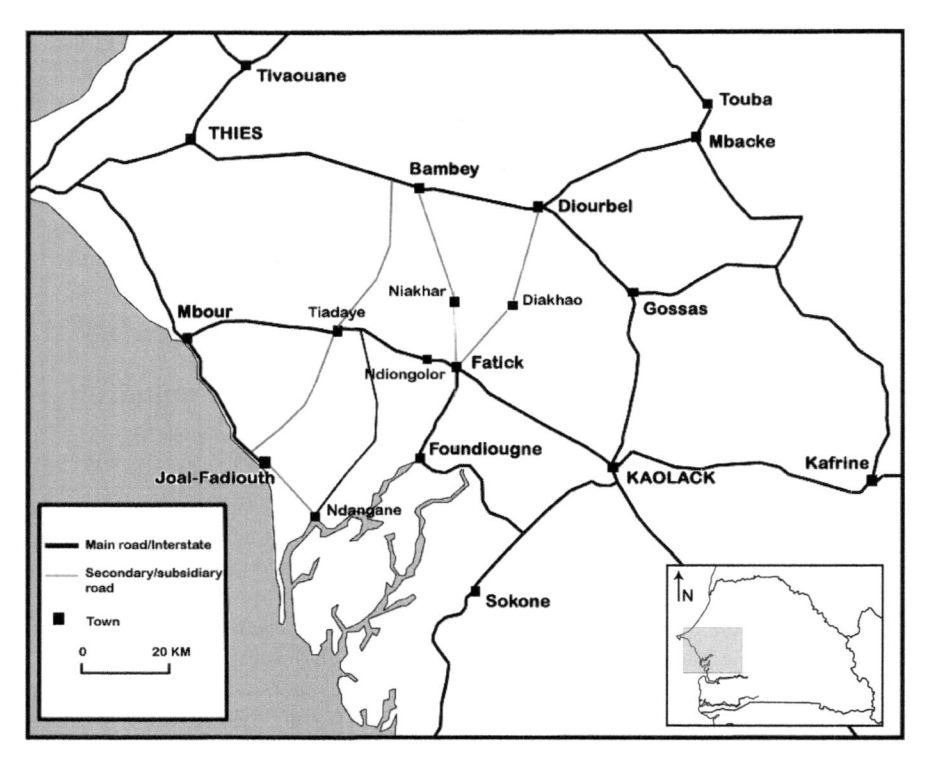

Fig. 9.1 The Siin region of Senegal

economists and officials planned to build colonial *mise-en-valeur* not on infrastructural development, "modernizing," or reorganizing local economies, but to pursue economic extraction on the cheap by using existing structures of production and local agricultural *savoir-faire*.

The small province of Siin in west-central Senegal was to play a prominent role in this economic scheme (Fig. 9.1). A modest political actor, the Siin was home to one of the most sophisticated agricultural ecologies in French West Africa. Siin's agrarian world formed a complex edifice of land rights, labor sharing, and field rotation combining multicrop cultivation, animal husbandry, and regenerative fallows integrated into a broader cosmology and symbolic economy. This agro-pastoral system permitted the achievement of comparatively high population densities and abundant crop production, a fact that did not escape colonial officials. Not surprisingly, the process of French economic expansion coincided with the birth of colonial ethnography, which, in time, paved the way for the deployment of new technologies of the state, practices of enumeration and codification, as well as modes of regulation designed to assist the proper conduct of colonial governance (Robinson 2000; cf. Cohn 1996). In this other kind of "putting to use," new forms of biopolitical knowledge and classificatory grids were overlaid onto colonized

Fig. 9.2 Postcard, "Serer from the vicinity of Nianing" (early 1900s) (Archives Nationales du Sénégal, Iconographie, #0615) http://www.archivesdusenegal.gouv.sn/cartes/0615.JPG

populations so as to identify existing "racial" assets and weave them into programs of economic development. In this context, the Serer, Siin's majority ethnic group, soon came to be perceived as one of the most successful peasantries of Senegal, a population of hardworking, conservative, and isolationist rural folk, wedded to their land, suspicious of change, and outside influences (Fig. 9.2).

The figure of the "typical peasant" probably emerged at the nexus of the colonial gaze and a more deeply rooted domain of socioeconomic practices among Serer populations, making difficult to say which of history or imagination holds primary authorship (Galvan 2004: Chap. 2; Richard 2007: 155–174). More significant, however, is the "truth effect" of this representational economy, which conveniently welded culture and race and recontextualized them into a landscape of bounded ethnic units – a *montage* that reveals more about French interests and anxieties than African identities. Juxtaposed against neighboring ethnic groups, the Serer peasant became a significant counterpart to French ideas of progress, modernization, and "civilization" (Conklin 1997). In this light, the Serer provided a compelling, multipurpose "other," whose traditional lifeways appeared at once compatible with and antithetic to colonial economic policies. This ambivalence is denoted in two contrasting colonial perspectives on the Serer, with some observers decrying their hostility to change as an obstacle to progress opposing it to the faculty of economic adaptation and cultural "assimilation" of Wolof populations (Geismar 1933; Reynier 1933; Rousseau 1928), and others also appealed to the romance of a pristine rural civilization, celebrated for its longevity, ingenuity, and symbiotic ties to the landscape (Galvan 2004: 49–50). This image also had pragmatic resonance for

French officials. Many indeed underscored that the Serer provided exactly the kind of small-scale production and agricultural diligence required by the project of *mise-en-valeur*. Thus, Bérenger-Féraud (1879: 279, 284) saw early on the promise of the Serer as both valuable producers and consumers for the colonial economy, who would supply "our commerce with products of serious value in very satisfying quantities," while becoming "very desirable tributaries for our commerce if we manage, through a series of long-term measures, to diminish their inclination for drunkenness and protect them against incursions from their neighbors, who under the pretext of converting them to Islam, devastate their country from time to time."

Economic development, in other words, also entailed cultivating the "native peasant within," even as imperial moral education demanded a radical transformation of colonized subjectivities and being-in-the-world (Comaroff and Comaroff 1997) – an impossible project demanding at once change and its opposite, a rural play on the not white/not quite contradiction (Bhabha 1994). These contradictions, in turn, are apparent in colonial reports that largely lamented the Serer's inability to fully convert to commodity farming, individual entrepreneurship, and modernity, even as the Siin dominated cash crop production in French West Africa at the height of the colonial period. And thus, as colonial officials and later scholars continued to portray the Siin as a bastion of cultural conservatism, a complex story of cultural transformations, compromises, and negotiations has gone largely undocumented (but see Galvan 2004; Guigou 1992; Reinwald 1997a, b for important exceptions).

The rest of this chapter essays a few reflections on these contradictions, particularly as generated by the colonial reconfiguration of Senegal's rural economy and integration of the region into a broader sphere of capitalist relations. Economic exploitation in Senegal was accompanied by the attempt to inculcate new affects of place and politics, new ideas of property and civility, new tastes and desires, as well as modes of sociality into African communities. The advent of peanut agriculture became enmeshed with and reliant on a broader sphere of colonial strategies, involving taxation, commoditization, monetization, legal codification, and labor movements.[7] While these technologies of government and the movements of capital they sanctioned entailed significant agricultural and social transformations, they were also mediated and modified by local social forms and perceptions.

Drawing on historical ethnography and archaeology, I explore the particular shapes that these entanglements acquired in the Siin province between the 1860s and 1930s. I pursue the trail of encounters between colonial state and subjects across a messy world of "multiple, indeterminate configurations of power and authority" (Hansen and Stepputat 2006: 302), bridged by tensions and compromises, where the rule of law had to be reestablished constantly in its engagement with local populations (Comaroff 1998; Cooper and Stoler 1997; Hansen and Stepputat 2005). The slippage between colonial policy and local realities, in turn, opened a space of action, where the conditions of colonial existence could be subverted and negotiated away from

---

[7]For important historical works on these questions in Francophone Africa, see Cooper (1996), Roberts (2005), and Roitman (2005).

official influence, where hegemony and orthodoxy dissolved into hybridity and heterodoxy (Bhabha 1994; Comaroff and Comaroff 1992; Hall 2000; Mbembe 2001; Schrire 1996).

My concern is with the material terrains on which colonial power plays were waged, the assemblages of authority and agency involved, and the traces of African cultural voices lingering in materiality yet lost to history and modern understandings (Smith 2004). Documenting these expressions requires attention to the Janus face of subjectivity: the condition of being subjected to a particular regime of rule *and* that of coming to occupy a particular understanding of oneself and mode of consciousness (Foucault 1994: 331). It also calls for careful analysis of the fashioning of subjective experiences in particular fields of culture, history, and material relations. Finally, it demands sensitivity to both the repressive and productive sides of power: the world of rules, discipline, and authority that constrains the will and deeds of historical agents, but which, in doing so, also creates conditions that enable new courses of action and imaginations.

In an effort to accommodate constraints of time and space, I take up one facet of the colonial narrative of labor, law, and commerce – namely, regimes of value and their material repertoires. Cultural economy is particularly germane to the study of Serer communities' engagement with the projects of colonial governance in that it represents one of the "contact zones" (Linke 2006), "targets," and "points of application" (Scott 1999: 25), where the technologies and forms of authority of the colonial state met previously existing structures of power as well as the cultural senses and sensibilities of African populations, where different domains of materiality clashed or interlocked (also Ferguson and Gupta 2002; Foucault 2007; Trouillot 2003). It is in this mosaic of familiar places and strange spaces – agricultural fields, stretches of landscapes, villages, market centers, administrative posts – that colonial capital flows converged on local worlds of cultural intimacy, where rural Africans reasoned with, contested, and compromised the reason of state (*raison d'état*) and logic of the market. But before getting to this story of culture and commodities, a bit of historical background is in order.

Peanuts, "The Market," and the Making of Colonial Sovereignty

The roots of colonial economy were planted in the course of the nineteenth century, building on the commercial networks and commodity circuits that had supplied the Atlantic era (Curtin 1975). After a brief boom in the first half of the nineteenth century (Curtin 1981), the gum commerce began to wane during the 1840s, thus opening an outlet for the peanut trade (Brooks 1975). With the developing soap industry and need for lubricant for industrial machinery in the metropole, peanut production soon escalated from a measly 1 metric ton in 1840 to 5,000 tons in 1850; in 1898, export reached 95,000 metric tons (Klein 1968: 36–38; Moitt 1989: 27) (Fig. 9.3). The growing weight of peanut cash cropping in the balance of trade occasioned a recentering of the Atlantic economy after 1850s from the Senegal River toward the

Fig. 9.3 Postcard, "Senegal, the peanut trade" (early 1900s) (Archives Nationales du Sénégal, Iconographie, #0424) http://www.archivesdusenegal.gouv.sn/cartes/0424.JPG

provinces of the "peanut basin," and the Siin-Saalum emerged as the primary producing region at the *fin-de-siècle*.

The introduction of peanuts dramatically altered the contours of economic and power relations in Siin. Cash cropping was a veritable instrument of social promotion for African peasantries (Mbodj 1978: 102–104), which freed trade and production from the moorings of customary privileges and eroded the economic order of the precolonial state (Klein 1979). Peasants were allowed to confront the market more directly as producers rather than through the intermediary of the *buur* (king), nobility, and other traditional authorities. Once beholden to aristocratic lords, peasants reclaimed the fruits of their labor, channeling the proceeds of foodstuff and peanut sales toward the acquisition of goods that were once restricted to social elites or limited in circulation because of their connection to Atlantic exchanges (imported cloth, beads and trinkets, manufactures) (but see Richard 2010; Searing 1993). Weapons became particularly prized as a protective measure against pillages, which further loosened peasants from the predatory grasp of kings and their enslaved armies (Klein 1968: 67; Mbodj 1978: 81).

In effect, with peanut cultivation came linkages to a broader sphere of goods and exchanges which enabled peasants to gradually replace *buurs* and *ceddos* (slave warriors) as beneficiaries of the external commerce by becoming instrumental, if unequal, agents of that economy. The threat of growing peasant economic independence triggered a period of unbridled reprisals, as local aristocracies sought to combat declining incomes and tap the newfound peanut wealth of the peasant world through pillaging and ransacking villages and imposing tribute and customs on the trade

(Curtin 1981: 86). On this background of social tensions, famines, and conflict, French military interventions and pacification between the 1850s and 1870s introduced further instability by destroying fields and torching down villages, policing trade, etc.

The era of the protectorate (1887–1924) ushered further major transitions in political power, bringing about transformations in chiefly authority, as well as a gradual decrease of the *ceddo* entourage and its eventual dilution into the growing mass of the peasantry toward the end of the 1890s (Noirot 1896; also Klein 1968: Chap. 8; Mbodj 1980). Crippled by anemic budgets and metropolitan penny-pinching, French administrators chose to exploit Serer sociopolitical structures and collaborate with local chiefs and monarchs to graft the armature of the colonial system onto local rural settings (Pélissier 1966: 202). French colonial rule, thus, created two effective spheres of administration: a level of former kings and chiefs doing the grunt work on the ground, overseen at a distance by a broader bureaucratic system made up of French administrators and governors. The aristocracy was left in place and operated until World War II under this régime of indirect administration. They were delegated institutional functions (levying fines, recruiting for *corvée* labor, administering simply judicial matters), tax collection duties, and monitored peanut cash cropping (Aujas 1929; Guy 1908: 308). By the late nineteenth century, considerable changes in the forms and distribution of power had been underway at the expense of "traditional" grassroot institutions, mostly land custodians/lineage heads (*lamaans*) and village authorities.

Colonialism also reframed local economies, social structures, and relations of production, introducing new administrative divisions, modes of taxation, and forced labor (often inducing migrations when colonial demands were too heavy); new systems of social and residential organization; an overall economic dependence on prices established in distant countries, on French commercial houses for loans, cash, and goods, as well as on migrant workers; and the growing influences of Islam and Catholicism (Galvan 2004; Klein 1968, 1979; Mbodj and Becker 1999). Although Senegal's dependence on the world market remained low until the late nineteenth century, colonial agriculture, need for cash to pay the head tax, and growing reliance on French products effectively tethered local lives to the fate of peanuts, generally at the expense of local modes of subsistence and industries (Noirot (1896), in Klein 1968: 174–175). Further, the penetration of *navétanes* (seasonal laborers) and growing agricultural presence of other ethnic groups followed the expansion of peanut agriculture (David 1980; Pélissier 1966: 204–205) and resulted in important changes on the social geography and occupation of space.

The lack of colonial personnel, budgetary shortages, and a need for bureaucratic frugality forced the colonial administration to craft a "hegemonic" political sphere by interpolating new institutions and forms of governance into a precolonial sphere of sovereignty and authority – and not an uncontested one at that. The result was a tense and complex social space, traversed by different planes of political action representing different political projects with different lines of force and extensions, whose contradictions provided fertile ground for the rise of divergent political effects and affinities. This very landscape provided the coded and charged social terrain across which colonial capital, commerce, and commodities moved, and the sites of their entanglement with Serer's social practices, forms of signification, and cultural economy – to wit, the sites whereon particular colonial subjects arose from the deployment of stately political rationalities and their entwinement with Serer's world-making practices.

Cash Crops, Commodities, and Regimes of Value

Like many rural societies in Africa (Klein 1980), the Siin economy in recent history has been predicated on what peasant scholars call a "subsistence ethic" and "safety-first" principle. Faced with a precarious environment and capricious seasonal rainfalls, Serer peasants have labored to ensure adequate and dependable grain yields, instead of maximizing agricultural production (see Bourgeau 1933: 36; Martin et al. 1980: 53; Reynier 1933: 5–6). During most of the colonial period, Siin farmers managed a continued focus on subsistence cereal and rarely allowed cash crop acreage to exceed that of surfaces planted in millet (Pélissier 1966).

As they toiled to meet subsistence needs, Siin peasants also worked toward accumulating a portfolio of maternal wealth. This "community of goods" was a form of family group insurance, which operated as a "safety net" against the uncertainties of weather and subsistence, a ceremonial fund applied toward the maintenance and reproduction of social networks, and capital that could be invested in production (Aujas 1931: 307–308; Gastellu 1981: 130). Though nominally a bilineal society, the Serer of Siin placed greater social emphasis on matrilineal descent and inheritance, and so building the "wealth of the maternal hut" (*halal a ndok yaay*) was the "finality of economic activity in the Serer milieu" (Gastellu 1974: 39; also Richard 2007: 174–187, 206–211).

These parallel economic logics found concrete expression in the agrarian landscape, where the harvests of selected fields went into feeding the members of "kitchens" (*ngak*, the basic locus of consumption/production) while another set of fields was cultivated to augment lineage wealth (Gastellu 1981; Guigou 1992; Reinwald 1997a, b). Historically, millet and rice fields were devoted to self-subsistence, with cereal surpluses channeled toward amassing maternal wealth (Bourgeau 1933: 36). The expansion of cash crops offered new opportunities for collective accumulation without compromising the existing subsistence economy (Gastellu 1974: 89). Agricultural production became increasingly compartmentalized. While millet farming continued to be directed toward food consumption, the cash proceeds of peanut sales went to satisfy the immediate needs in the *ngak* in the form of head tax, cloth purchases, and reimbursement of credit, before being routed toward matrilineal funds (ibid.: 49). Traditionally, collective accumulation was generally not invested in production; instead, millet surpluses were exchanged for cattle, the most highly regarded expression of wealth, generally in combination with jewelry and cloth (ibid.: 29). Cattle have historically been employed as a communal form of economic and symbolic capital, embodying the lineage's prestige and material wealth (Gastellu 1985; Richard 2007: 209). As a particularly liquid form of capital, convertible into social relations and spouses, cattle also played a pivotal role in local ceremonial exchanges and the building of alliances and obligations (Dupire et al. 1974; Guigou 1992: 189, 419).

Serer economic sensibilities, based on dual spheres of relations and circulation, were looked on with great suspicion by the French administration and merchant community (Galvan 2004): first, because they were seen as a primitive throwback barring the implementation of free market exchange and normalization of owner-ship arrangements along a European template of individualism, contract relations, divisible property, patrimonialism, and primogeniture; second, because the absence of a singular system of land title and holding weakened social control; and third, because the Serer would prove to be particularly adept at navigating the Byzantine networks of bilineal inheritance to evade debt/loan repayment and taxation (Dulphy 1939; Galvan 1997: 19–20). The standardization "effect" expected of the introduc-tion of new idioms of property, commodification, and monetization also aimed to foster new dispositions (industriousness) and a taste for commerce and French goods. These measures were put in place to encourage redoubled devotion to peanut production and intensification, and the use of agricultural proceeds to acquire every-thing else. Key, then, was to create a *need* for cash so as to increase peasant depen-dence on money and markets for social reproduction. The results turned out to be more mitigated in practice (also Roitman 2005).

At first sight, it is undeniable that Serer's commodity consumption increased dramatically after the 1860s. This period saw a dramatic increase and diversification in imported goods on archaeological sites. Alcohol consumption appears to have been significant, as suggested by the dominance of gin and wine bottle in material assemblages (Fig. 9.4).[8] At the same time, the acquisition of alcohol and other imported goods was not exactly a novel phenomenon in Siin, but one drawing on long-existing economic circuits. Not only had Serer's consumption practices been shaped by centuries of interaction with European commerce, but local communities had displayed a considerable amount of agency in commercial relations, as local régimes of value influenced the reception and incorporation of trade items and new forms of social distinction emerged in the process (Richard 2010). Wine, for instance, acquired a central role in the domain of elite ritual practice (feasting and ceremonies of investiture, in particular) while trade liquor was relegated to the more mundane theater of daily consumption, social prestations, labor parties, and ancestor worship.

---

[8]This lends some support to contemporary writings that lamented the prodigious consumption of alcohol in the region and debilitating effects of chronic drunkenness on Serer populations (Bérenger-Féraud 1879: 18–20, 279; Corre 1876–77: 598–599; Guy 1908: 305; Pinet-Laprade 1865: 154), as well as the darker repercussions of "civilization" (Carlus 1880: 105, 411). While these testimonies contain a probable amount of strategic distortion and ethnic defamation on the part of European observers, their consistency across colonial correspondence suggests a measure of historical truth, underwriting the central role of alcohol in processes of colonization (see Richard 2007: 166, 212–213, 215; also Dietler 2006). Archaeological and documentary evidence, however, also indi-cates some differences in alcohol and glass use/consumption across the Siin during the colonial period (Debien 1964: 549; Richard 2010).

Fig. 9.4 Imported liquor bottles, Diakhao region, mid-nineteenth century contexts and later

Alcohol became an intrinsic feature of rural sociality. In turn, local capacity for decision making and consumption choices stretched into the colonial era. Witness, for instance, in the 1890s, Ernest Noirot's (1896: 54–55) complaint that colonial authorities' attempt to replace alcohol with imported cloth and make the latter the chief means of barter was largely unsuccessful, since the Serer were unwilling to let go of liquor and preferred African cloth.

What then of common charges, such as those leveled by Reynier (1933: 1) who condemned the Serer for their "little inclination for commerce," lack of "adventurous mind," and "imperfectible" nature? At issue here is not so much that the Serer did not engage in commerce, but that they did so selectively without being drawn into the web of colonial dependence.

The Serer's relative success in preserving economic self-sufficiency was in part derived from their well-integrated agro-pastoral economy, which had sufficient flexibility to accommodate French imperial demands while retaining traditional forms of production (Pélissier 1953: 113). Although a marginal woman's crop at first (Gastellu 1974: 56), peanut was progressively worked in the agricultural cycle and found its place in the alternating millet–fallow rotations (Mbodj 1978: 303–308; Pélissier 1966: 246–250).[9] Mbodj (1980: 145) estimates that until the first decade of

---

[9]Expansion in the volume of cash crop exports offers telling evidence of peanuts' increasing role in Siin's economy. The amount of peanuts exported from the region rose from 8,000 tons in 1884 to 40,000 tons in 1909, and then more than doubled by 1914 to reach 100,000 tons. Cash crop exports reached a high plateau in the 1930s at an average of 250,000 tons a year, thereby making Siin-Saalum the premiere economic region in French West Africa (Klein 1979: 77–79; Mbodj 1978: 542–543).

1900s, Serer peasants produced enough to meet their subsistence needs and began to enter the cycle of food dependence only after that period. In fact, until the 1930s, millet continued to be grown for subsistence while peanuts were mainly cultivated for sale (Bourgeau 1933: 36; Gastellu 1974: 56–60): when prices to the producer slumped too low and the terms of trade proved too unfavorable, Serer peasants could respond to economic crises by reducing cash crop production, growing millet instead, and reinforcing their nutrient base with rice (Reinwald 1997b: 159).

Another factor, mentioned in practically every colonial report until the 1930s, was the aversion of Serer peasants for loans and credit purchases and their remarkably low levels of indebtedness compared to other ethnic groups (Reinwald 1997b: 157). These forms of refusal were assisted by the development of composite practices of property and conversion. The institution of land pawnship (*taile*), for instance, entailed the temporary transfer of land use rights for cash, providing one instance of renegotiation of colonial idioms of land management below the façade of the "law." Serer notions of inalienable matrilineal land were stretched to allow its cash convertibility and virtual commodification (Galvan 2004). This enabled Serer peasants to generate cash so as to meet the imperatives of taxation and social reproduction without compromising local management rights, forms of property, and commitment to the matrilineage. In turn, the reluctance to borrow both buttressed Serer resistance to full-scale peanut agriculture and slowed down the progress of commodification in the first third of the 20th century (Galvan 2004: 112–113). In this light, the effects of market forces and colonial economic policies proved much less disruptive on Serer's traditional agricultural economy than for their Wolof neighbors who embraced cash crop at the expense of cereal farming (Guigou 1992: 58; Pélissier 1966: 237).

At the same time, after the 1890s, trade in Siin *was* increasingly regulated by peanut production (Mbodj 1978: 548–552). Pressed by the exigencies of taxation, the need to purchase the basic commodities they no longer produced and the threat of *corvée* labor, peasants were left with little choice but to gradually enter the sphere of cash-mediated exchanges (Galvan 1997; Klein 1968: 186; Mbodj 1980; also Guyer 1995). Farmers reluctantly acquiesced, by increasing surfaces cultivable in peanuts, which tethered local subsistence to the fates of world market prices and climatic vagaries (Lericollais 1972; Mbodj 1978: 321–427). Growing reliance on monetized exchanges also had a profound impact on local consumption practices and moral economy (Bourgeau 1933: 55–56; Mbodj 1978: 102–104, 530; Reinwald 1997a). Trading points (*escales*) played a central role in making available manufactured goods that became integral part of the peasants' quotidian (Fig. 9.5), as more and more of the cash proceeds derived from peanut sales were used to purchase imported items and things, such as medicine, travel, or education (Galvan 1997: 22; also Bourgeau 1933: 55; Guy 1908: 313–314; Martin et al. 1980: 70).

These various transformations have left concrete echoes and signatures in the archaeological landscapes of the late nineteenth and early twentieth centuries. While sparse in regional material inventories prior to the 1850s, imported objects become a ubiquitous fixture of village remains of the colonial period. Along with trade alcohol, the rising presence of pharmaceutical containers, perfume bottles, molded beads, buttons, and metal hardware and cookware on regional sites (Richard 2007:

Fig. 9.5 Postcard, "Sine-Saloum, the Foundiougne escale" (early 1900s) (Archives Nationales du Sénégal, Iconographie, #0696) http://www.archivesdusenegal.gouv.sn/cartes/0696.JPG

Chap. 9) offers a material testimony of how Serer's understanding of the world and themselves in it was gradually recalibrated around commodity acquisition and changing forms of consumption.

The material underside of Serer's colonial subjectivities can also be felt in the restructuration of social space toward French trading and administrative centers, such as Fatick, Foundiougne, or Kaolack, where crops could be sold and converted into cash, food, or other purchasable goods (Aujas 1929; Klein 1968: 114–116, 150–152). We, thus, note a palpable increase of post-1870s settlements in the Fatick area, which seems to support archival evidence of a landscape in flux (Guigou 1992: 77–78), as the town began to pull local farmers and seasonal migrant labor in its commercial orbit. Other colonial investments, such as the development of transportation infrastructure, also influenced the Serer's residential landscape, their legacy still visible in many contemporary villages of the Siin hinterland that agglutinate in ribbons along primary and secondary roads.

From the economic realm, framed by new necessities of consumption and market exchange, commodities and money began to trickle into the sphere of socially significant transactions, causing a diversification of social payments at baptisms, weddings, or funerals and a related decrease in the symbolic prestige of cattle. After the 1930s, the terms of social and ritual reproduction in Siin were increasingly dictated by cash exchanges. More dramatically perhaps, the realm of imported manufactures became a terrain of struggle for the redefinition of ownership and inheritance, where social ontologies were tested, or in the case of matrilineal allegiances gradually unmade (Gravrand 1966).

Between Past and Postcolony: Siin and the Politics of Representation

To the architects of imperialism, Siin's built world was iconic of the cultural inferiority and lack of civility of African populations – a profoundly premodern, savage mode of existence out of which they should be lifted. The limited political, financial, and physical presence of France in Siin represented so many stumbling blocks to the disciplining and "advancement" of colonized populations. Instead, "commerce" – that most implacable force of social development – would provide the gospel and main vector of France's *mission civilisatrice*. In colonial rhetoric, conversion to the market and commodity farming (imposed through the artifices of commoditization, new legal proscriptions [*Code de l'Indigénat*], new notions of work, exchange, and property) would naturally reform the hearts and minds, cultures, and comportments of African subjects. When translated into the messier realm of practice, however, these injunctions often failed to deliver the promises of modernist "purification," begetting instead a proliferation of hybrid constructs and assemblages (Latour 1993).

Curiously, colonial authors have often failed to appreciate the profound transformations wrought by colonial capitalism in Siin, a "silence" (Trouillot 1995) perpetuated in today's ethnic imagination in Senegal, where the discourse of Serer-cum-backward peasant is well and alive. Even as sensitive a cultural analyst as Lericollais (1972: 117), writing on the Siin heartland of the 1960s, found it "striking to find only few traces of … 50 years of trading economy, when one draws up an inventory of the goods in a sérèr house, aside from a few tubs and cooking pots, a few dresses in chests, sometimes a few corrugated iron sheets on the roof." And yet, almost 100 years earlier, in a series of descriptions of coastal houses, Corre (1883; also Debien 1964) hinted that imported rifles, knifelets, hoes, and small trunks could be found alongside locally obtained calabashes, mortars and pestles, wooden and ceramic containers, mats, baskets, etc… (Fig. 9.6). In other words, trade imports not only seamlessly coexisted with local crafts, but were also probably quite central to daily activities, such as hunting, protection, and agriculture. Indeed, the mere ubiquity of mass-produced artifacts on the surface of villages dating to the colonial period provides quiet, but potent, reminders of peasants' binding attachments to a world beyond. Much like the liberal economists criticized by Marx (1973), most observers of Siin have tethered their gazes to objects and surface appearances – a sense of failed or unachieved commodification – and missed the complex array of historical relations and experiences underwriting the phenomenal world of the Serer. The rhetoric of conservatism, then, is less about resistance to change and innovation than it is a moral commentary on the (perceived) Serer's distance from modernity, colonial or otherwise.

But colonial modernity (of whatever national flavor), as this essay suggests, was never determinate or sedimented; it was an incomplete suite of experimental projects and ideological justifications for the expansion of imperial capitalisms and sovereignties. Always in the making, at once symbolic and sensible, yet no less violent

Fig. 9.6 Postcard, "Serer, preparation of a fermented millet beverage" (early 1900s) (Archives Nationales du Sénégal, Iconographie, #0348) http://www.archivesdusenegal.gouv.sn/cartes/0348. JPG Note the imported cast iron cauldrons in the foreground

and repressive, these projects and the architecture of order they supported collided with a mosaic of cultural topographies and practical terrains (Watts 1992). Much as in the Siin, these encounters produced fractured spaces of sovereignty and subjectivity that rewrote the experiences of all involved parties. Far from passive witnesses of history, African farmers emerged as particular subjects who navigated within the impositions of colonial law and commerce and the possibilities of culture and customary arrangements (cf. Watts 1993). Faced with changing social coordinates and calculi, Siin peasants worked to maintain a delicate balance between growing food and peanuts, acquiring objects while honoring matrilineal obligations, paying taxes and the costs of social reproduction while avoiding debt or famine, working within the terms of freehold property without giving up their notions of inalienable land, etc. In doing so, they retained a degree of social autonomy in the face of colonial encroachments, even as they were becoming more deeply enmeshed with the fate of global markets.

These mitigated experiences did not stop at the gates of postindependence Senegal. In fact, on some level, Serer peasants have had to contend with a no less formidable opponent in the form of the Senegalese state (Galvan 2004), which in the 1960s imposed rather drastic institutional land reforms that fully did away with precolonial tenure systems, regimes of management, and modes of conflict arbitration (Abelin 1979). Subsequent declines in world prices, ecological crises, rising cost of fertilizers and basic necessities, and growing urban recentering of Senegal (Lericollais 1999; Mbodj 1992) have pushed the Siin to an even more marginal position in the national imaginary, as the obverse face of Senegal's modernity.

Beyond acts of vain resistance and an increasing estrangement between the realm of official administration and local informal management, Serer villagers have responded to their worsening conditions by mobilizing cultural memory and reworking collective imaginations of the precolonial and postcolonial pasts to articulate a critical commentary on state legitimacy, citizens' rights, social justice, and state–subject relations (Galvan 2004). These projects, however, have often rested on a romanticization and glorification of different political institutions: customary authorities, the precolonial kingdom, the colonial state, or Islamic clerics. The present study might provide an alternative, perhaps complementary, stance of critique. Taking a deeper view of history may help us to illuminate the current postcolonial predicaments without invoking essentializations of culture or history inherited from earlier periods. Placed in a long trajectory of power, the historical fate of rural villagers in Siin can be understood as the product of a complex engagement with multiple configurations of authority and sovereignty, which have sought to control and constrain their freedom of choice while opening unsuspected horizons of cultural action. Understanding the dynamic modes of practice and forms of existence that arose from these historical junctures can help us to dispel contemporary stereotypes in Senegal and the politics of difference they authorize. More importantly, documenting how the terrain of cultural and political choices in Siin has been reconfigured in the *longue durée* of colonial/postcolonial history can offer some glimpses of the kinds of subjectivities and futures that these encounters with modern power have made possible (Mbembe 2001; Scott 1999; Weiss 2004).

Looking beyond West Africa to other geographic and archaeological contexts, the example of the Siin offers a reminder that history is always and perhaps inevitably an "argument about the present" (Holston 2008: 33–35). The material and discursive pasts we encounter in various archives leak into contemporary realities, and, through the recomposition and rearrangement of their elements over time, continue to structure possibilities of today and tomorrow. Placing colonial experiences in conversation with postcolonial conditions may help us survey the problem space of colonial history with fresh eyes and instruments in ways that locate salient historical questions *because of their enduring resonance in the present*. The project of colonial capitalism and how it has been historically formulated – in terms of totalities and determination, tradition and modernity, subsumption or autonomy, progress or tragedy – has indelibly stamped the shaping of political identities in the public sphere of colonized nations with lingering effects on the global present. Concurrently, charting the circuitry of material relations and articulations across the historical geography of colonialism can reveal how various framings of rule, economy, and identity crystallized at various conjectures. This mode of analysis can also expose how the fluency of social life often interrupted, contested, and contaminated the categories, technologies, and legacies of colonialism, and thus break the spell of colonialism and capitalism's coherence by attending to the vulnerabilities and instabilities on which these projects were built. As they push against the frame of habitual chronologies, historical determinations, and geographic delimitations, colonial assemblages of practices can help to write histories of colonial capitalism that respect the global gravity of capital and colony without making fetishes of them, that acknowledge the ubiquity of entanglement without reifying the local into the *locus primus* of history, that accept the power of categories without falling prey to their beguiling aura … These histories, above all, refuse the triviality of being simply about the long ago. As they rummage through the debris of colonialism, as they jostle and reorder its fragments, loosen them from the matrix of time, and smuggle them into the here and now, archaeology's histories have no choice but to accept their capacity to comment about the present and inspire new ways of imagining and transforming the worlds of tomorrow (e.g., Silliman 2009).

References

Abelin, Philippe. 1979 Domaine National et Développement au Sénégal. *Bulletin de l'IFAN* 41B(3): 508–538.

Aldrich, Robert. 2002 Imperial *Mise en Valeur* and *Mise en Scène*: Recent Works on French Colonialism. *The Historical Journal* 45(4): 917–936.

Aujas, L. 1929 La Région du Sine-Saloum: Le Port de Kaolack. *Bulletin du Comité d'Études Historiques et Scientifiques de l'A.O.F.* 12: 92–132.

Aujas, L. 1931 Les Sérères du Sénegal. *Bulletin du Comité d'Études Historiques et Scientifiques de l'A.O.F.* 14: 293–333.

Barry, Andrew, Thomas Osborne, and Nikolas Rose (editors). 1996 *Foucault and Political Reason: Liberalism, Neo-Liberalism, and Rationalities of Government*. University of Chicago Press, Chicago.

Bartelson, Jens. 2001 *The Critique of the State*. Cambridge University Press, New York.

Bérenger-Féraud, L.-J.-B. 1879 *Les Peuplades de la Sénégambie*. Ernest Leroux, Paris.

Bhabha, Homi. 1994 *The Location of Culture*. Routledge, London.

Blim, Michael. 2000 Capitalisms in Late Modernity. *Annual Review of Anthropology* 29: 25–38.

Boone, Catherine. 1992 *Merchant Capital and the Roots of State Power in Senegal, 1930–1945*. Cambridge University Press, Cambridge.

Bourgeau, J. 1933 Note sur la Coutume des Sérères du Sine et du Saloum. *Bulletin du Comité d'Études Historiques et Scientifiques de l'A.O.F.* 16: 1–65.

Brooks, George. 1975 Peanuts and Colonialism: Consequences of the Commercialization of Peanuts in West Africa, 1830–70. *Journal of African History* 16(1): 29–54.

Brown, Bill. 2004a *A Sense of Things: The Object Matter of American Literature*. University of Chicago Press, Chicago.

Brown, Bill (editor). 2004b *Things*. University of Chicago Press, Chicago.

Calhoun, Graig, Frederick Cooper, and Kevin W. Moore (editors). 2006 *Lessons of Empire: Imperial Histories and American Power*. The New Press, New York.

Çaliskan, Koray, and Michel Callon. 2009 Economization, Part 1: Shifting Attention from the Economy towards Processes of Economization. *Economy and Society* 38(3): 369–398.

Callon, Michel (editor). 1992 *The Laws of the Market*. Basil Blackwell, Malden, MA.

Carlus, J. 1880 Les Sérères de la Sénégambie. *Revue de Géographie* 6: 409–420; 7: 30–37, 98–105.

Chakrabarty, Dipesh. 2008 *Provincializing Europe: Postcolonial Thought and Historical Difference*. New edition. Princeton University Press, Princeton.

Cohn, Bernard. 1996 *Colonialism and its Forms of Knowledge*. Princeton University Press, Princeton.

Comaroff, John. 1998 Reflections on the Colonial State, in South Africa and Elsewhere: Factions, Fragments, Facts, and Fictions. *Social Identities* 4(3): 321–361.

Comaroff, John, and Jean Comaroff. 1992 *Ethnography and the Historical Imagination*. Westview Press, Boulder.

Comaroff, John, and Jean Comaroff. 1997 *Of Revelation and Revolution: The Dialectics of Modernity on a South African Frontier, Volume Two*. University of Chicago Press, Chicago.

Conklin, Alice. 1997 *A Mission to Civilize: The Republican Idea of Empire in France and West Africa, 1895 1930*. Stanford University Press, Stanford.

Cooper, Frederick. 1993 Africa and the World Economy. In *Confronting Historical Paradigms: Peasants, Labor, and the Capitalist World System in Africa and Latin America*, edited by Frederick Cooper, Allen F. Isaacman, Florencia E. Mallon, William Roseberry, and Steve J. Stern, pp. 84–201. University of Wisconsin Press, Madison.

Cooper, Frederick. 1996 *Decolonization and African Society: The Labor Question in French and British Africa*. Cambridge University Press, Cambridge.

Cooper, Frederick. 2004 Empire Multiplied. *Comparative Studies in Society and History* 46: 247–72.

Cooper, Frederick. 2005 *Colonialism in Question: Theory, Knowledge, History*. University of California Press, Berkeley.

Cooper, Frederick, and Ann Laura Stoler (editors). 1997 *Tensions of Empire: Colonial Cultures in a Bourgeois World*. Berkeley: University of California Press.

Coronil, Fernando. 2001 Smelling Like a Market. *American Historical Review* 106(1): 119–129.

Corre, A. 1883 Les Sérères de Joal et de Portudal. *Revue d'Ethnographie* 2: 1–20.

Curtin, Philip. 1975 *Economic Change in Precolonial Africa: Senegambia in the Era of the Slave Trade*. University of Wisconsin Press, Madison.

Curtin, Philip. 1981 The Abolition of the Slave Trade from Senegambia. In *The Abolition of the Atlantic Slave Trade: Origins and Effects in Europe, Africa, and the Americas*, edited by David Eltis and James Walvin, pp. 83–97. University of Wisconsin Press, Madison.

David, Philippe. 1980 *Les Navétanes*. Nouvelles Éditions Africaines, Paris.

Dawdy, Shannon. 2008 *Building the Devil's Empire: French Colonial New Orleans*. University of Chicago Press, Chicago.

Debien, G. 1964 Journal du Docteur Corre en Pays Sérère (Décembre 1876-Janvier 1877). *Bulletin de l'IFAN* 26B(3–4): 532–599.

Delle, James, Stephen Mrozowski, and Robert Paynter (editors). 2000 *Lines That Divide: Historical Archaeologies of Race, Class, and Gender*. University of Tennessee, Knoxville.

Dietler, Michael. 2006 Alcohol: Anthropological/Archaeological Perspectives. *Annual Review of Anthropology* 35: 229–249.

Dirks, Nicholas. 1992 *Colonialism and Culture*. University of Michigan Press, Ann Arbor.

Dulphy, M. 1939 Coutumes Sérère de la Petite Côte (1936). In *Coutumiers Juridiques de l'Afrique Occidentale Française, Tome I (Sénégal)*, pp. 237–321. Librarie Larose, Paris.

Dupire, Marguerite, André Lericollais, Bernard Delpech, and Jean-Marc Gastellu. 1974 Résidence, Tenure Foncière, Alliance dans une Société Bilinéaire (Serer du Sine et du Baol, Sénégal). *Cahiers d'Études Africaines* 14(3): 417–452.

Faidherbe, Léon. 1889 *Le Sénégal, la France dans l'Afrique Occidentale*. Hachette, Paris.

Ferguson, James, and Akhil Gupta. 2002 Spatializing States: Toward an Ethnography of Neoliberal Governmentality. *American Ethnologist* 29(4): 981–1002.

Foucault, Michel. 1994 *Power. Essential Works of Michel Foucault 1954–1984. Volume 3*, pp. 349–364. The New Press, New York.

Foucault, Michel. 2007 *Security, Territory, Population. Lectures at the Collège de France, 1977–1978*. Palgrave Macmillan, New York.

Galvan, Dennis. 1997 The Market Meets Sacred Fire: Land Pawning as Institutional Syncretism in Inter-War Senegal. *African Economic History* 25: 9–41.

Galvan, Dennis. 2004 *The State Must Be Our Master of Fire: How Peasants Craft Culturally Sustainable Development*. University of California Press, Berkeley.

Gastellu, Jean-Marc. 1974 L'Organisation du Travail en Milieu Serer Ol. In *Maintenance Sociale et Changement Économique au Sénégal. II. Pratique du Travail et Rééquilibres Sociaux en Milieu Serer*, edited by Jean-Marc Gastellu and Bernard Delpech, pp. 11–104. ORSTOM, Paris.

Gastellu, Jean-Marc. 1981 *L'Égalitarisme Économique des Serer du Sénégal*. ORSTOM, Paris.

Gastellu, Jean-Marc. 1985 Petit Traité de Matrilinéarité: L'Accumulation dans Deux Sociétés Rurales d'Afrique de l'Ouest. *Cahiers ORSTOM*, Série Sciences Humaines 21(4): 413–432.

Geismar, Léon. 1933 *Recueil des Coutumes Civiles des Races du Sénégal*. Imprimerie du Gouvernement, Saint-Louis.

Gidwani, Vinay. 2008 *Capital, Interrupted: Agrarian Development and the Politics of Work in India*. University of Minnesota Press, Minneapolis.

Gravrand, Henri. 1966 Dynamisme Interne de la Famille Serer. *Afrique Documents* 85–86: 95–122.

Guigou, Brigitte. 1992 *Les Changements du Système Familial et Matrimonial: Les Sérères du Sine (Sénégal)*. *Unpublished Ph.D. dissertation, École des Hautes Études en Sciences Sociales*, Paris, France.

Guy, Camille. 1908 Le Sine-Saloum. *La Géographie* 18: 297–314.

Guyer, Jane (editor). 1995 *Money Matters: Instability, Values and Social Payments in the Modern History of West African Communities*. Heinemann, Portsmouth.

Hall, Martin. 2000 *Archaeology and the Modern World: Colonial Transcripts in South Africa and the Chesapeake*. Routledge, New York.

Hamilakis, Yannis, and Philip Duke. 2007 *Archaeology and Capitalism: From Ethics to Politics*. Left Coast Press, Walnut Creek, CA.

Hansen, Thomas Blom, and Finn Stepputat (editors). 2005 *Sovereign Bodies. Citizens, Migrants and States in the Postcolonial World*. Princeton University Press, Princeton.

Hansen, Thomas Blom, and Finn Stepputat. 2006 Sovereignty Revisited. *Annual Review of Anthropology* 35: 295–315.

Hardy, Georges. 1921 *La Mise en Valeur du Sénégal de 1817 à 1854*. Larose, Paris.

Holston, James. 2008 *Insurgent Citizenship: Disjunction of Democracy and Modernity in Brazil*. Princeton University Press, Princeton, NJ.

Johnson, Matthew. 1996 *The Archaeology of Capitalism*. Blackwell Publishers, Cambridge, MA.

Kelly, Ken G. 2009 Where is the Caribbean? French Colonial Archaeology in the English Lake. *International Journal of Historical Archaeology* 13: 80–93.

Klein, Martin. 1968 *Islam and Imperialism in Senegal: The Sine-Saloum, 1847–1914*. Stanford University Press, Stanford.

Klein, Martin. 1979 Colonial Rule and Structural Change. In *The Political Economy of Underdevelopment: Dependence in Senegal*, edited by Rita Cruise O'Brien, pp. 65–99. Sage Publications, Beverly Hills.

Klein, Martin (editor). 1980 *Peasants in Africa: Historical and Contemporary Perspectives*. Sage Publications, Beverly Hills.

Latour, Bruno. 1993 *We Have Never Been Modern*. Harvard University Press. Cambridge.

Lawrance, Benjamin N., Emily Osborn, and Richard (editors). 2006 *Intermediaries, Interpreters, and Clerks: African Employees in the Making of Colonial Africa*. University of Wisconsin Press, Madison, WI.

Linke, Uli. 2006 Contact Zones: Rethinking the Sensual Life of the State. *Anthropological Theory* 6(2): 205–225.

Leone, Mark, and Parker Potter (editors). 1999 *Historical Archaeologies of Capitalism*. Plenum Press, New York.

Lericollais, André. 1972 *Sob: Étude Géographique d'un Terroir Sérèr (Sénégal)*. Mouton & Co, Paris.

Lericollais, André (editor). 1999 *Paysans Sereer: Dynamiques Agraires er Mobilités au Sénégal*. Éditions de l'IRD, Paris.

Marx, Karl. 1973 [1939] *Grundrisse: Introduction to the Critique of Political Economy*. Penguin Books Ltd., Baltimore.

Marseille, Jacques. 1984 *Empire Colonial et Capitalisme Français: Histoire d'un Divorce*. Albin Michel, Paris.

Martin, Victor, Charles Becker, and Mohamed Mbodj. 1980 Trois Documents d'Ernest Noirot sur l'Histoire des Royaumes du Siin et du Saloum. *Bulletin de l'IFAN* 42B(1): 37–85.

Mbembe, Achille. 2001 *On the Postcolony*. University of California Press, Berkeley.

Mbodj, Mohamed. 1978 *Un Exemple d'Économie Coloniale: Le Sine-Saloum et l'Arachide, 1887–1940*. Unpublished Ph.D. dissertation, Université Paris VII, Paris.

Mbodj, Mohamed. 1980 Sénégal et Dépendance: Le Sine-Saloum et l'Arachide, 1887–1940. In *Sociétés Paysannes du Tiers-Monde*, edited by Catherine Coquery-Vidrovitch, pp. 139–154. Presses Universitaires de Lille, Lille.

Mbodj, Mohamed. 1992 La Crise Trentenaire de l'Économie Arachidière. In *Sénégal: Trajectoires d'un État*, edited by Momar-Coumba Diop, pp. 95–135. Karthala, Paris.

Mbodj, Mohamed, and Charles Becker. 1999 De la Traite à la Crise Agricole. Historique des Échanges Commerciaux dans le Sine. In *Paysans Sereer: Dynamiques Agraires et Mobilités au Sénégal*, edited by André Lericollais, pp. 96–116. Éditions de l'IRD, Paris.

McGuire, Randall, and Robert Paynter (editors). 1991 *Archaeology of Inequality*. Blackwell Publishers, Cambridge, MA.

Moitt, Bernard. 1989 Slavery and Emancipation in Senegal's Peanut Basin: The Nineteenth and Twentieth Centuries. *International Journal of African Historical Studies* 22(1): 27–50.

Moore, Donald. 2005 *Suffering for Territory: Race, Place, and Power in Zimbabwe*. Duke University Press, Durham, NC.

Monteilhet, J. 1916 Documents Relatifs à l'Histoire du Sénegal. *Bulletin du Comité d'Études Historiques et Scientifiques de l'A.O.F.* 1916: 62–119.

Morgan, Marston. 2009 *New Societies in the South Pacific: An Ethnography of French Sovereignty in New Caledonia (1834–2014)*. Unpublished Ph.D. dissertation, Department of Anthropology, University of Chicago, Chicago.

Noirot, Ernest. 1896 Rapport Politique et Économique (10 April 1896). Archives Nationales du Sénégal, 13 G 327, No. 5.

Pagden, Anthony. 1995 *Lords of All the World: Ideologies of Empire, in Spain, Britain and France, c. 1500–1800*. Yale University Press, New Haven, CT.

Pélissier, Paul. 1953 Les Paysans Sérères: Essai sur la Formation d'un Terroir du Sénégal. *Cahiers d'Outre-Mer* 22: 105–127.

Pélissier, Paul. 1966 *Paysans du Sénégal: Les Civilisations Agraires to Cayor à la Casamance*. Imprimerie Fabrègue, Saint-Irieix.

Pinet-Laprade, Émile. 1865 Notice sur les Sérères. *Annuaire du Sénégal et Dépendances* 1865: 121–179.

Reinwald, Brigitte. 1997a Changing Family Strategies as a Response to Colonial Challenge: Microanalytic Observations on Siin/Senegal 1890–1960. *History of the Family* 2(2): 183–195.

Reinwald, Brigitte. 1997b "Though the Earth Does Not Lie": Agricultural Transitions in Siin (Senegal) during Colonial Rule. *Paideuma* 43: 143–169.

Reynier, Marcel. 1933 Cercle du Sine-Saloum (Kaolack): Rapport Politique Annuel. Archives Nationales du Sénégal, 2 G 33/70.

Richard, François. 2007 *From Cosaan to Colony: Exploring Archaeological Landscape Formations and Socio-Political Complexity in the Siin (Senegal), AD 500–1900*. Unpublished Ph.D. dissertation, Department of Anthropology, Syracuse University, Syracuse, NY.

Richard, François. 2010 Re-Charting Atlantic Encounters: Object Trajectories and Histories of Value in the Siin (Senegal) and Senegambia. *Archaeological Dialogues* 17(1): 1–27.

Richard, François. N.d. In Pursuit of 'Vernacular Cosmopolitanisms': Historical Archaeology in Senegal and the Material Contours of the African Atlantic. Submitted to *International Journal of Historical Archaeology*.

Roberts, Richard. 2005 *Litigants and Households: African Disputes and Colonial Courts in the French Soudan 1895–1912*. Heinemann, Portsmouth.

Robinson, David. 2000 *Paths of Accommodation: Muslim Societies and French Colonial Authorities in Senegal and Mauritania, 1880–1920*. Ohio University Press, Athens.

Roitman, Janet. 2005 *Fiscal Disobedience: An Anthropology of Economic Regulation in Central Africa*. Princeton University Press, Princeton.

Rousseau, R. 1928 Notes sur l'Habitat Rural au Sénégal (en 1928). Archives Nationales du Sénégal, 1 G 26/104.

Schrire, Carmel. 1996 *Digging through Darkness: Chronicles of an Archaeologist*. University of Virginia, Charlottesville.

Scott, David. 1999 *Refashioning Futures: Criticism after Postcoloniality*. Princeton University Press, Princeton.

Sahlins, Marshall. 1994 Cosmologies of Capitalism: The Trans-Pacific Sector of 'The World System.' In *Culture/Power/History: A Reader in Contemporary Social Theory*, edited by

Nicholas B. Dirks, Geoff Eley, and Sherry B. Ortner, pp. 412–455. Princeton University Press, Princeton.

Searing, James. 1993 *West African Slavery and Atlantic Commerce: The Senegal River Valley, 1700–1860*. Cambridge University Press, New York.

Silliman, Stephen. 2005 Cultural Contact or Colonialism? Challenges in the Archaeology of Native North America. *American Antiquity* 70(1): 55–74.

Silliman, Stephen. 2009 Change and Continuity, Practice and Memory: Native American Persistence in Colonial England. *American Antiquity* 74(2): 211–230.

Smith, Adam. 2004 The End of the Essential Archaeological Subject. *Archaeological Dialogues* 11(1): 1–20.

Stahl, Ann B. 2001 *Making History in Banda: Anthropological Visions of Africa's Past*. Cambridge University Press, New York.

Stoler, Ann L. 1995a *Capitalism and Confrontation in Sumatra's Plantation Belt, 1870–1979*. Second edition. University of Michigan Press, Ann Arbor, MI.

Stoler, Ann L. 1995b *Race and the Education of Desire: Foucault's* History of Sexuality *and the Colonial Order of Things*. Duke University Press, Durham, NC.

Stoler, Ann L., Carole McGranahan, and Peter C. Perdue (editors). 2007 *Imperial Formations*. School for Advanced Research, Santa Fe, NM.

Taussig, Michael. 1987 *Shamanism, Colonialism, and the Wild Man: A Study in Terror and Healing*. University of Chicago Press, Chicago.

Thomas, Nicholas. 1994 *Colonialism's Culture: Anthropology, Travel, Government*. Princeton University Press, Princeton.

Trouillot, Michel-Rolph. 1995 *Silencing the Past: Power and the Production of History*. Beacon Press, Boston.

Trouillot, Michel-Rolph. 2003 *Global Transformations: Anthropology and the Modern World*. Palgrave Macmillan, New York.

Voss, Barbara. 2008 *The Archaeology of Ethnogenesis: Race and Sexuality in Colonial San Francisco*. Berkeley: University of California Press.

Watts, Michael. 1992 Capitalisms, Crises and Cultures I: Notes toward a Totality of Fragments. In *Reworking Modernity: Capitalisms and Symbolic Discontent*, edited by Allan Pred and John Michael Watts, pp 1–19. Rutgers University Press, New Brunswick.

Watts, Michael. 1993 Idioms of Land and Labor: Producing Politics and Rice in Senegambia. In *Land in African Agrarian Systems*, edited by Thomas J. Bassett and Donald E. Crummey, pp. 157–193. University of Wisconsin Press, Madison.

Weate, Jeremy. 2003 Achille Mbembe and the Postcolony: Going beyond the Text. *Research in African Literatures* 34(4): 27–41.

Weiss, Brad (editor). 2004 *Producing African Futures: Ritual and Reproduction in a Neoliberal Age*. Brill, Leiden.

Chapter 10
Fictive Capital and Artifacts: The Diamond Rush of Nineteenth-Century South Africa

The 50 years between 1950 and 2000 are not remarkable compared with the period 1850 to 1914 – when flows of merchandise trade, capital investment and labor migration were all comparable to or greater than those of today.

(Hirst and Thompson 2002: 248)

Introduction

This chapter explores the culture of the nineteenth-century Diamond Fields in South Africa. The Diamond Fields began with the diamond rush, which convened a population of speculative subjectivities from all over southern Africa and the world. Even as this diamond mining site came to be about the brute mechanisms of organizing and disciplining labor, the fields were also about the fantasies that condensed a population committed to the dream of profit without labor, and extracting easy wealth from the ground. The fascinating undercurrent of speculative energies that underwrote the events of the Diamond Fields echoes aspects of today's new economy. The contemporary scope and speed of economic globalization provoke different questions about what it means to understand an economic culture or how economic beliefs shape cultures (and vice versa). Rather than questions about how factories order laboring bodies, or how their commodities demarcate class or map the rise of mass consumption (topics that have comprised the traditional remit of much historical archaeology in the past) economically minded anthropological literature has increasingly come to pose questions in terms of information economies, bubble markets, volatile speculative booms, and virtualized spheres of exchange (e.g., Castells 1996; Harvey 1999;

L. Weiss (✉)
Archaeology Center and Department of Anthropology,
Stanford University, Palo Alto, CA, USA
e-mail: lw2004@caa.columbia.edu

S.K. Croucher and L. Weiss (eds.), *The Archaeology of Capitalism in Colonial Contexts*,
Contributions To Global Historical Archaeology, DOI 10.1007/978-1-4614-0192-6_10,
© Springer Science+Business Media, LLC 2011

LiPuma and Lee 2004). It is timely for historical archaeologists to ask questions about the material precursors of late capitalism, speculative communities, and even deindustrialization (Purser 1999). It is also timely to ask whether our contemporary speculative economic culture has truly freed itself from the legacy of its colonial roots.

North American historical archaeology has a strong tradition of exploring the workings of capital (Leone 1995; McGuire and Paynter 1991; Mrozowski 1991; Paynter 2000). The archaeological record has traditionally provided a mode of empirically chronicling the unrecorded regional effects (and local refashionings) of capitalism's systematic expansion of commodity circuits, structured spaces, and labor regimens (Patterson 2003: 123). If some archaeological projects suffered from the biases incurred from the Eurocentric epistemologies of Marx, critical theory or Foucault (Wilkie and Bartoy 2000), at the same time, such materialist and critical historical archaeologies continue to shape our disciplinary challenge (e.g., Palus et al. 2006). If Marx's ghost casts a long shadow on the archaeological engagement with capitalism, then it so also does raise enduring questions about the colonial context (Patterson 2003). Without attentiveness to the dynamics of power and cultural practices in the colonial or nonmetropolitan context, our invocation of capitalism would remain an abstraction. The Eurocentric abstraction of capital, as if it were conceivable as some monolithic self-regulating force, discrete from the practices, cultures, and ideas at the "peripheries," never existed in practice (Chakrabarty 2000a, b; Polanyi 2001). As such, historical archaeology has become increasingly sensitive to the "fragmentation, contradiction, and conflict" inherent within each and every case-study pursued (Hall and Silliman 2006: 14). Increasingly, engaging with questions of capital means engaging with the challenge of postcolonial theory – forcing questions about the ability of purely Western epistemes to comprehensively document identity, culture, capitalism, or even history itself (Croucher 2006, 2010; Hall 2000; Liebmann and Rizvi 2008; Silliman 2005).[1]

Inspired by these critical and postcolonial motivations, my research applies a somewhat unconventional set of questions about late capitalism to the nineteenth colonial context, questions about the animating force of speculation rather than industrialization or labor production, and the volatile context this produced for the diamond rush community. I suggest that the 1886 segregation of the diamond mining fields (traditionally construed as a tactic employed to conserve a pool of "cheap" labor) was important for illustrating the complex interplay of speculative subjectivities and beliefs about race, criminality, and violence. Just as Hegel's writing of *Phenomenology of Spirit* (representing Marx's dialectic at its most abstract and universalizing) was steeped in the "historically unthinkable" events of the Haitian Revolution (Buck-Morss 2009), and so also do the immutable "laws" of finance capital have their own "unthinkable" historical precedents in the colonies.

There are a number of globally dispersed sites of gold or diamond discovery that I think are worth grouping, for the purpose of historical inquiry, as "rush sites." The early culture of many mineral rush sites were often forged in a combination of unbridled economic expectations and the comparative laxity of colonial administration,

---

[1] Though the application of postcolonial theory itself not always successfully evades monolithic readings (e.g., see Horning, Chap. 3).

which often materialized a virulent, even "mutant" form of capitalism. Within such environments, what can emerge is a rapidly shifting and essentially lawless landscape connecting strangers in unprecedented forms of exchange and economic translation, strangers equally motivated by fantasies of easy wealth as well as the desperate avoidance of risk at every turn in the colonial gamble. Archaeological investigations of colonial rush sites contribute an important vantage on speculative populations, particularly as these communities conceived of themselves as "sojourners" with little attention to their municipal future (Douglass 1998; Hardesty 2005). In a sense, rush sites manifested microcosms of speculative capitalism before it was formalized and named as such through a system of economic laws, standardized formats, or market protocols. Rush sites can reveal the centrality of structuring race and labor to even the most abstract domains of speculative value and market "laws" both before and after they are monopolized.

My archaeological research centers on the public spaces of the late nineteenth-century Diamond Fields of South Africa. By comparison to the protracted Dutch and British engagement with the agricultural and pastoral trading economies of the Cape (preceding the events of the diamond rush by over two centuries), the diamond rush was an ephemeral event lasting only approximately two decades before monopolization (Turrell 1982; Worger 1987). Yet, the discovery of diamonds (and the subsequent discovery of gold) was to be a formative event in the course of colonization at the Cape, and the news of the diamond rush had a global reach in the early 1870s. Thus, the brief decades of the rush encampment were explosive and turbulent, and the largely unlegislated environment of the rush camp enabled its speculative way of life to powerfully demarcate rapid shifts in the social and cultural environment of the fields. The most dramatic transformation of the early diggings was the product of prospector (and investor) anxieties about the illicit diamond trade. The illicit diamond trade had always existed on the fields, yet increasingly, every dip in diamonds prices on the fields, as well as mounting bankruptcy among small-scale and poorly capitalized diamond prospectors led to the belief that this trade was proliferating wildly. Ultimately, growing anxiety about illicit trade precipitated the extreme measure of curbing all contact between black laborers working in the diamond diggings and diamond buyers working in the peripheral canteens and hotels – ultimately resulting in the segregation of the worker population under the company oversight of De Beers in 1886 (Worger 1987: 144).

This act of racially sequestering the diamond diggers on the fields not only directly affected those who were segregated, but decisively changed the culture on the public spaces on the fields more generally (the public spaces constituting the social nexus of the fields stretching along scattered hundreds of canteens, hotels, and eating houses). The shift in the canteen culture, which occurs in the wake of segregation, is difficult to assess from the archival records, yet my archaeological excavation of one such rural canteen and hotel indicates a distinct change in the assemblage, and the introduction of a more professional and formal tone to a space that had previously signaled a distinctly informal fusion of colonizer-colonized practices and trade. The goal of this chapter is to explain how the zealous quality of the speculative vision on the fields was at the root of these changes. The dashed communal fantasy of easy profits transferred directly to the vilification of the spaces of suspected interracial illicit diamond trade. The story of the Diamond Fields is certainly unique, ephemeral and lodged in the particular colonial dynamics of nineteenth-century southern Africa. Yet it also demonstrates that cultures of unfettered economic expectation such as Susan Strange's "casino capitalism" (1986) do not derive from an imagined global "nowhere," dispensed according to metropolitan financial orthodoxy. These cultures of speculative fever, "market malaise" and attendant social violence and racial divisions of communities, were importantly forged in the "peripheries." The violent and disruptive events of the so-called colonial periphery deserve a second look, as it was these events that effectively educated metropolitan centers and institutions about the social limit-horizons for handling investor risk and securing commodity flows.[2] The lesson of the unsustainable trajectory of such beliefs about profit, race and criminality, is a lesson that was forged in the tragedy of the colonial landscape.

The events of the Diamond Fields illustrate the delicate yet determinative relationship between abstract and seemingly immaterial principles of global capital and the local cultures of circulation on the so-called economic periphery (Chakrabarty 2000a, b; Croucher, Chap. 8; Hauser, Chap. 6; Richard, Chap. 9). The story of the Diamond Fields provincializes the typically Eurocentric story of capitalism, illustrating how the acceleration of imperial investment during the emergence of finance capital was always interwoven with the subtleties and frustrations of local small-scale practices in the colonial "peripheries." On the Diamond Fields, it was the anxiety about illicitly traded diamonds (both actually occurring trade as well as the proliferation of rumors marking its own sort of fictive capital) that came to transform zones of previous cultural hybridity and informal exchange into a carefully segregated company town. The racial separation that the diamond laborers underwent had a corresponding effect on the broader Diamond Field community, which can be observed through correlative shifts in the material culture at the Half-Way House Hotel and Canteen, as I shall discuss through the lens of excavated data.

The Diamond Fields and Illegal Diamond Buying

The diamond rush took off in the early 1870s, producing a sprawling tent city of thousands who had traveled from all over the world and southern Africa to the northern frontier of the British Cape Colony (what is now the Northern Cape of South Africa). The Diamond Fields first emerged as a hasty and rapidly shifting encampment at the confluence of the Harts and Vaal rivers. As a result of a flurry of contestations over land rights, the diamondiferous region was almost immediately assimilated within the larger British protectorate of Griqualand West in 1871. The development of the Diamond

---

[2]This connection between metropolitan economic policies and economic cultures in the colonies is inspired by Dipesh Chakrabarty's project of provincializing Europe, which is an attempt to single out individuals and cultural practices which embody a constant interruption to the so-called "totalizing thrust" of capital without reducing such people or communities to the passive status of 'precapitalist' (Chakrabarty 2000a, b: 66).

Fields was not a singular event, however, and there were many other such global encampments of mineral rush occurring in colonial landscapes from the American West to Australia to South America (Hardesty 2005; Dixon 2005; Lawrence 2000; Knapp and Herbert 1998). These rush sites, typically occurring in colonial frontier landscapes, often bore a distinct relationship to the investments of metropolitan centers of finance – a relationship broadly characterized at the time as imperialism (Hobson 1900). Traditionally, it has been the metropolitan centers that have been construed as the "invisible hand" behind the development and monopolization of such rush sites. Yet, at least in the instance of the Diamond Fields, the shape of events that unfolded over the last few decades of the nineteenth century had a great deal to do with the practices of the Mfengu, Pedi, Southern Sotho, Zulu, Tsonga, and Thlaping laborers (among many other southern African migrants) who had established an entrepreneurial and often illicit diamond trade with European "fences" and diamond buyers on the fields.

The illicit exchange of diamonds, or "IDB," was typically described as occurring between African laborers who had obtained diamonds from the claims in which they were hired to work in and European traders running eating houses, hotels, and canteens – particularly on establishments on the western outskirts of the Diamond Fields. For reasons of local geology (leaving the majority of diamondiferous soil embedded in sedimentary levels difficult to excavate through individual means) as well as the vagaries of fluctuating international market prices, prospectors began to see fewer and fewer diamonds emerging from their claims and smaller and smaller profits. Increasingly, either the failure to procure diamonds from the claims, or the dramatic dips in the prices paid for diamonds produced a powerful cartography of suspicion. The communally held utopia of easily acquired wealth snapped into a nightmare vision of stolen diamonds, flowing through the fields and sold in canteen back rooms. This anxiety initially produced a series of vigilante raids and mounting demonstrations of mob violence among diamond diggers. This growing tension, in turn, gave way to a complex system of "trapping" illicit traders and the establishment of a detective department devoted to the curtailment of IDB (Worger 1987). The practice of trapping came to focus specifically on peripheral public eating and drinking establishments, rumored to be the main site of these illicit transactions (such as the Half-Way House Canteen). Public spaces where Pedi, Tsonga, Sotho, or Thlaping laborers could mingle with Griqua traders, French, British, Prussian, or Boer prospectors became presumed trading depots for the elusive fictive capital of the stolen diamond. As such, these public spaces became dangerous sites of potential violence, as "diggers began to be alive to the enormous losses they were sustaining through the robberies of their native servants" (Matthews 1887: 187). Many of the newspaper accounts and travelogues fueled these suspicions, describing eating houses that were kept explicitly for the purpose of procuring new sources of diamonds from naïve laborers "fresh" on the fields. Often, the owners would employ a group of men to feel out potential clients (*ibid.*).

My excavation of one such roadside hotel and canteen (the Half-Way House Hotel) on the periphery of the diggings offers a new vantage upon the actual character of the rural establishments, which ringed the center of the fields and lining the roads leading to the fields. Through archaeological analysis of the material culture of the tableware and the hotel décor, a more fine-grained representation of the submerged sorts of social practices that would have enshrouded this much-discussed illicit trade emerges. The archaeological remains of the early hotel in the years preceding the segregation of the fields, suggest a complex blending of "respectable" and expedient culture. The surprising emphasis on such forms of propriety evidenced by the ceramic assemblage perhaps indicates one way in which it was the "respectable" ambience that, in itself, worked to camouflage illicit transactions and contributed to how difficult it was to root out the illicit trade. As such, it is of particular interest to better understand how this emergent hybrid public space and its repertoire of behaviors and exchanges would have been shaped by the subsequent segregation of the Diamond Fields. While the first object of interest in a discussion of illicit trade would seem to be the contraband itself, it is, provocatively, through understanding the material culture that formed the bedrock of daily life within which illicit trade and black markets were enacted that we can better discern the particular practices and transgressions that make such economic practices important sites of subversion (Casella 2000; Hauser 2008).

The Stock Exchange: The Xhosa Cattle Killing

Contrary to colonial assumption, to the perspective of the southern Africans living on the fields, the diamond rush was far from the first explosive speculative event that had struck the southern African landscape. Mining, particularly of gold, had been a part of southern African for most of the previous millennia (Miller et al. 2000; Pikirayi 2001). Among migrant laborers leaving for and returning from the Diamond Fields, there was a widespread African epithet for the fields: "the white man's Nongqawuse" (Bundy 1979: 73). Nongqawuse was the Gcaleka prophetess who in 1856 had proclaimed imminent salvation from cattle sickness and the hands of warring settlers (specifically on February 18, 1857), on condition that the Xhosa people universally sacrificed their crops and cattle. Fascinatingly, after thousands of cattle had been slaughtered, and her prophecy failed to realize during the "initial disappointment," there were nonetheless widespread believers who insisted that any failure was the consequence of those who hadn't properly sacrificed their cattle or prepared their new granaries. Reports of fabulous sightings in which deliverance was imminent had a remarkable persistence. The detailed descriptions of these sightings and rumors often bore an uncanny resemblance to the fantasies of those diamond diggers who arrived on the fields, particularly as the soil itself was believed to contain immense brimming riches enough for everyone, with reports among Nongqawuse's followers that, "the horns of oxen... have been seen peeping from the reeds and some had heard the bellowing of cattle impatient to rise from underground" (Peires 1989: 132). The tragic similarity between this anticipated ancestral deliverance of the Xhosa people, where "there were to be no unfulfilled wants and desires of any kind" (Peires 1989: 133), and the euphoric speculative fantasies of diamond prospectors was the ineradicable and desperate suspicions about one's neighbors, which proliferated as these subterranean specters failed the grasp of even the most fervent sacrifices of these believers.

Echoing the subsequent wave of diamond rushers, Nongqawuse's vision invoked the specter of an ever-receding horizon of redemption. Thus, *if* the entrance could only be found, discussed Nongqawuse's believers, this very source of limitless cows and oxen could rejuvenate all the beleaguered Xhosa people. Only 10 years later, diamond prospectors, inspired by the emancipatory vision of the diamond gamble excitedly pursued a nomadic range of phantom encampments, continually pitching and repitching their tents according to the ever-changing rumors about the greatest source of diamonds. Fascinatingly, these two millennial visions ostensibly participated in economies that were not merely incommensurable but even antithetical. In the instance of Nongqawuse's vision, "the Englishman's money… would change into fire and destroy all who possessed it" (Peires 1989: 104). Approximately 15 years later, "special" diamond courts on the fields rapidly enacted new laws to prosecute illicit diamond traders, readily dispensing with the legal cornerstone of presumed innocence. The very presence of a diamond on an African body instantly rendered this individual a criminal before the colonial court.

The suggestion of some transposable quality within the speculative frenzy spurred by Nongqawuse's vision and this new vision of the diamondiferous soils of the northern territories was fascinating as it did not derive from any merging regime of value, rather what was coalesced by these two respective currencies (that of cattle and cash) was the powerful force of a shared speculative vision that exceeded the limits of actually existing markets. It was the (destructive) expectations and beliefs elicited by the prospect of incalculable wealth that pervaded both regimes of value and prompted such a direct comparison. Such speculative landscapes were spawned from a shared vision of deliverance from want and the depredations of physical labor, and a fantasy release from the depredations of ever expanding markets. The divisions that emerged between those who had believed in Nongqawuse's prophecies and those who had not believed smoldered for generations to come (divisions that would have been particularly active dynamic at the time of the diamond rush); resentment and suspicions proliferated about those who, in inadequately sacrificing their cattle, or in secretly selling their corn rather than burning it, may have prevented the attainment of foretold riches. The translation from Nongqawuse's prophecy to capitalism's fantasy, the creative destruction of speculative fervor (enacted through sacrifice and consumption by Xhosa and prospectors, respectively) and, finally, the uncontrollable suspicion dividing communities, was immediately relayed among those laborers who shrewdly spoke of traveling to "the white man's Nongqawuse." While many African laborers on the Diamond Fields came to personally profit (and many acquired remarkable riches and properties in the earliest days), those Mfengu, Themba, and Xhosa survivors of the Eastern Cape cattle-killings who personally came to the "white man's Nongqawuse" were signaling that they did not merely come to labor but also to knowledgably exploit this speculative culture's ability to produce market opportunities for buyers and sellers (Bundy 1979: 73), whether through simply trading marked up produce, firewood and meat, or as dealers in a burgeoning economy of illicit diamonds. It was the ostensible figure of the African "laborer" who immediately provided economic commentary on the destructive effects of speculative capital, a vision that was to reshape local (and ultimately metropolitan) sensibilities about how diamonds could be profitably extracted.

Hotels and Kitchen Counters on the Diamond Fields

Despite its official status as a British Protectorate, however, the culture of the early fields encampment was marked by a prevailing cultural hybridity and an uncertainty about legality and sovereignty, which accelerated the blurring of the traditional Victorian registers of class, race, and gender [to some degree a rather unsurprising state of affairs for a city literally "honeycombed with cesspool," traversed by roving dogs, flies and with the approaching roads practically lined with rotting animal carcasses (Matthews 1887: 107)]. No space condensed or seemed to speed up the social confusion quite as much as the suburban canteens and hotels, which ringed the diggings. It is important to emphasize that the illegal diamond buying trade did exist, and illicit traders were frequently trapped through sting operations undertaken by a detective department devoted to the rooting out of IDB. Court transcripts provide a picture in which collaborations between European canteen and eating-house owners and African "touts" were deployed through the rubric of hospitality, proprietors feeding or offering gifts to African diggers, in a ritual that would sometimes lead to black market business (Resident Magistrate 1877a, b). These touts would identify potential sellers and connect then with receivers at canteens, bars outside the diggings, and resultantly such locales were frequently reviled as "clearing houses for IDB [Illegal Diamond Buying]" (Doughty 1963: 145). Over the course of the 1870s, as these spaces increasingly became the focus of vigilante justice, causing incidents where "whole crowd[s] of miners [would march]... in a body to the tent, shop or canteen of the accused, smashed it up and set it on fire" (*ibid.*).

The ambience of hospitality and the public spaces of the fields, thus, evidently bore a complex relationship to the illicit diamond trade. In order to further examine this subtle relationship, I conducted an excavation one such suburban canteen and hotel called The Half-Way House (named as it was located approximately halfway between the early river diggings and the subsequent larger "dry diggings"). The hotel was run by several different individuals dissident enough to be mentioned in the archival record as such. For instance, one of the first references to the proprietor's wife in 1873 depicts her as "raving" on polemical issues such as "squatters' rights," an issue that became a common conflict between those who had obtained rights from the local Griqua cultivator chiefs, and who were subsequently forced to purchase title upon British annexation (Boyle 1873: 110). Other proprietors expressed similarly independent-minded ideas, a German owner was recorded in Sir Charles Warren's *On the Veldt in the Seventies* as critiquing the local Berlin Mission Society as nothing more than a "profiteering racket" adding that he would never run such a business as the Half-Way House in Europe as it "would not be respectable"

(Warren 1902: 319). Diamonds were frequently observed being brought to this canteen (*ibid*). Given the vigilante climate on the fields, such an isolated canteen and hotel must have come under increasing pressure to demonstrate its regularity and propriety as a business.

It is unsurprising, then, that the sorts of advertisements put in the local newspapers were often defensive in tone, one advertisement insisting that the proprietors did not sell liquor to Africans without the required legal note, and maintaining (somewhat dubiously), that they provided all the comforts of "an English home" (The Diamond News and Griqualand West Government Gazette 1872). In light of these facts, the everyday material culture of the canteen comes to take on an interesting light with regard to these broader social tensions. Would the proprietors have sought to emulate proper bourgeois Victorian décor and service and, if so, why? What role might this sort of aspirational décor serve at this time, given the general atmosphere of rising distrust on the fields? Because newspaper advertisements and travel guides of the time indicate that everything necessary to emulate a proper table service was available at local stores and canteens for reasonable prices from the earliest years of the Diamond Fields, the choices of the Half-Way House Hotel suffered from less of the material constraints of other of these sorts of mineral rush sites in America and Australia. Yet, at the same time, as with other mineral rushers, these prospectors largely considered themselves "sojourners" (Hardesty 2005: 82) and would have also, thus, been constrained by the transience of their project. As one travel guide suggested, it would be possible to open a small canteen with as little as 50 pounds in one's pocket (Payton 1872: 130), so the material culture of the hotels and canteens was constituted by the dual influence of a provisional culture, mixed with the heady spirit of anticipated luxury and conspicuous consumption among its clientele.

The Archaeology of the Half-Way House Hotel

In 2005, I excavated the middens of the 1870s Half-Way House with the assistance of local archaeologists and historians at the Kimberley McGregor museum.[3] Analysis of the early ceramic assemblage evidenced an extensive variety of transfer patterns and colors, though the choices were generally suggestive of the fashion for the classical revival style commonly represented with motifs such as laurel wreaths, vases, acanthus leaves, columned pilasters, palmettes, Greek key "Turco" designs, and Corinthian borders (Sussman 1979: 112, 234), as well as cherubs and figures or landscapes in classical style (Majewski and Schiffer 2001: 35) (Fig. 10.1).

The predominance of transfer print British industrial wares was in line with the Cape Town fashion for British wares (Malan 2003); however, the enormous diversity

---

[3]For a detailed discussion of the excavation and its findings, see chapters V and VI in my doctoral dissertation (Weiss 2009). Ceramic analysis was undertaken at the Historical Archaeology Research Center at the University of Cape Town.

Fig. 10.1 Classical motifs present in the tableware assemblage; classical cameo and cherub borders with laurel wreathes

of patterns (upward of 25 for an approximately 10 year span) suggests the probability of mismatched wares being in use at any one time during the early years at the hotel. The ceramic assemblage also revealed the presence of the much less highly regarded sponge wares (often with notable scraping on them) (Brooks 2003: 134; Croucher 2006: 317). The nicety involved in the table service, insofar as it was not conducted in the far more pragmatic and ubiquitous tin enamel as at other hotels employed on the Diamond Fields (Macnish 1969: 237), and the difficulty of transporting and sustaining relatively high proportion of high-fired white wares and porcelain tea wares (not exactly the most "frontier ready" services (Lawrence and Shepherd 2006: 74)) indicate that the deployment of this sort of aspirational décor, however uneven, was important to the sorts of stranger socialities that were emergent at this rural hotel.

At the same time, many aspects of the assemblage, when considered within the context of a busy roadside hotel and canteen, indicate that the Half-Way House Hotel was necessarily a site engaging in much informal enactment of meal and refreshment service. Notably, in contrast to the typical domestic table, in spite of the presence of a good deal of serving platters, serving tureens were absent from the early hotel's assemblage. The absence of tureens, coupled with the predominance of nondomesticated faunal remains and largely unimproved domestic species, suggests a significant degree of improvisational meal service, as well as the likelihood of a kitchen-based (and thus largely unsynchronized or formal) meal service. This would have suited the somewhat disorganized arrivals and departures of travelers as well as the pace of opportunistic trade with local Griqua or Boer farmers and hunters (Voigt 2007).

While archival reports indicate that such peripheral canteens were frequented by Pedia, Thlaping, Sotho, and Mfengu laborers, the archaeological evidence implies that the cross-racial mingling at these establishments were not only for refreshment but also frequently for trade. Dark blue and Venetian glass beads further suggests the presence of barter between local economies of cattle and settler economies of cash (Comaroff and Comaroff 2006a); a broken barrel keg key indicates the sale of "take-away" brandy ("Cape Smoke"), noted in the travelogues to be a favorite among impoverished wage laborers and local Griqua (Payton 1872: 130). The surprising presence of bat-eared fox and jackal tarsals indicate that there was the presence of opportunistic pelt-trading, with the likelihood that there was the presence of informal barter and exchange between proprietors, prospectors, and traders. Medicated wines and good amounts of soda codds, on the contrary, indicate the typical Victorian concern with health and convalescing. Intriguingly, this early hotel assemblage typifies no one set of cultural practices monolithically, but would seem to represent many diverse and travel-contingent needs, as well as a good deal of trade and service improvisations. This sort of social hybridity (Hall 1992), in which local economies, informal trade, barter, negotiation of wage labor, and other such interactions were ongoing and pervasive (these activities went on day and night as many traversed the roads at all hours), suggests the broader culture of a mobile and hybrid community.[4]

Discussion

To some extent, the assemblage of the hotel represents these peripheral locales as having been sustained by informal trading and exchange networks. Yet at the same time, the presence of transfer-ware sets carrying motifs popular in the northern metropole also works against the archivally derived assumptions about rural canteens and eating houses, as being nothing more than "shocking dens of vice" (Holub 1881: 73). It is difficult to construe the need for the effort by proprietors to create matching sets of classical imagery if the pursuits of the clientele were utterly countercultural, and solely focused on criminal trade. Rather, the material culture suggests an unexpectedly easy blending of "respectable" table service and substitutions derived from local and/or illegible trade sources. Interestingly, the more domestic or bourgeois qualities of the ceramic assemblage indicate the possibility that these home-style niceties effectively camouflaged illicit exchanges, and were coalesced, however unevenly, in hopes of deflecting rumors and suspicions of

---

[4]While the Half-Way House makes a remarkable example of such peripheral diggings hotels and eating houses, further archaeological examination of these roadside sites would be extremely important to better understand the range and difference in these roadside and periurban locales at the Diamond Fields.

illicit diamond trade at these locales. At the very least, evidence of these material gestures toward propriety and Victorian fashion undermines the assumption that criminal entrepôts, locales, and figures of illicit diamond trade were easily distinguishable from more respectable businesses and enterprises, which aspired to the moral scheme of Victorian culture and the bourgeois lifestyle.

This point has been central to some recent anthropological work on global economic networks and moral economies. In *Fiscal Disobedience*, Janet Roitman's ethnographic research in Central Africa suggests that just as often as criminal communities, bandits or smuggling networks constitute Hobsbawm's "anti-societies" (in conscious moral opposition to the status quo), they also "seek a certain mode of integration...." (Roitman 2005: 181). Roitman's work excavates the perplexingly seamless interweaving of criminal practice and more traditional social or class aspirations.[5] Read against the archival vilification of peripheral canteens, it is significant to consider what this assemblage collectively evidences – which is how difficult it would have been to have definitively identified when and how such sites were housing criminal activity and when, on the contrary, they were simply pursuing a "regular" service. As the illicit diamond trade was, in many respects, an attempt by any and every participant in the diamond diggings to "get in" on the gamble, the illicit trade went to the heart of a broader cultural impetus that was the raison d'être of the fields and other such speculative encampments. The fact that even the wealthiest men and women on the fields participated in illegal diamond buying (Herbert 1972: 59) was what initially compelled the community to orchestrate "sting operations." It was the confounding inability to navigate this community according to the recognizable repertoires of respectability; the inability effectively discerns which members of the community were transgressing the lines between criminality and class that propelled broader efforts to mechanically segregate out those workers who came into contact with diamondiferous soil and those willing recipients of illicit diamonds.

These public spaces quite probably became routes for illicit diamond trade precisely because they provided such an unobjectionable and inscrutable backdrop for the mixing of unacquainted diamond diggers and buyers. The mingling of those sections of the rush community who were predisposed to transgressive financial strategies and exchanges, and who held very little emotional investment in the proprieties of the present, mirrored a material affect observed in the careless deployment of familial-style Victorian decor. Those who flocked to the rush sites

---

[5]Interestingly, this seamlessness subjectivity straddling criminal and noncriminal affect was abstractly conceived as "homo oeconomicus" by the Chicago neoliberal economic theorists. "The criminal is a rational-economic individual who invests, expects a certain profit and risks making a loss. From the angle of homo oeconomicus, there is no fundamental difference between murder and a parking offence" (Lemke 2001:10). The initial archaeological evidence from the hotel site certainly bears out this neoliberal assertion that, for those purely speculating and calculating subjects, there was no irreparable rupture between criminality and entrepreneurial activity (except for degrees of risk).

felt themselves to be participating in a new abstract, fluid, and less moralized cultures of circulation, a new world of money – the speculative culture so well documented in the late nineteenth-century metropole (Holway 2002; Itzkowitz 2002; Poovey 2003).

The very motto of the Diamond Fields, *Spero Meliora* (I hope for better things) (Beet 1931: 23), was fitting for the "white man's Nongqawuse." Local subjectivities were only half-lodged in the present and half-lodged in the future, which seemed to produce an environment reflecting the failure to commit to either the social aspirations of more typical bourgeois domestic lifestyles, or the criminal enterprises of the frontier gambler. This, I would suggest, not only was the state of affairs at communal hotels sites on the outskirts of early rush communities but also represents an important broader affect of the late nineteenth century as it came to coagulate into the moral economy of abstract wealth and finance capital. Tacking between the material evidence and the written evidence, we understand better the quality of the concern that British officials and elite financiers were experiencing with such black market sites. With the specter of a destabilizing black market for diamonds, such places and their "unreadability" according to any sort of intact form of policing, began to mobilize profound changes, first in surveillance tactics, with South Africa's first undercover police orchestrated "sting" operations, as well as with pass laws, and new criminal laws preventing Africans from owning claims or selling diamonds at all (Smalberger 1976a, b).

This is why, rather than the definitive presence of one or another form of aspirational sentiment or décor, it was the easy slippage between several social registers that typifies this particular assemblage, its admixture of high and low, its denotation of informal service as well as some signatures of more formal table service mirror its clientele's readiness for change and mobility. As Donald Hardesty writes in reference to the gold rush of the American West, these mining sites comprised individuals "who do not expect to live permanently in their new environment…they are "sojourners'" (Hardesty 2005: 82). In the spirit of Hardesty's insight, rather than parsing these sorts of assemblages into one or another class category, I attempt to delineate a characteristic inconsistency to better understand how individuals within this community felt themselves to be less constrained by proscribed class boundaries (Wurst 2006).

The proprietors seemed to mirror this straddling of different worlds, mentioning that he could never have entered into such a business (as running the roadside canteen and hotel) in Germany, as it was not "respectable"(Warren 1902). When pressed, the proprietor expressed a fascinating contradiction, "he also said he began to like the country, and thought he might stay, his reason for liking it being that the people are more free here than in Germany" (*ibid.*). We can see that rush communities were being transformed as much by their emergent local cultures and its attendant "freedoms," as they were constrained by colonial governmental edicts or metropolitan trends (Lucas 2004: 193). Many of these changes, no doubt, were effected through the complex exchanges of illicit diamonds, inextricable from social exchanges in barrooms and eating houses, rescripting ever-widening spheres of culturally hybrid and entrepreneurial sensibilities.

Archaeology in the Wake of Segregation

So, moving from these local circumstances back to the corporate-colonial structures, it is important to keep in mind that "the global system of colonialism played out in a myriad local circumstances – has always [the] … imminence of violence" (Hall 2000: 65). What happened in the 1880s on the Diamond Fields would change forever the course of mining in South African history, and produce a landscape hauntingly familiar to those who endured apartheid's indignities. As a result of insecurity over the specter of rampant diamond theft and illicit trade, when the diamond claims were increasingly consolidated, monopolist Cecil Rhodes of De Beers attempted to mollify the conservative banking orthodoxy of primary shareholders such as Nathanial Rothschild by swiftly implementing stricter security measures for searching and housing workers. As a culmination of this, in 1886, De Beers (along with several other mining companies) imposed the strict racial segregation of miners and the compounding of African workers in bachelor-style dormitories that were architecturally based on slave barracks in the Brazilian Diamond Fields (Turrell 1982: 57). The climate in rural canteens and hotels seem to have been affected by these community-wide changes, as evidenced by a shift in the sorts of material culture in the hotel's post 1880 assemblage. The social practices that were taking root at such places, the free mixing of high and low trade, speculators from southern Africa, Europe, and the Cape Colony, was what had to change – in the minds of metropolitan shareholders and claim-side gamblers alike.

The story of the harsh spatial dictates of the panoptical compounds and the worker housing is a familiar colonial narrative (Weiss 2011). What is interesting to be able to examine in greater detail, are the shifts that the hotel underwent in the wake of these dramatic community changes. Perhaps the single most notable shift in the ceramic assemblage is the emergence of plain or banded ironstone "hotel-wares," usurping the previous predominance of a variety of transfer-print tableware (Fig. 10.2).

Plain ironstone wares and banded wares were, by comparison, almost completely absent in the earlier hotel assemblage despite their widespread availability at that time. These "ironstone china" wares came to be popularly known as "hotel ware" or "commercial ware" as a result of their popularity with "large steamship companies, hotels, clubs, colleges and other places where hard usage has to be undergone" (Jewitt 1878: 317).[6] Ironstone china took off in popularity in America in the late nineteenth century – sparking off a domestic industry for the ware (Barker and Majewski 2006: 217). These wares were popular as they resembled the French porcelains in vogue at this time, while being considerably less expensive (*ibid.*). These wares have been traditionally grouped with other white refined wares as households and hotels frequently used these wares interchangeably to create the effect of a

---

[6]Ironstone "china" was actually a type of earthenware, but so named as it was renowned for its extreme hardness and durability, "for it is not easy to break even a plate" (Jewitt 1878:317).

Fig. 10.2 Plain ironstone saucer from the late Half-Way House Hotel

matched dinner service (Bell 2005; Brooks 2003: 124; Lawrence 2000: 132).[7] The plainness of the decoration of these ironstones, despite the fact that ironstone dishes were most often available in very colorful patterns (Miller 2005: 7), marks a dramatic departure from the previous aesthetic choices surrounding the hotel's table and meal services.

Importantly, the plainness of decoration type denotes an environment with a more homogenized, professionalized, and "sanitized-looking" system of presenting service to clientele. Tables set with matching patterns of banded plates and tureens, alternating with white-ware would have presented diners with a very different visual cue from the previous hotel's assemblage (punctuated as it had been with images of cherubic and classical vistas, matrimonial floral sprays, and feminine cameos). Importantly, these ironstone and banded wares are almost exclusively found in the form of individual plates and saucers that the guests would have eaten off of directly. Further separating the client from the proprietor's "hearth," as it were, is the emergence of serving tureens and platters that emerge in the assemblage, which indicates

---

[7]This ware are distinct from a ware-type known as "white granite" which was a mid nineteenth century ironstone manufactured for export to North America See (Malan 2003: 196).

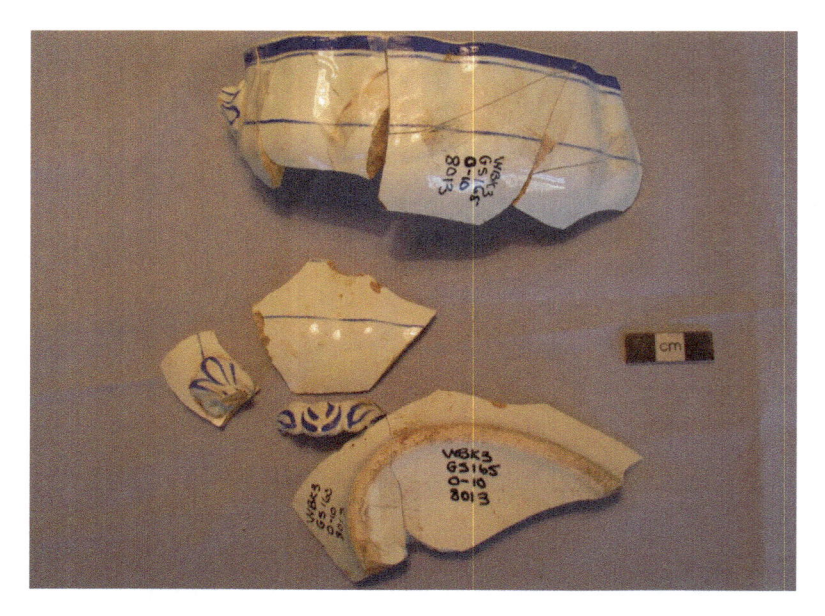

Fig. 10.3 Partially refitted *blue* banded tureen from the late Half-Way House Hotel

a reduced likelihood of any part of the meal service being served directly out of the kitchen. The tureens were minimally decorated by comparison to the predominating tureen styles of the time period (Fig. 10.3) and while there continue to be the presence of *kommetjes* and other such less formal service vessels, their numbers are noticeably reduced.[8]

The fact that the undecorated ironstone vessels predominate the most individual component of the tableware (plates and saucers – which diners would have been directly eating from, as opposed to tureens, or serving vessels) suggests an incipient distinction between the client's immediate tableware and tableware that might participate in the intimate or domestic style of the establishment – thus personally relating to (or used by) the staff and proprietors. In an important sense, with this distinction emerging between the kitchen and the dining room, there emerged a professionalized signature to the hotel service; the subdued and minimalist tone to the tableware assemblage, lacking the preceding inflections of collective or "home-style" atmosphere, correlates with the appearance of more formalized stemwares, pressed glass bowls, and a multiplication of the tea services. The general shift in the character of the assemblage could be described as shifting from a domestic and informal atmosphere, to a more service-oriented and recognizably hotel-like assemblage,

---

[8]To give a quantitative sense of the ceramic assemblage, MNV estimates for the early hotel show decorated wares comprised 45 out of a total of 65 vessels and miscellaneous items, with no undecorated wares and no tureens. Estimates from the later hotel show a reduction in decorated wares (to 53 out of a total of 100 vessels) as well as the MNV estimate of 4 tureens, and 16 undecorated plain ironstone ware vessels.

which more than likely coincided with a far less diverse clientele as a result of the segregation of the fields. The emergence of serving tureens not only indicates the possibility of a shift in food preparation at the hotel, but more definitively suggests that a change in the form of meal service had occurred, "from the kitchen" to something more like what was called "*service à la française*,"[9] necessitating the simultaneous deployment of tureens, emphasizing the presentation of an abundant variety of courses at the table (Flanders 2004: 273). *Service à la française* came to be in demand in the American colonies in the late nineteenth century (Wall 1994: 121), and may have experienced a similarly delayed reception in southern Africa as was the case with many other ceramic fashions (Lucas 2004: 105; Malan 2003).[10] Continental-style meal service were not unknown on the Diamond Fields, where *table d'hôte* was practiced (Trollope 1878: 78).[11] While this meal service might ostensibly have allowed for a more relaxed or communal sort of dining arrangement, it is also true that the lack of regularity of meal start times for clients came to mean that residents and diners could, to some degree, experience a good deal of more privacy in their dining.

What becomes relevant to ask, in terms of the dramatic shift in the tableware signature at the hotel, is whether the sort of culture at the dining table would have taken a similar turn toward the more individuated service. Over the 1880s and 1890s, a distinct shift comes to be perceptible in hotel advertisements that increasingly stress the potentially individuated nature of the amenities, so, while including reference to the somewhat common *table d'hôte* service, ads would emphasize "table d'hôte with *separate tables*" (Murray 1894: 256) and also listing special rates for "private suppers" (The Independent 1877). Taking the fact that drinking and eating had constituted, in many important respects, the core of the incipient sociality that defined the early Diamond Fields, these seemingly minor or subtle shifts in the collective ambience of the hotel and canteen space indicate profound changes in the way that social fluidity was expressed, which, in turn, had very direct implications for the way that exchange could be undertaken at such locales. The business practices at hotels on the Diamond Fields had come to revolve mainly around (more licit) profit motives and professionalized service rather than operating from any motive or belief in an informal family style in which the inner transactions of the hotel were readily observable or available to customers. For instance, Diamond Field hotel advertisements increasingly came to list their amenities as including "Sample Rooms" – specialized hotel rooms that could be turned into temporary entrepreneurial spaces in which traveling salesmen could formally conduct trade and display their wares to customers (Sandoval-Strauss 2007: 82). The commercial

---

[9] Service *vice à la française* would have been quite different from what was, at that time, becoming increasingly fashionable in the European metropole, service *à la russe* – which had come to be synonymous with pretension and required an enormous serving staff (Flanders 2004: 275).

[10] The ironstone, insofar as its plainness was suggestive of the popular French porcelain again suggests the possibility of a broader emulation of French-styled service.

[11] *Table d'hôte* was a communal and fixed priced meal service offered during a set period, which would have afforded a roadside establishment much-needed flexibility in terms of service times.

practice and exchange that went on at these hotels had come to take on a much more formalized register. No longer conducted within the informal guise of home-style intimacy or hospitality to strangers, trade had come to be conducted within an entrepreneurial register – as an overtly commercial sort of social enterprise, and to this end, rooms, dining service and interactions more generally could be described as having become compartmentalized and formalized to the point where they no longer operated at cross-purposes to the forces of financial consolidation or imperial rule more generally.

The narrowing of public spaces, such as those discussed at the Half-Way House Hotel, associated with the fields is a fascinating phenomenon to consider, one which is often submerged within broader discussions of the emergence of early apartheid landscapes. It is important to keep in mind that the segregated landscapes took on its broadest social significance insofar as there came to be fewer and fewer conceivable alternatives to its strictly bifurcated landscape. In a fundamental sense, those social divides that have come to be the hallmark of apartheid landscapes became determinative in the case that hotels, canteens, and eating houses were forced to relinquish any thick claim to a shared private sphere, no longer eliciting the possibility easy stranger sociality of the Half-Way House and ultimately vanquishing the intense provocation that the fictive capital of these indistinct spheres raised. Such spaces came to delineate a more professional orthodoxy for entrepreneurial activity, the boundaries of privacy gradually took on greater definition and ultimately became imaginable according to the institutional dictates of the De Beers company.

Conclusion

In many ways, the story of the Diamond Fields and its transformation into a company town is more than a story about the rise of industrial capitalism, though it was, importantly, also this. The archaeology of the public zones of trade and social hybridity reveal the extent to which a precocious speculative ethos, one that in the contemporary climate of neoliberalism is recognized to, "favors speculation, play, and gambling over virtuous labour and wealth" (Comaroff and Comaroff 2006b: 14), precipitated larger political transformations far from the metropolitan banking centers, such as The City in London, Dutch stock exchanges, or even Cape Town. These nineteenth-century enclaves of casino capitalism carried within their spaces a twinned capacity; on the one hand, the heady blend of risk and profit and emergent cultures of circulation forged new social freedoms; on the other hand, these spaces also proliferated the destructive mirage of phantom exchange, ever-elusive fictive capital. Within a comparably short span of time, a dramatically divided and increasingly corporatized social landscape replaced such public spaces on the fields, transforming roadside canteens and hotels such as the Half-Way House in the process. The example of the Diamond Fields fleshes out this intimate and complicated connection between the structure of modernity's racialized political practices and communities mobilized around the fantasy of limitless wealth. Apartheid had traditionally been understood in the context of industrial capitalism as an attempt to secure the availability of cheap labor (Atmore and Marks 1974; Johnstone 1970; Wolpe 1972), but in the case of the diamond rush, and arguably the gold fields as well, the commodification of African labor also participated in what Achille Mbembe terms a "spectral power" in which "profit and delirium had to be so closely connected as to constantly trigger the vertiginous capacity of the native to be both a thing and a metonym of something else" (Mbembe 2004: 382). This is the power of fictive capital known to proliferate in the trails of speculative frenzy, and whose volatility comes to have an accordingly devastating effect on the landscapes and communities left in its wake.

Returning to the question of capitalism and colonialism, how can we understand the relationship of colonial imperialism to this landscape of proliferating identities and these zones of illicit trade? In many ways, our ideas about capital have always emerged from the struggles over identity and freedom in the market "margins." Foucault quotes a private letter in which Marx chided Engels, saying, "You know very well where we found our idea of class struggle; we found it in the work of the French historians who talked about the race struggle" (Foucault 2003: 80). Foucault goes on to elaborate how revolutionary discourse emerged from this modern form of historical documentation, one that marked a rupture from traditional historical narrative formats of sovereign territories or Roman-juridical tradition, becoming a discourse inscribed within the more epic terms of race and biology. Similarly, it was in the colonies where "profit and delirium" exploded, allowing the fictive capital (so iconic of the speculative ferment of nineteenth finance capital) to come unhinged from the constraints of monetary policies, the proprietary domains of banks and the traditions of financial institutions. As the Xhosa and Mfengu migrant laborers so adroitly observed, the Diamond Fields epitomized the doomed cultural form of speculative expectation elicited by the colonial lure of easy wealth.

In its material assemblages, its architectures, and dramatic segregation, the Diamond Fields is a testament to the ways in which the culture of "casino capitalism" (even as it was not yet to the speed or tempo of today's markets) was nonetheless an animating force both compelling extreme risk-taking as well as extreme attempts to thwart such risk-taking in the colonies. It was a force that extended from metropole to periphery and back again, and a force shaped by the speculative subjectivities of southern Africans and Europeans alike. The diamond produced a cartography riddled with the intoxicating promise of novel financial aristocracies and unlimited social freedoms. The public spaces of the fields, the hotels and eating houses so reviled in later years, were not only meting out cups of tea and plates of stew to their patrons and guests but in the process they were also lubricating the emergent workings of an illicit economy, one which was, in turn, inspired by dreams and fantasies as much as calculation and economic risk. As a result of the camouflage of the material culture, it was an illicit economy in equal parts domestic and public, prosaic and dangerous. The history of these mobile and polyvalent colonial publics that intrudes upon the metropolitan histories of capital, their materialities, and their mutations tell a deeper story about the ardent hopes and fantasies that always exceed and reshape the laws of the marketplace.

References

Advertisement. 1872 "Cogin's Hope Hotel: Half Way House." *The Diamond News and Griqualand West Government Gazette*. February 21.

Advertisement. 1877 "Phoenix Dining Saloon". *The Independent*. November 2.

Atmore, A., and Shula Marks. 1974 The Imperial Factor in South Africa in the Nineteenth Century: Towards a Reassessment. *Journal of Imperial and Commonwealth History* 3(1): 105–39.

Barker, D., and T. Majewski. 2006 Ceramic studies in historical archaeology. *In* The Cambridge Companion to Historical Archaeology. D. Hicks and M.C. Beaudry, eds. Pp. 205–234. Cambridge: Cambridge University Press.

Beet, George. 1931 *The Grand Old Days of the Diamond Fields*. Cape Town: Maskew Miller, Ltd.

Bell, Alison. 2005 *Consumption in a Company Town: Conspicuous Display, Restraint, and Pleasure in a Nineteenth-Century Virginia Iron-Mining Community*. Upland Archaeology in the East.

Boyle, Frederick. 1873 *To The Cape For Diamonds*. London: Simon and Hall.

Brooks, Alisdair. 2003 Crossing Offa's Dyke: British ideologies and late eighteenth- and nineteenth-century ceramics in Wales. *In* Archaeologies of the British: Explorations of identity in Great Britain and its colonies 1600–1945. S. Lawrence, ed. Pp. 119–37. London: Routledge.

Buck-Morss, Susan. 2009 *Hegel, Haiti and Universal History*. Pittsburgh, Pa.: University of Pittsburgh Press.

Bundy, Colin. 1979 *The Rise and Fall of the South African Peasantry*. London: Heinemann.

Casella, Eleanor. 2000 "Doing trade": A Sexual Economy of Nineteenth-Century Australian Female Convict Prisons. *World Archaeology* 32(2): 209–221.

Castells, Manuel. 1996 *The Rise of Network Society*. Oxford: Blackwell.

Chakrabarty, Dipesh. 2000a *Provincializing Europe: Postcolonial Thought and Historical Difference*. Princeton, N.J.: Princeton University Press.

Chakrabarty, Dipesh. 2000b *Universalism and Belonging in the Logic of Capital*. Public Culture 12(3): 653–78.

Comaroff, Jean, and John Comaroff. 2006a *Beasts, Banknotes and the Colour of Money in Colonial South Africa*. Archaeological Dialogues 12(2): 107–32.

Comaroff, Jean, and John L. Comaroff. 2006b *Law and Disorder in the Postcolony: An introduction*. Chicago: University of Chicago Press.

Croucher, Sarah K. 2006 Plantations on Zanzibar: An Archaeological Approach to Complex Identities. Ph.D. Dissertation, Department of Anthropology, University of Manchester.

Croucher, Sarah K. 2010 Cultural Identity, Colonial and Postcolonial Archaeologies. *In* Handbook of Postcolonial Archaeology. J. Lydon and U.Z. Rizvi, eds. Walnut Creek, CA: Left Coast Press.

Dixon, Kelly J. 2005 *Boomtown Saloons Archaeology and History in Virginia City*. Reno: University of Nevada Press.

Doughty, Oswald. 1963 *Early Diamond Days. The Opening of the Diamond Fields in South Africa*. Longmans: London.

Douglass, William A. 1998 The Mining Camp as Community. *In* Social Approaches to an Industrial Past: The Archaeology and Anthropology of Mining. B. Knapp and V.C. Pigott, eds. Pp. 97–108. London: Routledge.

Flanders, J. 2004 *Inside the Victorian home: a portrait of domestic life in Victorian England*. New York: W.W. Norton.

Foucault, Michel. 2003 *Society must be defended: Lectures at the Collège de France, 1975–76*. M. Bertani, A. Fontana, F. Ewald, and D. Macey, transl. New York: Picador.

Hall, Martin. 1992 Small Things and the Mobile, Conflictual Fusion of Power, Fear, and Desire. *In* The Art and Mystery of Historical Archaeology, Essays in Honor of J. Deetz. A.E. Yentsch and M.C. Beaudry, eds. Pp. 373–98. Boca Raton, FL.: CRC Press.

Hall, Martin. 2000 *Archaeology and the Modern World: Colonial Transcripts in South Africa and the Chesapeake*. London: Routledge.

Hall, Martin, and Stephen Silliman. 2006 Introduction: Archaeology of the Modern World. *In* Historical Archaeology. M. Hall and S. Silliman, eds. Pp. 1–22. London: Blackwell.

Hardesty, Donald. 2005 *Mining Rushes and Landscape Learning in the Modern World*. *In* Colonization of Unfamiliar Landscapes: The Archaeology of Adaptation. M. Rockman and J. Steele, eds. Pp. 81–96. New York: Routledge.

Harvey, David. 1999 *The Limits to Capital*. New York: Verso.

Hauser, Mark. 2008 *An Archaeology of Black Markets: Local Ceramics and Economies in Eighteenth- Century Jamaica*. Gainesville: University Press of Florida.

Herbert, Ivor. 1972 *The Diamond Diggers: South Africa 1866 to the 1970's*. London: Tom Stacey.

Hirst, Paul, and Grahame Thompson. 2002 *The Future of Globalization*. Cooperation and Conflict 37(3): 247–265.

Hobson, J. A. 1900 *Capitalism and Imperialism in South Africa*. Contemporary Review 77(Jan/June): 1–17.

Holub, Emil. 1881 *Seven Years in South Africa: Travels, Researches, and Hunting Adventures, Between the Diamond-Fields and the Zambesi (1872–79)*. London: Samson Low.

Holway, Tatianan M. 2002 A *"Capital Idea": Dickens, Speculation, and Victorian Economies of Representation*. Unpublished Ph.D. dissertation, Department of English and Comparative Literature, Columbia University, New York.

Itzkowitz, David C. 2002 Fair Enterprise or Extravagant Speculation: Investment, Speculation, and Gambling in Victorian England. *Victorian Studies* 45: 121–47.

Jewitt, Llewellynn. 1878 *The Ceramic Art of Great Britain from Pre-Historic Times to the Present Day...Pottery and Porcelain works*. London: Virtue and Co. Limited.

Johnstone, Frederick. 1970 White Prosperity and White Supremacy in South Africa Today. *African Affairs* 69(275): 124–140.

Knapp, Bernard, V. C. Pigott, and E. W. Herbert. 1998 *Social Approaches to an Industrial Past the Archaeology and Anthropology of Mining*. London: Routledge.

Lawrence, Susan. 2000 *Dolly's Creek*. Carlton South, Vic.: Melbourne University Press.

Lawrence, Susan, and Nick Shepherd. 2006 *Historical Archaeology and Colonialism*. *In* The Cambridge Companion to Historical Archaeology. D. Hicks and M.C. Beaudry, eds. Pp. 69–86. Cambridge: Cambridge University Press.

Lemke, Thomas. 2001 The Birth of Biopolitics: Michel Foucault's Lecture at the College de France on Neo-Liberal Governmentality. *Economy and Society* 30(2): 190–207.

Leone, Mark. 1995 A Historical Archaeology of Capitalism. *American Anthropologist* 97(2): 251–68.

Liebmann, Matthew, and Uzma Z. Rizvi. 2008 *Archaeology and the Postcolonial Critique*. Lanham, MD: AltaMira Press.

LiPuma, Edward, and Benjamin Lee. 2004 *Financial Derivatives and the Globalization of Risk*. Durham: Duke University Press.

Lucas, Gavin. 2004 *An Archaeology of Colonial Identity: Power and Material Culture in the Dwars Valley, South Africa*. New York: Kluwer Academic/Plenum Publishers.

Macnish, James T. 1969 *Graves and Guineas:* Cape Town: C. Struik.

Majewski, Teresita, and Michael B. Schiffer. 2001 Beyond Consumption: Toward an Archaeology of Consumerism. *In* Archaeologies of the Contemporary Past. V. Buchli and G. Lucas, eds. Pp. 25–50. London: Routledge.

Malan, Antonia. 2003 Nineteenth Century Ceramics in Cape Town, South Africa. *In* Archaeologies of the British: exploration of identity in Great Britain and its colonies, 1600–1945. S. Lawrence, ed. Pp. 191–210. London: Routledge.

Matthews, J. W. 1887 *Ingwadi Yami*. Johannesburg: Africana Book Society.

Mbembe, Achille. 2004 Aesthetics of Superfluity. *Public Culture* 16(3): 373–405.

McGuire, Randall H., and Robert Paynter. 1991 *The Archaeology of Inequality*. Cambridge, MA.: Blackwell.

Miller, Duncan, Nirdev Desai, and Julia Lee-Thorp. 2000 Indigenous Gold Mining in Southern Africa: A Review. *South African Archaeological Society, Goodwin Series* 8: 91–9.

Miller, Judith. 2005 *Miller's Antiques Encyclopedia*. London: Mitchell Beazley.

Mrozowski, Stephen A. 1991 Landscape of Inequality. *In* The Archaeology of Inequality. R. McGuire and R. Paynter, eds. Pp. 79–101. Cambridge, MA.: Blackwell.

Murray, Richard. 1894. *South African Remniscences.* Cape Town: J.C. Juta & Co.

Palus, Matthew, Mark Leone, and Matthew Cochran. 2006 Critical Archaeology: Politics Past and Present. *In* Historical Archaeology. M. Hall and S.W. Silliman, eds. Pp. 84–106. Malden, MA: Blackwell.

Patterson, T. C. 2003 *Marx's Ghost: Conversations with Archaeologists.* Oxford: Berg.

Paynter, Robert. 2000 Historical Archaeology and the Post-Columbian World of North America. *Journal of Archaeological Research* 8(3): 169–217.

Payton, Charles Alfred, Sir. 1872 *The Diamond Diggings of South Africa: A Personal and Practical Account.* London: Horace Cox.

Peires, J. B. 1989 *The dead Will Arise: Nongqawuse and the Great Xhosa Cattle Killing Movement of 1856–7.* London: James Currey.

Pikirayi, Innocent. 2001 *The Zimbabwe Culture: Origins and Decline of Southern Zambezian States.* Walnut Creek, Calif.: AltaMira Press.

Polanyi, Karl. 2001 *The Great Transformation: The Political and Economic Origins of our Time.* Boston, MA: Beacon Press.

Poovey, Mary. 2003 *The Financial System in Nineteenth-Century Britain.* Oxford: Oxford University Press.

Purser, Margaret. 1999 Ex Occidente Lux? An Archaeology of Later Capitalism in the Nineteenth Century West. *In* Historical Archaeologies of Capitalism. M.P. Leone and P.B. Potter, eds. Pp. 115–142. New York: Springer.

Resident Magistrate. 1877a "Illicit Diamond Buying". *In* The Independent. Diamond Fields.

Resident Magistrate. 1877b "Inducing to Steal". *In* The Independent. Diamond Fields.

Roitman, Janet. 2005 *Fiscal Disobedience: An Anthropology of Economic Regulation in Central Africa.* Princeton, NJ: Princeton University Press.

Sandoval-Strauss, A. K. 2007 *Hotel: An American History.* New Haven, CT: Yale University Press.

Silliman, Stephen W. 2005 Culture Contact or Colonialism? Challenges in the Archaeology of Native North America. *American Antiquity* 70(1): 55–74.

Smalberger, John M. 1976a *Pass laws, Convict Labor and the Compound System: A Preliminary Overview of Labour Relations in Kimberley 1872–1888.* Unpublished manuscript on file, UCT Manuscripts and Archives, Cape Town. BC 635 820 1.4.

Smalberger, John M. 1976b The Role of the Diamond-Mining Industry in the Development of the Pass-Law System in South Africa. *The International Journal of African Historical Studies* IX (3):419–34.

Strange, Susan. 1986 *Casino Capitalism.* New York: Blackwell.

Sussman, Lynne. 1979 *Spode/Copeland Transfer-Printed Patterns Found at 20 Hudson's Bay Company Sites.* Ottawa: Parks Canada, National Historic Parks and Sites Branch; Hull.

Trollope, Anthony. 1878 *South Africa.* London: Chapman and Hall.

Turrell, Robert Vicat. 1982 Kimberley: Labour and Compounds, 1871–1888. *In* Industrialisation and Social Change in South Africa: African Class Formation, Culture and Consciousness 1870–1930. S. Marks and R. Rathbone, eds. Pp. 45–76. London: Longman group Ltd.

Voigt, Elizabeth. 2007 *Country Fare at Wildebeestkuil, Northern Cape.* Kimberley: Unpublished Faunal Report: McGregor Museum.

Wall, Diana. 1994 Family Dinners and Social Teas: Ceramics and Domestic Rituals. *In* Everyday Life in the Early Republic. C. Hutchins, ed. Pp. 249–84. Winterthur, Delaware: Winterthur Museum.

Warren, Charles. 1902 *On the Veldt in the Seventies.* London: Isbister & Co.

Weiss, L. 2009 *Fictive Capital and Economies of Desire: A Case Study of Illegal Diamond Buying and Apartheid Landscapes in 19th century Southern Africa,* Ph.D. dissertation, Department of Anthropology, Columbia University, New York.

Weiss, L. 2011 The Currency of Intimacy: Transformations of the Domestic Sphere on the late Nineteenth Century Diamond Fields. *In* Intimate Encounters:. B. Voss and E. Casella, eds. Cambridge: Cambridge University Press.

Wilkie, Laurie A., and Kevin M. Bartoy. 2000 A Critical Archaeology Revisited. *Current Anthropology*. 41(5): 747–77.

Wolpe, Howard. 1972 Capitalism and Cheap Labour Power in South Africa: From Segregation to Apartheid. *Economy and Society* 1:425–52.

Worger, William H. 1987 *South Africa's City of Diamonds: Mine Workers and Monopoly Capitalism in Kimberley*, 1867–1895. New Haven: Yale University Press.

Wurst, LouAnn. 2006 A Class all its Own: Explorations of Class Formation and Conflict. *In* Historical Archaeology. M. Hall and S. Silliman, eds. Pp. 190–206. Malden, MA: Blackwell Publishing.

Chapter 11
Considering Colonialism and Capitalism in Australian Historical Archaeology: Two Case Studies of Culture Contact from the Pastoral Domain

Alistair G. Paterson

Introduction

> The great northward stream of settlers could now be likened unto one of those real, erratic, perplexing Australian streams that flowed into the outback; fed by the wet fertile districts, swollen by the good seasons, gathering momentum as it ran swiftly among the ranges, fanning out broadly and thinly onto the saltbush plains, transforming all that it touched with an illusion of goodness and then, as the seasons changed, slowly, ebbing, dying, leaving as far as the outermost margins of its reach the scar of its momentary presence. (Meinig 1988: 92)

The geographer Donald Meinig was describing the nineteenth-century push by white settlers into increasingly arid parts of inland Australia – one explorer would describe this challenging desert country in a blunt Australian manner: "the country … is perfectly worthless and would not feed a bandicoot."[1] Despite its challenges, vast parts of the continent were settled (or invaded, depending on one's perspective) by sheep and cattle farmers involving various degrees and forms of cross-cultural contacts between settlers and Aboriginal peoples. Over 200 Australian indigenous societies, each with distinct languages and customs, came into contact with the settlers. Sheep and cattle pastoral stations were sometimes the key locations for these contacts.

In this chapter, I use two regional archaeological studies of pastoralism to explore colonization and colonialism in Australia. Along the way, I consider some essential components of these ventures, themes common to studies of colonial settings more broadly, such as access to labor, gender roles, power differentials, the importance

[1] The explorer was Alfred W. Howitt, who was a keen ethnographer of Aboriginal life in Central Australia (Howitt 1859) and probably most famous for leading an expedition to recover the bodies of transcontinental explorers, Burke and Wills, who died in Central Australia of starvation. A bandicoot is a retiring native marsupial with the size of a cat.

A.G. Paterson (✉)
School of Social and Cultural Studies, The University of Western Australia,
Perth, WA, Australia
e-mail: alistair.paterson@uwa.edu.au

S.K. Croucher and L. Weiss (eds.), *The Archaeology of Capitalism in Colonial Contexts*,   243
Contributions To Global Historical Archaeology, DOI 10.1007/978-1-4614-0192-6_11,
© Springer Science+Business Media, LLC 2011

of making a profit, ideology as a tool of resistance and dominance, and the role of commodities and materiality in demonstrations of status and identity.

As demonstrated in the chapters in this volume, colonization and colonialism are the core themes of archaeological research into the diasporas of colonial Europeans in the second millennium and the ensuing entanglement with indigenous societies. Michael Rowland's review of the archaeology of colonialism begins: "The immediate associations of colonialism are with intrusions, conquests, economic exploitation and the domination of indigenous peoples" (Rowlands 1998: 327). Following this point, this chapter focuses on the indigenous and cross-cultural aspects of the colonial pastoral industries in Australia. While the categories of colonized/colonizer and exploiter/ exploited are often true, this chapter attempts to add some texture to a binary perception that arises from examining the interface between two different cultures in contact. I refer to a great shift in Australian society from hunter-gatherer lifeways to a modern nation state; however, this is not to imply that it was an even process but rather a broad setting in which a multitude of individual interactions occurred.

To begin with, it is important to recognize the differences between colonization and colonialism and consider culture contacts. A recent definition is as relevant to Australia as anywhere else:

> Colonisation involves the expansion of one state or polity into the territory of another and the establishments of settlements subject to that parent state. Expansion may be accomplished by conquest or by trade, and includes political, economic, social, cultural, and psychological dimensions. Colonialism is the process by which new societies emerge in both the new territories and the core because of colonisation, and the new systems of relationships that result (Lawrence and Shepherd 2006: 69).

One of the promises of these topics of study for both anthropologists and archaeologists has been the core theme of power relations – although colonization has been more popular with archaeologists than colonialism (Rowlands 1998: 327), at least until recently (Gosden 2000, 2004; Silliman 2005). Across the globe, from Greenland to Australia, both prehistoric and historical colonizations have been studied by archaeologists. Colonization invites us to think of the efforts of individuals, communities, families, and societies and the mechanisms of colonization. The cross-cultural and ideational aspects of colonization have often been less prominent: "Colonisation has been used to refer to both territorial and commercial incentives but proved vague and elusive in detailing the relationships between homeland and diasporic communities and between colonisers and colonised" (Rowlands 1998: 327).

Colonialism is different to colonization in that it requires a minimum of two parties, one the colonial power with which others must reckon. Thus, colonialism is often bimodal with colonizer and colonized; however, colonial contexts are often more complicated. To take one example, working in colonial California, Barbara Voss (2005) describes a population comprising native Californians and more recent migrants of mixed Spanish, African, and Mexican descent, further delineated by Spanish racial designations known as the *sistemas de castas*. Working on the northern Californian coast, Kent Lightfoot and colleagues at Fort Ross have revealed a complex colonial mix of Aluet, native Californians, and Russians they describe as constituting a "pluralistic" setting (Lightfoot et al. 1998), rather than merely bicultural.

Colonialism is largely about power differentials, typically highlighting differences between a colonizing culture and indigenous people, although other forced migrants (such as slaves) or voluntary migrants are also part of the history of colonial-era power relationships. Key colonial relationships are often cross-cultural, and in recent decades archaeologists have detailed the interactions between "indigenous people and the expanding European mercantilist and capitalist world economy and political sphere in the last half millennium" (Silliman 2005: 55). The archaeology of culture contact has, for various reasons, been popularized in different parts of the world, and my aim is not to review that topic here other than to note that in many places there existed (and may still exist) disciplinary boundaries between "history" and "prehistory" that need to be acknowledged (Lightfoot 1995). A consequence of this in Australia, perhaps like North America prior to the 1990s, has been that much historical archaeology operated with little attention to indigenous archaeology and much prehistory was uninterested in the historical period. This was hardly a positive environment to study colonialism, although it has since changed (see below). Another issue posed by studying colonialism is that in addition to understanding how ideology and power were used in the past, the discipline of archaeology too has a "colonial culture" (McNiven and Russell 2005). In Australia, like elsewhere, this recognition has led to a more reflexive review of archaeological practices (Horning, Chap. 3).

Clearly, cultures are seldom totally isolated; however, the study of certain forms of culture contact, where very different societies encounter each other, raises the issue of power: "Cultures are always in contact ... Colonialism brings a new quality (or rather inequality) to human relations" (Gosden 2004: 5). This seems to be very relevant in colonial contexts, where Europeans came into contact with indigenous peoples. One core aspect of colonialism in the last millennium is its geographical reach, whereby previously distant communities came into contact through voluntary and involuntary means. These contacts involved seismic demographic shifts, for example the Spanish conquest of the Americas, the Atlantic slave trade, the European–Asian power struggles for control of the trade of Asian products. In many places, migrants overwhelmed and outnumbered indigenous people, such as in many American contexts and in Australasia and Southern Africa.

Both colonialism and culture contact are suited to anthropological and archaeological analyses. As expressed by Gosden and others, a key aspect of colonialism is material, as objects themselves are part of power and status differentials. "Analyses of colonialism increasingly stress the non-verbal, tactile dimensions of social practice: the exchange of objects, the arrangement and disposition of bodies, clothes, buildings, and tools in agricultural practices, medical and religious performances, regimes of domesticity and kinship, physical discipline, and the construction of landscape" (Pels 1997: 169). This potential seems particularly significant, where culture contact occurred between literature and nonliterature societies, where the resulting data gap was magnified by the fact that many nonliterature indigenous societies left behind no (or very few) accounts. To compound this situation, the often dramatic and tragic historical events resulted in knowledge of these and earlier times to be lost. This is especially evident, where people were victim to diseases, warfare, and removal from traditional country and resources and were unable to continue traditional practices. This is where archaeology is important. Archaeology can be a significant way to understand change, as it provides a basis for reconstructing the nature of precolonial societies (Lightfoot 1995; Rowlands 1998; Stahl 1994; Silliman 2005). In fact, change was a central expectation of colonialism. Europeans argued that indigenous societies needed to change or be lost – this core concept is expressed by the station manager at Strangways Springs in Central Australia (one of this chapter's two case studies), John Oastler, when he stated: "To break these wild tribes into something like obedience, and to teach them that the law of ownership of property, and that their laws must give way to the white man's law, was the most difficult task" (Oastler 1908: 205).

Historical archaeology has identified a range of shared topics as a result, as expressed by Charles Orser:

> They [colonialism, Eurocentrism, modernism, and capitalism] exist at every site, every laboratory table, within every map and chart made. Sometimes one is pushed to the forefront to be the subject of analysis. At other times, they may all hang back like ghost-writers, ever present but unacknowledged and unnamed. Regardless, each subject pervades historical archaeology and so must be acknowledged, understood, and challenged (Orser 1996: 57).

Clearly, these things – colonialism, Eurocentrism, modernism, and capitalism, as well as globalization – are the focus for much historical archaeology; particularly in North America and increasingly in Europe and elsewhere, there has been a strong research interest in capitalism, different status groups, different ethnic groups, ideology, issues of power and domination, and gender. However, parallel to these broad picture and shared attributes of the "modern world," archaeology also is potentially local and contextualised, in fact the primary nature of archaeological evidence is localized. In Australasia, there has been much research that contributes to understandings of colonization and the colonial era while less focus has been implicitly directed toward issues of capitalism, status, and class. Additionally, there has been less of a disciplinary "shake-up" as experienced by anthropology (Pels 2008), although archaeology has been transformed by a greater involvement in political aspects of research and collaboration with indigenous Australians. In what follows, I hope a "thick description" (Hall [*sensu* Geertz], Chap. 13; see also Richard, Chap. 9) of two instances of early stages of colonialism, when dealing with "otherness" was paramount, situates Australia in a larger comparative setting.

I begin with a review of Australian archaeological studies of colonization, colonialism, and capitalism before considering the case studies. The review is intended to consider differences between Australia and other places, particularly North America. There are good reasons for considering comparisons, given broad similarities in the historical setting. Australia is one of many places European settlement *first* occurred only in recent centuries. As one of many modern states originating as "settler societies" then intercultural relationships become a core issue on tracking the development between past and present society. The abruptness of contact in Australia is akin to southern Africa, Canada, or Argentina: part of the abruptness was economic given the differences between hunter-foragers and farmers.

When considering the driest continent (after Antarctica), environmental impacts deriving from the massive shift in land use should be part of equation – although that level of interdisciplinary understanding remains largely in the future. The environment is considered in the case studies here only as a determining factor in locational choices, not in any substantial manner.

Colonization, Colonialism, and Capitalism in Australian Archaeology

Historical archaeology in Australia, since its earliest projects in the 1960s, engaged with the results of the British colonization and colonial contexts in Australia. Early archaeological research was directed to the evidence for British colonization and its successes, failures, and form. Indeed, the earliest doctoral thesis in Australian historical archaeology studied an early nineteenth-century British fort at Port Essington in Northern Australia (Allen 2008). Early interest in models for colonization was proposed (Birmingham and Jeans 1983; with responses Bairstow 1984; Egloff 1994), but was not followed up by later archaeologists, despite a strong research interest in the prehistoric colonization of Australia and Oceania.

Colonial Australia was a popular research topic in the 1980s around the bicentennial of British colonization (Birmingham 1975; Birmingham 1988). While 1788 saw British colonization and the systematic process of the assumption of Aboriginal Australia, earlier contacts included Dutch encounters – shipwrecks and exploration – in the seventeenth and eighteenth centuries and seasonal contact with island Southeast Asian trepang harvesters in parts of coastal Northern Australia from the seventeenth century onward. However, for our discussion, the period after 1788 is most relevant.

Foundation studies into early colonial industries and society provided the basis for the interpretation of the archaeology of colonial Australia. Early colonial industries studied by archaeologists included the first potters (Birmingham 1975; Jack 1985), colonial mining (Gaughwin 1992 and dedicated issues of *Australasian Historical Archaeology*), transfer of European power systems to Australia (Pearson 1996), pioneer technologies (Birmingham et al. 1979, 1983), sheep- and cattle-raising industries (Davidson 1994; Walker 1995), timber getting (Davies 2006), whaling and sealing (Lawrence and Staniforth 1998), and early agricultural ventures, such as in Van Diemen's Land (now Tasmania, Murray 1988) and New South Wales (Bairstow 2003; Connah 2007). Some colonial enterprises made use of unfree convict labor until transportation ended; other industries did not. As argued below, indigenous labor was also important. Together, these studies contributed along a broad front to our understanding of colonial Australia and constituted an important first phase for the nascent discipline. Second-phase topics include thornier issues, such as colonialism, capitalism, and historical culture contact.

Attempts to understand colonialism in Australia have been influenced by developments in theory in the social sciences and humanities more broadly. The Swiss Family Robinson model for colonization (Birmingham and Jeans 1983) was a collaboration between a geographer (Jeans) and a historical archaeologist (Birmingham). More recently in historical archaeology, the influence of anthropologically informed studies of material culture, particularly the work of Nicholas Thomas (1991, 1994), is evident. The use of material culture to interpret colonial contexts has also been pursued by examining colonial collectors (Gosden 2000; Gosden and Knowles 2001) and the Aboriginal production of items that came to be the focus of collectors (Taçon et al. 2003; Harrison 2003). Another focus is the consumption of mass-produced wares, such as ceramics in colonial settings: like elsewhere (c.f. Croucher, Chap. 8), in Australia, these dominate archaeological assemblages, and their interpretation requires nuanced understandings of both functional and other needs in their purchase and use (see Crook 2008 for recent work on the cost, value, and quality of consumables).

The study of capitalism, particularly popular in North American archaeology, is also important although a less implicit aspect of archaeological research. Aspects of capitalism, such as relative access to labor and wealth, and differentials related to class and status have been considered from archaeological perspectives in studies of both rural industries and of urban contexts. A particular focus has been urban societies in colonial Sydney and Melbourne (Murray 2004a, b) while investigations into poorer communities potentially provide a parallel to studies of colonial elites (Connah 2007). This work is in part a response to work elsewhere in the world, such as in Five Points (Cantwell and Wall 2001). The archaeology of capitalism is of course not just of the poor, but also involves the study of labor, power, and social relations, as well as production, ideological struggle, and the evidence for different social groups. Capitalism has rarely been the primary focus of archaeological research, with the exception of Heather Burke's study of the New England (NSW) town of Armidale (Burke 1999) which used architectural analysis to demark the rise of rural elite. Instead in Australia, research has studied consumption and production in Australia and the ways Australia was part of global movements of goods. Maritime archaeology has been significant in this regard (Staniforth 1987; Souter 2007) as the evidence for transported goods from maritime sites is different to the evidence from terrestrial archaeological sites. Other work has examined the archaeological evidence for labor and its inequalities, ranging from the organization of unfree or underpaid labor, be it Aboriginal (Smith 2000; Paterson 2005, 2008; Harrison 2004; Gill and Paterson 2007) or convict (Karskens 1986; Connah 2007). Responses to labor conditions by workers have also been studied at strikers' camps (Egloff et al. 1991), walk-off sites (Paterson et al. 2003), and within settlements (Davies 2006), inviting comparisons with other archaeological studies of workers' relations.

The provision of labor in colonial settings involved culture contact, what Hall (Chap. 13) describes as places of "transgression." A sold body of work in culture contact in colonial Australia between Aboriginal and non-Aboriginal people now exists (see papers in Torrence and Clarke 2000; Clarke and Paterson 2003;

Harrison and Williamson 2004; Murray 2004a, b; Lydon 2005; Paterson and Wilson 2009). It is important to consider how effectively a focus on capitalism handles the often vast differences between colonists and indigene, particularly given the respective culturally (and, indeed, spatially) located values of commodities, labor, and time. For example, core issues, such as the production and access to goods and the commodification of time and labor, are potentially vastly different depending on cultural perspective. To take the example from Strangways Springs (below), the pastoralists demanded Aboriginal labor and knowledge; yet from an indigenous perspective, this deal also allowed maintained access to traditional "country" with all the benefits – real, social, and spiritual – this may have meant at a time when the structure of Aboriginal networks and society were under attack. In colonial Australia, Aboriginal people constituted a social group often with little power who held roles as laborers, consumers, and targets for ideological transformation (comparable with Richard, Chap. 9). Australia is, thus, comparable to other settings, as studies of culture contact often focus on the interface between different societies – *typically*, Europeans and non-Europeans somewhere on the planet after the fifteenth century. This was largely the case in Australia, although other ethnicities, such as Chinese and South Asian migrants, also were part of the fabric of colonial frontiers. To summarize then, the transformation of Aboriginal societies saw changes in each indigenous community's ability to maintain traditional lifeways and economy, access country, travel, trade, and self-determine; saw exposure to diseases; meant power struggles with white Australians and roles within new economic and political orders.

Culture Contact as an Element of Colonial Projects: The Australian Pastoral Domain

In the remainder of this chapter, I consider two regions in nineteenth-century colonial Australia, where pastoralists were the primary colonists. This research emphasizes pastoral stations as a setting for colonization, colonialism, labor differentials, and cross-cultural engagements and sees the pastoral domain as a setting for colonialism and as a means to introduce capitalism into regions previously occupied by indigenous Aboriginal Australians practicing hunter-foraging lifeways. These two studies are based on Central Australia and Northwest Western Australia.

Both studies for this chapter consider sheep stations, a major element of Australia's history. For a century, income from wool exports dominated the national economy, and Australia grew wealthy as a result – by 1950, the nation was said to be "riding on the sheep's back." Cattle too were significant, yet less so in the early years of the settings discussed here. The themes of colonial pastoral Australia – the "bush" – entered the national psyche, perhaps simply shown by the ongoing value of the ballad *Waltzing Matilda* (lyrics Banjo Paterson and music Christina Macpherson).

Oh there once was a swagman camped in the billabong,
Under the shade of a Coolibah tree,
And he sang as he looked at the old billy boiling,
Who'll come a waltzing Matilda with me?[2]

Today, the ballad is a de facto national anthem and popular at sporting and military functions. It is full of elements of nineteenth-century Australian rural life, such as swag (a bed roll), billabong (a cutoff river bed), jumbuck (a wild sheep), and squatter (originally referred to farmers on land not legally entitled to them). The ballad *may* refer to social tensions in pastoral Australia in the late nineteenth century, when economic depression and general unemployment had resulted in conflicts across rural Australia with workers' strikes in Queensland in the early 1890s. (The swagman, being harassed by mounted police, chooses death in the billabong.) Whether a simple ditty or social commentary, Paterson's ballad reminds us of a time when laconic stockmen were the core characters in Australian life. But, when depicted, these pastoral identities were often white. Less popularized was the fact that the roots of the pastoral industries in *some* parts of Australia reside in cross-cultural encounters, dependent on various forms of cheap or unfree indigenous labor, and are imbedded in the power differentials that characterize work and industrial production more widely.

The first study is Strangways Springs in Central Australia. In this research, the development of the pastoral station was investigated through the documentary and archaeological records. From these data, the ways that station work came to define a socialized and spatially segregated pastoral domain were revealed. This case study is based on several years of archaeological investigations to provide a thick description of the early years of this colonial sheep station (Paterson 2003, 2005, 2008). The evidence for indigenous labor and shifts in Aboriginal activities following the arrival of white pastoralists is revealed through an analysis of archaeological sites across the landscape from precontact and historical eras. This suggests the extent to which the economically successful sheep station, today a cattle station of over 23,000 km^2, was in part built on foundations of indigenous labor and knowledge.

The second case study of the pastoral industry considers the European colonization in the 1860s of the Pilbara region of Western Australia, also a relatively late frontier from a British perspective. Archaeological research into the region is being conducted within the "Historical Archaeology of the Pilbara Project" (Paterson 2006; Paterson and Wilson 2009). The archaeological recording of the earliest settlements provides a regional case study in colonization. An outcome was identifying the archaeological fingerprint of various strata in the colonial settings (masters, servants, free labor) and indigenous responses to colonization.

The research had two general concerns: (1) How did hunter-gatherers fare in a capitalist world? and (2) How did white colonists and their descendents understand their lives and their attempts at survival, economic stability and growth, claim to country, access to workers, and dominion over the frontier?

---

[2]This is the first verse in its most widely accepted wording. A general discussion of the poem is available on Wikipedia.

Water and Work: The Physical, Observed, and Remembered Culture of Colonialism at Strangways Springs, Central Australia

ADELAIDE, Monday. The diamond drill has tapped water 25 miles north of Strangways Springs, at a depth of 210 ft. It is running over the surface at the rate of 1,600 gallons an hour. The water is of better quality than that of the previous bores. *The Argus* (Melbourne, Victoria), 16 November 1886.

Central Australia was a barrier to European colonization until pastoralists began their intrusions from the late 1850s. The arid regions were home to desert societies, many who would become known internationally through early ethnographic reports. Before ethnographers were pastoralists: "How wonderful it would be [anthropologist Edward Stirling], wistfully reflected, to access the memories of 'those early pioneers and settlers who for years lived in close association with the natives at a time when their customs were still uninfluenced by general contact with the Europeans" (Stirling 1896: 2; cited in Rowse 1998: 16). Stirling was describing what happened at many pastoral stations, where traditional lives of Aboriginal Australians changed following the arrival of pastoralists.

Life in the Far North of South Australia was about water, work, and power. Around Strangways Springs, the various salt lakes, river courses, rock holes, and artesian springs provided water in a landscape comprising sand dunes, saltbush and grass plains, and stony deserts. The focus for this discussion is Strangways Springs Station in the southwestern Lake Eyre Basin, northern South Australia (Fig. 11.1), where from ca. 1860 interaction between Aboriginal people and Europeans occurred primarily in the pastoral domain. This was one of the earliest stations in Central Australia. The springs were fed by the largest artesian basin on earth: the Lake Eyre Basin. Lake Eyre is Australia's largest lake when it fills; however, this occurs only a handful of times a century, most of the time it is a vast salt pan.

The settlers arrived in Arabana peoples' country, where people had lived for millennia with a hunter-foraging lifestyle maximizing the variables of the harsh environment. This was the heart of Arabana people's country and at a crossroads for trade networks. People had long relied on the artesian springs (Fig. 11.2), as indicated by dense assemblages of archaeological material, mainly stone artifacts (Paterson 2008).[3] When other parts of the landscape could be used, they were, with a preference for occupation sites on sandy surfaces close to water sources. Some Arabana people, and their neighbors, became involved with the pastoralists. This was the case at Strangways Springs Station, for in 1875, a mere decade after the arrival of British settlers at Strangways Springs Station, the visiting ethnographer F.J. Gillen wrote that "all the shepherds employed at this station are Niggers[sic] ... and do just as well as the whites" (Gillen 1995: 49).

---

[3]The earliest radiocarbon date from Strangways Springs is 560 ± 75 BP (Florek 1993) and in the region 21,884 cal. BP (Magee and Miller 1998). Both dates are from material in hearths.

Fig. 11.1 Map of Australia showing the key regions and sites referred to

Water allowed the pastoralists to raise sheep, although they struggled in drier years to keep animals alive. Yet, in good years, the stock thrived. Heavy dirt hung to the fleece when shorn, and it was hard to get enough water to wash it away – a labor-intensive process called scouring. During the earliest years, pastoralists relied heavily on artesian waters; however, the Australian desert had never felt hooves and the dramatic impact on delicate ecosystems and landforms around the springs was seen immediately. Pastoralists were reliant on the same water that Aboriginal people used most regularly. To get their flocks out to pastures, pastoralists relied on Arabana people to tell them where rain had fallen. Consequently, in the early years, the spatial organization of the pastoral station mimicked precontact Aboriginal land use patterns.

The archaeological deposits across the landscape allowed for an analysis of land use patterns prior to contact and from the earliest years of the station onward. In the period 1860–1900, Strangways Springs head station – a collection of stone buildings,

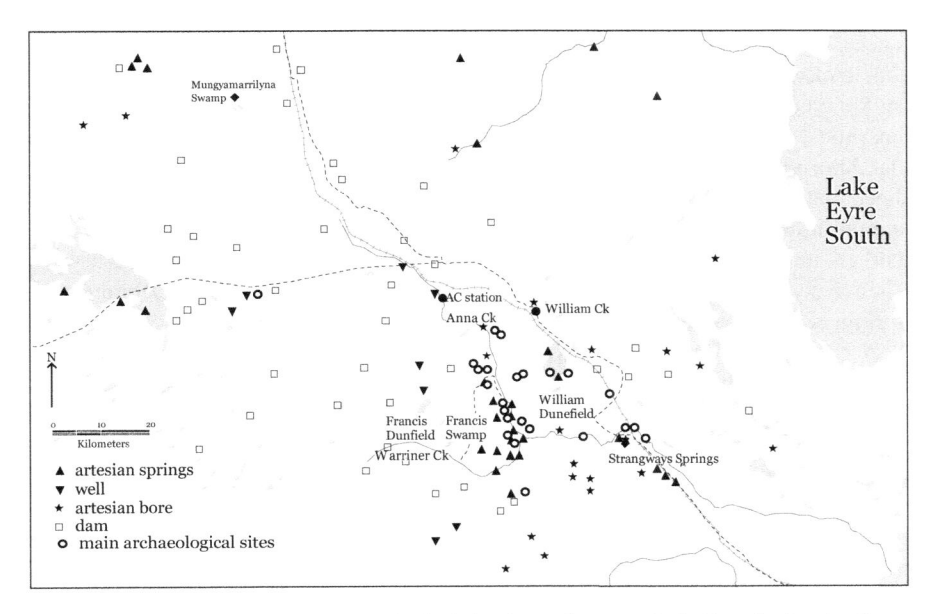

Fig. 11.2 Map showing the key archaeological sites in southwestern Lake Eyre Basin: significant places, artesian springs, and location of dams, bores, and wells

yards, camps, and work sites spread out along a stony ridge overlooking the plain and Warriner Creek – was the primary setting for pastoral work, white activities, and culture contact with Arabana people. The archaeological deposits at houses, worksites, and campsites of both the settlers and Arabana allowed for a detailed analysis of the places where people lived and worked. A series of surveys, assisted by historical sources, located other sites across the vast station landscape, including Aboriginal camps, outstations where animals were tended by small communities of both white and Aboriginal people, and the various sheep station infrastructure that came to be built, such as yards and fences, windmills, dams, roadways, shearing sheds, and residential working sites. Fortunately, the South Australian archives held letters and paperwork from the earliest years of the station (1860s–1880s). Particularly useful was the regular correspondence between managers and owners detailing the running of the station, workforce, Aboriginal people, and finances of the station.

One clear finding of the study was the manner in which the pastoral station was organized and operated over time. The first two decades of the station were clearly a "learning stage" for the pastoralists, who sometime suffered heavy stock losses. They relied heavily on "natural" waters, like artesian springs or water collected following rainfall. To improve their chances, a network of outstations was established to spread their stock. During this period, there were no fences and the flocks required intensive shepherding to protect them from getting lost, hunted, or killed by dogs. (In many places, where European sheep farmers settled across the world, they initially had no fences, and thus relied on shepherding on the pen range, a form of animal husbandry akin to medieval practices.) Outstations were built with small yards into which animals could be herded at night for protection from Aboriginal hunters and dingoes. Small huts housed workers; the archaeological records from camp and work sites reveal that Aboriginal people camped nearby, presumably attracted to the outstations. The sheep that survived were shorn, and then the washed fleeces had to be transported by animal-drawn carts over tracks hundreds of kilometers through tough country. The workers on the station were both white and Aboriginal. The 1860s were hard years when many pastoral stations were abandoned across the region; however, Strangways Springs was not and appears to have made a profit.

A railway line into Central Australia in the 1880s improved transport. By the 1880s, the first phase of the pastoral station was over, and the next phase was characterized by investment. Expensive water drilling equipment allowed access to artesian water in greater quantities. The organization of the pastoral station changed, becoming centered around new wells and increasingly compartmentalized into large paddocks by fences built and then maintained by dedicated fence-building laborers (Fig. 11.2). Shepherds were replaced by "doggers" (dingo hunters) and fencers while the demand for lambers, shearers, and wool cleaners remained. At this time, the first head station at Strangways Springs was replaced by a new larger head station at Anna Creek (the name of the station today). Clearly, the sheep industry was paying off, driven by demands for Australian wool in the factories of industrialized Britain.

The study revealed how the early toehold at Strangways Springs was consolidated by access to labor, profit, suitable expenditure, and technological and transport improvements. The analysis of both documents and archaeological sites revealed a strong level of Aboriginal involvement in the pastoral station. Aboriginal people remained the majority of workers for at least the initial decades matching the seasonal demand for shepherding and animal tending. It was hard to get reliable workers to come to remote Australia, especially with other opportunities in Australia like the Victorian goldfields. From the earliest years of the stations, Aboriginal male and female children were indoctrinated into pastoral work and these "henchmen and shepherdesses" – as the pastoralists wrote of them – acted as intermediaries between the station and the wider indigenous community. It is not clear how these workers became involved with the pastoralists, nor all of the services they fulfilled. Station workers were also members of traditional society beholden to cultural doctrines, such as initiation rites. The first generation of workers grew to adulthood within the pastoral domain (Fig. 11.3). Hunter-gatherers became reliable tenders of animal herders almost immediately – although would not have immediately forgone hunting and foraging. However, work and the payment for work – in food rations and clothing typically – changed them. For example, an analysis of the historical camps suggests that there was a decreased reliance on the staple of ground seeds (*nardoo*): presumably replaced by flour.

The evidence suggests different types and degrees of interpersonal engagement. The pastoralists provide some insights about Arabana people that they relied on for work. When there was a demand for labor – during lambing, shearing, and wool

Fig. 11.3 Aboriginal workers at Strangways Springs: Mr. and Mrs. William Rowdy and their son, residents of Anna Creek (ca. 1898)

washing – Aboriginal workers tended to make up the necessary workforce. The pastoralists distinguished between those Arabana people with whom they were in contact (normally referred to in the possessive as "ours") and nonstation indigenous people often termed "wild." During the early years of the station, the pastoral domain was constantly entered by "wild" or foreign Aboriginals, often on long expeditions to trade or conduct revenge missions (*pinyaroo*). The Lake Eyre Basin was an active network of long-distance trade routes through which valuable items, like ochre, grinding stones, *pituri* (a plant), and information, flowed (McBryde 1987). The pastoral domain acted in competition to these networks – pastoralists did not want their stock being hunted and clearly begrudged the disruption to the pastoral domain. Over time, an idea of "inside" and "outside" firmed, and fewer surprise visits occurred.

The analysis of settlements, both white and Aboriginal, provides some understanding of the activities and material dimensions of life on the station. One key finding was that Aboriginal people had access to a similar range of types of material culture as whites – this included clothing, protective material for shelters, smoking pipes, ceramics and glassware, and tools. That said, the amount of material was greater at the head station complex where whites lived, and one suspects that function shifted – for example, bottles that held spirits probably became useful containers and sources for glass flakes rather than for alcohol.

The study of this pastoral domain provided a strong set of evidence for the involvement of some Aboriginal people in the pastoral domain while others were not. Within the domain, they provided valuable labor and knowledge cheaply, and probably this underpinned the eventual monetary success of the station.

Situating Belonging: Records of Colonization in the Northwest of Western Australia

The Northwest of Australia is a vast arid region extending from inland deserts through rocky inland ranges to a coastal plain with numerous offshore islands. Like Central Australia, the Northwest was first colonized by whites only after the mid nineteenth century. The region was remote from both the eastern seaboard and Perth, the capital of Western Australia. Early visitors to the Northwest included Dutch, French, and British explorers, whalers (mainly from the USA), and the first terrestrial exploratory party in 1860. Within a few years, Anglo–Australian colonization was underway with a trickle of colonists, stock, and provisions primarily through the port of Cossack (Fig. 11.1). The difficulties faced by settlers were sometimes prohibitive while the rewards for some were encouraging. Experience from colonial Australia suggested that local Aboriginal people would need consideration:

> The settlement of Gregory's Land [Northwest] may now be considered as certain, and the newly discovered territory bids fair to be to Western Australia what Port Phillip was to New South Wales. From the account furnished by Mr. Padbury ... it will be at once seen that the trip of the *Tien Tsin* has been altogether successful, the pioneer party, with their stock, having been landed in safety. The country is reported to be of excellent quality, water abundant, the native quiet, and, when Mr. Padbury left, everything was going on as well as could be wished. The natives are described to be quiet; having a taste for tobacco and a horror of horned stock. The former they ate in any quantity, of the latter they entertained great fear, decamping as soon as they were landed, and not reappearing at the time the vessel left. This state of affairs cannot however be expected to last long, and when they begin to appreciate the flavour of beef and when mutton, disagreements between the black and white occupants of the soil will probably commence. *The Inquirer and Commercial News*, 3 June 1863.

Within a short time, a handful of sheep stations were established across the interior (Fig. 11.1). The discovery of pearlshell saw the development of a pearling fleet that, for the first two decades, relied heavily on Aboriginal labor, and later, from the 1880s, used divers from various East Asian countries. Pearlshell products were highly valued by European manufacturers of decorative items, such as buttons.

Coastal Aboriginal people were in greatest contact with the earlier colonists. Other people well inland from colonial settlements were less in contact with the whites, although many became workers or ran afoul of the law and ended up being imprisoned, particularly for hunting stock or absconding from work. In the Dampier Archipelago, the local indigenous people did not survive; they were subject to a massacre in the early years of colonization. Other groups survived, although with reduced access to traditional country. Some inland people were actually drawn into the coastal zone of primary culture contact. The transformation of power was assisted by colonial laws – particularly the *Master and Servant Act* – that were designed to facilitate cheap indigenous workers for pastoralists, many of whom were also pearlers.

Until this project, no archaeological research has been conducted on the colonial sites (except Reynolds 1987). Archaeological recording of eight of the earliest pastoral stations has revealed details of the organization of the pastoral head stations, as well as Aboriginal activities at them. The evidence for Aboriginal

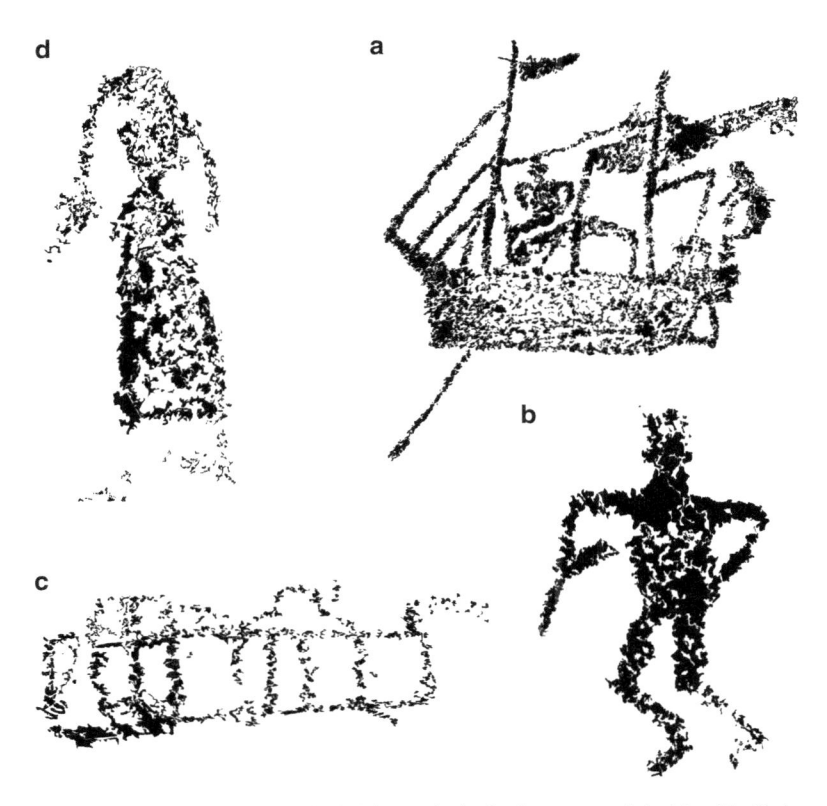

Fig. 11.4 Indigenous depictions of colonial times: clockwise from upper right (**a**) a ship (Inthanoona Station); (**b**) a man with gun (Inthanoona); (**c**) a smithy building (Springs); (**d**) a woman in a long dress (Springs Station)

participation in the pastoral head stations suggests a regional pattern, whereby Aboriginal people were physically available for work. There is, however, little documentary nor photographic evidence such as that for Strangways Springs – there are few faces and few names, neither black nor white.

The largest colonial settlement was the port of Cossack, where the archaeological record reveals substantial campsites, where Aboriginal people camped adjacent to the European and Asian townsites. They relied heavily on collecting local shellfish, had some access to European commodities, and may have been occasionally involved in the pearling fleet. Aboriginal people were enmeshed with both Europeans and Asians (Carson 2003). The indigenous production of flaked glass artifacts reveals how new materials, such as glass, were incorporated into existing technological material traditions in an intensive fashion in the multiethnic zone (Wilson 2005).

A significant finding was of indigenous accounts of colonial life on Ngarluma people's country (Fig. 11.4). At four of the head station sites, there were historical rock engravings, a continuation of much older practice dating back thousands of years in the region (Paterson and Wilson 2009). The historical art at the pastoral stations suggests: (1) the presence of Aboriginal people and the continuation of rock engraving as narrative form; (2) that some art was produced with sight and hearing of the station and was thus probably not restricted to certain viewers, such as initiates; (3) a tendency for historical themed imagery to be located close to Europeans; (4) that a tight range of historical themes were worthy of depiction, including Europeans (male and female) and their clothes, horses, guns, pipes, hats, houses, and ships; (5) a potential shift toward more hastily executed historical art being less deeply engraved perhaps reflecting the greater time demands for those involved in pastoral work; and (6) a focus on certain aspect of the pastoral world over others – there are few sheep or goats for example, but many horses, and other images suggest a tendency to show guns (often being fired) and aspects of riding culture. The analysis of this assemblage is provided elsewhere (Paterson and Wilson 2009).

If, as argued, the laws of the colonial frontier were intended to allow pastoralists access to cheap Aboriginal laborers, then the archaeological record reveals something of this, with Aboriginal camps and contact-era rock engravings at early pastoral sites. In addition to the work at pastoral sites, both white pastoralists and Aborigines were involved with the pearling fleet. This is reported in historical accounts, one example provided by Donald McRae, the manager at Old Woodbrook Station, who wrote in the late 1870s: "I was very busy getting my darkies together for pearling. I have got a very good crowd this season, nearly forty and would have done good things if it had not been for these new regulations which will throw us back a bit" (McRae 1881). The exploitative relationship between pearlers and pastoralists as late as the 1890s was described by Arthur Bligh in his colorful account, *The Golden Quest*:

> The method of obtaining this labour is better imagined than described. It is sufficient to say it was crude. Many of the pearlers also owned blocks of country on which they usually ran sheep and cattle. On the runs the owners mainly used the old men and all the women and children to work and care for the stock, while the young men were diving … this generation of young men soon died out (Bligh 1984[1958]: 35).

The archaeological record at the pastoral sites provides information on the organization of the pastoral domain – the selection of locations in the environment was driven by concerns about water and pasture, ease of transport, and proximity of other stations. The abandonment of early head stations as dominant nodes across the colonial frontier suggests a reorganization of the sheep industry and the end of the first phase of the pastoral domain: possibly, some stations had been too close to each other and thus too small for profitable stock raising while others were in inaccessible regions. It is not clear in this study what role, if any, Aboriginal labor and environmental changes had in these changes.

Beyond culture contact, the archaeological sites provide information about frontier consumption patterns in a setting, where all goods had to be transported by ship, presumably at high cost. The voyage from Perth was hazardous and took many weeks. The analysis of the eight stations in the HAPP suggests that some stations had greater access to expensive imported consumer goods. The highest consumption was reported at the early Old Sherlock Station homestead, where a much larger relative proportion of the assemblage was devoted to decorated ceramics and luxury items.

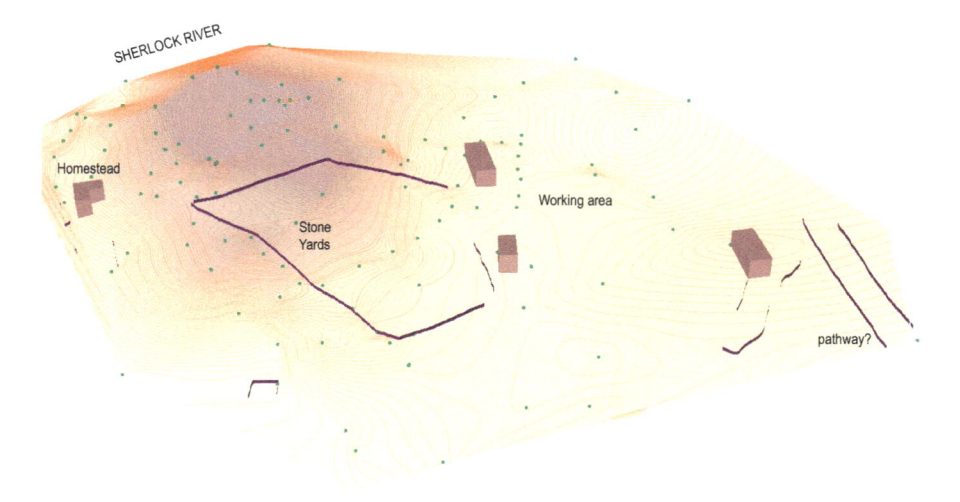

Fig. 11.5 Plan of Old Sherlock Station showing workers and residents separated by a low hill

The homestead was abandoned in the late 1880s following a fire after which a new head station was established at another site; thus, the archaeology provides a good insight into the first 20 years of the frontier sheep station. An intersite spatial analysis suggests that the greatest range of ceramic wares was found near what is interpreted as the house for the station manager, although transfer printed ceramics were used across the station by all workers (Fig. 11.5). The workers' precinct was characterized by communal stone buildings for work and living. The main house for the owner manager used high weight, high cost, and imported luxuries – such as wrought iron work presumably for a verandah, white marble and black slate stone for decoration of small formal rooms, such as the drawing room. The emphasis on tasteful consumption and wealth in this far-removed settlement seemed surprising, presumably this was part of deliberate process of social advancement aimed at fellow station owners, managers, and staff. Further spatial analysis of this and Inthanoona and Springs stations suggests strong spatial patterning in the archaeological record possibly related to difference between high-status residents (managers and owners) and low-status workers (both white and Aboriginal) (Smith 2008).

The material record of consumption and identity stands as complementary record to historical sources, which are very rare for the Northwest in the nineteenth century. Thus, archaeology provides fine-grained detail for a region, where little documentary evidence has survived. The indigenous rock art seems particularly significant given the great changes that occurred across indigenous society with the arrival of outsiders and their impact on Aboriginal life. Aboriginal people are still present in the region, and in some cases now hold Native Title over the land taken from them. The detail of the archaeological record appears to link people not only to long-held cultural ties to country, but also to historical narratives related to the arrival of whites. The character of British colonists requires further attention, as well as study into how colonization unfolded – this too seems well-suited to archaeological analyses, particularly into how different communities functioned and were organized along lines of ethnicity and status.

Conclusions

These instances of capitalist enterprises in Central and Northwestern raise further questions: Who was working? How was affordable labor gained? How did these regions involved in forms of mono-production relate to global economic forces? How important were cultural contacts and negotiations? In Australia, a dramatic transfer in the custodianship of country occurred, although much later than elsewhere. For example, in Europe, studies have focused on the late medieval transfer of land, its custodians, and its uses (Johnson 1996). In pastoral Australia, power differentials existed between Aboriginal people and others; employers and laborers; free and unfree individuals; those who have access to capital and those who did not; and high-status individuals and low-status individuals. Australia is considered to be a very egalitarian society, yet perhaps these studies reveal differentials in colonial society that do not fit comfortably with this idea.

An implication of these studies is that indigenous agency, often overlooked or hidden in colonial overviews, is potentially available in other ways – meeting the challenge of understanding those "people without history" Europeans encountered across the world (Wolf 1982). Important differentials occurred in colonial Australia, and we are beginning to better understand how some indigenous people "choose to resist, proactively or reactively, the emerging colonial order; others will choose to collude with the colonizers in such a way as to assist in the development of the colony while creating a niche for themselves in the emerging power structure" (Delle 1999: 13, cited in Jordan 2009: 34). An interesting aspect of Australian studies is that there is little discussion of the process of creolization. Perhaps this form of ethnogenesis did not occur in Australia as it did in other regions, although there are exceptions to this in the work of Lynette Russell on mixed sealing communities (Russell 2005). As argued here, the pastoral domain is a hybrid creation, although with great inequalities within it, and it is not convincingly clear if any "new" society grew out of a result of this fusion or not. I believe that the role of Aboriginal knowledge of landscape and environment in some contexts, like Strangways Springs and the Northwest, was significant and that the economic success of the pastoralists relied on their use of indigenous knowledge, as well as access to cheap labor. With work came new roles for males and females, and clearly gender is part of this shift that occurred in colonial work settings.

Another aspect of colonialism and power relationships is resistance. Resistance was employed as a strategy across Australia, sometime successfully. The ways that negotiation was employed and perhaps resulted in survival are less explicit, yet clearly a significant strategy. Maybe a key aspect is the demand for labor: if Aboriginal people were needed, then there was some power in that, despite the gross inequities. In many regions across Australia, Aboriginal people were pastoral workers until, somewhat perversely, the well-intentioned movement for equal wages in the mid-twentieth century had the effect of pushing indigenous people off stations and into towns across rural Australia.

Like elsewhere, the pastoral frontier was a place of consumption, with the archaeological record revealing how manufactured goods made their way into various colonial settings, opening a traditional Marxian interpretive model to include both settler and indigenous values. In many instances of culture contact around the world, Europeans traded across cross-cultural frontiers with groups with clear status differentials – in such cases, new items gravitate to high-status contexts in archaeological records. Aboriginal Australian societies were fairly egalitarian; thus, it is perhaps less clear in Australia what value goods had beyond functionality and curiosity – although again more nuanced studies of cross-cultural values of objects are coming forward (Harrison 2006; Jones 2007). Beyond artifacts, a sense of the importance of key elements of the colonial world from an indigenous perspective is suggested in contact rock art. In the Northwest and elsewhere in Australia, this includes new things, such as objects and novel activities, married with the maintenance of traditional motifs (Tacon et al. 2010).

The pastoral domain in Australia invites landscape approaches interested in transformations, both environmental and ideological. While studies like Leone's (1988) study of William Paca's garden have been popular, there are not many studies which link ideology to the material expression of pastoral Australia, although I suspect it is possible, as suggested by the heavy investment made at Old Sherlock Station and the fine-grained trends in status suggested in the distribution of archaeological material across these landscapes (see also Connah 2007; Smith 2008).

The binary concepts of "colonizer" and "colonized" equated with "Englishman" and "Aborigine" probably still dominate popular understanding of colonial Australia. The processes of culture contact over time as described here are significant tools to move forward from this simple idea and match up with studies in Australian history and anthropology. This is important in modern Australia as differences between Aboriginal Australia and the rest of Australia are still a strong focus of debate about land rights, human rights, self-determination, environmental and cultural resource management, regional and urban developments, and the role of past events in contemporary Australia. Today, Australia asks: Should there be a national reconciliation process? But things are not so clearly two-sided as they seem. There were differences in the ways that various Aboriginal people interacted with non-Aboriginal settlers – as shown for the pastoral domains in these studies, individuals were differentially committed to or resisted pastoralists, and some individuals held key roles in cross-cultural discussions and negotiations. Neither group is clear-cut: although dominated by British migrants, non-Aboriginal settlers came from diverse backgrounds across Europe and South and East Asia. Aboriginal communities often were an amalgamation of various surviving indigenous societies. Nor did all Aboriginal people assist each other, some capitalized by working their closer relationships with settlers. The ideas of the colonial landscape derived from Aboriginal and settler origins. For example, the pastoral industry was an icon of egalitarian Australia in the nineteenth and twentieth centuries, yet its roots lay in Aboriginal country, indigenous knowledge, a mimicry of resource use, competition between people and animals for precious resources, the ability to access capital, and differentials of power, ability, and wealth. The role of subalterns – both Aboriginal and not – in the creation of modern nation states can be in part measured archaeologically. Australia often looks to precontact indigenous society when it thinks of the Aboriginal past; however, there were important events in the contact period that help explain people – of Aboriginal and non-Aboriginal origins – in modern Australia. It may be easy to overstate this case, as in many places there was much less of a link between early settlers and Aboriginal people, and certainly over time the presence of Aboriginal people became spatially restricted – however, this extends beyond the scope of this chapter.

Part of the potential significance of these investigations is to modern communities. The situation described by Lightfoot (2005) for Native Americans in California finds parallels in Australia, where communities are expected to demonstrate their attachment to places almost despite the events of the colonial era and despite whatever strategies their ancestors took in these cross-cultural contexts. Native Title largely rests on demonstrations of precontact knowledge and practice (see papers in Lilley 2000). In a famous decision related to Yorta Yorta peoples' land claims, such claims could be washed away by the "tide of history" (Justice Olney, The Members of the Yorta Yorta Aboriginal Community v The State of Victoria & Ors [1998]).[4] Thus, knowledge of colonial events has direct implications for people in the present.

As a history of labor, it is interesting to point out that in the Pilbara in the 1940s Aboriginal works staged a massive strike and brought the sheep stations to a halt for a time. Aborigines had been paid in rations and clothes until the 1920s, and the minimum wage thereafter – they were paid less than whites. A grassroot movement led to a general strike involving 800 workers from many stations – the strike started on May Day 1946 and lasted 3 years. This was a major event in the recognition of Aboriginal rights and part of the shift toward being granted Australian citizenship, which only occurred in the 1960s.

To conclude with an anecdote, a few years ago I was involved in a collaborative project in central Northern Territory, where I was interested in the potential study of the precontact and colonial-era archaeological sites in the Murchison and Davenport

---

[4] Justice Olney found in his determination of native title that:

Where a clan or group has continued to acknowledge the laws and (so far as practicable) to observe the customs based on the traditions of that clan or group, whereby their traditional connection with the land has been substantially maintained, the traditional community title of that clan or group can be said to remain in existence. However, when the tide of history has washed away any real acknowledgment of traditional law and any real observance of traditional customs, the foundation of native title has disappeared. A native title which has ceased with the abandoning of laws and customs based on tradition cannot be revived for contemporary recognition.

[i] ... dispossession of the original inhabitants and their descendants has continued to the present time ... (para 121) ... The tide of history has undoubtedly washed away any traditional rights that the indigenous people may have previously exercised ... (18 December 1998)

ranges, a dominant set of landforms in the region. My colleague, a geographer, had interests in the range of historical activities in the ranges, such as pastoralism and mining, as well as environmental issues and indigenous involvement in these economic activities. The third project director was a Warumungu elder Murphy Kennedy (deceased). When we sat down to plan the fieldwork, we discussed which archaeological sites to target. While I was interested in the early contact-era sites, Murphy had radically different interests. Murphy and his family had identified the importance of a "walk-off" site – this was a campsite, where in the 1970s the local community people had lived after they left the local pastoral station in the era of equal rights for Aboriginal workers (Bell 1978). When wage equality was made law, many Aboriginal people were forced off sheep and cattle stations, and perhaps off their traditional country, to live in towns and other settlements. The walk-off camp was a place, where Murphy and his family lived for a time. Murphy though we should record the archaeology at the site, which we did (Paterson et al. 2003). Some interesting discoveries from that investigation related to site formation processes (Deacon 2002); but I suspect what was most important – not so much as scientific research but more as political and social action – was the use of archaeology to examine material aspects of *recent life* in what was clearly a landscape, where power was in flux – long-held notions of land ownership, Aboriginal people in Australia, and the environment were changing, and these sites were physical expressions of a time when race and racism, history, and reconciliation were big issues. They still are.

References

Allen, J. 2008 *Port Essington: the historical archaeology of a north Australian nineteenth century military outpost*. Studies in Australasian historical archaeology. Sydney University Press in association with the Australasian Society for Historical Archaeology, Sydney.

Bairstow, D. 1984 The Swiss Family Robinson Model: A Comment and Appraisal. *The Australian Journal of Historical Archaeology* 2:2.

Bairstow, D. 2003 *A Million Pounds, a Million Acres: The Pioneer Settlement of the Australian Agricultural Company*. Cremorne, N.S.W.

Bell, D. 1978 For our families: the Kurundi walk-off and the Ngurrantiji venture. *Aboriginal History* 2:32–62.

Birmingham, J. 1975 The Archaeological Contribution to Nineteenth-century History: Some Australian Case Studies. *World Archaeology* 7(3):306–317.

Birmingham, J. 1988 An Introduction: Colonial Perceptions and Archaeological Contexts. In *Archaeology and Colonisation: Australia in the World Context*, edited by J. Birmingham, D. Bairstow and A. Wilson, pp. 11–24. Australasian Society for Historical Archaeology, Sydney.

Birmingham, J., R. I. Jack and D. N. Jeans. 1979 *Australian Pioneer Technology: Sites and Relics: Towards an Industrial Archaeology of Australia*. Heinemann Educational Australia, Richmond, Vic.

Birmingham, J., R. I. Jack and D. N. Jeans. 1983 *Industrial Archaeology in Australia: Rural Industry*. Heinemann, Melbourne.

Birmingham, J. and D. Jeans. 1983 The Swiss Family Robinson and the archaeology of colonisations. *Australian Journal of Historical Archaeology* 1:3–14.

Bligh, A. C. V. 1984 [1958] *The Golden Quest*. facsimilie ed. Hesperian Press, Carlisle, Western Australia.

Burke, H. 1999 *Meaning and Ideology in Historical Archaeology: Style, Social Identity, and Capitalism in an Australian Town*. Contributions to global historical archaeology. Kluwer Academic/Plenum Publisher, New York.

Cantwell, A.E., and D. Wall. 2001 *Unearthing Gotham: the Archaeology of New York City*. Yale University Press, New Haven.

Carson, A. 2003 *Ah Kim's Garden: Ethnicity in the Archaeological Record at Cossack, Western Australia*. Unpublished Honours thesis, University of Western Australia.

Clarke, A. and A. G. Paterson. 2003 Cross-Cultural Archaeology: An Introduction. *Archaeology in Oceania* 38(2):49–51.

Connah, G. 2007 *The Same Under a Different Sky? A Country Estate in Nineteenth-Century New South Wales*. British Archaeological Reports, International Series 1625. Archeopress, Oxford.

Crook, P. 2008 'Superior Quality': Exploring the nature of cost, quality and value in historical archaeology. Unpublished PhD thesis, La Trobe University. Bundoora, Victoria.

Davidson, B. R. 1994 The development of the pastoral industry in Australia during the nineteenth century. In *Pastoralists at the Periphery: Herders in a Capitalist World*, edited by C. Chang and H. A. Koster. vol. 79–95. The University and Arizona Press, Tucson.

Davies, P. 2006 *Henry's Mill: The Historical Archaeology of a Forest Community*. BAR international series 1558: Studies in Contemporary and Historical Archaeology 2, Archeopress, Oxford.

Deacon, J. 2002 *A Spatial Analysis of Ngurrutiji, an Aboriginal Historic Site in Central Australia*, Unpublished Honours thesis, University of Western Australia.

Delle, J. A. 1999 'A good and easy speculation': spatial conflict, collusion and resistance in late sixteenth-century Munster, Ireland. *International Journal of Historical Archaeology* 3(1):11–35.

Egloff, B. J. 1994 From Swiss Family Robinson to Sir Russell Drysdale: towards changing the tone of historical archaeology in Australia. *Australian Archaeology* 39:1–9.

Egloff, B. J., M. O'Sullivan and J. Ramsay. 1991 Archaeology of the 1891 shearer's war: the main strike camp at Barcaldine, Queensland. *Australian Historical Archaeology* 9:63–75.

Florek, S. 1993 *Archaeology of the Mound Spring Campsites near Lake Eyre in South Australia*. Unpublished PhD thesis, University of Sydney.

Gaughwin, D. 1992 Trade, Capital and the Development of the Extractive Industries of Northeast Tasmania. *The Australian Journal of Historical Archaeology* 10:55–64.

Gill, N. and A. G. Paterson. 2007 A Work in Progress: Aboriginal People and Pastoral Cultural Heritage in Australia. In *Loving a Sunburned Country? Geographies of Australian Heritages*, edited by R. Jones and B. Shaw, pp. 113–131. Ashgate, Aldershot.

Gillen, R. S., Ed. 1995 *F.J. Gillen's First Diary 1875: Adelaide to Alice Springs, March to June*. Wakefield Press, Adelaide.

Gosden, C. 2000 Varieties of colonial experience: material culture and colonialism in West New Britain Province, Papua New Guinea. In *Australian Archaeologist: Collected Papers in Honour of Jim Allen*, edited by A. Anderson and T. Murray, pp. 161–170. Coombs Academic Publishing, The Australian National University, Canberra.

Gosden, C. 2004 *Archaeology and Colonialism: Cultural Contact from 5000 B.C. to the Present*. Topics in contemporary archaeology. Cambridge University Press, Cambridge.

Gosden, C. and C. Knowles. 2001 *Collecting Colonialism: Material Culture and Colonial Change*. Berg, Oxford.

Harrison, R. 2003 'The magical virtue of these sharp things': colonialism, mimesis and knapped bottle glass artefacts in Australia. *Journal of Material Culture* 8(3):311–336.

Harrison, R. 2004 *Shared Landscapes: Archaeologies of Attachment and the Pastoral Industry in New South Wales*. Studies in the Cultural Construction of Open Space. UNSW Press, Sydney.

Harrison, R. 2006 An Artefact of Colonial Desire? Kimberley Points and the Technologies of Enchantment. *Current Anthropology* 47(1):63–88.

Harrison, R. and C. Williamson. 2004 *After Captain Cook: the Archaeology of the Recent Indigenous Past in Australia*. AltaMira Press, Walnut Creek.

Howitt, A. W. 1859 Diary kept by A.W. Howitt on journey to Davenport Range Sept. 21, 1859 to Oct. 31, 1859. In *MS 9356 14a and 14b, 'A.W. Howitt Papers: Incomplete letters; misc. material'*, La Trobe Library, Melbourne.

Jack, R. I. 1985 The archaeology of colonial Australia. In *Comparative Studies in the Archaeology of Colonialism*, edited by S. L. Dyson, pp. 153–176. BAR International Series 233, British Archaeological Reports, Oxford.

Johnson, M. 1996 *An Archaeology of Capitalism*. Blackwell, Oxford.

Jones, P. G. 2007 *Ochre and Rust: Artefacts and Encounters on Australian Frontiers*. Wakefield Press, Kent Town, South Australia.

Jordan, K. A. 2009 Colonies, Colonialism, and Cultural Entanglement: The Archaeology of Postcolumbian Intercultural Relations In *International Handbook of Historical Archaeology*, edited by T. Majewski and D. Gaimster, pp. 31–49. Springer, New York.

Karskens, G. 1986 Defiance, Deference and Diligence: Three Views of Convicts in New South Wales Road Gangs. *The Australian Journal of Historical Archaeology* 4:17–28.

Lawrence, S. and N. Shepherd. 2006 Historical archaeology and colonialism. In *The Cambridge Companion to Historical Archaeology*, edited by D. Hicks and M. Beaudry, pp. 69–86. Cambridge University Press, Cambridge.

Lawrence, S. and M. Staniforth (editors). 1998 *The Archaeology of Whaling in Southern Australia and New Zealand*. Brolga Press, for the Australasian Society for Historical Archaeology and the Australian Institute of Maritime Archaeology Special Publication No. 10, Canberra.

Leone, M. 1988 The relationship between archaeological data and the documentary record: eighteenth-century gardens in Annapolis. *Historical Archaeology* 22:29.

Lightfoot, K. G. 1995 Culture contact studies: redefining the relationship between prehistoric and historical archaeology. *American Antiquity* 60(2):199–217.

Lightfoot, K. G. 2005 *Indians, Missionaries, and Merchants: The Legacy of Colonial Encounters on the Californian Frontiers*. University of California Press, Berkeley.

Lightfoot, K. G., A. Martinez, et al. 1998 Daily practice and material culture in pluralistic social settings: an archaeological study of culture change and persistence from Fort Ross, California. *American Antiquity* 63(2):199–122.

Lilley, I. 2000 *Native Title and the Transformation of Archaeology in the Postcolonial World*. Oceania monograph, 50. University of Sydney, Sydney.

Lydon, J. 2005 *Eye Contact: Photographing Indigenous Australians*. Duke University Press, Durham.

Magee, J. W. and G. H. Miller. 1998 Lake Eyre palaeohydrology from 60 ka to the present: beach ridges and glacial maximum aridity. *Palaeogeography, Palaeoclimatology, Palaeoecology* 144:307–329.

McBryde, I. 1987 Goods from another country: exchange networks and the people of the Lake Eyre Basin. In *Australians to 1788*, edited by D. J. Mulvaney and J. P. White, pp. 253–274. Fairfax Syme & Weldon Associates, Broadway, NSW.

McNiven, I. and L. Russell. 2005 *Appropriated Pasts: Indigenous Peoples and the Colonial Culture of Archaeology*. Walnut Creek, AltaMira Press.

McRae, D. 1881 Letters MS 287A. In *31/7/1881*. Perth: Western Australian Archives.

Meinig, D. W. 1988 *On the Margins of the Good Earth: The South Australian Wheat Frontier 1869–1884*. South Australian Government Printer, Adelaide.

Murray, T. 1988 Beyond the Ramparts of the Unknown: The Historical Archaeology of the Van Diemen's Land Company. In *Archaeology and Colonisation: Australia in the World Context*, edited by J. Birmingham, D. Bairstow and A. Wilson, pp. 99–108. The Australian Society for Historical Archaeology Incorporated, Sydney.

Murray, T. 2004 *The Archaeology of Contact in Settler Societies*. Cambridge University Press, Cambridge.

Murray, T. 2004 Exploring the archaeology of a vanished Melbourne community at 'Little Lon'. In *Archaeology from Australia*, edited by T. Murray, pp. 116–130. vol. 1. Australian Scholarly Publishing, Melbourne.

Oastler, J. 1908 Administration of Justice in the Back Blocks. *The Honorary Magistrate,* 1904–1907: 208–209. Mortlock Library of South Australiana, Adelaide.

Orser Jr, C. E. 1996 *A Historical Archaeology of the Modern World.* Plenum Press, New York.

Paterson, A. G. 2003 The Texture of Agency: An Example of Culture-Contact in Central Australia. *Archaeology in Oceania* 38(2):52–65.

Paterson, A. G. 2005 Early pastoral landscapes and culture contact in central Australia. *Historical Archaeology* 39(3):28–48.

Paterson, A. G. 2006 Towards a Historical Archaeology of Western Australia's Northwest. *Australasian Historical Archaeology* 24:99–111.

Paterson, A. G. 2008 *The Lost Legions: Culture Contact in Colonial Australia.* Indigenous archaeologies series. AltaMira Press, Lanham, MD.

Paterson, A. G., N. Gill and M. Kennedy. 2003 An Archaeology of Historical Reality? A Case Study of the Recent Past. *Australian Archaeology* 57:82–89.

Paterson, A. G. and A. Wilson. 2009 Indigenous Perceptions of Contact at Inthanoona, Northwest Western Australia. *Archaeology in Oceania* 44:98–110.

Pearson, W. 1996 Water Power in a Dry Continent: The Transfer of Watermill Technology from Britain to Australia in the Nineteenth Century. *Australasian Historical Archaeology* 14:46–62.

Pels, P. 1997 The anthropology of colonialism: culture, history, and the emergence of Western Governmentality. *Annual Review of Anthropology* 26:163–183.

Pels, P. 2008 What has anthropology learned from the anthropology of colonialism? *Social Anthropology* 16(3):280–299.

Reynolds, R. 1987 The Indenoona contact site: A preliminary report of an engraving site in the Pilbara region of Western Australia. *Australian Archaeology* 25:80–87.

Rowlands, M. J. 1998 The archaeology of colonialism. In *Social Transformations in Archaeology: Global and Local Perspectives.* K. Kristiansen and M. J. Rowlands, pp. 327–333. Routledge, London.

Rowse, T. 1998 *White Flour, White Power: From Rations to Citizenship in Central Australia.* Cambridge University Press, Cambridge.

Russell, L. 2005 Kangaroo Island sealers and their descendants: Ethnic and gender ambiguities in the archaeology of a creolised community. *Australian Archaeology* 60:1–5.

Silliman, S. 2005 Culture contact or colonialism? Challenges in the Archaeology of native North America. *American Antiquity* 70(1):55–74.

Smith, P. A. 2000 Station camps: legislation, labour relations and rations on pastoral leases in the Kimberley region, Western Australia. *Aboriginal History* 24:75–97.

Smith, S. 2008 *Early Pilbara Headstations: Spatiality and Social Relations.* Unpublished Honours thesis, University of Western Australia.

Souter, C. 2007 *Archaeology of the Iron Barque Sepia: An Investigation of Cargo Assemblages.* Unpublished Masters thesis, University of Western Australia.

Stahl, A. B. 1994 Change and continuity in the Banda area, Ghana: the direct historical approach. *Journal of Field Archaeology* 21:181–203.

Staniforth, M. 1987 The Casks from the Wreck of the William Salthouse. *The Australian Journal of Historical Archaeology* 5:21–28.

Stirling, E. C. 1896 Anthropology. *Report on the Work of the Horn Scientific Expedition to Central Australia.* B. Spencer (ed), vol.4, pp. 1–157.

Taçon, P. S. C., B. South and S. Hooper. 2003 Depicting cross-cultural interaction: figurative designs in wood, earth and stone from south-east Australia. *Archaeology in Oceania* 38(2):89–101.

Tacon, P. S. C., A. G. Paterson, et al. (2010) Picturing Change and Changing Pictures: Contact Rock Art of Australia. In *A Companion to Rock Art,* edited by J. McDonald and P. Veth. Oxford, Blackwell Publishing.

Thomas, N. 1991 *Entangled Objects: Exchange, Material Culture, and Colonialism in the Pacific.* Harvard University Press, Cambridge, Massachusetts.

Thomas, N. 1994 *Colonialism's Culture: Anthropology, Travel and Government.* Princeton University Press, Princeton, New Jersey.

Torrence, R. and A. Clarke. 2000 Negotiating difference: practice makes theory for contemporary archaeology in Oceania. In *The archaeology of difference: negotiating cross-cultural engagements in Oceania*, edited by R. Torrence and A. Clarke, pp. 1–31. Routledge, London.

Voss, B. L. 2005 From Casta to Californio: Social Identity and the Archaeology of Culture Contact. *American Anthropologist* 107(3):461–474.

Walker, M. 1995 The landscape of pastoralism. In *Pastoral technology and the National Estate*, edited by A. I. Inc., pp. 57–64. Australian Heritage Commission, Canberra.

Wilson, M. 2005 *Variation Amongst Glass Artefact Assemblages at Cossack, Western Australia*, Unpublished Masters thesis, University of Western Australia.

Wolf, E. R. 1982 *Europe and the People Without History*. University of California Press, Berkeley.

Chapter 12
Infrastructure and the Conduct of Government: Annexation of the Eastport Community into the City of Annapolis During the Twentieth Century

Matthew Palus

Introduction

The historical archaeology of sanitation reform in the USA describes a continuum between households that are "off the grid" – infrastructurally self-contained and relatively independent in regards to the management of waste and water – and households that are integrated into the "networked infrastructure" (Graham and Marvin 2001: 8) of municipal sanitary systems. Many have realized that there is a crucial relationship between these variables and local governance; discussion of privy abandonment and sanitation reform often follows a sequence of public laws authorizing certain privy forms and means of disposing of night soil and other waste (Demeter 1994; Ford 1994; Geismar 1993; Howson 1992/1993; Meyer 2004; Mrozowski et al. 1989; Parrington 1983; Stone 1979; Stottman 1995, 2000). Embedded in this narrative, wherein regulation and governance prompt an improvement in sanitation and public health, are many taken for granteds regarding the nature of government and the relationships that governance implies: the action of power to bring about regulation, observation, and surveillance of households and populations, abstractions and epistemologies of government, and so forth. Taken together, these matters remind us that government itself has a history, that there are styles of government from region to region and period to period, and that archaeological features, like privies and sewers – which produced this visibility of government in the first place – might allow us to expose these styles of local/regional/state government and increase the scope of urban historical archaeology beyond the house lot or the city block. "Because much of contemporary urban life is precisely *about* the widening and intensifying use of networked infrastructures to extend social power, the study of the configuration, management and use of such networks needs to be at the centre, not the periphery, of our theories and analyses of the city and the metropolis" (Graham and Marvin 2001: 34).

M. Palus (✉)
Department of Anthropology, University of Maryland, College Park, MD, USA
e-mail: matthew.palus@gmail.com

S.K. Croucher and L. Weiss (eds.), *The Archaeology of Capitalism in Colonial Contexts*, 269
Contributions To Global Historical Archaeology, DOI 10.1007/978-1-4614-0192-6_12,
© Springer Science+Business Media, LLC 2011

I propose that the extension of government through technologies of infrastructure in this North American context is homologous to the vision of capitalism in colonial contexts that gives this volume its theme. "Politics is also technics. The 'art of government' is part and parcel with the 'technologies of government'" (Henman 2006: 206). Peter Pels extends this notion in his review of the anthropology of colonialism, drawing a strong connection between Western governmentality, read as "a set of universalistic technologies of domination – a *Statistik* or 'state-craft'" (Pels 1997: 165), and the contexts and processes of colonialism that the contributors to this volume address. While there are important differences, perhaps most notably the militarization and overt repression that is present in colonial contexts, aspects of governmentality and especially the technical basis for operationalizing knowledge represent a commonality across these contexts. For most of anthropology, the problematization of government begins with Foucault's historical essay on the emergence of governmentality and liberalism (Foucault 1991) which is included in Sharma and Gupta's more recent reader *The Anthropology of the State* (Sharma and Gupta 2006). The themes and concepts that have emerged from this literature can help historical archaeologists in North America to find new focus in questions of government and power; the resulting engagement between "Western" or "local" and "colonial" or "foreign" contexts would be more closely aligned with the very hybrid nature of colonialism itself. Technology has long been a focus of anthropological investigations into the histories of colonialism (Kaplan 1995; Mrázek 2002; Pemberton 1994; Scott 1998). What are the historical and cultural implications of similar techniques being applied both to Western and colonial contexts? Is the framework of internal colonization (e.g., Caprotti 2007, 2008; Pfaffenberger 1990) legitimately applied to the history of government and its techniques in Western settings? How are the outcomes of projects of modernization – really projects to promote economic development that produce a surplus of consequences (Ferguson 1994) – comparable across these contexts? Are these projects executed simultaneously or is one modeled after the successes of the other? To explore these questions, I present accounts of the development of sanitary infrastructure in Annapolis, Maryland, and also of a gradual transition in the way that the City of Annapolis was governed, which hinged upon new discursive and technical apparatuses of which sanitation was a part.

Annapolis is a medium-sized city on the Severn River, one of seven rivers flowing east that contribute to the vast estuary of the Chesapeake Bay. Annapolis was settled during the seventeenth century and became the capital for the Maryland colony in 1694; it was an economic power as well as a political center for the colony during the mid-eighteenth century, and is still the capital of Maryland and home to the state government. During the early nineteenth century, Annapolis was overshadowed economically by Baltimore to the north, which experienced greater industrial development and also had a far deeper port and greater shipping capacity (Leone 2005: 5–6). Annapolis faced considerable economic decline, which Matthews (2002) addresses very closely. Events in Annapolis during the nineteenth and early twentieth centuries, including its reconfiguration as a historic city and a showcase for Maryland's colonial heritage, even its eventual gentrification, occur against a backdrop of deep economic fretfulness. Matthews relates the earliest efforts to

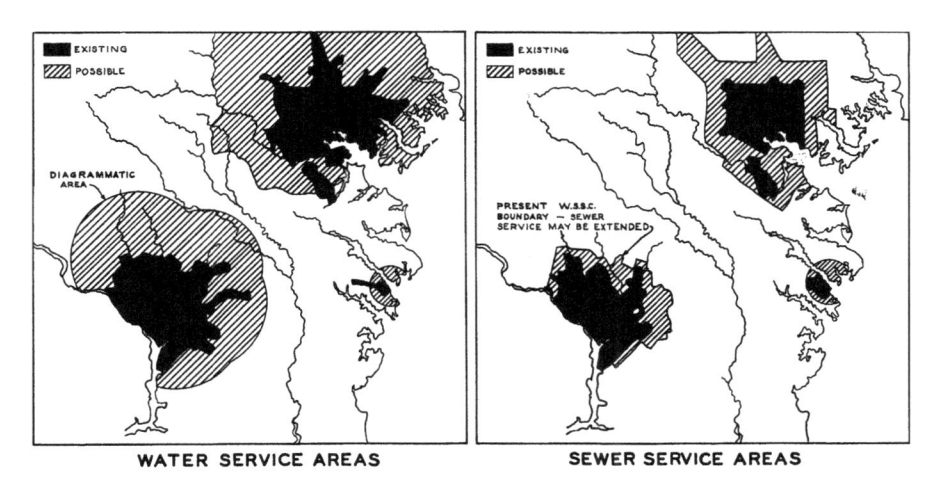

WATER SERVICE AREAS   **SEWER SERVICE AREAS**

Fig. 12.1 Detail of a regional plan published in 1937, depicting networked water and sewer infrastructure for Annapolis (*east*), Baltimore (*north*), and Washington D.C. (*west*) (Maryland State Planning Commission 1937: 52)

modernize Annapolis as explicit attempts to tie the city more securely into the political economy for the region in terms of transit and shipping, but also in the provision of urban infrastructure that would attract industry. Elites in Annapolis invested in the industrialization of light and water, with the establishment of gas light and municipal water utilities during the mid-nineteenth century (Matthews 2002: 23–25, 99–113). An extensive infrastructural network developed in Annapolis over the second half of the nineteenth century and the first part of the twentieth, but on a much smaller scale than neighboring Baltimore or Washington D.C. (Fig. 12.1).

The historical installation of broad municipal services in Annapolis, and arguably other places, constituted a new city that was buried under, erected over, and extended throughout the old. Utilities traced out existing relationships between people and institutions, and just as importantly they fixed those relationships in new ways with material forms. But further, the infrastructural networks that penetrated homes and at some point inevitably articulated with bodies also established an entirely new relationship among persons, things, and wider society. As material culture, the apparatuses for moving sewage and clean drinking water around the city performed in ways that material culture never had before. These networks were predicated on and incorporated new forms of authority, and engaged people in distinctive ways (e.g., Hughes 1983; Marcuse 1982; Schivelbusch 1988). In short, networks of utilities give evidence to a new materiality that developed during the later nineteenth century and came to define governed urban life (Graham and Marvin 2001; Osborne 1996; Palus 2005). This materiality was not limited to urban places, but rather extended to include rural areas during the early twentieth century, for instance with rural electrification, telephone, or irrigation networks (Fitsgerald 2002; Kline 2000). As these technologies were introduced in rural or urban contexts, there was a meeting of different materialities or different "object worlds"

(Meskell 2004: 2) such that one order of things, one system for organizing people, their homes and material lives, and their communities and their government was displaced or hybridized with another (after Castree 2006).

In the State of Maryland, government is historically trim with few governmental units or jurisdictions outside of the state government and the municipalities, the latter including counties and cities to whom a generous degree of "home rule" is delegated by the state (Spencer 1965: 2–4). Governmental authority in the USA is structured by a federation in which the federated states share their sovereignty with the federal government under the U.S. Constitution. A state in this context has much the same meaning as a state or a province in many other countries. Under the 10th Amendment to the U.S. Constitution, powers not specifically delegated to the federal government and not prohibited to the states are reserved for state governments. Individual state constitutions establish the delegation of powers to increasingly local levels of government. Counties represent the basic administrative division within most states and enclose large territories of urban and rural development. County governments in Maryland, as in many of the states, developed primarily around juridical and administrative record-keeping functions, such as registering ownership of land. In contrast, cities incorporated as municipalities are historically service-oriented in ways that the counties are not and provided for "regulation of public conduct and public health, the construction and maintenance of public thoroughfares and buildings, and ... the provision of limited protective – fire and police – services" (Spencer 1965: 6).

Urban archaeology in other North American settings has already demonstrated that the regulation of public conduct and public health has an origin that can be located archaeologically as well as discursively. In the archaeological studies referenced earlier in this introduction, the historical discourses on what Martin Melosi (2000) calls the "sanitary idea" or Graham and Martin's related notion of a "modern infrastructural ideal" (2001: 43) are used to explain the abandonment of privies and vaults as a system for managing wastes, and the embrace of networked infrastructure as the underpinnings of urban political economy. Considered more broadly, the regulation of conduct, exemplified here in the project of promoting public health, could also connect the historical modernization of municipal government with the modernization of its infrastructure. Authority is translated into material networks, becoming both unavoidable and to the extent that it is buried and forgotten, invisible (Williams 2008). In this sense, the sources and expressions of local governmental authority changed during the early twentieth century in a way that can be located archaeologically.

The substance of this paper is an examination of public services, specifically networked water, and sanitation infrastructure as the material culture of a political annexation, just as infrastructural improvements frequently represent a constituent material component of colonization. In 1951, the City of Annapolis annexed a neighboring community called Eastport and several other neighboring communities that had grown up around it over the nineteenth and twentieth centuries (Evening Capital [EC] 1950a). I consider the legal annexation of the Eastport community as the culmination of a long-term process, and I locate its foundations in the provision of public utilities, viewing infrastructural improvements as the gradual extension of government into new territory and more importantly the enclosure of new populations.

In particular, I look at a large sanitation project that took place between 1933 and 1937, which included both Annapolis and its newly constituted "metropolitan area," under the authority of an entirely new level of government between county and city, designated in 1931 as the Annapolis Metropolitan Sewerage Commission. The Eastport community, as part of the suburban fringe, was effectively governed by the City of Annapolis before it was annexed politically not only by the services that Annapolis provided, but also by the administrative apparatus that accompanied services. In the early twentieth century, the Annapolis city government was transitioning from a system rooted in nineteenth-century patronage toward liberal government. Documentary and archaeological data on construction of sewer, water, and storm drain infrastructure during the early twentieth century make this transition especially visible and open up these styles of government to discussion.

In looking at Eastport, I propose a frame in which disparate services are taken together as the materiality of its annexation and ultimately suggest that governmentality has its own materiality, which is legible in public utilities during the later nineteenth and early twentieth centuries. In other words, I suggest an examination of these features as the material culture of governing a population, rather than placing them immediately into the cultural context of sanitation. This is to say that sewers are about sanitation, but they are also about governing and power. The archaeological literature on sanitation and public health bore this possibility already; this essay presents my attempt to apply it in order to reveal "how the outcomes of planned social interventions can end up coming together into powerful constellations of control that were never intended and in some cases never even recognized" (Ferguson 1994: 19).

Eastport's Trajectory to Annexation

The community of Eastport is located on the western shore of the Severn River, on the first peninsula south of Annapolis called Horn Point (Fig. 12.2). In 1868, it was platted with 256 home sites on just over 100 acres of land by the Mutual Building Association of Annapolis, a corporation of investors from Annapolis and the surrounding county. Over the later nineteenth and early twentieth centuries, the neighborhood filled in with homes, churches, and businesses. Diverse classes settled there with emphasis on the maritime trades, such as boat building, oystering, and oyster shucking and packing. However, Eastport was also a pool of labor and domestic workers for neighboring Annapolis, and especially its major employer, the United States Naval Academy, a training center founded in Annapolis in 1845 as the naval equivalent to the U.S. military academy for the army at West Point. Thirty percent of Eastport households had at least one member employed at the Naval Academy at the time of the 1930 U.S. Census (Census 1930). Eastport existed as a distinct community in Anne Arundel County under the jurisdiction of the county government until it was annexed into the City of Annapolis in 1951 along with a number of other communities, making Annapolis the fourth largest city in the state of Maryland (Abdo et al. 1996: 4).

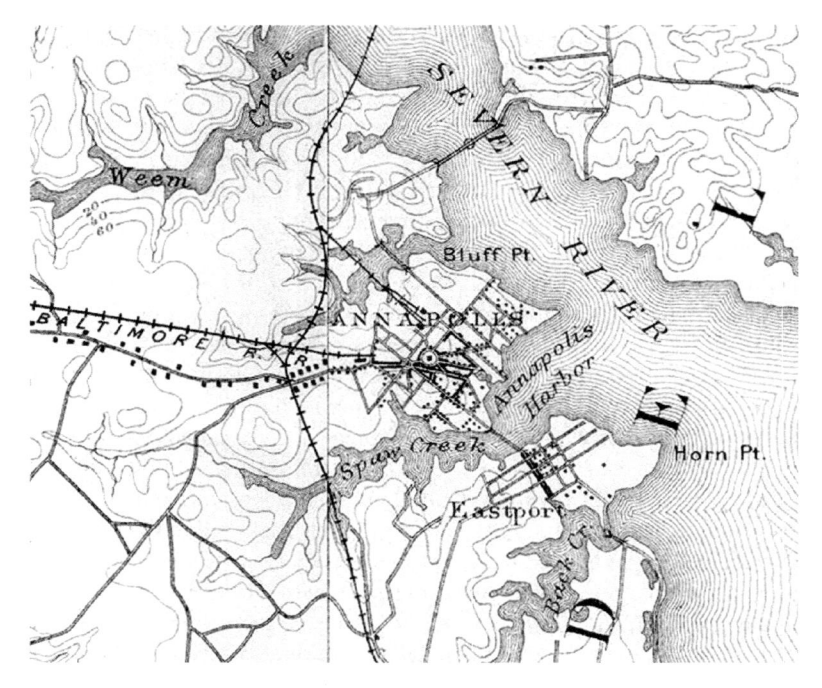

Fig. 12.2 Detail of 1892 topographic map depicting development and waterways around Annapolis and Eastport, also called Horn Point (U.S. Geological Survey 1892)

There was a minor building boom during the mid-1880s when a glass factory was established in Horn Point and a number of glass blowers settled in the neighborhood with their families. By 1886, there was a public school in Horn Point, several stores, and a shoemaker, in addition to the glass factory (EC 1886c). Back Creek was bridged in 1886, connecting Horn Point with agricultural land and beaches further south and creating a direct route for truck farmers and excursionists traveling between Annapolis and an area further south called Bay Ridge (EC 1886a). Opined a writer for the *Evening Capital*, a newspaper founded in Annapolis in 1884, "This village is assuming great proportions compared to what it has been some years back, and its close proximity to Annapolis, and its easy access, will no doubt, in the near future, be made an annex to the 'Ancient city'" (EC 1886b). This speculation on annexation – whether figurative or literal – is important because it establishes that the possibility of annexation and the presumed relationship between settlement in Horn Point and the growth of capital in Annapolis were alive in local discourses from the earliest development of the Eastport community. Settlers in Horn Point addressed this notion in a very direct way when they moved to incorporate their village in 1887, but the idea of annexation, and the discursive link between settlement and development in Horn Point/Eastport, and the accumulation of capital in Annapolis never faded, even where annexation itself was viewed negatively.

For instance, a meeting of Horn Point residents was held in May of 1887, in which local patriarch Charles J. Murphy stated his position on incorporating as an independent town:

> You are well aware that our village is growing in size and importance every day ... The question will be submitted to you tonight as to whether this village shall at some future time become a part of the city of Annapolis, and I trust that before you vote upon this question that you will give it deep thought as it must have a lasting effect upon your prosperity in the future. And I would also state that in the future this little meeting, simple as it may appear to us now, will be referred to as the pioneer meeting of what, may, at some time, become a great commercial city ... In regard to the matter of annexation to the city of Annapolis, I oppose such an act, for we cannot possibly reap any advantages there from ... and should this village be annexed to the adjoining city our taxes would be nearly doubled without any equivalent return for the same. (EC 1887)

As indicated in Murphy's comments (reminiscent of certain scenes in Paul Thomas Anderson's 2007 film *There Will Be Blood*), the premier matter that was voted on at the meeting was "Shall the village of Horn Point become now, or at any future time, a part of the corporation of Annapolis city?" The vote went unanimously against (EC 1887). While the seeming democracy of this moment may argue against the comparison with colonial contexts, plainly annexation was accomplished, and I argue here that infrastructure was the vehicle.

Beyond the seeming importance of Eastport as a zone for capital to grow outside of Annapolis, the living space that was opened up in Horn Point by its subdivision in 1868 created a historically important opportunity for African Americans to obtain homes, land, and therein prosperity. Few African Americans participated in the speculative moment that saw all land in Eastport transferred from the Mutual Building Association to other ownership between 1868 and 1900.[1] Yet census data reported between 1910 and 1930 show consistent increases in African American homeownership, until African Americans in Eastport match the rate of homeownership reported among families within the community that were enumerated as "white" (Palus forthcoming). By 1930, African American homeownership in Eastport far outstripped rates reported for African Americans in the City of Annapolis and also surrounding Anne Arundel County. Generally in Maryland, the rate of African American homeownership is higher in rural areas than in urban centers, such as Baltimore, perhaps revealing the degree to which suburban development created such opportunities. Slightly more than 60% of African American households in Eastport owned or mortgaged their homes in 1930, compared with 44% of African American households throughout the surrounding county and 22% of those

---

[1] This assessment of African American land acquisition in Eastport before 1900 comes from examination of grantor records available in the land records office of Anne Arundel County, in Annapolis, Maryland. Data was compiled from deed instruments filed with the county between 1868 and 1900 to produce a list of grantees acquiring land from the Mutual Building Association. Grantees were then identified by race using relevant censuses and city directories for Annapolis and its vicinity. From a total of 90 deed instruments, only two appeared to document the transfer of land to African American ownership.

in the City of Annapolis (Census 1910, 1920, 1930; Rogers 1918: 466–501; Steuart 1922: 1,282–1,283; Steuart 1933: 573–589).

There is generally a pattern of metropolitan population growth in Maryland between 1930 and 1960. In the development of several heavily populated urbanized counties, including Baltimore County surrounding the City of Baltimore, Prince George's County, and Montgomery County surrounding Washington, D.C., and Anne Arundel County surrounding Annapolis, population growth occurs outside of incorporated municipalities rather than within them (Spencer 1965: 8–11). This pattern accurately describes circumstances in the Annapolis area, where suburban expansion took place beyond its corporate limits within a series of neighboring unincorporated communities, like Eastport. Overall, in Maryland, the response to this pattern of metropolitan population growth was considerable transformation in the operation of government and the reallocation of authority:

> ... the reallocation of functional responsibilities, the creation of special districts, the establishment of new intergovernmental agencies and cooperative programs, and, of primary importance, the entrance of some county governments into what has previously been a traditional responsibility of municipal government. (Spencer 1965: 12)

By way of example, the State of Maryland approved an act allowing the creation of a Sanitary Commission in Anne Arundel County in 1922, granting the commission authority to lay out sanitation districts and to construct water and sewerage systems. That act specifically excluded the City of Annapolis from the authority of this commission, and the first county sanitary districts were set up further north in Anne Arundel County in communities closer to Baltimore (Maryland 1924). The creation of the Annapolis Metropolitan Sewerage District in 1931 would be another example of these coping strategies, allowing services to be provided to a population living largely outside of incorporated towns.

At the same time, it must be recognized that suburban populations, like those persons settling in the Eastport community, elected to take up residence outside of incorporated cities. The belt of development surrounding Annapolis, Baltimore, Washington D.C., and other urban centers in the region became semiautonomous zones, where African American wealth and political capital were concentrated (Johnson 2002). Such suburban communities, whatever their racial composition, are economically bound to adjacent urban markets, but they represent sovereign spaces as well. The *absence* of infrastructure is part of what makes them so. Households utilizing wells and privies have a tangible independence; they refuse the commodification of water resources and also elide the scriptural onus that accompanies networked infrastructure. These are households that leave a smaller historical footprint, a population that is less clearly visible to the apparatuses for governing because they are not so firmly engaged with the instrumentation that renders population visible. The expansion of service on a regional scale, as illustrated in Fig. 12.1 above, encloses and finally makes visible these spaces of suburban sovereignty, capturing population and wealth for the city to govern.

While special-purpose metropolitan districts assert a new level of government between the city and the county, the problem of providing services to suburban population can also be resolved through outright annexation of land. Annexation was the dominant mode of city growth during the nineteenth century, and other forms of city–county consolidation were influential in concept from ca. 1900 to 1945; however, the legislative maneuvers necessary to build these new entities were difficult to complete (Horan and Taylor 1977: xiii–xvi). Several annexations took place in Baltimore during the nineteenth and twentieth centuries. Population growth just outside of the corporate limits in Baltimore County resulted in a "Belt" of settlement around Baltimore with over 40,000 inhabitants by the mid-1880s. Efforts within the city to annex this territory began early in the second half of the nineteenth century. The State Constitution enacted in 1864 prohibited the transfer of territory from one county to another without the consent of the people in the territory, signified with a referendum vote on the annexation (Arnold 1978: 113–115). By this measure, Baltimore County and the City of Baltimore, which was treated like another county, campaigned for votes with the promise of services:

> City leaders were almost always anxious to expand the municipal tax base and political power, but during most of the nineteenth and twentieth centuries had to secure the consent of those to be annexed. The city thus had to make its offer attractive enough to win suburban favor, but no so attractive as to endanger municipal finances. (Arnold 1978: 109)

A referendum on annexation of "The Belt" into the City of Baltimore failed in 1874, but passed by a popular vote in 1888 with the added conditions of partial tax amnesty and tax freezes for 12 years following annexation. In anticipation of the 1920 census and with an eye on its standing among other American cities, Baltimore worked toward another annexation that was accomplished in 1918. This second annexation was accomplished through an act of the State Legislature, the "Greater Baltimore Bill," following a challenge to the constitutional requirement for a referendum on county-to-city as opposed to county-to-county transfers of territory (Arnold 1978).

There are few constitutional controls on the Maryland state government, where legislating the local is concerned. Conversely, because the Maryland Constitution prohibits little in the way of local legislation, much is accomplished at the local level through proposals to the legislature of "general–local" laws, often submitted by a senator or delegate from the county who acts as a legislative chief within that jurisdiction (Spencer 1965: 16). In other words, localities act through the state's power to legislate the local to accomplish desired programs at home, submitting legislative acts through their local delegates. This pattern was seen throughout the government records for the City of Annapolis during the later nineteenth and early twentieth centuries, where the legal councilor for the city drafts and submits state legislation addressing extraordinarily local concerns. The apparent relationship and interplay between municipal government in Annapolis and the state's lawmakers do not owe especially to Annapolis' role as state capital and home to the legislature, but rather describe the relationship of state power to local government throughout Maryland.

The intervention of the state government during the 1920s and 1930s was crucial in the conception and creation of the Annapolis Metropolitan Sewerage District and arguably in the reform and transformation of local government that accompanied this new governmental entity. Federal dollars fed into the project as well, though the district was established on paper and underway well before the organization of the Works Projects Administration (WPA), a federal agency created to promote economic recovery during the Great Depression by putting the unemployed to work largely on public projects. Federally funded public work projects during the Great Depression enabled many small- and medium-sized cities in the USA to install sanitation infrastructure and provide for treatment of sewage (Melosi 2000: 162–163, 210–211), but it is not clear to what degree federal intervention enabled the construction of new sanitation infrastructure in Annapolis during this period. Overall federal involvement in sanitation projects in Annapolis increased after 1934, beginning with some investment from the Civil Works Administration (CWA), precursor to the WPA (Annapolis 1935, 01/08/1934; McWilliams 2009).

Eastport, thus, developed as part of the suburban fringe of Annapolis, and the context for the annexation of Eastport is the "metropolitanization" of Annapolis. Metropolitanization is a trend in municipal government that began in the USA during the early twentieth century. It is a movement to improve the efficiency of government by reorganizing jurisdiction and authority and mapping a new governmental entity onto a complicated historical topography (Miller 2002; Sancton 2000; Stephens and Wikstrom 2000). I argue that constructions like sewer and water infrastructure at once materialize governmental power as it was extended into Eastport, and moreover that they lend themselves toward a certain kind of government. This discussion, therefore, draws together a complex formed from three things: first, a move from Annapolis seen as a small town with tight boundaries on its jurisdiction and authority toward Annapolis seen as a metropole; second, the modernization of Annapolis' government such that it came to resemble the form of rule that Foucault termed "governmentality" (1991); and third, the physical infrastructure that was put into the ground, as an archaeological trace and an apparatus that is central to both of these. I am composing a reply to a question posed by Mitchell Dean in his 1999 text on governmentality: "by what means, mechanisms, procedures, instruments, tactics, techniques, technologies and vocabularies is authority constituted and rule accomplished?" (1999: 31) Here, Dean is specifically addressing the style of government, its instrumentation, and, arguably, its materializations.

Governmentality, Techni, and Liberalism

Starting in the second half of the nineteenth century, there was an intensification and elaboration of government in Annapolis, an increase in the number and variety of governmental mechanisms aimed at providing for the health, safety, and security of the city's population. Especially relevant to Eastport is the documentary and archaeological data on two of these mechanisms and their infrastructural expressions: municipal water and sewer systems, which developed in Annapolis during the late 1860s and were extended into Eastport during the 1920s and 1930s. These systems each manifested concerns for cleanliness and public health, and they reflected the growing influence of the "sanitary idea" (Melosi 2000) in Annapolis during the later nineteenth century. However, this essay is not centered on changing ideologies of health and sanitation or even the idea of "improvement" as Tarlow has recently described it (2007), but rather takes these municipal services as a way to explore changing ideas about American government and their resulting implicitly racialized materialities.

This account of governmentality is drawn closely from Foucault's 1991 essay designating liberal government as a problematic and Colin Gordon's (1991) introduction to the volume in which it appears (Burchell et al. 1991), as well as other works published alongside these. I also rely on Mitchell Dean's text *Governmentality: Power and Rule in Modern Society* (Dean 1999), which is an extremely useful primer and reference. Matthew Hannah's *Governmentality and the Mastery of Territory in Nineteenth-Century America* (2000) influenced my approach as a historical study of the emergence of the U.S. Census as a tool of rational government in the second half of the nineteenth century, and this paper borrows from his framework as well. David Kazanjian's *The Colonizing Trick* (Kazanjian 2003) also exemplifies the contradictions inherent in nineteenth-century American governmentality – particularly in racialized notions of citizenship – and provides important context for my analysis of the material politics between Annapolis and Eastport.

The concept of governmentality is one that Foucault develops in his later scholarship, as an extension of his research into personal discipline (1977) and biopower (1990: 140–144) as complementary techniques of power that are crucial to the development of capitalism. Governmentality is the natural extension and eventual conclusion of Foucault's interest in this subject. Following Foucault (1991: 102–104), Mitchell Dean writes that:

> … 'governmentality' marks the emergence of a distinctly new form of thinking about and exercising power in certain societies … This form of power is bound up with the discovery of a new reality, the economy, and concerned with a new object, the population. Governmentality emerges in Western European societies in the 'early modern period' when the art of government of the state becomes a distinct activity, and when the forms of knowledge and techniques of the human and social sciences become integral to it. (Dean 1999: 19)

Thus, the core elements marking the historical emergence of governmentality are: first, the invention and institution of political economy, which resituates the source of wealth from land to production and duplicates at a societal scale what had heretofore been conceptualized as the wealth of families governed by a patriarch; second, the discovery through social science of population and the functioning of political economy as a natural fact with measurable parameters, combined with the emergence of social statistics as the "science of the state" (Foucault 1991: 96; also see Pels 1997: 165); and third, the expansion of the apparatus of security which incorporates the institutions implicated in Foucault's theories of discipline and biopower, but also includes the apparatus of economic regulation and fields of policy (Dean 1999: 9–39; Foucault 1991; Gordon 1991; Hannah 2000: 17–25). The "governmentalization of government" is the historical process at work; population is the object of governmental rule (Dean 1999: 19), but people are not governmentalized, governments are.

Geographer Matthew Hannah (2000) has used Foucault's theory of governmentality to explore the connections between the U.S. Census, western territorial expansion, and American government during the second half of the nineteenth century. Hannah's work chronicles the efforts of Francis A. Walker (1840–1897), who was superintendent over the U.S. Census in 1870 and 1880 and who, according to Hannah, "was probably the single most important early American proponent of what we would now call governmentality" (2000: 3). Walker's work to mold the census into an instrument for scientific governance reveals the state of government in nineteenth-century America vis-à-vis Foucault's theories. Hannah describes the tension between waning paternalism and emerging government by experts over the period of his study, ca. 1850–1900. In effect, he describes the emergence of a governmentalized federal state at the end of the nineteenth century, highlighting the census as a premier tool for envisioning the nation as a territory with a population and an economy to be administered.

Hannah's research inspires this question: If the federal state is not markedly governmentalized before the end of the nineteenth century – Hannah's thesis is that the national census was transformed into an instrument for liberal government through Francis A. Walker's vision – what of state and municipal governments? When do they begin to conceive of their citizenry as a population to be administered? When do they develop the instrumentation and the tactics to carry out this project? Sewer and water infrastructure, their representations, and the discourses that surround them promise to help us to detect similar transformations at these local levels. Like the census, they are a part of the instrumentation of the state, a part of what Foucault calls the apparatus of security. This observation suggests the value of a governmentality framework for interpreting the traces of public services and utilities infrastructure that archaeologists so frequently encounter in contexts from the later nineteenth century to the middle of the twentieth century (cf. Barry 1996; Osborne 1996).

Governmentality has clear relevance for histories of colonialism and its importance extends into recent contexts as well, as further consequences of liberalism continue to erupt. Governmentality is one of the themes that emerges from James Ferguson's influential study of development and its many meanings, as it was applied during one project in Lesotho in southern Africa during the 1970s and 1980s (Ferguson 1994). In that context, he concluded:

> … the 'development' apparatus in Lesotho is not a machine for eliminating poverty that is incidentally involved with the state bureaucracy; it is a machine for reinforcing and expanding the exercise of bureaucratic state power, which incidentally takes 'poverty' as its point of entry – launching an intervention that may have no effect on the poverty but does in fact have other concrete effects. Such a result may be no part of the planners' intentions – indeed, it almost never is – but resultant systems have an intelligibility of their own. (Ferguson 1994: 255–256)

The present study holds to a very similar conception of the relationship between elaboration in networked public services and the expansion and intensification of governance as an outcome.

Other scholars have been drawn to networked infrastructure as a rich point for analyzing neoliberal policies in postcolonial settings (Harris 2009; Harvey 2005; Ioris 2007; Larner and Laurie 2010; McCarthy and Prudham 2004; Sangameswaran 2009; Walker et al. 2008). In his account of the development and more recent privatization of water for drinking, irrigation, and hydroelectric power in Brazil, Antonio

Ioris proposes that "Utility privatization is one of the main ordeals neoliberal globalization policies impose on countries in the global South" (Ioris 2007: 39). The present study, which registers a transformation in government in Annapolis as a shift toward classical economic liberalism, is largely anterior to the discourses of development that are the focus of anthropological research on neoliberalism. The resources and infrastructural capital being privatized under neoliberal economic policies (e.g., Harris 2009; Ioris 2007; Sangameswaran 2009) were first assembled under a somewhat different ethos, as part and parcel of liberal governance earlier in the twentieth century. What draws these instances together – programs of development, privatization, and direct colonial applications of technical apparatuses – are the techniques applied in the production of knowledge and the specific mode of statecraft that takes political economy for the object of governmental projects.

Caprotti (2007, 2008) uses the expression "internal colonialism" to describe the modernization projects of fascist Italy, specifically the creation of a series of New Towns and the frequently coerced relocation of Italian citizens to "colonize" a region of reclaimed marshland south of Rome called the Pontine Marshes, beginning in 1928 and continuing throughout the 1930s (2007: 85, 116). He writes,

> The Pontine Marshes project was a deeply modern enterprise imbued with all the defining characteristics of a modern meta-project: reliance on technology and technical-scientific knowledge, a progress-based conceptualization of the project, the fetishism of technology, and the use of statistics and the 'objective' sciences to justify what were in reality social projects. (Caprotti 2007: 183)

The projects Caprotti describes are linked with those fascist projects that González-Ruibal approaches in Ethiopia (2008), and elsewhere designates as the failures of modernity (2006), and yet the reclamation and resettlement of the Pontine Marshes, which mobilized technologies of infrastructure, statistical knowledge, and specifically fascist discourses of planning and modernity, produced viable communities rather than ruin, albeit representing an engagement with modernity that was at times "uneasy" (Caprotti 2007: 98). Both of these perspectives remind us that social and material expressions of modernity are at all times imperfect, and these studies promote this focus as a point of entry for historical archaeological inquiry: modernity, in success and failure, is never without its surpluses of consequence and meaning and never seamless. In the Pontine Marshes project, Caprotti finds this seam large enough to climb inside; in the context of U.S. history, racial ideology and the ongoing formation of racial meanings promote the same availability to critical analysis.

While Caprotti does not follow this line of analysis, it could be said that the project to reclaim and settle the Pontine Marshes promoted or performed the governmentalization of the fascist Italian state through the exercise of techniques of government similar to those described in this chapter, especially the application of social and demographic statistics in service to authoritarian projects to manage population (Caprotti 2007: 122–126). Thus, "the regime's planning institutions constructed urban, rural, and agricultural realities embodied in the colonists who, willing or not, came to populate this vast socio-technological experiment" (Caprotti 2007: 167).

It is difficult to parse the understanding of liberalism that is promoted by the notion of governmentality from discussions of neoliberal policies in the contemporary global economy. For Foucault, liberalism signifies a pervading governmental apparatus of knowledge and control. Neoliberalism, in contrast, references privatization of erstwhile public assets. How can these liberalisms be reconciled? For Foucault, the apparatus of security works with some subtlety, despite its tendency to broaden its every operation. It safeguards, but does not interfere in the flows of capital, in concept if not in execution. Foucault, therefore, challenges us to consider neoliberalism in historical terms, as one moment in a broader genealogy of capital and its organization.

Public Works, Patronage, and Liberal Government in Annapolis

Governmentalization in Annapolis is a long-term process and it is expressed more clearly in some areas of the city government than in others. For instance, the operation of the city's water utility, established in 1865 (Annapolis Water Company 1867), followed Foucault's model of liberal government very closely while over the same term of years, municipal sewers were frequently installed through the intercession of city council members as favors to their constituency, rather than being applied to improving sanitation in a systematic way. The archaeological data also show that wells and privies were still in use in Annapolis at the turn of the twentieth century, indicating redundancy with and perhaps class- and race-based access to networked sanitary systems developing since the 1860s (Palus 2009: 191–200, Appendix D).

Wells, privies, and cisterns were maintained for use in Eastport well into the twentieth century. Where only a few public wells remained in Annapolis after 1900, water was still being pumped from Eastport wells until the late 1920s and perhaps in some cases as recently as the 1960s (Palus 2009). House-to-house plans of the sewer system installed in Eastport between 1934 and 1937 show exactly how each dwelling was connected with municipal water and sewer infrastructure, and the plans also show which houses were not connected to the sanitary system at all (Fig. 12.3). Quantitative analysis of these plans clearly reveals that service broke down along lines of race and to a lesser degree along lines of class. This has bearing on the question of how Eastport was governed and eventually annexed by Annapolis. Does uneven service imply uneven governance or perhaps resistance to governance and annexation?

Hannah (2000) posits patronage as the historical antecedent and ongoing countertrend to governmentality. The operation of patronage as a style of government in Annapolis can be illustrated from the minutes of the meetings of the Mayor and City Council, as in the following excerpted passages from three different meetings in 1927 and 1928:

> Alderman Tucker brought before the Council request of Mr. Mayer for extension of sewer in Spa View Heights to connect the new house now under construction. After some discussion Alderman Phipps made a motion which was adopted that this be referred to the Street Committee with power to act and if favorable that it advertise for bids (Annapolis 1927: 200).

> Alderman Fisher stated that people living on Wagner Street could get water only after midnight and it would be impossible for a man desiring to do so, to install a heating plant on account of the water supply, the street having a supply pipe of only 1 1/2, and requested that

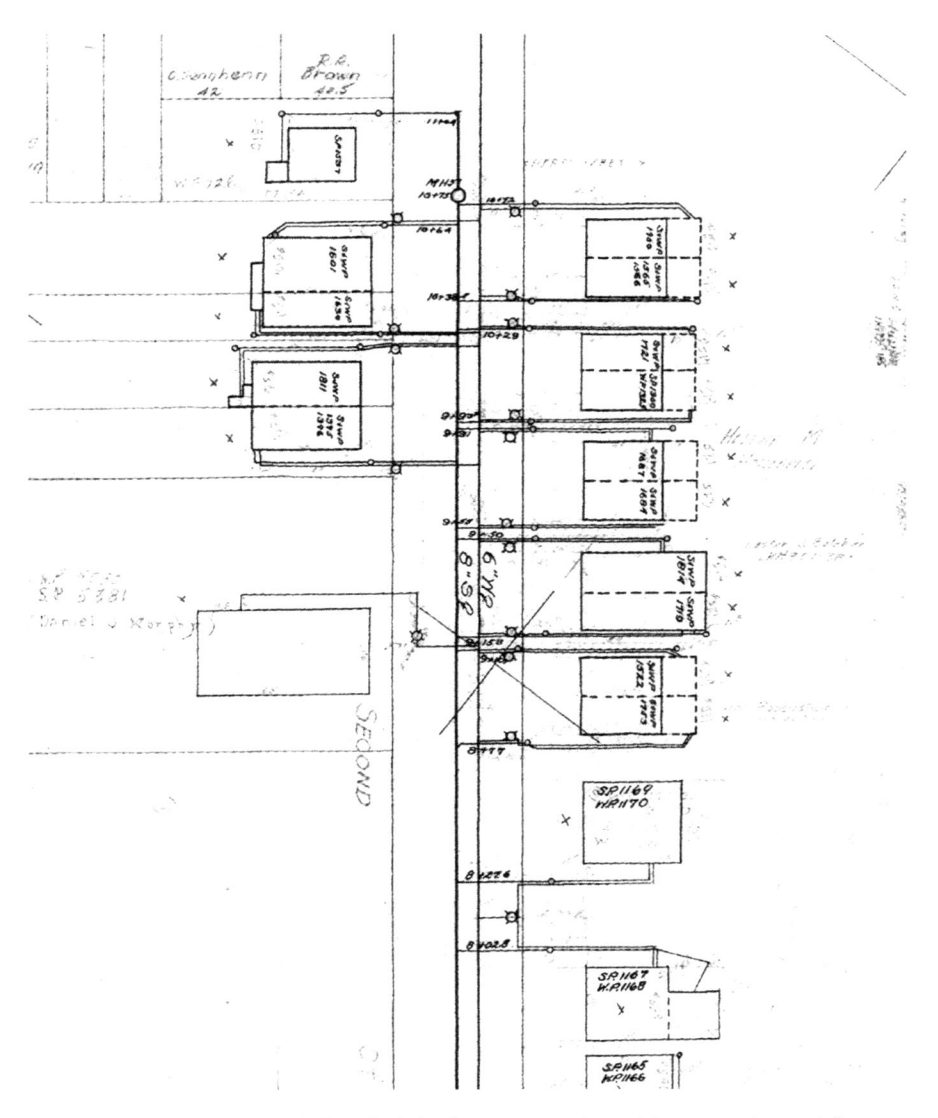

Fig. 12.3 Detail of street-level plans depicting house connections with sewer and water infrastructure installed in Eastport between 1927 and 1937 (Annapolis Metropolitan Sewerage Commission 1932–1937; courtesy of the City of Annapolis Department of Public Works)

the members of the City Council now on the water board look into this matter so that the existing condition can be remedied as soon as possible. (Annapolis 1927: 126)

Mr. Keith Worthington of Monroe Court addressed the Board and stated he was speaking not only for himself but for others living in Munroe Court saying that when it rained the water would back up in their cellars and requested that the street be paved and in his opinion this would remedy the nuisance of having water in their cellars every time it rained. This was also referred to the Street Committee. (Annapolis 1928: 196)

These passages address the state of Annapolis' infrastructure, but more important here is the structure of these and similar requests. In contrast to this style of government, where citizens go to the City Council and ask for things often with support from one council member or another, the installation of sanitary infrastructure in Annapolis and its wider metropolitan area during the 1930s begins to reveal an entirely different epistemology of government.

There was a perceivable change in the conduct of government in the city of Annapolis as the municipal infrastructure serving the city and its suburban fringe was enlarged and elaborated. The conduct of government was by degrees disarticulated from established social networks that gave shape to the power of the city council throughout the nineteenth century. Rather than meeting face-to-face with their representatives in city council chambers, people in Annapolis contacted the city government more and more through the mediation of municipal services as, for instance, municipal water and sewers introduced new routines and embedded people within new relationships of surveillance, administration, and power. Policy, regulation, and the more *impersonal* operation of bureaucracy began to replace patronage as the guiding principle of government. And, there is a material trace of the ongoing "governmentalization of government" in Annapolis in the public services that were set in place during the later nineteenth and early twentieth centuries.

In 1925, the city council had begun to discuss improvements to the existing water reservoir for Annapolis and its distribution network, asking "Is Annapolis ever going to be called on to furnish water to the U.S. Naval Academy, Eastport, West Annapolis, and all suburban sections? If so, when and on what terms?" (Smith 1925: 17) Plans for improvements were drawn up by 1927; later in that same year, the city council met with a representative of the State Health Department who laid out the possibilities for a metropolitan sewer and water district (Annapolis 1927: 66–67). From 1927 onward, the two efforts grew into one project, with improvements to existing water and sewer infrastructure and the extension of service to neighboring communities outside of the corporate limits of the city. The Maryland State Board of Health was instrumental in this, for instance calling together a conference that included representatives of the Annapolis city council, commissioners of the surrounding county, and members of the Annapolis Water Board to discuss the future metropolitanization of Annapolis and the relationship that these various agencies would have (Annapolis 1926: 3–4).

A plan for the Annapolis Metropolitan Sewerage District printed in 1931 depicts the territory that the new sewerage commission would oversee (Burwell 1931; Wolman 1926) and encloses all of the communities that were annexed by the City of Annapolis in 1951 (Fig. 12.4). Scale plans of the sewer, water, and storm drain networks were also made, with deed references, customer numbers, and the locations of individual house connections depicted for every structure that received service (Fig. 12.3 above). In addition to this, there is a photographic record of this sewer building project (Commission 1932–1937; Doyel 2008: 184) which largely seems directed at protecting sanitation authorities from liability for damage to property resulting from installation work, but also closely documented the construction of the first sewage treatment plant for the sewerage district and a pumping station

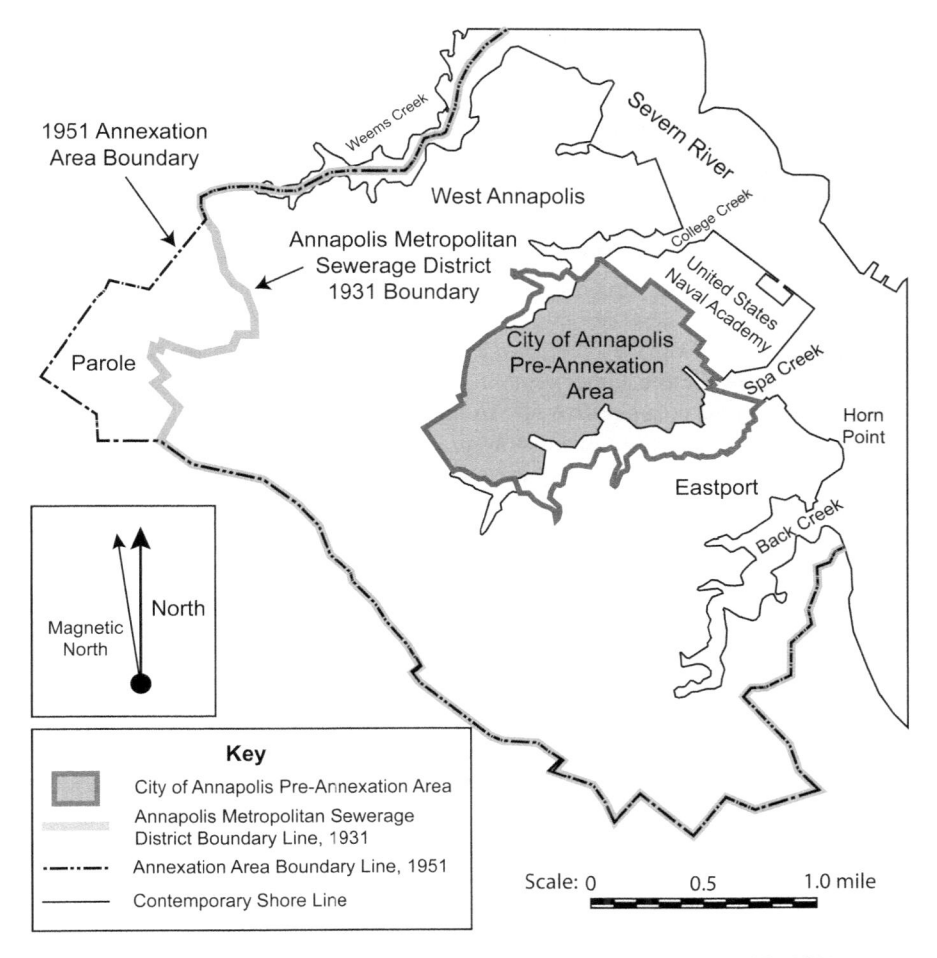

Fig. 12.4 Overlay comparing the Annapolis Metropolitan Sewerage District and the 1951 annexation area, including Eastport and other adjacent communities (source: Burwell 1931; EC 1950b)

located in Eastport. This extensive documentation is itself an important component of liberal government in that it produced a new visibility for this population and fixed Eastport within an administrative apparatus; when we consider the "discovery of population" in Eastport and the instrumentation of the state, this is precisely what we are talking about.

The role of the Maryland State Board of Health in this project is central to an understanding of the "governmentalization of government" in Annapolis. In essence, this transition away from the patronage system, where sewer lines were asked for and sometimes received, was promoted by the state government. Similarly, some of the elements of liberal government were absent in Annapolis, but were present at the state level. For instance, the state health board promulgated regulations, and more importantly it conducted surveys of sanitary conditions across the state, creating a new and different visibility for sewerage as a factor in public health.

"As-built" plans of Eastport's sewer, water, and storm drain infrastructure were produced by the Annapolis Metropolitan Sewerage Commission between 1932 and 1937 (Annapolis Metropolitan Sewerage Commission 1932–1937), though Sanborn Company insurance maps (1930) and the above mentioned photographic record for the project indicate that municipal water was introduced to Eastport starting in 1927 and sewer lines were installed starting in 1934. These plans detail house connections to sewer and water infrastructure and show a variety of ways in which houses accommodated these new services. For instance, in many cases, sewer and water connections extend from the street, past the house, and into a small addition depicted at the rear of the structure. Other structures introduce these services directly into the front of the residence, suggestive of a different accommodation for plumbing as a new component of dwelling. Interestingly, at 11 households, the plans show sewer and water lines extending to a privy or small outbuilding at the rear of the lot, sometimes with no connections made to the dwelling at all. There are 132 homes without service, around 16% of the homes depicted on the as-built plans.

The 1930 U.S. Census introduces demographic information to this data (Census 1930). In all, 594 households were enumerated in Eastport during the 1930 census, and many households were identified by their street address. A proportion of these, equaling 244 households, could be linked across these two records.[2] Cross-tabulating data from the sewer and water plans with the race variable in the 1930 census draws out some relevant patterns in how these services, and the populations that they serviced, may have been racialized. Population is being discovered in these representations, which then become tools for governing; the services are racialized, but the population being administered is also racialized by these instruments in new ways. In this sense, networked infrastructure and its sustaining discourses are techniques of government that make manifest racial differences in the population under governance. The 244 enumerated households in the sample include 66 African–American families and 177 households coded as "white," including a small number of European immigrants. One-third of these African–American households were not connected to municipal sewer or water. A much smaller proportion of white households were without service; eight and a half percent were not connected to city sewer, and a little more than 12% were without running water (15 and 22 households, respectively). Several plumbed privies occurred at both African–American and white-identified households.

---

[2]The fit between these two records is a theoretically challenging issue. Street addresses were not recorded for households on a number of residential streets in Eastport during the 1930 census. House numbers do not appear consistently in Sanborn fire insurance maps made for Eastport in 1930 either, and it is possible that house numbers were not assigned universally at that time. What is at stake here, however, is the historical visibility of a proportion of Eastport's residents. Transparency to the historical record implies transparency to the apparatuses of governing that depended on these same records. "The finitude of the state's power to act is an immediate consequence of the limitation of its power to know." (Dean 1999: 16) How the state knows, its instrumentation for knowing, is also how it governs.

Because infrastructure, like municipal water and sewers, define the color line so clearly, we can consider these technologies as racial materialities, as race-in-process, by looking at how municipal services were apportioned and how these services identified people more clearly to their racial types. The sanitary system as an apparatus of security becomes a part of the ongoing construction of race, even as the sanitary system emerges from the changes in how Annapolis was governed at the end of the nineteenth century and early in the twentieth. Furthermore, if services like municipal sewers can be described as the material culture of government, what does the relative rate of connection and disconnection signal about how communities of different races in Eastport were governed? How is the relationship between each household and the municipal infrastructure the work of agency? (cf. Ford 1994).

This last consideration becomes a central interpretive concern. If a far greater proportion of African–American households were not accessing municipal services from Annapolis, does this mark them as victims of systematic disinvestment, victims of the economic violence that constrained opportunities for African Americans after their emancipation from slavery, and promote their continuing poverty? Or can it also – not instead of – mark them as resistors to their own incorporation as a governable population, resistors to the commodification of water as a natural resource, resistors to the terms of their governance being suddenly changed, and ultimately as resistors to their annexation into the City of Annapolis?

Conclusion

In a recent commentary, Noel Castree writes, "neoliberal practices always … exist in a more-than-neoliberal context," resulting in "unevenness in terms of process and outcome: neoliberalisations in the plural" (Castree 2006: 3). Each case in this plurality can be read as "a qualitatively distinct phenomenon in its own right: namely, an articulation between certain neoliberal policies and a raft of other social and natural phenomenon" (2006: 4). Legal implementation of racial ideology in the USA during the early twentieth century exemplifies the sorts of concerns articulating with, in this instance, the implementation of progressive reform in government that is designated by the notions of liberalism and governmentality. When the metropolitan-wide sanitation project described above is compared with earlier styles of service, real contrast reveals the advancing yet incomplete "governmentalization of the state" (Foucault 1991: 103) in this local context. This case exposes the hierarchical relationship between the city government of Annapolis and the Maryland state government emergent during the early twentieth century, in that this Depression-era sewer building program was largely prompted by action at the level of the state. Just as the City of Annapolis extended its political power to neighboring Eastport, it was itself subject to new and profuse state powers over the same period of time.

Many would anticipate that access to services will be racialized and that the extent of services provided to Eastport will be incomplete, exposing class and color lines. In the context of this research – which sees a convergence of government and public services infrastructure – lack of coverage in public services may suggest a curious gap in the governance of this community and the in-fact racialization of government. Importantly, the rate of homeownership among African Americans in Eastport is approximately equal to that of white households in the community at the time of the 1930 census, around 60%, far above what is seen historically in Annapolis and across the state (Palus 2009: 300–320; Schweninger 1990: 180). This helps us to interpret the disparity in service. African Americans in Eastport wielded substantial economic power. Rather than representing a neglected population, the void may just as well indicate an exit from the multiform tactics of governance that are implied by service. Interpretation of the racialization of utilities and the partiality of the program of governing become some of the most crucial elements of this history. This creates the opportunity to take apart the elements of rational government as Foucault and others have portrayed it and reimagine aspects of Eastport's social history according to that model.

This new materiality, inextricably linked with government, is predicated on social control through exhaustive knowledge of population, which is produced by the wider infrastructure that becomes a sort of machine for rendering population visible and regularizing behaviors. However, this apparatus is in places blind, which is partly a consequence of race. In that there are racial differences, utility lines retrace the color line and intensify the meaning of racial identifications. I propose that racial differences embedded in certain public services in Eastport can yield an account of African–American agency, resistance, and ultimately the achievement of a measure of autonomy and self-determination, rather than yielding only an account of structural, race-based disenfranchisement. Disconnection suggests the agentive capacity to push away from governance and defend the limited sovereignty that suburban settlement presented to African Americans prior to this intensification of government, this deployment of new and elaborate apparatuses, and this burgeoning imperative to govern.

The emergence of that imperative is marked here most conspicuously by the new instrumentation providing for economic security. Infrastructure for water and sanitary sewers were only a portion of the overall networked infrastructure put in place in Annapolis during the later nineteenth and early twentieth centuries, as in other contexts for urban modernization. The locus for technical modernization is not only where archaeologists find it with the abandonment of much of the infrastructure for the earlier nineteenth century, exemplified here in the archaeological features comprising filled wells and privies. It manifests as well in the discourses of government, in the representations of population that guided development, and in the very corpus of historical records that make historical archaeology distinctly compelling but also challenging. That base of knowledge is enabled by an apparatus that is contiguous with the physical infrastructure and also more distantly contiguous with the techniques and discourses of colonial administration.

Acknowledgments I would like to thank Lindsay Weiss and Sarah Croucher for giving me an opportunity to present these ideas at the meeting of the Society for Historical Archaeology in Albuquerque in 2008, and also for their suggestions toward shaping this piece for publication. Historians Jane McWilliams and Jean Russo allowed me to make use of their primary documentary research on public utilities in Annapolis, which was a crucial supplement to my own limited time in the archives. Paul Lackey in the Annapolis Department of Public Works provided copies of original plans of the sewer and water infrastructure in Eastport. Historic photographs of the 1930s sewer project are held by Thomas and Pamela Dawson of Edgewater, Maryland, and were loaned to me by Ginger Doyel, as she was preparing her own book about the Eastport neighborhood. I am also grateful for encouragement and assistance received from Nan Rothschild, Mark Leone, Christopher Matthews, Lynn Meskell, Paul Mullins, Jenn Babiarz, Martin Hall, and others who have pulled for me. It all helped.

References

Abdo, Gaith, Gilda Anroman, Brian Jay Dyson, John Harmon, Terrie Hruzd, Carl Morgan and Trish Radigan. 1996 *Eastport Neighborhood Study, Annapolis, Maryland.* University of Maryland College Park, College Park.

Annapolis, Mayor and City Council of. 1926 Proceedings of the Mayor and Aldermen of Annapolis, Volume 23. On file, Maryland State Archives M49-23 (1/22/2/5) Original Municipal Records, Mayor and City Council of Annapolis., Annapolis.

Annapolis, Mayor and City Council of. 1927 Proceedings of the Mayor and Aldermen of Annapolis, Volume 23. MSA M49-23 (1/22/2/5) Original Municipal Records, Mayor and City Council of Annapolis. Maryland State Archive, Annapolis. Maryland State Archive, Annapolis.

Annapolis, Mayor and City Council of. 1928 Proceedings of the Mayor and Aldermen of Annapolis, Volume 23. Original Municipal Records, Mayor and City Council of Annapolis. Maryland State Archive, Annapolis.

Annapolis, Mayor and City Council of. 1935 Proceedings of the Mayor and Aldermen of Annapolis, Volume 24 (1931–1935). Original Municipal Records, Mayor and City Council of Annapolis. Maryland State Archive, Annapolis.

Annapolis Metropolitan Sewerage Commission. 1932–1937 Eastport Sewer, Water and Storm Drains, Detail Drawings. On File, Department of Public Works, Annapolis, Maryland.

Annapolis Water Company. 1867 The First Report of the President and Directors of the Annapolis Water Company to the Stockholders; and the Report of the Engineer, Annapolis, February 12, 1867. On file, Annapolis Department of Public Works, Annapolis, Maryland.

Arnold, Joseph L. 1978 Suburban Growth and Municipal Annexation in Baltimore, 1745–1918. *Maryland Historical Magazine* 73(2):109–128.

Barry, Andrew. 1996 Lines of Communication and Spaces of Rule. In *Foucault and Political Reason: Liberalism, Neo-liberalism and Rationalities of Government*, edited by Andrew Barry, Thomas Osborne and Nikolas Rose, pp. 123–141. University of Chicago Press, Chicago.

Burchell, Graham, Colin Gordon and Peter Miller (editors). 1991 *The Foucault Effect: Studies in Governmentality.* University of Chicago Press, Chicago.

Burwell, Robert L. 1931 Annapolis Metropolitan Sewerage Commission, Annapolis Metropolitan Sewerage District, Annapolis.

Caprotti, Federico. 2007 *Mussolini's Cities: Internal Colonialism in Italy, 1930–1939.* Cambria Press, Youngstown, New York.

Caprotti, Federico. 2008 Internal Colonisation, Hegemony and Coercion: Investigating Migration in Southern Lazio, Italy, in the 1930s. *Geoforum* 39(2):942–957.

Castree, Noel. 2006 Commentary: From Neoliberalism to Neoliberalisation: Consolations, Confusions, and Necessary Illusions. *Environment and Planning A* 38(1):1–6.

Census, United States Bureau of the. 1910 Thirteenth Census of the United States: 1910 Population. Anne Arundel County, Maryland. Special Collections. University of Maryland College Park, College Park.

Census, United States Bureau of the. 1920 Fourteenth Census of the United States: 1920 – Census. Anne Arundel County, Maryland. Special Collections. University of Maryland College Park, College Park.

Census, United States Bureau of the. 1930 Fifteenth Census of the United States: 1930, Population Schedule. Anne Arundel County, Enumeration District 2–37. Special Collections. University of Maryland College Park, College Park.

Dean, Mitchell. 1999 *Governmentality: Power and Rule in Modern Society.* Sage Publications, London.

Demeter, Stephen C. 1994 Nineteenth-Century Sanitation Technology in Urban Detroit. *Michigan Archaeologist* 40(1):1–24.

Doyel, Ginger. 2008 *Over the Bridge: A History of Eastport and Annapolis.* Annapolis Maritime Museum, Annapolis.

Evening Capital (EC). 1886a Back Creek Bridge, 09/22/1886, 5(116):3. Annapolis, Maryland.

Evening Capital (EC). 1886b Horn Point Improvements, 11/08/1886, 5(156):3. Annapolis, Maryland.

Evening Capital (EC). 1886c Putting in their Work, 09/09/1886, 5(105):3. Annapolis, Maryland.

Evening Capital (EC). 1887 Horn Point Waking Up, 05/28/1887, 7(14):3. Annapolis, Maryland.

Evening Capital (EC). 1950a Greater Annapolis Voted; City to Become Fourth Largest in Maryland. Evening Capital, 05/24/1950, 71(120). Annapolis, Maryland.

Evening Capital (EC). 1950b Proposed Greater Annapolis; Voters to Decide Annexation Issue in Election on May 23. Evening Capital, 05/15/1950, 71(112). Annapolis, Maryland.

Ferguson, James. 1994 *The Anti-Politics Machine: "Development," Depoliticization, and Bureaucratic Power in Lesotho.* University of Minnesota Press, Minneapolis.

Fitsgerald, Deborah. 2002 Book Review: Consumers in the Country: Technology and Social Change in Rural America. *Technology and Culture* 43(1):163–165.

Ford, Benjamin. 1994 Health and Sanitation in Postbellum Harpers Ferry. *Historical Archaeology* 28(4):49–61.

Foucault, Michel. 1977 *Discipline and Punish: The Birth of the Prison.* Penguin, London.

Foucault, Michel. 1990 *The History of Sexuality Volume 1: An Introduction.* Translated by Robert Hurley 1. 3 vols. Vintage Books, New York.

Foucault, Michel. 1991 Governmentality. In *The Foucault Effect: Studies in Governmentality,* edited by Graham Burchell, Colin Gordon and Peter Miller, pp. 87–104. University of Chicago Press, Chicago.

Geismar, Joan H. 1993 Where is Night Soil? Thoughts on an Urban Privy. *Historical Archaeology* 27(2):57–70.

González-Ruibal, Alfredo. 2006 The Dream of Reason: An Archaeology of the Failures of Modernity in Ethiopia. *Journal of Social Archaeology* 6(2):175–201.

González-Ruibal, Alfredo. 2008 Time to Destroy: An Archaeology of Supermodernity. *Current Anthropology* 49(2):247–279.

Gordon, Colin. 1991 Governmental Rationality: An Introduction. In *The Foucault Effect: Studies in Governmentality,* edited by Graham Burchell, Colin Gordon and Peter Miller, pp. 1–51. University of Chicago Press, Chicago.

Graham, Stephen and Simon Marvin. 2001 *Splintering Urbanism: Networked Infrastructures, Technological Mobilities and the Urban Condition.* Routledge, London.

Hannah, Matthew G. 2000 *Governmentality and Mastering Territory in Nineteenth-Century America.* Cambridge University Press, Cambridge.

Harris, Leila M. 2009 Gender and Emergent Water Governance: Comparative Overview of Neoliberalized Natures and Gender Dimensions of Privatization, Devolution and Marketization. *Gender, Place & Culture* 16(4):387–408.

Harvey, Penelope. 2005 The Materiality of State-Effects: An Ethnography of a Road in the Peruvian Andes. In *State Formation: Anthropological Perspectives,* edited by Christian Krohn-Hansen and Knut G. Nustad, pp. 123–141. Pluto Press, London.

Henman, Paul. 2006 Segmentation and Conditionality: Technological Reconfigurations of Social Policy. In *Analysing Social Policy: A Governmental Approach,* edited by Greg Marston and Catherine McDonald, pp. 205–222. Edward Elgar, Cheltenham, UK.

Horan, James F. and G. Thomas Taylor, Jr. 1977 *Experiments in Metropolitan Government.* Praeger Publishers, New York.

Howson, Jean. 1992/1993 The Archaeology of 19th-Century Health and Hygiene at the Sullivan Street Site in New York City. *Northeast Historical Archaeology* 21/22:137–160.

Hughes, Thomas P. 1983 *Networks of Power: Electrification in Western Society, 1880–1930.* Johns Hopkins University Press, Baltimore.

Ioris, Antonio A. R. 2007 The Troubled Waters of Brazil: Nature Commodification and Social Exclusion. *Capitalism Nature Socialism* 18(1):28–50.

Johnson, Valerie C. 2002 *Black Power in the Suburbs: The Myth or Reality of African American Suburban Political Incorporation.* SUNY Series in African American Studies. State University of New York Press, Albany.

Kaplan, Martha. 1995 Panopticon in Poona: An Essay on Foucault and Colonialism. *Cultural Anthropology* 10(1):85–98.

Kazanjian, David. 2003 *The Colonizing Trick: National Culture and Imperial Citizenship in Early America.* University of Minnesota Press, Minneapolis.

Kline, Ronald R. 2000 *Consumers in the Country: Technology and Social Change in Rural America.* Revisiting Rural America. Johns Hopkins University Press, Baltimore.

Larner, Wendy and Nina Laurie. 2010 Travelling Technocrats, Embodied Knowledges: Globalising Privatization in Telecoms and Water. *Geoforum* 41(2):218–226.

Leone, Mark P. 2005 *The Archaeology of Liberty in an American Capital: Excavations in Annapolis.* University of California Press, Berkeley.

Marcuse, Herbert. 1982 Some Social Implications of Modern Technology. In *The Essential Frankfurt School Reader*, edited by Andrew Arato and Eike Gebhardt, pp. 138–162. Continuum, New York.

Maryland, State of. 1924 Chapter 168. In *The Annotated Code of the Public General Laws of Maryland*, edited by George P. Bagby. Lord Baltimore Press, Baltimore.

Maryland State Planning Commission. 1937 *Regional Planning Part IV: Baltimore-Washington-Annapolis Area.* Johns Hopkins University, Baltimore.

Matthews, Christopher N. 2002 *An Archaeology of History and Tradition: Moments of Danger in the Annapolis Landscape.* Kluwer Academic/Plenum Publishers, New York.

McCarthy, James and Scott Prudham. 2004 Neoliberal Nature and the Nature of Neoliberalism. *Geoforum* 35(3):2004.

McWilliams, Jane W. 2009 Annapolis History Chronology. Electronic File.

Melosi, Martin V. 2000 *The Sanitary City: Urban Infrastructure in America from Colonial Times to the Present.* Johns Hopkins University Press, Baltimore.

Meskell, Lynn M. 2004 *Object Worlds in Ancient Egypt: Material Biographies Past and Present.* Berg, Oxford.

Meyer, Michael D. 2004 Sidebar: From Chamber Pots to Privies that Flush. In *Putting the "There" There: Historical Archaeologies of West Oakland* (I-880 Cypress Freeway Replacement Project, Interpretive Report No. 2), edited by Mary Praetzellis and Adrian Praetzellis, pp. 164–166. Anthropological Studies Center, Sonoma State University, Rohnert Park, CA.

Miller, David Y. 2002 *The Regional Governing of Metropolitan America.* Essentials of Public Policy and Administration Series. Westview Press, Boulder, CO.

Mrázek, Rudolph. 2002 *Engineers of Happy Land: Technology and Nationalism in a Colony.* Princeton University Press, Princeton.

Mrozowski, Stephen A., E. L. Bell, M. C. Beaudry, D. B. Landon and G. K. Kelso. 1989 Living on the Boott: Health and Well Being in a Boardinghouse Population. Theme Issue, The Archaeology of Public Health. *World Archaeology* 21(2):298–319.

Osborne, Thomas. 1996 Security and Vitality: Drains, Liberalism and Power in the Nineteenth Century. In *Foucault and Political Reason: Liberalism, Neo-liberalism and Rationalities of Government*, edited by Andrew Barry, Thomas Osborne and Nikolas Rose, pp. 99–121. University of Chicago Press, Chicago.

Palus, Matthew M. 2005 Building an Architecture of Power: Electricity in Annapolis, Maryland in the 19th and 20th Centuries. In *Archaeologies of Materiality*, edited by Lynn M Meskell, pp. 162–189. Blackwell Publishing, Oxford.

Palus, Matthew M. 2009 *Materialities of Government: A Historical Archaeology of Infrastructure in Annapolis and Eastport, 1865–1951.* Ph.D. Dissertation, Columbia University, New York.

Palus, Matthew M. forthcoming Infrastructure and African American Achievement in Annapolis, Maryland During the Early 20th Century. In *The Materiality of Freedom*, edited by Jodi Barnes. University of South Carolina Press, Columbia.

Parrington, Michael. 1983 The History and Archaeology of Philadelphia Roads, Streets, and Utility Lines. *Pennsylvania Archaeologist* 53(3):15–31.

Pels, Peter. 1997 The Anthropology of Colonialism: Culture, History, and the Emergence of Western Governmentality. *Annual Review of Anthropology* 26:163–183.

Pemberton, John. 1994 *On the Subject of "Java."* Cornell University Press, Ithaca.

Pfaffenberger, Bryan. 1990 The Harsh Facts of Hydraulics: Technology and Society in Sri Lanka's Colonization Schemes. *Technology and Culture* 31(3):361–397.

Rogers, Samual L. 1918 *Negro Population, 1790–1915.* U.S. Department of Commerce, Bureau of the Census. Government Printing Office, Washington, D.C.

Sanborn Map Company. 1930 Annapolis, Maryland. Map accessed through ProQuest, LLC, copyright held by Environmental Data Resources, Inc., Milford, CT.

Sancton, Andrew. 2000 *Merger Mania: The Assault on Local Government.* McGill-Queen's University Press, Montreal.

Sangameswaran, Priya. 2009 Neoliberalism and Water Reforms in Western India: Commercialization, Self-Sufficiency, and Regulatory Bodies. *Geoforum* 40(2):228–238.

Schivelbusch, Wolfgang. 1988 *Disenchanted Night: The Industrialization of Light in the Nineteenth Century.* University of California Press, Berkeley.

Schweninger, Loren. 1990 *Black Property Owners in the South, 1790–1915.* Blacks in the New World. University of Illinois Press, Urbana, IL.

Scott, James C. 1998 *Seeing Like a State: How Certain Schemes to Improve the Human Condition have Failed.* Yale University Press, New Haven.

Sharma, Aradhana and Akhil Gupta (editors). 2006 *The Anthropology of the State.* Blackwell Publishing, Oxford.

Smith, Charles W. 1925 Report of the Mayor of Annapolis on the State of the City's Finances from July 1, 1924 to June 30, 1925, with Statement of the Sinking Fund. Charles W. Smith, Mayor. On file, Maryland State Archive M102-2 (1/22/4/26) City of Annapolis, Annapolis Mayor & Aldermen, Reports and Minutes (Mayor's Report, 1894–1959), Annapolis.

Spencer, Jean E. 1965 *Contemporary Local Government in Maryland.* Bureau of Governmental Research, College of Business and Public Administration, University of Maryland, College Park, MD.

Stephens, G. Ross and Nelson Wikstrom. 2000 *Metropolitan Government and Governance: Theoretical Perspectives, Empirical Analysis, and the Future.* Oxford University Press, Oxford.

Steuart, W. M. 1922 Fourteenth Census of the United States Taken in the Year 1920, Volume II: Population 1920, General Report and Analytical Tables. U.S. Department of Commerce, Bureau of the Census. Government Printing Office, Washington, D.C.

Steuart, W. M. 1933 Fifteenth Census of the United States: 1930, Population, Volume VI: Families (Reports by States, Giving Statistics for Families, Dwellings and Homes, by Counties, for Urban and Rural Areas and for Urban Places of 2,500 or More). Government Printing Office, Washington, D.C.

Stone, May N. 1979 The Plumbing Paradox: American Attitudes Toward Late Nineteenth-Century Domestic Sanitary Arrangements. *Winterthur Portfolio* 14(3):283–309.

Stottman, M. Jay. 1995 Towards a Greater Understanding of Privy Vault Architecture. In *Historical Archaeology in Kentucky*, edited by Kim A McBride, Stephen W McBride and David Pollack. Kentucky Heritage Council, Frankfort, KY.

Stottman, M. Jay. 2000 Out of Sight, Out of Mind: Privy Architecture and the Perception of Sanitation. *Historical Archaeology* 34(1):39–61.

Survey, U.S. Geological. 1892 U.S.G.S. Owensville Sheet, Surveyed 1890. General Printing Office, Washington, D.C.

Tarlow, Sarah. 2007 *The Archaeology of Improvement in Britain, 1750–1850.* Cambridge University Press, Cambridge.

Walker, Margath, Susan M. Roberts, John Paul III Jones and Oliver Fröhling. 2008 Neoliberal Development Through Technical Assistance: Constructing Communities of Entrepreneurial Subjects in Oaxaca, Mexico. *Geoforum* 39(1):527–542.

Williams, Rosalind. 2008 *Notes on the Underground: An Essay on Technology, Society, and the Imagination.* The MIT Press, Cambridge.

Wolman, Abel. 1926 Letter from Abel Wolman, Chief Engineer, Maryland State Department of Health, Baltimore, to Mayor Allen B. Howard, Annapolis, Maryland, April 12, 1926. Maryland State Archives, Annapolis.

Chapter 13
New Subjectivities: Capitalist, Colonial Subject, and Archaeologist

Martin Hall

If any one person is to be emblematic of the dilemmas of historical archaeology today, there is surely no better than Leonidas Posada Gaviria, the material man of later nineteenth-century Bogotá who "made a fortune by supplying to the modernized needs and gentrified tastes of his fellow citizens." Felipe Gaitán-Ammann paints a provocative word picture of this champion of the world of things: "as Leonidas Posada Gaviria's life unfolds before our eyes, the city of Bogotá reveals to us as a complex heterotopic space in which politically decolonized agents succeeded in manipulating the strings of the capitalist system so as to reproduce conditions of coloniality through pre-capitalist forms of inequality and social interaction" (Gaitán-Ammann, Chap. 7).

On the other side of town, give or take a few decades, a water cistern had fallen into disuse and was accumulating rubbish at the Quinta de Bolivar, preserving "colorful debris of coarse lead-glazed earthenwares, medicine flasks, wine bottles, piles of faunal remains, and the first archaeological toothbrush excavated in Colombia." How can the connection with the life of Posada Gaviria be made and given meaning? What do the ceramics found in a water cistern on an estate combined with the biography of a merchant running a glass and dinnerware shop on a commercial street in Bogotá reveal about capitalism and colonialism that is not already known? And why the toothbrush?

There is a richness in these encounters with the past that is itself exotic and a world away from the austere measurement of clay tobacco pipe fragments and musket shot that defined an earlier historical archaeology. Such are the possibilities for an archaeology of Jamaican markets, mapped out by Mark Hauser, in which ceramics could be used to ply between the inventiveness of their makers, situated in local networks of exchange within an oppressive plantation regime of control, and the global system of distribution in which cargoes of slaves and of commodities crossed each other's paths across the Atlantic (Hauser, Chap. 6). Or an archaeology of the Russian–American Company, which ruled Alaska from 1799 until 1867 and which extracted exotic goods

M. Hall (✉)
University of Salford, Salford, Greater Manchester, UK
e-mail: Martin.Hall@salford.ac.uk

S.K. Croucher and L. Weiss (eds.), *The Archaeology of Capitalism in Colonial Contexts*, 295
Contributions To Global Historical Archaeology, DOI 10.1007/978-1-4614-0192-6_13,
© Springer Science+Business Media, LLC 2011

of high value in Europe through various regimes of exploitation and forced labor that can be traced through their material remnants (Crowell, Chap. 4). Or the archaeology of change in the late Ottoman Empire mapped out in settlement design in Transjordan (Carroll, Chap. 5). Or the archaeology of colonialism in nineteenth-century Australia, as indigenous communities encounter colonial settlers at remote sheep stations (Paterson, Chap. 11). Or, again, the encounter on the Californian coast in 1579 between the wrecked crew of the *San Agustín* and the Coast Miwok, who may have taken the Spanish as the dead returned and appropriated the Asian porcelains from the wreck for use in Kuksu – Ghost Dance – ceremonies (Russell, Chap. 2).

But with this heady travelogue comes an unease. As the spotlight pans from Colombia to Jamaica to Transjordan to California to Australia to Alaska, is this perhaps a spectacle of the exotic performed for the benefit of us, its participants? And here, Audrey Horning serves as our conscience, asking after James Deetz whether a good deal of historical archaeology is not just "the most expensive way in the world of finding out what we already know" (Horning, Chap. 3).

Recasting Horning's critique, is not the exchange of reports from the field itself a sumptuary activity through which a professional elite extends and reproduces its reputational capital? (see Appadurai 1986 on sumptuary value; David 1998 on the circulation of reputational value in academic life). Is perhaps the way in which information from faraway places is brought back to the center of the contemporary capitalist world to be woven into theory and redistributed and resold in high-priced journals not an equivalent to exporting peanuts from Senegal to make industrial lubricants in Europe in order to manufacture the commodities which are then sold back to the Senegalese (Richard, Chap. 9)? Leonidas Posada Gaviria understood the money to be made through the sale and circulation of elite goods and became rich. Perhaps, had he lived a century later, he would have made a good archaeologist.

There are three ways of avoiding the sumptuary allure of the past, and the particular value of the papers in this collection is the way in which they demonstrate the value of each of them. The first is through a deep grounding in the evidence, allowing its fissures and contradictions to challenge the assumed and presumed. The second is through an engagement with theory, plying between the abstract and the empirical to advance interpretation. The third is through engagement – taking a stand and making explicit the inevitable connection between the present and the past.

François Richard's chapter provides a thoughtful response to Audrey Horning's challenge to the value of what we all do. Richard sees the importance of evidence – "the 'dense circuitry' of people, spaces, and things" – as historicizing the ways in which power is configured in subjecting people to particular regimes (in this context, colonialism) and also in "coming to occupy a particular understanding of oneself and mode of consciousness." There is value in this dual engagement with evidence, directed at understanding both the subjectivity of the colonial subject and the subjectivity of the contemporary interpreter: "placing colonial experiences in conversation with postcolonial conditions may help us survey the problem space of colonial history with fresh eyes and instruments, in ways that locate salient historical questions *because of their enduring resonance in the present*" (Richard, Chap. 9, original emphasis).

Similarly, Lynda Carroll's close study of a small part of the Jordanian landscape at Wadi Hisban allows "for new discourses to help explore the daily lives of Ottoman subjects who lived under the shadow of the state … local interactions between state and subjects, as they both engaged in and challenged processes of capitalism and colonialism." During the nineteenth century, land use reforms had attempted to transform "primitive" Badu pastoralists into "productive subjects of the state." But settlement patterns revealed a history differing from the formal transcript: "the model of changing settlement, and the construction of large farms, has been thus far been constructed based on top down models of change, initiation from the policies of the state through colonial attitudes, or as the result of capitalist exploitation through the investments of merchant settlers." Throughout this discourse, Bedu remain largely passive recipients of both of these global structures. However, at Qasr Hisban, the natural and built landscapes provide an alternative story (Carroll, Chap. 5).

Aron Crowell demonstrates the qualities of thick description in his account of the traces of Russian colonialism in the material world of Alaska, "blue Orthodox domes" that "float above scores of southern Alaskan villages from Kodiak to the Yukon River" and identity that "is perpetuated in Russian family names, loan words, foods, and customs such as Christmas season 'starring' processions and New Year celebrations … The comingling of Russian and indigenous blood and culture laid the foundation for a complexly layered contemporary ethnicity that echoes the 'double consciousness' of indigenous Latin America." Crowell's interpretation of the evidence suggests a complex set of circumstances for which "archaeology is positioned to generate unique insights into social and cultural change among these overlooked strata of colonial society, where creolization unfolded through the daily interaction of men and women, colonizers and indigenes" (Crowell, Chap. 4).

Sarah Croucher provides a similar example from her fieldwork in Islamic Africa. She is forced out of the conventional frame of European capitalist/colonial interpretations by the simple necessities of working within a different cosmological orbit. Her work is a deep engagement with the materiality of the East African coast, running from Sofala in Mozambique to Mogadishu in Somalia. Here, it "is impossible to slot capitalist relations into any single 'type' of capitalism. We cannot say that colonial powers on Zanzibar were merchant capitalists and therefore place all cultural iterations of capitalism as analogous to those of seventeenth-century European merchants … Likewise, we cannot take the dominant mode of capitalism in Europe at the time as the 'core' of capitalism, and dismiss cultural practices embedded within capitalist modes on Zanzibar as simply a reaction in a 'periphery,' where capitalism is an external force and unchanged by Zanzibari practices … The cultural exchanges which traversed the commodity chain are perhaps as important to note as the economic relations and it is in these that we see the particularities of the manner in which understandings of capitalism on Zanzibar were shaped by the particular cultural context of the island, and the way in which the practices of Zanzibaris were also integral to the shaping of the wider capitalist world" (Croucher, Chap. 8).

Thick description, of course, engages continually with theory, and to deny theory is just another theoretical view of the world. There are two theoretical strands that run through the papers in this collection; abstracted, they give us a sense of the current frontier of the discipline as it pushes on into the jungle of the yet-to-be-understood. The first strand can be termed "material expressions," and the second, "places of transgression."

Matthew Palus introduces the notion of material expression by taking us into the twentieth-century sewers of Annapolis. His case is both simple and compelling – that we can "see" government at work (governability) through the fabric of public utilities: "towards the end of the nineteenth century, the city government of Annapolis extended its authority over urban infrastructure in new ways. The installation and management of sewer and water infrastructure became a new governmental function. Through these technologies the city government regulated the conduct of its citizens more intensively, and the regulation of conduct, exemplified here in the promotion of public health, connects the historical modernization of government in Annapolis with the modernization of its infrastructure" (Palus, Chap. 12).

There is a significant opportunity here for urban comparison of a large scale. For example, there can be an immediate cross-reference to nineteenth-century Cape Town, where a newly emerged landlord class, enriched from the compensation that came with the end of slavery and seeking maximum rentals with minimum investment, clashed with the merchant classes of Empire, who sought public investment in municipal improvement. This political struggle was expressed in the case for and against water utilities and provision for sewage disposal, with the factions cast, respectively, as the "Dirty Party" and the "Clean Party" (Bickford-Smith 1995).

One way of sharpening these explorations of material expression is to think of objects as being ascribed qualities of authenticity (Hall 2006). Whether Zanzibari ceramic sets, Alaskan religious icons, or American sewers, these systems of things grant durability to meaning and map out social orders: trade connections, reciprocal obligations, common identity, civic order. This is what the Coast Miwok saw in 1579 when the *San Agustín* washed ashore – the dead had returned for a fleeting visit, leaving behind them a cargo of objects that were the authentic embodiment of their presence and which could be circulated for years to come as a part of the Ghost Dance ceremonies (Russell, Chap. 2).

The second theoretical strand – places of transgression – gives the concept of material expression a more explicitly spatial dimension and directs attention to opposition, suppression, and subversion as ways of understanding the structures of dominant orders. This approach now has a respectable lineage in historical archaeology that tracks back to critiques of the totalizing structuralist and normative approaches of the 1970s and 1980s (see Leone 1988 and Hall 1992 for early critiques). It is nicely framed by François Richard in his essay on Francophone West African colonialism. Contact zones in Senegal, Richard writes, are places "where the technologies and forms of authority of the colonial state met previously existing structures of power as well as the cultural senses and sensibilities of African populations, where different domains of materiality clashed or interlocked ... It is in this mosaic of familiar places and strange spaces – agricultural fields, stretches of landscapes, villages, market centers, administrative posts – that colonial capital flows converged on local worlds of cultural intimacy, where rural Africans reasoned with, contested, and compromised the reason of state (*raison d'état*) and logic of the market" (Richard, Chap. 9).

For his part, Alistair Paterson uses two case studies of pastoralism to explore colonial contact and creolization in Australia. His aim is to get deeper into what has often been assumed to be a simple conflict, driven by economic interests, and to do this by adding "some texture to a binary perception that arises from examining the interface between two different cultures in contact." Paterson shows how Strangeways Springs in Central Australia was in part built on foundations of indigenous labor and knowledge while in the Pilbara region of Western Australia, the archaeological record provides information on the organization of the pastoral domain. "An implication of these studies is that indigenous agency, often overlooked or hidden in colonial overviews, is potentially available in other ways – meeting the challenge of understanding those 'people without history' Europeans encountered across the world" (Paterson, Chap. 11).

Lynda Carroll's study of changing settlement patterns in Transjordan, Mark Hauser's discussion of Caribbean markets, and Lindsay Weiss's work on nineteenth-century South African diamond fields show how this line of interpretation continues to open up our understanding of the past.

Carroll's focus is on the late Ottoman Empire and the ways in which large-scale agriculture sought to displace Bedouin nomadism. By looking at the architecture of settlement, she can suggest how the dominant intent of the commercially oriented farmers – many of them absentee landlords – was subverted by resilient nomadic communities who persisted in using opportunities for cultural survival. There were, for example, particular opportunities in the caves that are characteristic of the desert landscape: "in Transjordan, caves dot the landscape of Transjordan. Throughout the Ottoman period, caves were used for storage, for housing animals, and even as domestic spaces. These were often used as permanent features of the landscape around which tribal migrations were tethered to, through the course of their cyclical migrations … caves in Transjordan often became clandestine spaces, to provide activity areas that remained outside of the view of the state. The mobility of Bedu, especially before the Tanzimat, made it easy to circumvent state monitoring efforts. The use of caves, along with their ability to move camp, was part of a strategy used to underrepresent produce, hide taxable livestock, or even hide potential conscripts" (Carroll, Chap. 5).

Hauser skillfully uses the documentary evidence and faint material traces to show how markets in pre-emancipation Jamaica may have violated the aspirations of plantation owners and colonial officials to maintain total control. Course earthenware pots – yabbas – were distributed by street marketers or higglers: "market activity undertaken by higglers embodied the local economy, in that the trade was one of island-produced goods and the islands' shores circumscribed the flow of the commodities. The higglers themselves were also local, in that they had mastered the various physical and economic geographies of Jamaica. They could move seamlessly between plantation and city and between provision ground and market": "for the enslaved, circumscribed by the obligations of laboring on plantation grounds six days a week, the distances traversed by higglers were great. Conversely, for the planters who did not know the provision ground trails or the unwritten rules of the informal trade, the higglers' knowledge was equally 'esoteric.' Such knowledge made a higgler a potentially dangerous sort of person who could control the market and pass information outside the gaze of the planter." This gives the capitalist relations of the market a dual function; markets "provided the infrastructure that enabled planters to have enslaved Africans use their own labor to feed and fend for themselves. Second they created the infrastructure through which the loosely linked network of higglers and markets not only circulated goods, but also perhaps information. The markets provided a space for information to be passed, solidarities to be built, and social action to be orchestrated" (Hauser, Chap. 6).

This is the classic carnivalesque of Bakhtin (1984). As such, it also allows the possibilities in the critiques of Bakhtin's work; that a delimited space, such as market (allowed on specified days and in a bounded place), may in reality be within the frame of Foucault's panopticon; that the controlled opportunity for the colonial subject to let off steam and to believe there was an opportunity for resistance was in itself part of the processes of control (Stallybrass and White 1986).

Lindsay Weiss's work with the diamond fields provides a model instance of the ways in which material assemblages from places of transgression can be used in direct interpretation of social and political life, illuminating that which is beyond the reach of verbal evidence. She shows how the early days of the diamond rush created spaces in which established orders broke down and "accelerated the blurring of the traditional Victorian registers of class, race and gender (to some degree a rather unsurprising state of affairs for a city literally 'honeycombed with cesspool,' traversed by roving dogs, flies and with the approaching roads practically lined with rotting animal carcasses)" (Weiss, Chap. 10).

Weiss sees the particular archaeological potential in the places that offered housing to the transitory population of the early diamond field: "no space condensed or seemed to speed up the social confusion quite as much as the suburban canteens and hotels, which ringed the diggings." This is expressed in the material assemblage from one such place, an assemblage from the early phase of the hotel which "typi-fies no one set of cultural practices monolithically, but would seem to represent many diverse and travel-contingent needs, as well as a good deal of trade and service improvisations. This sort of social hybridity … in which local economies, informal trade, barter, negotiation of wage labor and other such interactions were ongoing and pervasive (these activities went on day and night as many traversed the roads at all hours), suggest the broader culture of a mobile and hybrid community" (Weiss, Chap. 10).

Thus, the material assemblage challenges the verbal evidence and reveals some of the dimensions of transgression: "over the 1880s and 1890s, a distinct shift comes to be perceptible in hotel advertisements which increasingly stress the potentially individuated nature of the amenities, so, while including reference to the somewhat common *table d'hôte* service, ads would emphasize 'table d'hôte with *separate tables*' … and also listing special rates for 'private suppers' … Taking the fact that drinking and eating had constituted, in many important respects, the core of the incipient sociality that defined the early Diamond Fields, these seemingly minor or subtle shifts in the collective ambience of the hotel and canteen space indicate profound changes in the way that social fluidity was expressed which, in turn, had very direct implications for the way that exchange could be undertaken at such locales.

The business practices at hotels on the Diamond Fields had come to revolve mainly around (more licit) profit motives and professionalized service rather than operating from any motive or belief in an informal family style in which the inner transactions of the hotel were readily observable or available to customers" (Weiss, Chap. 10).

Cases such as these clearly show the iterative power of theory, as we move between particular circumstances and abstracted principles. Horning, though, adds a vital rider, the danger of slipping into a totalizing narrative that collapses all accounts of colonialism into a common set of uniform terms: "for those of us engaged in comparative analysis … there is one overarching caution that must be acknowledged: To know the archaeology of inequality and oppression in one part of the modern world is not to know it in another, except in the most superficial of fashions. In the case of Northern Ireland, the ability of surprising insights to emerge from seemingly familiar landscapes is surely a more powerful tool of engagement than assertions equating 'Irish peasants' with enslaved African Americans, an abstract equation as likely to confuse or alienate contemporary Northern Irish of both traditions as it would offend the descendants of those millions of Africans who endured the Middle Passage, the horrors of enslavement, and centuries of race-based discrimination" (Horning, Chap. 3).

Finally, and to return to the niggling question asked by Audrey Horning, is there any point to all of this? To put this another way, what is the connection between the past and the present? Do the studies in this collection serve in a tournament of value in which the prizes are research grants, appointments, and – ultimately – tenure? Or is the point rather the relationship between these constructed pasts and the present?

In raising this issue, Horning makes clear the importance of "positionality," of the stand taken by the interpreter of the past: "the need for self-reflexivity and an explicit ethical position is a necessity for responsible archaeology in a postcolonial, post-modern age, yet I've always hoped that my own position was obvious in the questions I ask. I want to prioritize other people's stories over my own, but accept that as a kind of self-justifying subterfuge suggestive of a latent attachment to scientific objectivity exacerbated by an over-developed (Western?) sense of privacy. It is a question of balance – if we employ personal narrative, we run the risk of further privileging the author's voice while exposing individual agendas" (Horning, Chap. 3).

Bent Flyvbjerg addresses the question of positionality through his provocative concept of "situational ethics": "the objective is to balance instrumental rationality with value rationality by increasing the capacity of individuals, organisations and society to think and act in value–rational terms … researchers … take their point of departure in their attitude to the situation in the society being studied. They seek to ensure that such an attitude is not based on idiosyncratic morality or personal preferences, but instead on a common view among a specific reference group to which the researchers refer" (Flyvbjerg 2001: 130. See also Hall 2005).

For Horning, this translates into a clear agenda: "the archaeology I conduct in Northern Ireland specifically focuses upon early modern British expansion. I am interested in examining late medieval Irish life and the subsequent interactions between the Irish and the (mainly) English and Scots who settled in Ireland as part of the late sixteenth and early seventeenth-century processes of plantation. I do so in full recognition that this period and these interactions remain contested and constitute the root of the dichotomous historical memories that gave rise to the Troubles and which continue to structure everyday life. I believe that a better understanding of the complexities of the early modern period in Ireland, which includes a consideration of the entwined forces of capitalism and colonialism, can provoke and enhance understanding between today's two traditions and contribute to the construction of some form of shared, peaceful future" (Horning, Chap. 3).

Alistair Paterson similarly demonstrates the richness of an awareness of positionality in the reflective anecdote with which he ends his chapter. Planning fieldwork in central Northern Territory with Murphy Kennedy, a Warumungu elder, Paterson recalls that "we discussed which archaeological sites to target. While I was interested in the early contact-era sites, Murphy had radically different interests. Murphy and his family had identified the importance of a 'walk-off' site – this was a campsite where in the 1970s the local community had lived after they left the local pastoral station in the era of equal rights for Aboriginal workers … Murphy though we should record the archaeology at the site, which we did. Some interesting discoveries from that investigation related to site formation processes; but I suspect what was most important – not so much as scientific research but more as political and social action – was the use of archaeology to examine material aspects of *recent life* in what was a clear landscape where power was in flux – long held notions of land ownership, Aboriginal people in Australia, and the environment were changing, and these sites were physical expressions of a time when race and racism, history, and reconciliation were big issues. They still are" (Paterson, Chap. 11).

Running through all of these chapters is a consistent critique of colonialism and economic forms and the dangers of totalizing interpretations that deny the valency of agency and local context. Taken together, they hover at the edge of a theory of our own, an archaeologist Baudrillard or Bourdieu or Bhabha who can pull together the strands into a theory of nonverbal representation of meaning. They lurk in the wings of the contemporary political stage, criticizing capitalism and implying the connection with today's world of goods, laying bare colonialism, and almost making the connection with the new empire of our own times.

In this, their authors both survey where we are now and anticipate where we may go next. Like Leonidas Posada Gaviria, they survey the heterotopic space of the world of ideas, knowing the potential of material culture but wondering just how to extract its full value.

References

Appadurai, A. 1986 Commodities and the politics of value. *The Social Life of Things*, edited by Arjun Appadurai, pp. 3–63. Cambridge, Cambridge University Press.

Bakhtin, M. 1984 *Rabelais and his World*. Bloomington, Indiana University Press.

Bickford-Smith, V. 1995 *Ethnic Pride and Racial Prejudice in Victorian Cape Town*. Cambridge, Cambridge University Press.

David, P. 1998 Communication norms and the collective cognitive performance of 'invisible colleges'. In *Creation and transfer of knowledge: institutions and incentives*, edited by G. B. Navaretti, P. Dasgupta, K.-G. Maler and D. Siniscalco, pp. 115–163. Heidelberg, Springer-Verlag.

Flyvbjerg, B. 2001 *Making Social Science Matter: Why social inquiry fails and how it can succeed again*. Cambridge, Cambridge University Press.

Hall, M. 1992 Small things and the mobile, conflictual fusion of power, fear and desire. In *The Art and Mystery of Historical Archaeology. Essays in Honor of James Deetz,* edited by A. Yentsch and M. Beaudry, pp. 373–399. Boca Raton, CRC Press.

Hall, M. 2005 Situational ethics and engaged practice: the case of archaeology in Africa. In *Embedding Ethics*, edited by P. Pels and L. Meskell, pp. 169–194. London, Berg.

Hall, M. 2006 The reappearance of the authentic. In *Museum Frictions: Public Cultures/Global Transformations*, edited by I. Karp, C. Kratz, L. Szwaja and T. Ybarra-Frausto., pp. 70–101. Durham, Duke University Press.

Leone, M. 1988 The Georgian order as the order of merchant capitalism in Annapolis, Maryland. In *The Recovery of Meaning. Historical Archaeology in the Eastern United States,* edited by M. Leone and P. Potter, pp. 235–261. Washington, Smithsonian Institution.

Stallybrass, P. and A. White. 1986 *The Politics and Poetics of Transgression*. Ithaca, Cornell University Press.

Index